staff meals from chanterelle

Staff Meals from Chanterelle

David Waltuck
and Melicia Phillips

Photographs by Maria Robledo

workman publishing | new york

Cover and book design by Barbara Balch
Cover and book photographs by Maria Robledo

Library of Congress Cataloging-in-Publication Data
Waltuck, David.
   [Staff meals from Chanterelle cookbook]
   David Waltuck's staff meals from Chanterelle cookbook / by David
Waltuck & Melicia Phillips.
     p.cm.
   ISBN 0-7611-1698-2
    1. Cookery. 2. Chanterelle (Restaurant) I. Title: Staff meals from
   Chanterelle cookbook. II. Phillips, Melicia. III. Title.
   TX714 .W264 2000
   641.5'09747'1--dc21   00-034984

Workman books are available at special discounts when purchased in bulk for premiums and sales promotions as well as for fund-raising or educational use. Special editions or book excerpts can be created to specification. For details, contact the Special Sales Director at the address below.

Workman Publishing Company, Inc.
708 Broadway
New York, NY 10003-9555
www.workman.com

Manufactured in the United States of America
First printing October 2000
10 9 8 7 6 5 4 3 2

FROM DAVID

I dedicate this book to my families. First to my real family, to my wonderful kids, Sara and Jake, and especially to my wife Karen, whose love and support, tempered with good advice and worthwhile criticism, have sustained me through so much. Secondly, to my equally real Chanterelle family, and that means everyone that I have had the pleasure of working, eating, drinking, and generally spending an awful lot of time with in the twenty plus years of Chanterelle's existence.

acknowledgments

Bringing this book into the world turned out to be a much bigger task than originally planned. What was intended as a one-year project took six years. I would never claim to have done this by myself, in fact I find that almost everything that I do, I do as a collaboration. So I would like to thank a few of the people who have been instrumental in putting this book together.

First, thanks to my coauthor Melicia Phillips who conceived this book and helped make it a reality.

Thanks to everyone at Workman Publishing for their support and assistance, especially Joni Miller, without whom this book would never have been, and my editor Suzanne Rafer, who deserves a medal for patience and for keeping the faith as we went wildly over schedule. Thanks to Barbara Balch for her perfect design and to Maria Robledo for the honest photos, taken in hectic, behind-the-scenes conditions at Chanterelle.

I would never claim that any of the recipes in this book (or any other book for that matter) are totally original, but some of them have been directly contributed by family and friends. So, I'd like to thank Aunt Fanny, Aunt Gertie, Nina Fraas, Leonard Lopate, and Michael Klug for their generous recipe contributions. Thanks goes as well to Frank Duba for faithful recipe testing and to Evelyn Dotson for both recipe development and testing.

Thanks also to my friend Bill Katz, who, though not involved in the making of this book, has always been part of Chanterelle. More than a designer, his esthetic is everywhere.

And of course, thanks to my family for their encouragement and endurance.

Staff Meals from Chanterelle

contents

Introduction: A Brief History of Chanterelle, xi

soup <small>2</small>

The perfect one-dish meal for any busy family. Enjoy aromatic Creamy Tomato Mint Soup, a thick Split Pea Soup with Ham, and a Mussel Soup redolent with saffron.

beef,veal,lamb <small>42</small>

A wide selection of slow-simmered stews, stir-fries, and roasts. There's comforting Cottage Pie, tender Roasted Veal Shank, exotic Lamb Tagine with Prunes and Honey, and spectacular Beef Fillets with Star Anise.

pork <small>98</small>

Pork is a staff favorite and we welcome it often in the form of Pork Goulash, Oven-Roasted Barbecued Ribs, Chinese-Style Meatballs, and Montana Fried "Pork Chop" Sandwiches.

poultry <small>140</small>

The backbone of any family meal, chicken comes to our table roasted with root vegetables or stuffed with basil, in a potpie or as Melicia's Chicken and Dumplings. This chapter also includes an aromatic Thai Duck Curry and two luscious braised rabbit dishes.

seafood <small>210</small>

There's a mix of front-of-the-house dishes and staff meals here. Ginger Pickled Salmon with Wasabi Sauce, Monkfish with Roast Shallots and Garlic, Shrimp with Black Bean Sauce, and Deviled Crab Cakes are all here, as well as Fish 'n' Chips—of course.

pasta 252

We love pasta and serve up bowlfuls of Linguine with Clam Sauce, Spaghetti with Potatoes and Greens, and Cheese Tortellini with Sun-Dried Tomato Cream. Here, too, is a Shrimp Fried Rice that makes use of leftovers, and a favorite Risotto with Porcini.

sides,salads 300

Easy accompaniments include a Spiced Applesauce, old-fashioned Braised Red Cabbage, Summertime Creamed Corn, Warm Lentil Salad, irresistible Vidalia Onion Fritters, and a particular favorite, Everyday Mashed Potatoes.

dressings,dips 346

A selection of quick, versatile dressings, including Green Goddess, Caesar, Blue Cheese, and Creamy Italian, plus a full range of flavorful mayonnaises turn fresh greens and vegetables into something really special.

brunch,breads 374

Invite friends for leisurely weekend brunch and linger over Chanterelle Breakfast Scones, Challah French Toast, Half-Inch-High Buttermilk Pancakes, or Shirred Eggs with Smithfield Ham and Tarragon. Later in the day, accompany meals with Garlic Bread or piping hot Indian Chapati.

desserts 406

Staff favorites include brownies (naturally), Zesty Cranberry Soup, Summertime Ginger Shortcakes, and platefuls of cookies—especially those loaded with plenty of chocolate chips and peanut butter.

Conversion Table 434

Index 435

Staff Meals from Chanterelle

"Good food and plenty of it"

—*slogan on Chanterelle staff sweatshirt*

a brief history of chanterelle

In 1979, SoHo was a neighborhood in transition, not yet the chic, tourist-driven quarter it is today, teeming with boutiques, galleries, clubs, and restaurants. Although it was *the* place for art galleries and many artists lived and worked in lofts on the upper floors of its turn-of-the-century commercial buildings, the area was still quite industrial. During the day a steady stream of trucks rumbled along the narrow cobblestone streets, making deliveries and pickups at textile dealers, tool-and-die factories, boiler shops, paper box companies, glass cutters, and knife sharpeners. There was only a handful of places to eat and a scattering of retail shops that catered mainly to local residents. At night the streets were virtually deserted.

My wife Karen and I were only in our early twenties, but the vision of the type of restaurant we wanted to create was firm and clear in our minds. We chose a small storefront on the isolated corner of Grand and Greene Streets, establishing Chanterelle amid the wonderful old cast-iron buildings that have long been SoHo's architectural hallmark. Most recently the site of a bodega, the premises had originally housed a corset factory and showroom. Our choice of location raised a few eyebrows, but in the late 1970s aspiring restaurateurs and would-be gallery owners could take advantage of low rents in "fringe" neighborhoods (and even gain a certain cachet by doing so). Most importantly, Karen and I felt that if we were faithful to our beliefs about cuisine and service, our clientele would find us. Happily, this turned out to be true.

It took six arduous months for us to make the necessary renovations—painstakingly repairing the cast-iron facade with ball-peen hammers, restoring the ornate mid-nineteenth-century pressed-tin ceiling, fixing the inset antique mirrors, stripping and refinishing the decrepit mahogany wainscoting and columns, and building a kitchen from scratch. We painted the walls a pale, soothing, peachy yellow color reminiscent of chanterelle

mushrooms, laid an expanse of discreet gray carpet, and, contrary to fashion, left the walls unadorned except for the original architectural decorations and inset mirrors. Three big brass chandeliers added the finishing touch.

One of our main goals was to create an atmosphere in which people could enjoy all the pleasures of the table—food, wine, and conversation—without distraction. We envisioned each table in the dining room as its own intimate world, all of its needs unintimidatingly anticipated and fulfilled by our bright staff. And no music—only the congenial hum of our guests' conversations, punctuated by the clink of glasses and silverware. Since we felt that displaying art on the walls would draw diners' eyes up and away from their meal, we put artworks by contemporary American artists (some well-established, others up-and-coming) on our menu covers. The first had a print by the great TriBeCa-based sculptor Marisol. Since then we have been honored to feature works by a wide range of distinguished artists, photographers, musicians, and writers, among them Roy Lichtenstein, Cy Twombley, Jennifer Bartlett, Ellsworth Kelly, Donald Evans, John Cage, Virgil Thomson, Keith Haring, Francesco Clemente, Louise Nevelson, and Allen Ginsberg. We change Chanterelle's menu cover twice a year, and the appearance of a new featured artwork is always a special moment for us and for our guests. Each "retired" menu is framed and added to the gallery of covers exhibited in the small anteroom near Chanterelle's reception area.

With high hopes, a waitstaff of only two, and no funds in reserve (a cardinal sin for a restaurant start-up), Karen and I opened Chanterelle on November 14, 1979, serving a modest tasting menu and an à la carte menu that featured lobster with Sauternes and curry, as well as the grilled seafood sausage that has become my signature dish. We didn't anticipate being busy right away, so I cooked alone, without a sous chef. Our first customers were friends, family, artists, gallery owners, and our investors. But one evening only a week or so later, I suddenly found myself with a booked-solid dining room filled with restaurant reviewers, noted personalities, and other chefs. Like all new restaurants, we hadn't yet worked out all the kinks, and everything took longer to leave the kitchen than it was supposed to. As I rushed like a madman to keep everyone fed and happy, I could feel the palpable anticipation (and restlessness) of all those hungry food professionals and other avid eaters. At one point, I opened the oven door to remove some eagerly awaited racks of lamb only to find them cold and raw—the oven wasn't turned on! And that was just the beginning.

Of course, we survived that awful yet comical night. (Comical, that is, in retrospect; at the time it was a chef's worst nightmare come true.) A short while later Chanterelle received a very favorable review in *New York* magazine's "End of the Decade" issue. The restaurant took off and the realization of our dreams began. In 1989, after a successful ten-year run in the original SoHo location, we moved Chanterelle to a more spacious home in TriBeCa's historic Mercantile Exchange building on Harrison Street.

In many respects, only our address has changed. The restaurant is still situated on a corner in a turn-of-the-century building, the staff remains intelligent and attentive, each month's new menu is always handwritten in Karen's elegant, sweeping script, and my cooking continues to evolve.

THE CHANTERELLE FAMILY From the beginning, Karen and I made a conscious decision to devote ourselves to Chanterelle, and we have never regretted our choice. The restaurant is our second home, and our children Sara and Jake are not only Waltucks but also a part of the greater Chanterelle family, along with everyone who works with us.

Restaurant employees typically work very long hours together as a close-knit team so it's not all that surprising that staffs often develop into "families." We're pleased that this is especially true of Chanterelle. It's inevitable really, since employees usually spend more time with each other at the restaurant than they do with their "real" families and loved ones. We have always tried to nurture this unique closeness and to create a comfortable and agreeable work atmosphere in which it can flourish.

BEHIND THE KITCHEN DOOR In many ways restaurants are like the theater—a lot goes on behind the scenes that's never seen by the audience. This is a more than apt analogy—both restaurant owners and theater people routinely refer to the front and back of the house. To our clients, Chanterelle is a well-regarded restaurant with a deep commitment to pleasing them. But as refined as our restaurant is, when it comes to the back of the house, in a real sense Chanterelle is also very much a mom-and-pop operation (in fact, the staff often calls me Pops).

Over the years, both clients and friends have been intrigued by back-of-the-house life at Chanterelle, often asking about what actually goes on. People are especially curious about what chefs and other food professionals eat in "real life." Do Karen and I, our cooks, the waitstaff, and our other indispensable staff eat the same meals we serve to our clients? Do we gather around the table every afternoon feasting on foie gras, lobster, and truffles? Hardly, but we do eat very well.

The time the Chanterelle staff spends together over a meal is pretty much an expanded version of what it's like when any hardworking family tries to take an enjoyable and sociable break from their hectic schedule. We relax around the table and schmooze, but we also sample new dishes I'm developing and go over the evening's special dishes or new menu. (Chanterelle's menu changes completely every four weeks. The only exception is my grilled seafood sausage, which is always on the menu.) We are lucky to have this time together, because while it's a restaurant world tradition for staff to eat together as a family, in reality this doesn't happen often these days.

OUR FAMILY MEAL At Chanterelle, the employee table is set each afternoon at 4:30 by the waitstaff, who pull the dining room tables together to form one long banquet-style table that's covered with white cloths and set with silver. Karen and I almost always eat with our staff, and family members often join us, too. We always have plenty of food, so both the planned and unplanned eaters are well fed. These days our family table is likely to accommodate about twenty-five people. It seems like an astonishing number when we look back and remember that our first staff meal more than twenty years ago was at a table set for six! It's fun when our friends and family join us at the table. And there's no denying the staff rather mischievously relishes the opportunity to scrutinize someone's new boyfriend or meet somebody's mother. (After just such a meal, one of our long-standing waitstaff rolled her eyes and murmured under her breath, "Well, *that* explains a lot!")

We have weekly rituals, too. On Saturdays, our children come to the staff meal with Karen's parents, Gaby and Paul, and I always try to cook a few extra-special dishes for their enjoyment. Friday was always the day my father, Murray, showed up, and I made it a point to prepare something I knew he especially liked.

Over the years, our staff meal has given us a chance to learn about each other's lives. We share good and bad times, commiserate over breakups, celebrate newfound loves, and generally stay tuned-in to life's ups and downs. Sometimes it's a bit like a soap opera, but with very good food. Time together like this has also given us the sweet gift of seeing long-term affections develop. For example, my father took quite an interest in our staff, many of whom were staff-slash-something else (actors, dancers, writers, photographers, artists, you name it). He was a regular at their performances, exhibitions, or book signings, and he made it a point to visit the new restaurants of former Chanterelle employees when they moved on to their own restaurant kitchens. My father died in 1994, and even now it is bittersweet to see him still so deeply missed.

SUPPER IS SERVED Staff meals at Chanterelle are a mosaic of flavors as diverse as the people they nourish. Ours is always a very ample table. In fact, the motto on our staff sweatshirts is "Good food and plenty of it." Restaurant work is very physical, and plenty of good food ensures we'll have the stamina to do our best. There are always prodigious portions of side dishes such as rice, noodles, or couscous, and an enormous salad of mixed greens. Our main courses, as you'll soon be

able to taste for yourself, range from international in inspiration to resolutely all-American. Many are one-pot recipes that require a minimum of active supervision once they've started to cook—you can just let the pot simmer on the stove, filling your home with wonderful aromas. The result will be good things to eat such as Moroccan lamb shanks, beer-braised short ribs, chicken gumbo, and Hungarian-style stuffed cabbage, each a staff meal favorite. Satisfying, unfussy dishes like these have pleased generations of families, and they'll bring pleasure to yours, too.

These days I'm no longer the only one preparing our staff meal. As Chanterelle has become more successful, our staff has also grown larger and my responsibilities have expanded beyond the daily routine of the restaurant, so now I trade off with the other cooks. When it's my turn, we're likely to eat a dish like chicken with black mushrooms and Chinese sausage because I enjoy shopping in Chinatown, which is only a few blocks from the restaurant. Each of the other cooks brings his or her unique touch and ethnicity to the staff menu, introducing new flavors and reacquainting us with old favorites, too.

Today many families struggle to find the time and energy to cook a nice meal. I know the feeling—sometimes the demanding schedule of a busy professional kitchen makes preparing the big staff meal at Chanterelle a challenge for me, too. But in even the fullest, most hectic lives there should always be room for the delights of a tasty home-cooked meal. No succumbing to takeout, no peculiar smorgasbord meals culled from a salad bar. There is no substitute for the real thing. You'll find many of the recipes in this book well suited to busy families, big or small. Some recipes require only quick sautéing, some simply simmer on top of the stove, while others, whose flavors improve with age, are meant to be prepared in largish quantities so there'll be enough for several meals.

I truly love to cook—anything, anytime, anywhere. As a professional, I enjoy preparing the more formal, sophisticated food that has brought such pleasure to Chanterelle's clients for more than twenty years. But equally satisfying is the cooking that feeds *my* soul and makes *me* happy—the informal, intensely flavored meals I share with my family and friends. I hope my recipes will bring the same pleasure to your table.

—DAVID WALTUCK

staff meals from chanterelle

Soup

Soup is the perfect meal for busy families with tight schedules. Most require only one big pot, and once the ingredients are combined they require little tending as they cook. The recipes here are meant to be enjoyed as satisfying main-course dishes. At Chanterelle, for example, our staff meal is often a hearty soup, such as a beef-rich borscht, served with some good crusty bread and a salad. Some of these soups will provide two family meals, which makes them ideal as planned leftovers. All are delicious the first time around, but like most soups they'll gain even greater depth of flavor with reheating.

Another nice thing about soups is that they encourage creativity—which, after all, is one of the most pleasurable aspects of cooking.

Hot Beef Borscht for Aunt Gertie

When **I was little**, my aunt Gertie talked frequently about a hot beef borscht with garlic that she had eaten during her own childhood. Although her taste memory of it was vivid, no matter how hard she tried she was never able to make a version that matched the one she described so fondly. I think this richly beefy, slightly peppery borscht is what Aunt Gertie had in mind. Borscht is usually sweet and sour, with lemon juice as the traditional flavoring, but I also add vinegar—which contributes an appealing tanginess. Because this borscht contains meat, it should be served hot, not cold. Accompanied by thick-sliced rye bread, a cucumber or green salad, and a dish of sour cream, this makes a very satisfying meal. The sour cream is more than a garnish—it balances and smooths out the flavors. Like most soups, this borscht improves with age and reheating. However, caraway seeds will overwhelm the other flavors in reheated dishes, so add some of the seeds to the borscht each time you heat it, rather than all at once.

SERVES 6 AS A MAIN COURSE

3 pounds beef brisket

5 cups Beefed-Up Veal Stock (page 38), canned low-sodium
   chicken broth, or water

3 tablespoons rendered chicken fat (see box, page 143)
   or canola or other vegetable oil

1 large onion, sliced

2 large cloves garlic, minced

2½ quarts Chicken Stock (page 39) or canned low-sodium
   chicken broth

5 cups peeled and shredded uncooked beets
   (5 to 6 large beets)

⅓ cup fresh lemon juice

6 cups shredded cabbage (1- to 2-pound head)

7 tablespoons sugar

¼ cup red wine vinegar or cider vinegar

2 tablespoons coarse (kosher) salt

Freshly ground black pepper, to taste

1 tablespoon caraway seeds (optional)

1. Place the beef in a large saucepan and add the beef stock. It should cover the meat. Bring to a boil over high heat, then reduce the heat to low and simmer, partially covered, until the beef is tender, about 2 hours. Remove the beef from the liquid and let it cool. Reserve the stock. (This may be done a day ahead.) When it's cool, cut the meat into ½-inch dice.

2. Heat the chicken fat or oil in a large stockpot over medium heat. Add the onion and garlic and sauté, stirring occasionally, until lightly browned, about 10 minutes.

3. Add the reserved beef stock and the chicken stock, increase the heat to high, and bring to a boil. Reduce the heat to low and add the beets and lemon juice. Simmer, uncovered, until the beets are quite tender, about 30 minutes. At this point the beets should still be red, but they will have begun to give up their color to the broth.

4. Add the cut-up beef and cabbage, increase the heat to return the borscht to a simmer, then simmer, uncovered, until the cabbage is soft and the beef is heated through, about 10 minutes more. Season with the sugar, vinegar, salt, pepper, and caraway (if desired). Simmer for a couple of minutes to let the flavors blend, then taste and adjust the seasoning. Serve immediately.

Hot and Sour Soup

Soups are the epitome of **comfort food**, and this flavorful Hot and Sour Soup is no exception. Highly seasoned and thick with two types of dried mushrooms, lily buds, and beef, it is equally satisfying served on its own or accompanied by Stir-Fried Rice Noodles with Bean Sprouts and Scallions (page 282). The recipe, traditionally made with pork, was inspired by a beef-based version in Barbara Tropp's first cookbook, *The Modern Art of Chinese Cooking*. Beef gives the soup richer flavor, but you could substitute pork or chicken, or create an all-vegetable version. At first taste people assume the soup's spiciness comes from chile peppers, but it actually contains none. Black pepper, the original spice used in China to add heat to certain dishes, is the surprise stand-in.

Special ingredients like dried wood ears (also called tree ears or black fungus) and shiitake mushrooms have become increasingly available in large supermarkets, but for lily buds and black vinegar you'll probably need to visit a Chinese market. If necessary, the lily buds can be omitted, and balsamic vinegar can be substituted for the black vinegar. **SERVES 8 AS A MAIN COURSE**

3 ounces dried wood ear mushrooms

3 ounces dried shiitake mushrooms

3 ounces dried lily buds (optional)

1 beef flank steak (about 1¼ pounds), chilled in the freezer
 for 20 minutes to facilitate cutting

½ cup good-quality soy sauce, such as Kikkoman

4 teaspoons Asian sesame oil, plus additional
 for serving

1 tablespoon Chinese black vinegar
 (see box, page 49)

1 tablespoon dry sherry

1 teaspoon sugar

3 quarts Chicken Stock (page 39) or canned low-sodium
    chicken broth
2 tablespoons mushroom soy sauce
1 cup rice vinegar, or more to taste
1 tablespoon freshly ground black pepper,
    or to taste
½ teaspoon ground Szechuan pepper
Coarse (kosher) salt, to taste
6 tablespoons cornstarch
½ cup cold water
3 large eggs, beaten
10 scallions, white and green parts, trimmed and
    cut into ½-inch lengths

1. Place the wood ears, shiitakes, and lily buds (if desired) in separate bowls and cover each with boiling water. Let soak at room temperature for 30 minutes to soften.

2. Slice the chilled flank steak against the grain into ¼-inch strips, then cut each strip into ¼-inch dice. Combine ¼ cup of the regular soy sauce and 4 teaspoons sesame oil with the black vinegar, sherry, and sugar in a large bowl. Add the beef and toss to coat. Refrigerate, covered, for at least 2 hours and up to 24.

3. When you're ready to make the soup, drain the wood ears, shiitakes, and lily buds using a slotted spoon. Lift them from the water, leaving the grit behind. (Only the shiitake soaking water is worth using now or saving for another recipe; strain it through a strainer lined with several layers of cheesecloth and add it to the stockpot with the stock in step 4.) Trim and discard any hard parts from the wood ears and cut what remains into ½-inch pieces. Trim away any stems from the shiitakes and slice the caps into thin strips. Cut the lily buds in half lengthwise.

4. Bring the stock to a boil in a large, nonreactive stockpot over high heat. Add the mushrooms, mushroom soy sauce, and remaining ¼ cup soy sauce. Reduce the heat to low and simmer, uncovered, for 30 minutes, to allow the mushrooms to flavor the broth. Drain the flank steak and add, along with 1 cup rice vinegar and both the black and the Szechuan peppers. Simmer for 10 minutes. Add the lily buds and simmer until the beef is tender and the lily buds are heated through, 5 minutes more.

5. Taste and adjust the seasoning with salt, pepper, and vinegar if necessary. Whisk the cornstarch with the water to blend. When smooth, whisk it into the soup to thicken, about 1 minute (see Note).

6. To serve, bring the soup to a boil quickly and swirl in the beaten eggs with a whisk to form shreds of egg. Toss in the scallions and season with a little additional sesame oil. Serve immediately.

Note: The soup may be prepared through step 5 several days ahead. If you're doing so, refrigerate it, covered, and check the seasoning again before serving. You're looking for a balance of the strong flavors of vinegar and pepper.

dried wood ears and lily buds

Wood ear mushrooms, also called black tree fungi, tree ears, or cloud ears (a larger, less tender version), are cultivated on fallen tree trunks or wood that has been allowed to rot before the fungus grows on it. They look like little blackish brown chips or flakes and are often used in tandem with lily buds to add crunchy textural interest to stir-fries and soups, especially hot and sour soups.

Lily buds, also called tiger lily buds or golden needles, are another traditional hot and sour soup ingredient. They are valued more for their intriguingly chewy texture than for their delicate, tealike flavor. Long, thin, and a light golden color, they are actually the dried, unopened flowers of yellow and orange daylilies. When you're buying lily buds, avoid any that are brittle and brown (signs of age); look for flexible, golden ones.

Both wood ears and lily buds should be rehydrated before using. A long overnight soak in cold water works best. But if you're pressed for time, wood ears can be quickly reconstituted by pouring boiling water over them (for lily buds, use warm water). Let soak for 30 minutes; drain by lifting them from the soaking liquid with a slotted spoon. Trim off any hard parts before using.

Chicken Soup with Fresh Herbs

In this version of **my mother's** chicken soup I combine the best of two worlds—fine home cooking and fine restaurant cooking—to create a more intensely flavorful version of a classic comfort food. By cooking the chicken in chicken stock, rather than simply in water, you double the flavor. It's the same technique I use at Chanterelle to prepare consommé for the restaurant menu. The soup's richly concentrated taste is the very essence of the bird as well as a perfect vehicle for Homemade Matzoh Balls (page 11).

The matzoh balls can be poached right in the chicken soup toward the end of the final simmering, or poached separately in chicken stock in another pan, then drained and added to the soup just before serving. Either method results in good flavor, although poaching matzoh balls in the soup does make it cloudy and a little less appetizing looking. Since I always have plenty of chicken stock in the restaurant, I usually poach them separately.

SERVES 10 AS A MAIN COURSE

1 bunch fresh dill
1 bunch fresh chervil or 1 tablespoon chopped fresh tarragon leaves
1 bunch fresh flat-leaf parsley
4 quarts Chicken Stock (page 39) or canned low-sodium
   chicken broth
2 whole chickens (about 3½ pounds each), quartered
1 large onion, diced
8 large carrots, peeled and cut into 1-inch rounds
5 large parsnips, peeled and cut into ½-inch rounds
Coarse (kosher) salt and freshly ground black pepper, to taste
Homemade Matzoh Balls (recipe follows; optional)

1. Using butcher's twine, tie the dill, chervil, and parsley together in one big bunch. (If you're using tarragon, just sprinkle it in after you pour the stock into the pot.) Place the bunch of herbs in a very large stockpot along with the chicken stock and chicken pieces. Set the pot over high heat and bring to a boil, skimming the surface as the foam rises to the top. Reduce the heat to low, cover, and simmer the broth until the chickens are just cooked through, about 45 minutes. Test for doneness by piercing a thigh with a fork; the juices should run clear.

2. Carefully remove the chicken pieces from the broth and set aside to cool. Remove and discard the herb bundle.

3. Add the onion, carrots, and parsnips to the broth and return to a boil. Reduce the heat to low and simmer until the vegetables are very tender, about 30 minutes; a fork should pierce quite easily through a piece of carrot (see Note).

4. While the vegetables cook, remove the skin from the chicken pieces and pull the meat from the bones. Discard the skin and bones. Coarsely chop the meat and add it to the soup, simmering it for 10 minutes longer to reheat. Remove the pot from the heat and season with salt and freshly ground pepper. Serve immediately.

Note: If you're planning to cook the matzoh balls in the soup, add the batter in step 3, after the vegetables have been simmering for about 20 minutes and before the chicken is added. The matzoh balls should take about 15 to 20 minutes to poach in the simmering soup; they'll bob to the surface when they're done. Add the chicken after the matzoh balls have cooked for 10 minutes.

   If you've cooked the matzoh balls separately and they're still warm, add them 5 minutes after you add the chicken. If the matzoh balls are cool, add them at the same time that you add the chicken.

Staff Meals from Chanterelle | s o u p

soup for sara

After several years of lunches centered on her fondness for peanut butter sandwiches, our daughter, Sara, suddenly discovered soup. So she and I began making soup together, tucking containers away in the freezer for her school lunches. She likes lentil and leek and potato, but her real favorite is chicken with fresh herbs and noodles or rice. Around noon in the wintertime, when I'm busy in the kitchen, I'll picture her sitting at a table of boisterous kids, quietly reading a book and sipping soup from her thermos.

Homemade Matzoh Balls

This is the matzoh ball recipe I make at home for my family and at the restaurant for staff meals. Sometimes I cheat a bit by adding just a little baking powder to the mixture to make it lighter and airier, but, of course, you wouldn't do this if the matzoh balls were to be served during Passover. I once transformed these simple **little dumplings** into an unexpected and luxurious treat on the menu at Chanterelle, adding lots of chopped black truffles to the mixture and forming elegant miniature matzoh balls to set afloat in cups of chicken consommé. To make this fancier version for a special occasion, just add as much chopped black truffle as you can afford to this recipe.

MAKES 1 DOZEN 2½- TO 3-INCH MATZOH BALLS

2 large egg yolks
¼ cup rendered chicken fat (see box, page 143),
    melted but not hot
½ cup warm Chicken Stock (page 39) or canned low-sodium
    chicken broth
¾ to 1 cup matzoh meal
½ teaspoon baking powder (optional)
2 tablespoons grated onion
1 tablespoon chopped mixed fresh herbs, such as
    flat-leaf parsley, dill, and chervil leaves
½ teaspoon coarse (kosher) salt
¼ teaspoon coarsely ground black pepper
3 large egg whites
5 quarts Chicken Stock, water, or a combination of both

1. Combine the egg yolks and chicken fat in a large bowl and beat with an electric mixer on medium speed until thickened. Add ½ cup warm chicken stock and continue beating. Mix in the matzoh meal, baking powder (if desired), onion, herbs, salt, and pepper. Set aside.

2. In a medium-size bowl using clean beaters, beat the egg whites with the mixer at medium-high speed until they reach soft peaks. Using a rubber spatula, fold the whites gently but thoroughly into the matzoh mixture, then refrigerate, covered, for 1 hour.

3. Place the chicken stock in a large stockpot and bring to a boil over medium-high heat.

4. Use your hands to roll the matzoh mixture into balls slightly smaller than a Ping-Pong ball (matzoh balls expand as they cook). When the stock is boiling, reduce the heat and carefully lower the matzoh balls into the liquid. Poach the matzoh balls in the simmering stock until they float to the surface, 15 to 20 minutes. Remove them from the stock and keep warm until you're ready to serve. If you're making them a day in advance, transfer the matzoh balls to a storage container and refrigerate, covered, until you're ready to reheat them in the soup.

Greek-Style Tripe Soup with Lemon

I love tripe. Someday I'm going to organize a **tripe lovers' convention.** I anticipate a skimpy turnout, however, since most people who didn't grow up with tripe dishes think they'll abhor it, and never bother trying it. Years ago, when I first began cooking in restaurants, I lived in a small apartment near Times Square. Exhausted and hungry at the end of a long shift, I often revived myself with a bowl of this soothing soup at one of the area's many inexpensive Greek restaurants. It's quite similar to avgolemono, a traditional, but tripeless, Greek soup also made with egg yolks and fresh lemon juice. The acidity of fresh lemon juice here balances the soup's richness, while the combination of egg yolks and cream whisked in at the end serves as a thickener. Serve with a simple tomato, olive, and cucumber salad and a rustic loaf of bread.

SERVES 8 TO 10 AS A MAIN COURSE

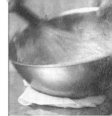

8 tablespoons (1 stick) unsalted butter

1 large onion, finely diced

6 cloves garlic, minced

¼ cup all-purpose flour

2 cups dry white wine

2½ quarts Chicken Stock (page 39) or canned low-sodium
   chicken broth

2 pounds beef tripe (see box, page 83),
   cut into ½-inch dice

5 medium carrots, peeled and cut into ¼-inch dice

3 leeks, white parts trimmed with some green attached,
   well rinsed, drained, and cut into ¼-inch dice

4 bay leaves

½ teaspoon dried thyme leaves

3 large egg yolks

1 cup heavy (or whipping) cream

Coarse (kosher) salt and freshly ground black pepper,
   to taste

Juice of 3 to 4 lemons

Chopped fresh flat-leaf parsley leaves, for garnish

1. Melt the butter in a large stockpot over medium-low heat. Add the onion and garlic and sweat slowly until soft and translucent but not browned, about 10 minutes.

2. Add the flour and cook, stirring frequently, for 10 to 15 minutes to develop a nutty aroma. Do not let the mixture brown. Whisk in the wine and increase the heat to medium. Add the chicken stock and bring to a simmer, whisking often, making sure there are no lumps. Add the tripe, carrots, leeks, bay leaves, and thyme and simmer, covered, until the tripe is as tender as you want it—about 1½ hours for a slightly resilient texture.

3. Combine the egg yolks and cream in a small bowl and whisk to blend. Reduce the heat under the soup to low; the soup should be barely simmering. Then whisk in the egg mixture. Continue to cook, stirring the soup constantly, until it thickens slightly. Don't let the soup get too hot or it will curdle. Remove the pot from the heat and season with salt, pepper, and lemon juice; the soup should be lemony, but not overpoweringly so. Remove the bay leaves and serve, garnished with chopped parsley.

Thai Shrimp Soup

My wife, Karen, and I love Thai food, which is one of the reasons we traveled to Thailand a few years ago. We were fascinated by the extraordinary quality of the cooking (and ingredients) everywhere we went, even at the Bangkok airport. In fact, we ate this **terrific-tasting version** of a classic Thai soup at the airport snack bar. Inspired as I was by Thai cuisine, I felt it wasn't quite right for the Chanterelle menu, so I experimented with ingredients and flavors for the Chanterelle staff, and eventually, little by little, some Thai influences made their way into the menu.

Here the light, elegant shrimp broth allows the haunting perfumes of lemongrass and kaffir lime leaves to come through beautifully. Cucumber Salad with Red Onion and Chinese Sausage (page 314) is a perfect accompaniment.

SERVES 4 AS A MAIN COURSE

2 tablespoons canola or other vegetable oil
1 small clove garlic, minced
6 stalks lemongrass, trimmed and sliced into very thin rounds
1½ pounds small or medium shrimp, peeled and
    deveined (reserve shells)
8 cups Chicken Stock (page 39) or canned low-sodium
    chicken broth
3 kaffir lime leaves
3 tablespoons Thai fish sauce (*nam pla*), or more to taste
3 tablespoons fresh lime juice, or more to taste
1 tablespoon good-quality soy sauce, such as Kikkoman
2 teaspoons chili-garlic sauce (*sambal oelek*)
1 can (8 ounces) straw mushrooms, drained (see Note)
1 cup thinly sliced green cabbage
6 scallions, white and green parts, trimmed and thinly sliced

1. Heat the oil in a medium-size saucepan over medium-high heat. Add the garlic and lemongrass, which should sizzle immediately in the oil. Stir the mixture

Staff Meals from Chanterelle | soup

until it's aromatic but not browned, about 45 seconds. Add the reserved shrimp shells and stir until the shells have turned opaque, about 2 minutes. Add the stock and kaffir lime leaves and bring to a boil over high heat.

2. Reduce the heat to low and simmer, uncovered, for 30 minutes, to let the stock reduce slightly and the flavors blend. Add 3 tablespoons each fish sauce and lime juice along with the soy sauce and chili sauce, and simmer for 10 minutes more. Remove the pan from the heat and strain the broth into a clean pot, pressing hard on the solids in the sieve.

3. To serve, bring the broth to a simmer. Add the straw mushrooms, cabbage, and shrimp. Simmer gently until the shrimp is just opaque, about 2 minutes. Remove the pan from the heat and add the scallions. Taste and adjust the seasoning, adding more fish sauce, lime juice, or chili sauce if needed. Serve immediately.

Note: Although we did find fresh straw mushrooms in Thailand, I have seen only the canned variety in the United States. These mushrooms are necessary to the look and feel of many Thai dishes. Although some might object to the canned version, preserved products are actually very typical in authentic Thai cuisine. You can substitute fresh cultivated white mushrooms if you like. The cooking time remains the same.

kaffir lime leaves

If you can imagine a pear-shaped lime with an exaggeratedly knobby surface, you know what a kaffir lime looks like. In Thai cooking the grated rind is used with aromatic spices in curries; the juice, as a flavoring for soups and dipping sauces. The fruit's shiny, dark green leaves are flat and supple, a bit waxy, and a little thicker than bay leaves. They impart a pungent, zesty lemon-lime flavor with a slightly floral note to a wide variety of Thai dishes. Sometimes labeled "wild lime leaves," kaffir lime leaves are available fresh, frozen, and dried at Asian markets as well as some specialty food shops and large supermarkets. Fresh leaves (your best choice) and frozen leaves have more flavor but can be difficult to find, depending on where you live.

If you can't find kaffir lime leaves, then add a combination of fresh lemon juice and a bit of grated ordinary lime zest to the dish just before serving.

New England Clam Chowder

As is the case with so many historical regional recipes, the "correct" method for making clam chowder is a subject of enormous controversy. Should this **beloved classic** be made with salt pork or bacon? Tomatoes? Potatoes? Herbs? Cream? Passions run high. And the problem is compounded by the fact that quite often cooks just can't seem to leave well enough alone, changing a classic dish for the sake of change rather than improvement.

This version of clam chowder is what I think of as the right one. It has few embellishments and is filled with a strong, presence. It can stand in splendid solitude as a wonderful one-pot meal, with the addition of just one special treat. If our pastry chef feels especially generous when we make a pot of chowder for our staff meal, if we beg and whine sufficiently, and—perhaps most important—if he plans to stay and eat with us, he'll whip up a batch of buttery Herbed Biscuits (page 382).

SERVES 4 AS A MAIN COURSE

18 cherrystone clams or other hard-shell clams

1 cup dry white wine

3 strips bacon, cut crosswise
   into 1/8-inch pieces

1 medium onion, diced (about 1 cup)

1 small clove garlic, minced

1 tablespoon all-purpose flour

2 cups water

1 teaspoon dried thyme leaves

2 bay leaves

Freshly ground black pepper, to taste

2 medium-size waxy potatoes, such as Yukon Gold,
   peeled and cut into ¼-inch cubes (about 2 cups)
1 cup heavy (or whipping) cream
Dash of Tabasco sauce

1. Using a stiff brush, scrub the clams under cold running water. Rinse them well in a colander, then place them in a medium-size, nonreactive saucepan or stockpot. Add the wine, cover the pan, and set it over high heat. Steam the clams until they open, 5 to 8 minutes. Start checking after 5 minutes, removing each clam to a bowl as it opens, using tongs. If any clam seems reluctant to open, give the shell a sharp rap with the tongs; that usually does the trick. Discard any clam that absolutely refuses to open. Set the clams aside to cool.

2. Pour the clam cooking liquid through a strainer lined with several layers of dampened cheesecloth into a small heatproof bowl. Set aside.

3. Rinse out the saucepan and wipe it dry. Add the bacon and cook over medium heat, stirring occasionally, until browned and crisp, about 5 minutes. Using a slotted spoon, remove the bacon to paper towels to drain.

4. Add the onion and garlic to the bacon drippings in the saucepan and sauté over medium heat, stirring occasionally, until translucent but not browned, about 5 minutes. Sprinkle in the flour and cook, stirring, for 2 minutes; be sure not to let the flour brown. Whisk in the reserved clam cooking liquid and the water, then add the thyme, bay leaves, and pepper. Bring to a boil, whisking occasionally, then reduce the heat to maintain a steady simmer. Cook, uncovered, for 15 minutes to reduce the liquid somewhat and blend the flavors.

5. Meanwhile, remove the cooled clams from the shells; discard the shells. Chop the meat coarsely, either by hand or by pulsing briefly in a food processor. Set aside.

6. Add the potatoes to the soup and return to a simmer. Cook, uncovered, until the potatoes are just tender, about 10 minutes.

7. Add the bacon to the soup along with the chopped clams, cream, and Tabasco. Cook until everything is heated through, 2 to 3 minutes; do not let the soup boil, or the clams will toughen. Taste for seasoning and adjust as necessary, then ladle into soup bowls and serve immediately.

Mussel Soup with Saffron

This is a heady soup **redolent of the sea** and richly infused with saffron and cream. Using the essence of mussel juice created by steaming the mussels in white wine adds an unusual dimension to the flavor. I like to use Prince Edward Island or other rope-cultured mussels, because they're a nice small size and I've found them to be tastier and cleaner than other mussels, but any mussels you can find will do just fine. Simple accompaniments, like a big green salad and a loaf of warm crusty bread, are all that's needed to turn this soup into a pleasant supper.

SERVES 6 TO 8 AS A MAIN COURSE

3 pounds mussels
1 bottle (750 ml) dry white wine, such
    as a Pinot Blanc or Chardonnay
2 tablespoons chopped shallots
1 tablespoon minced garlic
2 tablespoons unsalted butter
1 medium onion, cut into small dice
1 large carrot, peeled and cut into small dice
1 tablespoon all-purpose flour
½ teaspoon saffron threads, soaked (see box, page 174)
4 cups Chicken Stock (page 39) or canned low-sodium
    chicken broth
4 cups heavy (or whipping) cream
Coarse (kosher) salt, to taste (optional)
Pinch of cayenne pepper, or to taste
Fresh lemon juice, to taste
1 bunch chives, snipped, for garnish

1. Soak, clean, and debeard the mussels (see box, facing page).

2. Place the mussels in a medium-size, nonreactive saucepan or stockpot. Add the wine, shallots, and garlic. Cover the pan and place it over high heat. Steam the mussels until they open, about 5 to 8 minutes, shaking the pot occasionally to redistribute the mussels as they steam.

3. Using a slotted spoon, remove the mussels to a bowl and set them aside, discarding any that haven't opened. Pour the cooking liquid through a strainer lined with cheesecloth into a heatproof bowl and set aside. When the mussels are cool enough to handle, remove the meat from the shells, discarding the shells. Cover the mussels to keep them warm while you prepare the soup.

4. Rinse out the saucepan and wipe it dry. Add the butter and melt over medium-low heat. Add the onion and carrot and cook gently, stirring occasionally, until softened, about 5 minutes. Reduce the heat to low, stir in the flour, and continue cooking, stirring constantly, until the mixture develops a nutty aroma, about 5 minutes. Be careful not to let the flour brown.

5. Add the mussel cooking liquid, saffron, and chicken stock and whisk well. Bring to a boil over high heat and cook, uncovered, for 15 minutes, to reduce the liquid somewhat and blend the flavors. Reduce the heat so the liquid simmers briskly and whisk in the cream. Cook until slightly thickened, about 10 to 15 minutes, whisking occasionally. Taste the soup. If it's not the desired strength, continue simmering to reduce it and further concentrate the flavors. Taste again and season with salt (if necessary), cayenne, and lemon juice.

6. To serve, divide the mussels among soup plates and ladle the hot soup over them. Garnish with snipped chives.

cleaning mussels

Fill a bucket with cold water. Add the mussels and a handful of salt. Soak the for about an hour to dislodge the dirt and any grit from around the lip of the shells, then remove them from the water and place in a colander in the sink. Under cold running water, use a stiff brush to vigorously scrub off any remaining grit or barnacles from each mussel. Leave the hairy "beard" that protrudes from the side of each shell intact for now. Discard any mussels with open or broken shells. Just before you plan on cooking the mussels, use your fingers or the dull side of a paring knife to pull off the beards.

Pea Soup with Ham

This satisfying soup is **always a hit** both at home and at our staff meal. There are no shortcuts to making it, but the effort is well worth the tasty end result. It's best to plan on preparing this over a two-day period—fixing the ham stock the first day, and finishing the soup the next. Like many restaurant kitchens, we frequently have Smithfield ham trimmings on hand at Chanterelle; I often use 2 or 3 pounds of them for ham broth, but I also make it with the same amount of ham hocks. Since the ham is already quite salty on its own, I recommend using homemade Chicken Stock (page 39) here. It tends to be less salty than even low-sodium canned chicken broth.

SERVES 10 TO 12 AS A MAIN COURSE

FOR THE HAM STOCK:

3 or 4 ham hocks (2 to 3 pounds)

3 large carrots, unpeeled, cut into 1-inch pieces

3 large onions, unpeeled, cut into large chunks

About 5 quarts Chicken Stock (page 39), canned low-sodium
    chicken broth, or water, enough to cover the ham, carrots,
    and onions by 3 inches

FOR THE SOUP:

5 quarts ham stock, or more as needed

¼ cup canola or other vegetable oil

2 medium onions, cut into ¼-inch dice

4 large cloves garlic, minced

2 pounds green split peas

3 medium carrots, peeled and cut into ¼-inch slices

3 bay leaves

Coarse (kosher) salt and freshly ground black pepper, to taste

2 to 3 tablespoons unsalted butter, or to taste (optional)

Diced ham from the hocks, for garnish

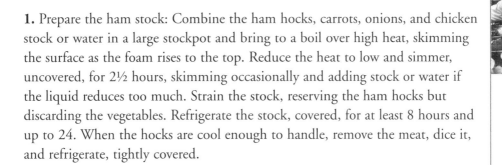

1. Prepare the ham stock: Combine the ham hocks, carrots, onions, and chicken stock or water in a large stockpot and bring to a boil over high heat, skimming the surface as the foam rises to the top. Reduce the heat to low and simmer, uncovered, for 2½ hours, skimming occasionally and adding stock or water if the liquid reduces too much. Strain the stock, reserving the ham hocks but discarding the vegetables. Refrigerate the stock, covered, for at least 8 hours and up to 24. When the hocks are cool enough to handle, remove the meat, dice it, and refrigerate, tightly covered.

2. When you're ready to prepare the soup, remove and discard the layer of fat on the surface of the ham stock. Heat the oil in a large stockpot over medium-low heat. Add the onions and garlic and sweat the vegetables, covered, until translucent but not browned, about 10 minutes, uncovering occasionally to stir.

3. Add the peas, carrots, bay leaves, and 5 quarts stock and bring to a boil over medium-high heat, stirring occasionally. Reduce the heat to low to maintain a steady simmer, then skim the surface of foam and debris. Simmer, uncovered, until the peas are tender, about 2 hours, stirring occasionally and scraping the bottom of the pot to make sure the soup isn't sticking. You may need to add more stock or water if the soup gets too thick. When it's done, the soup should be thick but not porridgelike.

4. Remove the soup from the heat and discard the bay leaves, then season with salt and pepper. Just before serving, I like to stir in a couple of tablespoons of butter to finish the soup. Ladle into bowls and garnish each with diced ham.

the best bay leaves

Fresh bay leaves are one of my favorite seasonings. I love their pungent, complex, up-front flavor with its hints of lavender, clove, and eucalyptus. Unfortunately, they're difficult to find, although you'll occasionally see them at specialty food shops or farmers' markets. If you're lucky enough to buy fresh leaves, let them age a day or so in a cool dark place before using, then break or bend each leaf to release its peppery flavor and perfume. Aromatic dried Turkish bay leaves are an excellent substitute for fresh bay. Be sure to read the label. If the origin isn't stated, you can assume the leaves are not Turkish. Always remove the leaves from the dish before serving.

Black Bean Soup

Robustly satisfying and easy to make, this is

my basic black bean soup. The recipe is simple and flexible, with
plenty of room for adjustments and extra touches of your own.
For example, in place of the bacon you could simmer a smoked
ham hock in the stock until tender, then dice the meat and add
it to the soup. Or you could expand the number and type of
vegetables, adding sweet peppers, leeks, or zucchini—or some
leafy greens like collards or bok choy. Throw in a few hot peppers,
a smoked or spicy sausage or two, or even a couple of hot dogs.
Almost anything goes. This version is thick with whole beans,
but a smoother consistency and a fancier, more refined soup can
be achieved by using half the amount of beans, then puréeing the
finished soup until it's smooth. Whether plain or fancy, the soup
needs only a simple lettuce and tomato salad and some piping-hot
Cornbread (page 381) to become a hunger-stanching supper.

Serve with its array of garnishes set out on the table in small
bowls. **SERVES 6 AS A MAIN COURSE**

2 cups dried black beans

6 cups cold water

3 tablespoons canola or other vegetable oil

4 ounces slab bacon, rind discarded, cut into ¼-inch dice

1 medium onion, peeled and cut into ¼-inch dice

1 large carrot, peeled and cut into ¼-inch dice

3 large cloves garlic, minced

8 cups Chicken Stock (page 39), canned low-sodium
    chicken broth, or water, or more as needed

4 bay leaves

Coarse (kosher) salt and freshly ground black pepper, to taste

½ teaspoon Tabasco sauce, or more to taste

1 tablespoon dry sherry or Madeira

Staff Meals from Chanterelle | soup

1 teaspoon wine vinegar, preferably sherry vinegar but
   white wine or red wine vinegar will do
For garnish: sour cream, diced onion, chopped fresh cilantro
   leaves, chopped hard-cooked egg

1. Pick over the beans, discarding any stones or bits of debris. Place the beans in a colander or strainer and rinse well under cold running water. Drain. Place the beans in a large stockpot or bowl, add the water (it should cover the beans by 2 inches), and soak for 8 hours or overnight in the refrigerator.

2. Heat the oil in a very large stockpot over medium-low heat. Add the bacon and sauté, stirring occasionally, until browned, about 15 minutes.

3. Add the onion, carrot, and garlic to the pot and sweat, uncovered, stirring occasionally, until the vegetables are soft but not browned, about 10 minutes.

4. Drain the soaked beans. Add them to the pot along with 8 cups stock and the bay leaves. Increase the heat to high and bring to a boil. Reduce the heat to medium low and simmer, uncovered, until the beans are tender and the vegetables have practically dissolved, 1 to 1½ hours. Stir the soup occasionally to make sure the beans aren't sticking to the bottom of the pot. If the soup becomes too thick, add additional stock or water. Most of the beans should keep their shape, but some will fall apart enough to thicken the soup.

5. Remove the pot from the heat and season with salt, pepper, Tabasco, dry sherry, and vinegar. Remove the bay leaves.

6. Ladle the soup into bowls and garnish with any combination you like of sour cream, diced onion, fresh cilantro leaves, and chopped hard-cooked egg.

Lentil Soup with Garlic Vinaigrette

Lentils come in a wide **array of colors** and sizes. My favorites are the tiny (about the size of a peppercorn) green French *lentilles de Puy,* which are grown on volcanic soil near the town of Le Puy in the mountainous region of the Auvergne. A bit firmer than brown lentils, they don't fall apart as easily, and I find their complex, slightly peppery taste intriguing. Look for them at specialty food stores. Of course, you can easily use the larger, more readily available brown lentils from the supermarket instead.

The simplicity of this soup allows the fine earthy flavor of the lentils to come through beautifully. If desired, you could further enhance the dish by simmering some smoked sausage or ham along with the lentils, adding an appealing depth of flavor.

A little garlic vinaigrette added to each bowl of soup before serving is an unexpected final touch. As an alternative garnish, you might add a swirl of salsa to each serving, or a dollop of sour cream mixed with Madras-style curry powder. **SERVES 8 TO 10 AS A MAIN COURSE**

FOR THE SOUP:

1 pound French de Puy (green) lentils or
   regular brown lentils

2 tablespoons olive oil

1 small onion, diced

2 large cloves garlic, minced

7 to 8 cups Chicken Stock (page 39) or canned low-sodium
   chicken broth

½ cup Tasty Basic Tomato Sauce (page 271) or good-quality
   commercial tomato sauce

2 bay leaves

½ teaspoon dried thyme leaves
1 large carrot, peeled and cut into ¼-inch dice

FOR THE VINAIGRETTE:

½ cup extra-virgin olive oil
¼ cup red wine vinegar
2 cloves garlic, minced

TO FINISH:

1 teaspoon red wine vinegar, or to taste
Coarse (kosher) salt and freshly ground
    black pepper, to taste

1. Pick over the lentils, discarding any stones or bits of debris. Rinse under cold running water and drain.

2. Heat the oil in a medium-large stockpot over medium-low heat. Add the onion and garlic and cook, stirring occasionally, until translucent but not browned, about 5 minutes.

3. Add the lentils, 7 cups of the stock, the tomato sauce, bay leaves, and thyme. Stir to mix, then increase the heat to high and bring to a boil. Reduce the heat to low to maintain a steady simmer and cook, partially covered, until the lentils are tender, about 45 minutes, uncovering occasionally to stir. You may need to add another cup of stock if the lentils absorb too much liquid. Stir in the carrot and simmer for 20 minutes more.

4. Meanwhile, make the vinaigrette: Combine the oil, vinegar, and garlic in a small bowl and whisk to blend.

5. When the soup is ready, remove it from the heat and season with the vinegar and salt and pepper. Ladle into soup bowls, then whisk the vinaigrette to reblend, and drizzle a tablespoonful over each portion. Serve immediately.

Mushroom-Barley Soup

Like many chefs, I have vivid **childhood memories** of my mother in her kitchen, and to this day I still remember how she prepared mushroom-barley soup. Compared to other dishes I watched her make, the whole process of making this particular soup seemed much more elaborate, like a ritual.

She made the soup the way they do in Jewish dairy restaurants, using for the broth the strained water she had soaked the mushrooms in, rather than adding meat stock. I recall watching, fascinated, as she made a brown roux, adding flour to butter, cooking it until it was quite dark, then using it to enrich and thicken the meatless soup. As for mushrooms, she used Polish dried mushrooms, even though they were expensive. They're hard to find these days, so I use dried porcini mushrooms imported from Italy, and for added flavor, I also use Chicken Stock (page 39) though this obviously makes the soup nondairy. **SERVES 8 AS A MAIN COURSE**

4 ounces dried porcini mushrooms

4 cups very warm water

2 medium leeks

3 tablespoons unsalted butter

2 carrots, peeled and cut into ¼-inch dice

2 medium onions, cut into ¼-inch dice

1 small clove garlic, minced

2 tablespoons all-purpose flour

10 cups Chicken Stock (page 39) or canned low-sodium
  chicken broth

2 bay leaves

½ cup pearl barley

Coarse (kosher) salt and freshly ground black pepper,
  to taste

1. Place the porcinis in a bowl and cover with the water. Let soak at room temperature for 30 minutes to soften.

2. Trim away and discard all but ½ inch of the green part from the leeks. Split the leeks lengthwise and rinse them well under cold running water to remove the grit. Drain and cut into ¼-inch dice.

3. Melt the butter in a medium-size saucepan over medium heat. Add the carrots, onions, leeks, and garlic. Sauté, stirring occasionally, until the onions and leeks are wilted and very lightly browned, about 10 minutes. Stir in the flour and cook, stirring constantly, for 5 minutes. The flour may brown slightly. Whisk in the chicken stock and increase the heat to high.

4. While the soup comes to a boil, lift the mushrooms from the soaking liquid with a slotted spoon and set aside. Strain the liquid into the soup through a strainer lined with several layers of cheesecloth and continue to bring to a boil. Add the bay leaves.

5. Rinse the soaked mushrooms and remove and discard any hard or gritty parts (see Note). Chop the mushrooms coarsely and add them to the soup. Add the barley and simmer, uncovered, stirring occasionally, until the barley is tender, about 45 minutes. Remove and discard the bay leaves. Season with salt and freshly ground pepper and serve.

Note: I rinse reconstituted dried porcinis because I find they're still likely to have some grit. This is not true of shiitakes.

bizarre breakfasts

To my way of thinking, breakfast is a state of mind rather than a traditional morning meal. I don't have anything against morning per se; I just don't especially like most breakfast foods. In fact, I'll eat virtually anything in the morning rather than face a bowl of cereal, a bagel or muffin, or bacon and eggs. I love a bowl of cold noodles in the morning, for example, or a meat loaf sandwich garnished with Cider Vinegar Slaw (page 310) or leftover Cooked Spinach Salad with Soy and Sesame (page 341). And practically any warm soup tastes good, though I have to say I'm very partial to Mushroom-Barley (page 26) and Chicken Soup with Fresh Herbs (page 9).

Panacea Vegetable Soup

The early winter season leading up to the insanity of the December holiday rush is our busiest time at the restaurant. The pace is frenetic, and we're all overworked and exhausted. Every so often I look around to find that almost everyone has the sniffles. At times like this we all need a big, **steaming, healthful** bowl of vegetable soup to clear our sinuses and bolster our morale. This gently flavored soup does the trick, so we dubbed it Panacea Vegetable Soup. When you're feeling frail, one bowl will make you feel like new. Be sure to add the vegetables in stages so that each cooks for the correct amount of time without getting too soft.

If you like your vegetable soup to include pasta, add ¼ cup orzo 20 minutes before the end of the cooking time.

SERVES 6 TO 8 AS A MAIN COURSE

3 leeks
3 tablespoons extra-virgin olive oil
1 medium onion, coarsely chopped (1½ cups)
6 cloves garlic, coarsely chopped
2½ quarts Chicken Stock (page 39) or canned low-sodium
    chicken broth
2 cups canned tomatoes with juice, tomatoes crushed by hand
2 bay leaves
¼ teaspoon dried oregano leaves
¼ teaspoon dried thyme leaves
4 carrots, peeled and cut into ¼-inch pieces
1 small butternut squash, peeled and cut into ½-inch pieces
1 yellow squash, cut into ½-inch pieces
1 zucchini, cut into ½-inch pieces
4 ounces green beans, trimmed and cut into ½-inch pieces
1 cup (well-packed) spinach, rinsed and spun dry

Staff Meals from Chanterelle

¼ small head green cabbage, shredded

1 can (15½ ounces) cannellini or red kidney beans,
  rinsed and drained

1 teaspoon red wine vinegar

1 tablespoon unsalted butter

Coarse (kosher) salt and freshly ground black pepper

Freshly grated Parmesan, for serving

1. Trim away and discard all but 2 inches of the green part from the leeks. Split the leeks lengthwise and rinse them well under cold running water to remove the grit. Drain and cut into ¼-inch-thick slices.

2. Heat the oil in a very large stockpot over medium heat. Add the onion, garlic, and leeks, reduce the heat to low, and sweat until the onions are translucent but not browned, 10 to 15 minutes.

3. Add the stock, tomatoes, bay leaves, oregano, and thyme, increase the heat to high, and bring to a boil. Then lower the heat to medium and simmer for 15 minutes. Add the carrots and simmer, uncovered, for 10 minutes. Add the butternut and yellow squashes, zucchini, and green beans and simmer, uncovered, for 15 minutes. Add the spinach, cabbage, and cannellini beans and continue simmering, uncovered, for 10 minutes more. The soup should be thick with vegetables that are tender but still hold their shape.

4. Remove the pot from the heat and discard the bay leaves. Add the vinegar, butter, and salt and pepper to taste. Taste and adjust the seasonings, if necessary, before serving. Pass the Parmesan at the table.

sweating vegetables

Sweating refers to slowly cooking sliced or diced ingredients in a small amount of fat, water, or stock over very low heat in a pan until they soften and release their juices but do not brown. Many cooks cover the pan, but I prefer to leave it uncovered so I can see what's going on. As the vegetables sweat, their flavors develop, becoming sweeter and more pronounced. When potatoes, carrots, onions, and leeks are used in combination with other ingredients, they are often sweated first.

Leek and Potato Soup

Like the New England Clam Chowder recipe on page 16, the flavor of this **hearty, filling classic** depends on the fine quality of the ingredients and the care taken in their preparation rather than on novelty. Be sure to use starchy Idaho (russet) potatoes for this soup rather than waxy ones. Waxy potatoes (round thin-skinned red potatoes or Yukon Golds, for example) will produce a gummy-textured soup, and this recipe is meant to make one that isn't too thick. Take care to sweat the vegetables slowly (see box, page 29), which allows their flavors to develop. And use a good chicken stock, preferably homemade. It's attention to details like these that separates an adequate cook from a good one. This is also why your guests will marvel at how such a simple soup can taste so delicious.

I like to add cream for a luxurious-tasting soup. If you decide not to use it, the soup will still be wonderful. However, don't be tempted to substitute milk, half-and-half, or even additional stock.

SERVES 8 AS A MAIN COURSE

3 bunches leeks (about 12)

4 tablespoons (½ stick) unsalted butter

2 large onions, coarsely chopped

4 large russet potatoes (about 2 pounds total),
    such as Idaho, peeled and cut into ½-inch dice

3 quarts Chicken Stock (page 39) or canned low-sodium
    chicken broth

2 cups heavy (or whipping) cream (optional)

Coarse (kosher) salt and freshly ground black
    pepper, to taste

1 bunch fresh chives, finely snipped, for garnish

1. Trim the leeks, leaving about 5 inches of green. Split the leeks lengthwise and rinse them well under cold running water to remove the grit. Drain and coarsely chop.

2. Melt the butter in a large stockpot over low heat. Add the leeks, onions, and potatoes, cover, and sweat the vegetables slowly for 30 minutes, uncovering occasionally to stir.

3. Add the chicken stock and increase the heat to high. Bring the mixture to a boil, then reduce the heat to maintain a steady simmer. Cook, stirring occasionally, until the vegetables are quite soft, about 30 to 40 minutes.

4. Pour the soup into a colander set over a second pot. Pass the vegetables through a food mill and return them to the stock in the pot. Stir to blend the soup, then bring it to a boil again. Cook over medium heat for 10 minutes, stirring often, to reduce the soup a bit and concentrate the flavors. Add the cream, if desired, and return the soup to a boil. Season to taste with salt and freshly ground pepper and garnish with a sprinkling of chives.

using a food mill

A food mill is the best piece of kitchen equipment for achieving the proper texture for Leek and Potato Soup (page 30) or Creamy Tomato Mint Soup (page 32). In contrast to a blender or food processor, which purées soups and sauces, a food mill simultaneously purées and strains out any bits of fiber, skin, or seeds. Depending on which perforated disk you use, the consistency of ingredients processed this way can range from extremely smooth to interestingly textured. Essentially the mill, which is set over a bowl, is a mechanical sieve consisting of an open-base, bowl-shaped hopper with a hand-cranked spring-loaded blade used to push ingredients through interchangeable disks (with small, medium, or large holes). The mills are made of plastic, aluminium, tinned steel, or stainless steel (the best choice) and are available at any well-stocked kitchenware store.

Staff Meals from Chanterelle | soup

Creamy Tomato Mint Soup

Although tomatoes and **aromatic herbs** always complement each other, tender sprigs of fresh mint seem to have a special affinity for tomatoes. In this soup the mint is a sprightly highlight that serves as a refreshing foil to the richness of the cream. Other fresh herbs, such as thyme or basil, can be substituted and the soup will still be very tasty, but you really owe it to yourself to make this recipe with mint at least once. As for the tomatoes, if it's summertime choose the ripest, freshest ones you can find (a pinch of sugar will bring out their natural sweetness); at other times of the year canned will do just fine. Serve with a basket of hot garlic bread and a tossed vegetable salad.

SERVES 8 AS A MAIN COURSE

3 tablespoons unsalted butter

1 medium onion, finely chopped (about 1 cup)

1 tablespoon minced garlic

1 tablespoon all-purpose flour

4 cups peeled, seeded, and coarsely chopped fresh ripe
    tomatoes (4 to 5 pounds; see box, page 33) or
    4 cups canned whole plum tomatoes with their juice
    (two 28-ounce cans)

8 cups Chicken Stock (page 39) or canned low-sodium
    chicken broth

2 tablespoons tomato paste

1 small (about 2 ounces) bunch fresh mint leaves,
    very coarsely chopped, stems discarded

2 cups heavy (or whipping) cream

Coarse (kosher) salt and freshly ground black pepper,
    to taste

Pinch of sugar (optional)

1. Melt the butter in a medium-large, nonreactive stockpot over low heat. Add the onion and garlic and sweat, stirring occasionally, until translucent but not browned, about 8 to 10 minutes.

2. Add the flour and cook, stirring, until the mixture develops a nutty aroma, about 10 minutes. Be careful not to let the flour brown.

3. Add the tomatoes, breaking them up against the side of the pot with a wooden spoon if they're canned. Add the stock, tomato paste, and mint and increase the heat to high. Bring to a boil, then reduce the heat to maintain a steady simmer. Cook, uncovered, stirring occasionally, until the tomatoes are very soft, about 30 minutes.

4. Pour the soup into a colander set over a second pot. Pass the tomatoes through a food mill and return them to the stock in the pot. Stir to blend the soup.

5. Whisk in the cream, then simmer, uncovered, whisking frequently, until the soup is well flavored and slightly thickened, about 15 minutes. Season with salt, pepper, and a pinch of sugar to highlight the sweetness of the tomatoes, if desired. Serve piping hot.

peeling and seeding tomatoes

While it's not essential to skin and seed the tomatoes you use in soup, it does ensure that there'll be no unsightly shriveled bits of tomato skin visible. Bring a pot of water to a boil. If it isn't large enough to hold all of the tomatoes, simply blanch a few at a time. With a sharp paring knife, cut a small, shallow X in the bottom of each tomato. Carefully ease the tomatoes into the boiling water and blanch until the edges of the Xs begin to curl up, about 30 seconds. Using a slotted spoon, remove the tomatoes from the pot to a colander and rinse under cold running water for about a minute. Using the paring knife or your fingers, pull off and discard the skin from each tomato, beginning at the X. The skin should come away easily; if it doesn't, return the tomato to the boiling water for a few more seconds. Core the tomatoes, then cut the peeled tomatoes in half crosswise and use your fingers to poke out the seeds. Discard the seeds. Riper tomatoes are the easiest to peel, but be careful not to blanch them too long or they will become mushy.

Butternut Squash and Bourbon Soup

This is **bright orange, bold**, and laced with bourbon. What more could you ask of a soup? The natural sweetness of the squash's creamy-textured flesh works in tandem with the bourbon's mellow caramelness to produce a luxuriously smooth, thick soup with lots of character. Although butternut is classified as a winter squash, it's available almost year-round these days, so there's no reason to let the season dictate when you make this soup. Occasionally the butternut squash sold in the summer is slightly less flavorful, but this is easily remedied by adding ½ teaspoon sugar to the squash as it simmers in the broth. Serve with roast chicken or Herbed Pinwheel Pork Loin (page 100) and a simple salad of mixed greens. **SERVES 8 AS A FIRST COURSE**

2 tablespoons unsalted butter

1 large onion, coarsely chopped

1 large butternut squash (3 to 3½ pounds), peeled, seeded, and cut into 1-inch chunks

6 cups Chicken Stock (page 39) or canned low-sodium chicken broth

¼ cup Wild Turkey or other excellent bourbon, plus additional for serving if desired

1 bay leaf

Coarse (kosher) salt and freshly ground black pepper, to taste

Fresh lemon juice, to taste

¼ cup heavy (or whipping) cream (optional)

1. Melt the butter in a medium-size stockpot over low heat. Add the chopped onion, cover, and slowly sweat the onion, uncovering occasionally to stir, until soft and translucent but not browned, about 8 minutes.

Staff Meals from Chanterelle | soup

2. Add the butternut squash, chicken stock, ¼ cup bourbon, and the bay leaf and increase the heat to high. Bring to a boil, then reduce the heat to low and simmer, uncovered, stirring occasionally, until the squash is quite soft and tender, about 25 minutes.

3. Remove and discard the bay leaf. Pour the soup into a colander set over a second pot. Working in batches, process the squash in a food processor or blender to a smooth purée. Stir the puréed squash into the stock in the pot.

4. Bring the soup to a simmer over medium heat, stirring occasionally. Continue simmering until the soup is the consistency of heavy cream, 5 to 10 minutes. Season to taste with salt and freshly ground pepper and a squirt of fresh lemon juice. For a richer-tasting soup, stir in 2 to 3 tablespoons of extra bourbon, the heavy cream, or both just before serving. Or you can drizzle the cream over the top of each bowl.

French Onion Soup

The **enveloping warmth** of this classic soup makes it the perfect antidote to a cold winter night. The onions are first cooked very slowly to concentrate their flavor, then caramelized over high heat to add subtle sweetness to the soup. The aroma of the onions languidly simmering in a broth infused with port, brandy, and white wine is the essence of French cooking. The port is a nontraditional touch inspired by James Beard's recipe for onion soup. It adds a supplemental bit of sweetness and helps give the broth a warm, rich color. For a quick garnish, top with crispy croutons (see box, page 356) and a sprinkling of freshly grated Parmesan. To serve the soup gratinéed as they do in French bistros, fill individual ovenproof bowls with hot soup and top with a thick slice of toasted French bread and a slice of Gruyère cheese. Place the bowls under the broiler until the cheese is melted, bubbly, and a bit browned. **SERVES 6 AS A MAIN COURSE**

2 tablespoons unsalted butter

1 tablespoon canola or other vegetable oil

5 large onions, peeled and sliced lengthwise (about 5 cups)

½ cup port

½ cup dry white wine

½ cup brandy

½ teaspoon sugar

8 cups Beefed-Up Veal Stock (page 38), Chicken Stock
    (page 39), or canned low-sodium beef or chicken broth

Coarse (kosher) salt and freshly ground black pepper, to taste

Crisp croutons (see box, page 356), for garnish

Freshly grated Parmesan, for garnish

1. Combine the butter and oil in a medium-large stockpot and heat over low heat. Add the onions and cook, uncovered, until brown but not crisp, about 30 minutes, stirring occasionally. Increase the heat to medium high and cook the onions, uncovered, stirring often, to further brown and caramelize them, 5 to 10 minutes more.

2. Stir in the port, white wine, and brandy and bring to a boil over high heat. Cook, uncovered, until reduced by half, about 5 minutes. Add the sugar and stock and bring to a boil, then lower the heat to a simmer. Cook the soup for 1 hour to allow the flavors to blend. Taste and season with salt and pepper. Serve, making sure each portion has a healthy amount of luscious onions. Top with the croutons and grated Parmesan.

how to ripen avocados

These days it's pretty unusual to find ripe, ready-to-use avocados at the store. However, ripening them yourself is simple. Two to three days before they're needed, buy the inevitably hard avocados, choosing those that feel heavy for their size when you heft them in the palm of your hand. Without crowding, place them in a brown paper bag along with an apple or tomato. (These fruits emit a harmless natural gas that speeds ripening.) Set the bag in a warm place away from direct sunlight and turn the bag once a day to ensure even ripening. The avocados should be ready to use within 3 days. You'll know they're ripe if they yield slightly to the touch when gently squeezed.

Chilled Avocado Soup

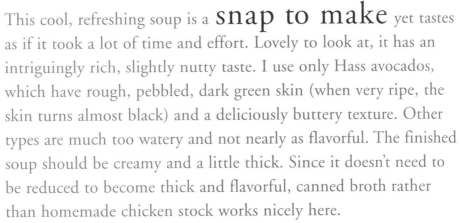

This cool, refreshing soup is a **snap to make** yet tastes as if it took a lot of time and effort. Lovely to look at, it has an intriguingly rich, slightly nutty taste. I use only Hass avocados, which have rough, pebbled, dark green skin (when very ripe, the skin turns almost black) and a deliciously buttery texture. Other types are much too watery and not nearly as flavorful. The finished soup should be creamy and a little thick. Since it doesn't need to be reduced to become thick and flavorful, canned broth rather than homemade chicken stock works nicely here.

Like any dish made with avocado, the soup's pale green color will darken when exposed to air for any period of time, so unless you're prepared to face khaki-colored food, serve within a few hours of preparation. The addition of fresh lime juice brightens the taste and slows discoloration. **SERVES 8 TO 10 AS A FIRST COURSE**

½ small onion, chopped
6 small ripe Hass avocados (about 2½ pounds total), peeled,
 pitted, and cut into chunks
6 cups canned low-sodium chicken broth
1 teaspoon coarse (kosher) salt
¼ teaspoon ground cumin, or to taste
Dash of Tabasco sauce
Juice of 1 lime
For garnish: chopped fresh cilantro leaves and diced tomato, or sour cream

Working in two batches, combine half of all the ingredients except the garnish in a food processor or blender; process until smooth. Transfer the purée to a large serving bowl. Repeat with the remaining half, then add to the serving bowl. Stir, taste, and adjust the seasonings. Refrigerate, covered, to chill. Serve cold or slightly chilled, topped with cilantro and tomato or a dollop of sour cream.

Beefed-Up Veal Stock

At Chanterelle I buy veal soup bones by the huge frozen boxful. These bones come **completely nude**—stripped entirely of any meat. Since you can't produce a flavorful stock from clean-as-a-whistle bones, I use beef shins cut through the bone in ¾-inch slices to beef up the flavor. If your veal bones have a little meat clinging to them, fine. But to ensure a greater depth of flavor, I recommend adding some beef.

This recipe makes a lot of stock, I know, and on top of that it involves a long, slow simmering time. But it's easy to prepare and will keep for months in the freezer. Still, truth be told, although I believe that it's best to make stock in large batches, you don't have to if your storage space is limited. The recipe is easy to halve or even quarter. If the vegetable amounts aren't exact, that's okay—stock making isn't rocket science. **MAKES ABOUT 12 QUARTS**

10 pounds veal bones, preferably with some meat left on
1- to 2-pound piece beef shin
¼ cup canola or other vegetable oil
3 large onions, unpeeled, cut into large chunks
4 carrots, unpeeled, cut into large chunks
3 heads garlic, cut in half through the cloves
12 to 15 quarts water

1. Preheat the oven to 400°F.

2. Place the veal bones and beef in a large, flameproof roasting pan and drizzle with the oil. Place the pan in the oven and roast the bones for 25 minutes, turning them after about 12 minutes. Add the onions, carrots, and garlic, distributing the vegetables evenly among the bones. Continue to roast until nicely browned but not burned or blackened, 45 minutes to 1 hour more.

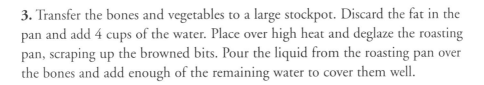

3. Transfer the bones and vegetables to a large stockpot. Discard the fat in the pan and add 4 cups of the water. Place over high heat and deglaze the roasting pan, scraping up the browned bits. Pour the liquid from the roasting pan over the bones and add enough of the remaining water to cover them well.

4. Bring the liquid to a boil over high heat, skimming the surface as the foam rises to the top. Then reduce the heat to low and simmer, partially covered, for 6 hours, skimming occasionally and adding water if it evaporates enough to uncover the bones.

5. Remove the bones and the meat and strain the stock through a fine-mesh sieve. At this point the meat and vegetables won't have much flavor, but if you're a fan of overboiled food, by all means nibble away; otherwise, discard them.

6. Let the stock cool before transferring it to storage containers. The stock will keep, covered, in the refrigerator for up to 4 days, and in the freezer for 6 months. Skim the fat off the top before proceeding with a recipe.

Chicken Stock

Restaurants make and use incredible quantities of chicken stock. In the kitchen at Chanterelle I literally cannot count the number of times a day we dip a ladleful or pour a flavorful stream of it into a pot. A good homemade chicken **stock is essential** to anyone who likes to cook and enjoys well-prepared food. For the sake of convenience, low-sodium canned chicken broth can be used in most recipes in this book, but the truth is that any dish prepared with your own homemade stock will taste better.

The simple flavorings in this chicken stock are my version of *mirepoix.* In the French cooking tradition this is a mixture of coarsely chopped aromatic vegetables, usually carrots, onions or leeks, and celery; turnips or parsnips are sometimes included as well. The vegetables enhance and provide flavor but are not

intended to become part of the final dish. I don't add celery here because I dislike it. Feel free to add a rib or two if you like.

MAKES ABOUT 9 QUARTS

10 pounds chicken necks, backs, and trimmings
3 large carrots, unpeeled, very roughly chopped
2 large onions, unpeeled, very roughly chopped
2 heads garlic, loose outer skins removed, cut crosswise in half
9 to 10 quarts cold water, or enough to cover

1. Combine all the ingredients in a stockpot that's big enough to hold everything comfortably; the water should cover the bones and vegetables by 3 to 4 inches. Bring to a boil over medium heat, skimming the surface as the foam rises to the top, then reduce the heat to low and simmer, uncovered, for at least 3 hours (4 is better). Add water if the stock seems to be reducing too much, and skim occasionally.

2. Remove the pot from the heat, let it cool, then strain the stock through a fine-mesh sieve into one or more storage containers. The stock will keep, covered, in the refrigerator for up to 4 days or frozen for up to 6 months. Skim the fat off the top before proceeding with a recipe.

degreasing chicken stock

The easiest, most effective way to degrease homemade stock is to strain it into a clean container and refrigerate it overnight. The fat will rise to the top, forming a solid layer that's easy to remove. At the restaurant, when we're in too much of a hurry to wait for the stock to chill, we use another method. Before we strain the stock, we place the pot off center on the burner and turn up the heat so the stock reaches a low boil. The liquid in the side of the pot that's resting on the burner will boil; the rest won't. Due to some mysterious law of physics, the fat from the liquid on the boiling side will move to the other side, where it can be carefully ladled off.

After degreasing, if you won't be using the entire amount of stock, simply strain it into a clean container and refrigerate. Any fat that remains can be removed the next day.

Fish Stock

This is a light, **mild-flavored** stock suitable for use in seafood-based soups and stews and in sauces that will be served over broiled or sautéed fish. In general I like my fish stock to be as neutral as possible, and so I use a minimum of ingredients. If I want to bump up the flavor with bay leaves or freshly ground black pepper, I add them when the stock is combined with other ingredients. Choose only non-oily fish for stock and remove the bitter-tasting gills from the fish heads using kitchen shears or a knife. **MAKES ABOUT 4 QUARTS**

4 pounds assorted nonoily fish trimmings, including heads
   (gills removed), bones, and scraps from white-fleshed fish
   such as halibut, flounder, cod, grouper, or striped bass
3 large carrots, cut into chunks
2 large onions, unpeeled, very roughly chopped
4 quarts cold water
2 cups dry white wine

1. Rinse all the fish trimmings, ridding them of any traces of blood and making sure that any skin on the heads or scraps is free of scales.

2. Combine all the ingredients in a stockpot that's big enough to hold everything comfortably; the liquid should cover the ingredients by 3 to 4 inches. Bring to a boil over medium heat, skimming the surface as the foam rises to the top, then reduce the heat to low and simmer, uncovered, for 25 minutes.

3. Remove the pot from the heat and strain the stock through a fine sieve into one or more containers. The stock may be refrigerated for up to 4 days or frozen for up to 6 months.

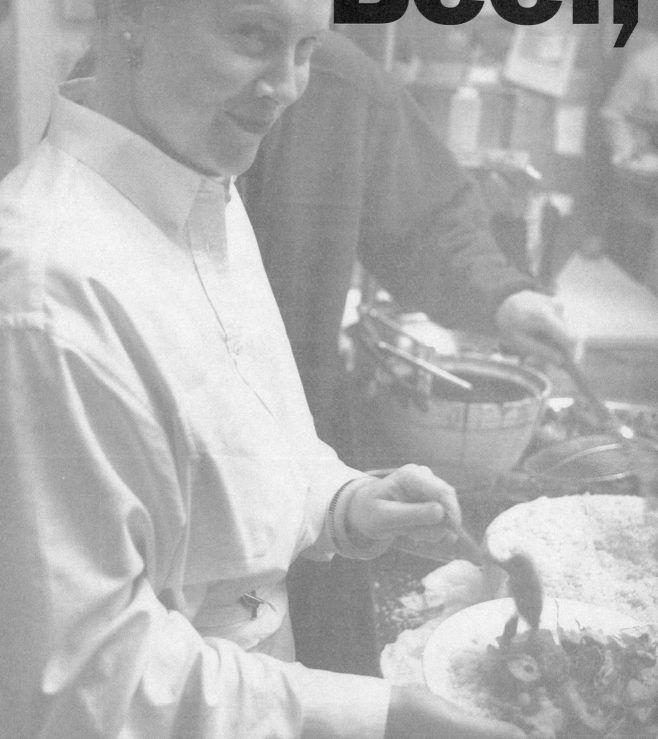

Beef,

Veal, Lamb

In this chapter you'll find the **one-pot** meat **dishes** that I cook at home for family and friends and at Chanterelle for the staff meals that lift our spirits and give us the stamina to face the evening rush. Like many American families, we eat red meat less often than in the past, but in cold weather we often seek the comfort of a slow-simmered stew, and there are still plenty of times, regardless of the season, when we unapologetically crave a good juicy hamburger.

For the most part, these are thrifty dishes created from less expensive cuts of beef, lamb, or veal, many tenderized through the use of flavorful marinades or leisurely braising, and all liberally seasoned. Beef, however, does lend itself to spectacular celebratory dishes as well, and while they don't

work as everyday fare, they do have a place at the occasional staff meal—and, of course, at the family table, too. For that reason, I have included a few front-of-the-house recipes that require a bit more effort in preparation, but they result in dishes that I believe will make welcome changes to your special-occasion repertoire.

Whether the meal calls for a wine-infused bistro version of Mom's Braised Brisket with Carrots (page 55), a succulent Lamb Tagine with Prunes and Honey (page 96), or a platter of Beef Fillets with Star Anise (page 52), you'll find that these are melt-in-your-mouth main dishes filled with character and good flavor. When paired with a green salad or vegetable and a piping-hot gratin, a steaming bowl of white rice, some mashed potatoes, or a side of orzo, there's no resisting pulling up a chair to the table and sitting down with friends or family.

Roast Beef Dinner

"Roast Beef, Medium, is not only a food. It is a Philosophy."

—Edna Ferber, *Roast Beef, Medium*

Every so often we just **have to indulge** in a delicious roast beef dinner, complete with all our favorite side dishes and plenty of piquant homemade Horseradish Sauce (page 369). Roasting a hefty-size piece of meat such as top round is a good way to serve a large family—or a restaurant staff! It's also a convenient excuse to consume unseemly quantities of mashed potatoes. If you can, plan to cook a roast that's larger than you'll need for one dinner so you'll have plenty of leftovers for sandwiches or hash the next day. **SERVES 6 TO 8**

FOR THE ROAST:

1 boneless top round beef roast (about 6 pounds),
    trimmed, rolled, and tied
Extra-virgin olive oil
Coarse (kosher) salt and freshly ground black pepper,
    to taste
2 large cloves garlic, minced

FOR THE ACCOMPANIMENTS:

Everyday Mashed Potatoes (page 334)
Fried Zucchini Coins (page 345)
Yummy Onions (page 325)
Horseradish Sauce (page 369)

1. Preheat the oven to 400°F.

2. Rub the roast all over with oil and season on all sides with salt and pepper. Place in a roasting pan and roast for 15 minutes, then reduce the oven temperature to 350°F and roast for 20 minutes more.

3. Remove the pan with the roast from the oven, leaving the oven on. Let the roast cool briefly, then rub it all over with the garlic, using either your fingertips (carefully) or a rubber spatula. Return the pan to the oven and finish roasting to the desired doneness, about 30 minutes more for rare to medium rare (120° to 130°F on an instant-read meat thermometer).

4. Transfer the roast to a platter and let stand, covered loosely with aluminum foil, in a warm place for at least 10 minutes before carving. Cut it into thin slices to serve, surrounded by bowls of the accompaniments.

roasting wisdom

The perfect roast requires just the right cut of beef. Top round, bottom round, rump roast, and eye round are all good choices and will make fine roasts. The cooking time and temperature for roast beef will depend a great deal on the cut of meat you've chosen, how it was butchered, and the oven temperature when it first goes into the oven. For the Roast Beef Dinner (page 45), I use a rump roast that's about 6 inches high at its thickest point and 10 inches long. With a starting oven temperature of 400°F, lowered after 15 minutes to 350°F, it takes a bit more than an hour for the roast to reach medium rare, the ideal degree of doneness for flavor and ease of slicing.

Since I trust my lips better than some inanimate thermometer, I judge doneness using a method that I don't necessarily recommend you try at home. I insert a metal skewer into the thickest part of the roast and leave it there for a few seconds. Then I remove the skewer and touch it to my lips; when it's quite warm but not really hot, the roast is ready to remove from the oven. A less daring—and more traditional—method would be to use a meat thermometer inserted in the thickest part of the roast, it should read around 120° to 130°F. Regardless of how you like your meat cooked, before slicing the roast, let it rest for 15 to 20 minutes after removing it from the oven. This gives the meat time to relax so the wonderful juices redistribute themselves. Doing so also ensures that the meat will be evenly rosy and fewer juices will be lost when it's carved.

Staff Meals from Chanterelle | b e e f , v e a l , l a m b

Lime-Marinated Flank Steak

Flank steak is an easy cut of beef to prepare, and the **price is right**. The grilled or broiled meat slices up nice and tender when cooked just to the right juicy redness. Cut at an angle against the grain, slices come out pleasantly wide and are especially good served hot over a room-temperature salad like the Cucumber Salad with Red Onion and Chinese Sausage (page 314). If you're in the mood for a simpler, yet satisfying, side dish, plain rice certainly fills the bill. A few sprigs of cilantro make a nice garnish. **SERVES 4**

3 cloves garlic, finely minced
¼ cup Thai fish sauce (nam pla)
¼ cup good-quality soy sauce, such as Kikkoman
Juice of 5 limes
¼ cup sugar
½ cup water
1 tablespoon hot red pepper flakes
1 beef flank steak (about 2 pounds), trimmed of fat

1. Place all the ingredients except the steak in a bowl and whisk to blend. Place the flank steak in a wide, shallow bowl and pour the marinade over it. Turn the meat, making sure it is completely coated with the marinade. Refrigerate, covered, for at least 4 hours and up to 24. Turn the meat occasionally as it marinates.

2. Preheat the grill to very high or preheat the broiler.

3. Remove the flank steak from the marinade and pat dry. Oil the grill rack, place the meat on the rack, and grill, making sure to watch the heat carefully; the sugar and soy sauce tend to cause the meat to blacken quickly. Flank steak is tender when cooked no more than medium rare, about 4 minutes per side.

4. Let the meat rest for 2 minutes, then slice thinly against the grain and serve.

Crispy Orange Beef

My version of this **Szechuan stir-fry** favorite uses a frying technique that's somewhat unorthodox but creates a dish as delicious as the original. Unlike a traditional stir-fry, the slightly spicy, sweet-yet-tangy orange sauce and the beef are prepared separately. The sauce can be made up to a week in advance and refrigerated. The flank steak (partially frozen first so it's easier to cut into thin, even slices) marinates overnight in a soy-sauce-based mixture. The marinated beef is then fried until it's browned and crispy, tossed with warmed orange sauce, and served immediately. To expand the number of servings for unexpected guests, quickly stir-fry green vegetables such as snow peas, zucchini, or asparagus and add them at the last minute. Crispy orange beef is so full of flavor that it needs nothing more than a big bowl of plain rice as an accompaniment. **SERVES 6 TO 8**

FOR THE BEEF AND MARINADE:

1 beef flank steak (2 pounds), trimmed of fat and
    partially frozen to facilitate slicing
¼ cup good-quality soy sauce,
    such as Kikkoman
1 tablespoon Chinese black vinegar or
    balsamic vinegar (see box, page 49)
1 tablespoon Asian sesame oil
1 tablespoon dry sherry
1 tablespoon sugar

FOR THE SAUCE:

2 tablespoons canola or other vegetable oil
2 large cloves garlic, minced
4 teaspoons grated fresh ginger
4 cups orange juice
½ cup rice vinegar, or more to taste

2 tablespoons orange-flavored liqueur, such as
Grand Marnier or Triple Sec

1 tablespoon dry sherry

4 large pieces dried orange or tangerine peel, softened
(see box, page 51)

4 cups Chicken Stock (page 39) or canned low-sodium
chicken broth

¼ cup sugar

3 tablespoons good-quality soy sauce, such as Kikkoman

2 tablespoons cornstarch

3 tablespoons cold water

Coarse (kosher) salt and freshly ground black pepper, to taste

TO FINISH:

2 tablespoons canola or other vegetable oil, plus
additional for deep-frying

6 whole dried red chiles, halved and seeded

Zest of 4 oranges, coarsely chopped or grated

2 ounces dried wood ear mushrooms, soaked as
directed on page 8, drained, then trimmed of
any hard parts and cut into ½-inch strips

½ cup all-purpose flour

½ cup cornstarch

chinese black vinegar

This dark vinegar, made from rice, wheat, millet, or sorghum, is mild yet deeply flavorful, with a slight hint of sweetness. In the north of China it's often used in the preparation of braised dishes and as a dipping sauce or table condiment. Since the darkest, richest-tasting examples are made in the province of Chiekiang, it is sometimes known as Chiekiang vinegar, and the labels of the best brands will include this geographical designation in various dialects (Chiekiang, Chinkiang, Chenkong, Chen-jung). Good brands to look for include Narcissus Yongchun Loagu, Tientsin Yongchun Loagu, and Gold-Plum Chinkiang Vinegar. In a pinch you can use a good balsamic vinegar as a substitute for black vinegar, although it's slightly sweeter.

1. Marinate the steak: Using a large, very sharp knife, slice the flank steak against the grain into ⅛-inch-thick slices. Cut each slice crosswise into two or three pieces and place in a large bowl. Prepare a marinade by combining the soy sauce, vinegar, sesame oil, sherry, and sugar, whisking until blended and the sugar is dissolved. Pour the marinade over the beef in the bowl and toss thoroughly to coat. Refrigerate, covered, for at least 6 hours and up to 12.

2. Meanwhile, prepare the sauce: Heat the oil in a small saucepan over medium heat. Add the garlic and ginger (they should sizzle on contact) and stir-fry until fragrant but not browned, about 45 seconds. Add the orange juice, ½ cup rice vinegar, liqueur, and sherry and bring to a boil over high heat. Reduce the heat to medium and cook until the liquid is reduced by half, 5 to 10 minutes.

3. Drain the dried orange peel well, then cut it into ½-inch pieces and add it to the reduced liquid in the saucepan along with the chicken stock, sugar, and soy sauce. Increase the heat to high and bring to a boil, then reduce the heat to medium and reduce the liquid again by half, about 10 minutes.

4. Whisk the cornstarch into the water to blend. When smooth, whisk it into the reduced liquid in the saucepan. Reduce the heat to low and cook, whisking occasionally, until the mixture is thickened, another 1 to 2 minutes (see Note). Remove the pan from the heat and season with salt, pepper, and a little additional vinegar, if desired. Strain the sauce and set aside.

5. When you're ready to serve, heat 2 tablespoons oil in a large skillet over high heat. Add the chiles and stir-fry quickly until aromatic and slightly blackened. Add the coarsely chopped orange zest and stir quickly for a few seconds, then add the reserved sauce and bring to a boil. Add the wood ear mushrooms and simmer to develop the flavors, about 5 minutes. Remove the skillet from the heat and set aside, covered, to keep warm.

6. Preheat the oven to its lowest setting.

7. Pour oil into a deep, heavy skillet to a depth of 4 inches and heat over medium-high heat to 375°F. Line a baking sheet with paper towels. Combine the flour and cornstarch in a shallow dish. Drain the beef from the marinade and dip, a few pieces at a time, in the flour mixture to coat on all sides, shaking off any excess. Add the coated beef to the hot oil in batches and fry until browned and quite crisp, about 5 minutes, turning as necessary with tongs; do not crowd the skillet. As the beef is done, transfer it with tongs to the prepared baking sheet and keep it warm in the oven.

8. When all the beef is cooked, place it in a large serving bowl and pour the heated sauce over it. Toss to coat and serve immediately.

Note: If you're not planning to use the sauce immediately, refrigerate it, tightly covered, for up to 1 week, omitting the thickening part of step 4. When you're ready to resume the recipe, reheat the sauce, thicken as directed in step 4, season, and strain, then proceed with step 5.

drying citrus peel

Although dried orange or tangerine peel is readily available at Asian markets, it's very easy to make your own. Choose oranges, tangerines, clementines, or mandarin oranges with fragrant, unblemished skins, avoiding any with a dull or dry-looking surface. Wash and dry the fruit well. Using a sharp paring knife, score the peel into quarters or eighths and remove it neatly. Place the pieces, outer-side down, on a cutting surface and scrape away all of the white pith with the paring knife (an old-fashioned serrated grapefruit spoon also works nicely) until the peel is translucent and you can see the little pores or oil sacs of the skin through it.

Arrange the peel, pith-side up, on a wire rack set in a warm, dry spot. Depending on the humidity, it will take the peel anywhere from 1 to 4 or 5 days to dry out. The dried pieces should be curled and slightly flexible and will have turned dark brown. Stored in a glass jar with a screw-top lid, the peel will last indefinitely. In fact, the older it gets, the more intense the flavor becomes.

Before using, soften the dried peel in warm water to cover for 10 minutes.

Beef Fillets with Star Anise

This is the summer special-occasion dish to beat all special-occasion dishes. I say "summer" because the best way to prepare these well-marinated steaks is on the grill, and for many of us that means summer. And as for the "special-occasion" part, anytime beef of this quality and amount is involved, it usually means something special is being celebrated.

Admittedly, this is not a staff-meal dish, but it's one I wanted very much to include because it's a favorite of mine. Actually, the real star here is the sauce, based on Chinese flavors. It marries beautifully with the tender beef, especially after the beef has been marinated in a compatibly flavored mixture just long enough so that its outer layer is permeated. Although the flavors are more exaggerated than they would be in a traditional Chinese dish, they infuse without overwhelming. Freshly steamed rice would accompany the steaks nicely. **SERVES 8**

FOR THE BEEF AND MARINADE:

2 cups good-quality soy sauce, such as Kikkoman
¼ cup balsamic vinegar
½ cup honey
2 tablespoons Chinese five-spice powder
2 tablespoons Asian sesame oil
1 tablespoon grated fresh ginger
8 beef fillet steaks (1½ inches thick; 8 to 10 ounces each)

FOR THE SAUCE:

¼ cup canola or other vegetable oil
1 large onion, unpeeled, roughly cut into chunks
3 medium carrots, unpeeled, roughly cut into chunks

3 heads garlic, cut in half through the cloves

1 piece (2 inches) fresh ginger, unpeeled, cut into ¼-inch slices

1 cup dry white wine

¾ cup dark soy sauce

4 ounces Chinese rock sugar or ½ cup (firmly packed)
   light brown sugar

4 large pieces dried orange or tangerine peel, softened
   (see box, page 51)

6 ounces whole star anise (about 2 cups; see box, page 54)

1 cinnamon stick (3 inches), broken in half

4 quarts Chicken Stock (page 39; see Note)

3 tablespoons beurre manié (see box, page 62)

1. Prepare the marinade: Place the soy sauce, vinegar, honey, five-spice powder, sesame oil, and ginger in a bowl and whisk until blended. Place the beef in a large roasting pan and pour the marinade over it. Turn the beef so that it's coated all over with the marinade. Refrigerate, covered, for 12 hours, turning the beef several times as it marinates.

2. Prepare the sauce: Heat the oil in a large stockpot over medium-high heat. Add the onion, carrots, garlic, and ginger and cook, stirring occasionally, until the vegetables are well browned, about 15 minutes.

3. Add the wine and soy sauce, increase the heat to high, and cook until the mixture is reduced by half, about 5 to 8 minutes. Add the rock sugar, orange peel, star anise, cinnamon stick, and chicken stock and bring to a boil. Reduce the heat and simmer the liquid for 1 hour.

4. Pour the sauce into a colander set over a second large pot, pushing down on the vegetables and spices to extract as much liquid as possible. Bring to a boil, then reduce the heat to medium high and boil until the liquid starts to thicken (it should be reduced by half and become more saucelike), about 30 minutes.

5. Meanwhile, preheat a grill to high or preheat the broiler.

6. Taste the sauce; it should be mildly sweet, salty, and redolent with the flavor of anise. Reduce the heat to medium, whisk in the *beurre manié,* and continue cooking the sauce, whisking frequently, until it has thickened enough to lightly

coat the back of a spoon, 5 minutes. Remove the sauce from the heat and set aside, covered to keep warm, while you grill the steaks.

7. Remove the steaks from the marinade and pat dry. Oil the grill rack, place the steaks on the rack, and grill, making sure you watch the heat carefully; the sugar and soy sauce tend to cause the meat to blacken quickly. If you like your steak rare, figure 4 to 6 minutes per side; for medium, 6 to 8 minutes per side.

8. Transfer the steaks to a platter or individual plates. Spoon the sauce over the steaks and serve immediately.

Note: This sauce calls for homemade stock only. You can get away with canned substitutes in other recipes, but for this one, please bring out the best from scratch.

Staff Meals from Chanterelle | beef, veal, lamb

two asian spices

Chinese five-spice powder is a strong-flavored mixture that contains—despite the name—anywhere from five to seven ground spices. It's used sparingly but to great effect in Chinese cooking, particularly in vegetable stir-fries, roasted or braised meats, and marinades for duck. Most versions contain cinnamon, Szechuan pepper, fennel seeds, ginger, cloves, and star anise (the flavor that generally comes through the most strongly). Just a pinch will do in most instances. I like to add it in place of cinnamon to blueberry muffins, apple pies or crisps, and rice pudding.

Fragrant and prettily shaped star anise, which looks like a reddish brown star, is a key ingredient in Chinese five-spice powder. On its own it's one of the few spices widely used in Chinese cooking, most often added whole to pork, duck, and poultry dishes. Star anise is the fruit of a small evergreen tree that grows in southern China and northern Vietnam. Its taste and fragrance are strong and licoricelike, with a hint of sweetness. Each eight-pointed pod contains a smaller, less intensely flavored seed. Look for star anise at Asian markets (a bulk bag costs around $1) and large supermarkets.

Mom's Braised Brisket with Carrots

This recipe is a combination of the braised brisket my mother, Jeanette, made and a version I enjoyed at a Paris bistro years ago. The difference between my mom's Jewish-style version and the French one is that my mother wouldn't dream of putting pig's feet in anything! But for this dish you want to create a **bold, rich sauce** that will practically make your lips stick together with each bite; here the extra flavor and gelatinous quality of the pig's feet make sure of that. Since I like pig's feet, I serve them right along with the brisket, carrots, and sauce. If that doesn't suit you, however, simply discard them. The prodigious amount of red wine I use is essential, but it needn't cost the earth. There are many good red wines available these days for less than $10, some even in the $5 range. Serve alongside buttered noodles or boiled potatoes to sop up the lovely sauce. **SERVES 8**

1 whole beef brisket (about 6 pounds)
3 pig's feet, split and chopped into large chunks
3 bottles (750 ml each) red wine (see Note)
½ cup brandy
7 tablespoons canola or other vegetable oil
3 large onions, coarsely chopped
3 large cloves garlic, minced
½ cup all-purpose flour
3 quarts Chicken Stock (page 39) or canned low-
    sodium chicken broth
5 bay leaves
2 tablespoons crushed dried mushrooms, such as shiitakes
1 teaspoon dried thyme leaves
12 medium-size carrots, peeled and cut into 2-inch lengths
Coarse (kosher) salt and freshly ground black pepper, to taste

1. Using a boning knife, divide the brisket in half horizontally, separating it along the natural division. Place the meat in a large, nonreactive roasting pan along with the pig's feet. Pour the wine and brandy over the meat, cover with plastic wrap, and marinate, in the refrigerator, for at least 8 hours and up to 24, turning the meat occasionally in the marinade.

2. When you're ready to proceed, heat 4 tablespoons of the oil in a large, non-reactive stockpot over medium heat. Add the onions and garlic and sauté, stirring occasionally, until lightly browned, about 15 minutes. Add the flour and cook, stirring constantly, until well incorporated into the onions and garlic and lightly browned, 8 to 10 minutes.

3. Remove the brisket from the marinade, pat dry with paper towels, and set aside on a platter. Add the marinade, with the pig's feet, to the stockpot. Increase the heat to medium and bring to a boil, stirring frequently.

4. Meanwhile, pour the remaining 3 tablespoons oil into a large skillet over high heat. Add the brisket and brown well on all sides, about 5 minutes per side.

5. Add the browned brisket to the stockpot along with the chicken stock, bay leaves, dried mushrooms, and thyme. Cover and bring to a boil over high heat, then reduce the heat to low and simmer, partially covered, until the meats are tender, about 2 to 2½ hours.

6. Remove the pot from the heat and transfer the brisket to a cutting board. When it's cool enough to handle, cut the brisket against the grain into ¼-inch slices and return them to the pot. Add the carrots, season with salt and pepper, and simmer, partially covered, until the carrots are tender, about another 20 minutes.

7. Remove the pot from the heat and discard the bay leaves. Arrange the brisket slices on a serving platter and spoon the carrots, pig's feet (if desired), and sauce over the meat to serve.

Note: Please don't overspend on the wine for this dish. What you want is one reminiscent of unsweetened grape juice. An inexpensive ($6 or so per bottle) Merlot from California or Chile is fine. Do not use a Cabernet. The long cooking will exaggerate its tannic flavor, and the resulting sauce will be too brown, not the deep luscious red it should be.

the benefits of braising

Braising is the ideal method for transforming inexpensive, not-so-tender cuts of meat such as oxtails, tripe, short ribs, and veal, beef, or lamb shanks into meltingly tender ones. The process is quite simple, and best of all it requires very little of a cook's time, since there's no fiddling with the food once all the ingredients are combined in the pot. The meat is patted dry with a paper towel, then nicely browned on all sides, and finally simmered slowly in a small amount of well-seasoned braising liquid in a good, heavy pot with a tight-fitting lid. The moist heat created inside the pot works wonders on the tough connective tissues of the meat, softening and tenderizing them. In addition, the meat's

own delicious juices unite with the braising liquid to add greater depth of flavor. It's important that the heat be evenly conducted, so use the heaviest pot in your kitchen, one that will just accommodate the ingredients without a lot of space to spare. A cast-iron pot, enameled or not, is a good choice, as would be a pricey, thick-sided one made of copper, if you're lucky enough to own one.

Braised dishes taste terrific served the same day they're made, but they're even better if allowed to rest for a day or two in the refrigerator so the flavors have time to mellow. Chilling also makes it easier to remove the fat from the surface before the dish is reheated.

Beef Short Ribs Braised in Beer

Short ribs have enjoyed something of a revival in the past few years for two very good reasons—their **succulent**, wonderfully beefy flavor and reasonable cost. This dish is a variation on *carbonnades à la flamande*, a traditional Belgian specialty in which chunks of beef stew meat are tenderized to the melting point by slow-cooking in a generous amount of Belgium's famous beer. Here short ribs receive a similarly transformational braising in a good dark beer, preferably one that's neither too bitter nor too sweet. I generally choose Brooklyn Brown Ale, but a strong Belgian beer, such as a robust Rodenbach red ale or Ichtegem's brown ale, or even a domestic one, such as Samuel Adams, would work just as well. By the time the ribs have finished cooking, the combination of thinly sliced, nearly caramelized onions, beer, and stock has created a mellow, flavorful, thick sauce with subtle hints of bitterness and sweetness. As you might expect, potatoes—mashed, or plain boiled—would be an ideal accompaniment. And there should be plenty of good crusty bread for mopping up every last speck of delicious sauce. **SERVES 6 TO 8**

¾ cup canola or other vegetable oil

5 to 6 pounds beef short ribs, trimmed of fat

4 large onions, halved lengthwise and cut crosswise into thin slices

2 tablespoons sugar

2 tablespoons all-purpose flour

4 bottles (12 ounces each) dark ale or beer

8 cups Chicken Stock (page 39) or canned low-sodium
   chicken broth

4 bay leaves

Coarse (kosher) salt and coarsely ground black pepper, to taste

1. Heat ½ cup of the oil in a very large, heavy, flameproof casserole or Dutch oven over medium-high heat. Add only enough of the short ribs to fit into the casserole without crowding and brown well on all sides, 4 to 5 minutes per side. As the ribs are browned, transfer them to a platter and continue browning the remaining ribs in batches.

2. When all the ribs are browned and removed from the casserole, discard the oil from the casserole, but do not wash it (you want to keep those flavorful brown bits). Return the casserole to the stove. Add the remaining ¼ cup oil and the onions and cook slowly, covered, over low heat until the onions are very soft but not browned, about 20 minutes.

3. Uncover the casserole and sprinkle the sugar over the onions. Cook, uncovered, stirring occasionally, until the onions have caramelized slightly and are just light brown in color, about 5 minutes. Sprinkle the flour over the onions and continue cooking, stirring frequently, until the flour turns light brown, 3 to 4 minutes. Add 1 bottle of the beer and increase the heat to medium high. Bring to a boil, scraping the bottom of the casserole with a wooden spoon to loosen any browned bits.

4. Return the ribs to the casserole along with the stock, remaining beer, and bay leaves. Bring to a boil, skimming the top occasionally, then reduce the heat to low and cook, tightly covered, until the meat is very tender, 1½ to 2 hours; you should be able to pull the bones from the meat with ease. Using tongs, transfer the ribs to a platter and let cool.

5. While the ribs cool, check the liquid in the casserole. If it's thick enough to coat the back of a spoon, it's ready to use as a sauce. If not, increase the heat to medium and reduce the liquid until it reaches the proper thickness. This may take up to an additional 15 minutes. Taste; the sauce should be slightly bitter, with a subtle, balancing touch of sweetness from the caramelized onions. Season with salt and pepper; remove and discard the bay leaves.

6. When the ribs are cool enough to handle, remove the meat from the bones. Discard the bones and return the meat to the casserole. Simmer until heated through, about 5 minutes. If you'll be serving immediately, skim the fat from the surface of the sauce; otherwise, refrigerate overnight and remove the hardened fat before reheating.

Beef Stew with Red Wine and Vegetables

On a cold winter day a good homemade stew is the culinary equivalent of a down parka. The depth of flavor in this one comes from just the right combination of compatible ingredients. The gelatin from the bacon rind adds texture to the silky sauce, the full-bodied red wine tenderizes and enriches all of the ingredients, and a healthy shot of brandy helps round out the flavors. You don't often find cauliflower in stew recipes, but I happen to love it, which is why it's used here, along with green beans. Both are added toward the end of the cooking time to impart a bit of crunch and more textural interest to the stew.

SERVES 6 TO 8

4 thick slices (4 ounces) slab bacon, rind removed,
   cut crosswise into ½-inch pieces

1 medium onion, diced

5 cloves garlic, minced

3 to 6 tablespoons canola or other vegetable oil

3½ pounds boneless beef chuck, trimmed of fat and
   cut into 1-inch cubes

1 bottle (750 ml) hearty, full-bodied red wine, such as
   Côtes-du-Rhône, a Spanish blend, or California Cabernet

½ cup brandy

7 cups Beefed-Up Veal Stock (page 38) or canned
   low-sodium beef broth

1 piece (3 inches square) bacon rind (optional)

3 bay leaves

1 teaspoon dried thyme leaves

1 to 2 tablespoons beurre manié (optional; see box, page 62)

4 large carrots, peeled and cut into ½-inch-thick rounds

2 large waxy potatoes, such as Yukon Gold,
    peeled and cut into 1-inch cubes

10 ounces fresh cultivated white mushrooms, halved or
    quartered if large

Coarse (kosher) salt and freshly ground black pepper, to taste

1½ cups cauliflower florets

4 ounces green beans, ends trimmed

1. Place the bacon in a large, heavy, flameproof casserole or Dutch oven and sauté over medium-low heat, stirring occasionally, until crisp, about 10 minutes. Add the onion and garlic; if there doesn't seem to be enough fat rendered from the bacon to sauté them, add a tablespoon of the oil as well. Sauté the onion and garlic until softened but not browned, about 5 minutes, stirring occasionally.

2. Meanwhile, heat 3 tablespoons of the oil in a large, heavy skillet over medium-high heat. Add only enough of the beef cubes to fit into the skillet without crowding and brown well on all sides, 4 to 5 minutes per side. As the beef browns, transfer it to the casserole with the bacon, onion, and garlic. Brown the remaining beef, in batches, adding more oil to the pan as necessary; don't let the bottom of the skillet burn.

3. When all the beef is browned and removed from the skillet, add 1 cup of the wine to the skillet and bring to a boil, scraping up the browned bits in the bottom of the pan. Pour the contents of the skillet into the casserole with the beef, along with the brandy and 2 cups of the wine. Increase the heat to high and reduce the liquid by two thirds, 15 to 20 minutes; watch carefully, because it may ignite.

choosing stew meat

Tender, richly flavorful, and juicy, beef chuck is an ideal choice for stew making. Any cut of chuck will be good, but if you have a choice opt for chuck-eye roast. And always avoid buying precut packaged stew meat at the supermarket; you'll get tastier results buying a large piece of chuck and taking the few extra minutes to cut it into pieces yourself.

4. Add the veal stock, bacon rind (if desired), bay leaves, and thyme and bring to a boil, then reduce the heat to very low. Cook the beef very gently, partially covered, for 1½ hours. If the liquid doesn't appear to be thickening at this point, whisk in some *beurre manié*.

5. Add the carrots, potatoes, and mushrooms and season with salt and pepper. Continue simmering until the meat and vegetables are tender, 30 minutes more.

6. Add the cauliflower and green beans and cook until crisp-tender, 6 to 8 minutes. Add the remaining wine (about ½ cup) and cook for 30 seconds more.

7. Remove the casserole from the heat, discarding the bay leaves and the bacon rind, if using. Adjust the seasoning with salt and pepper and serve.

beurre manié

Beurre manié (kneaded butter) is a mixture of equal parts softened unsalted butter and all-purpose flour that is thoroughly worked together to form a paste. It is used as a thickener for a variety of sauces and stews and, in particular, to slightly thicken the simmering gravies of braised meat dishes if they appear to be a bit too thin. It should be whisked quickly into the liquid, which then should be allowed to simmer until the flour loses its raw, starchy taste, at least 15 minutes more.

Pot-au-Feu

Pot-au-feu (translation: "**pot on fire**") is as much a generous statement of hospitality and sharing as it is a satisfying French cold-weather classic. It's a whole abundant meal from a single pot—a flavorful broth (given a bit of extra color and flavor from blackened onion), a delicious array of slow-simmered meats and poultry, and some nourishing vegetables.

Some people like to present the broth first, then serve the meat and vegetables as a separate course. But that seems too formal to me. First I ladle the delicious golden brown liquid from a tureen into the large, shallow bowl at each person's place, then I add a selection of sliced meats and vegetables to the broth. Potatoes boiled in their skins are a perfect accompaniment. Just before serving the pot-au-feu, set out a pepper grinder and small bowls of condiments such as coarse sea salt, cornichons, Dijon mustard, and Green Sauce (page 364). And don't forget a bottle of a simple red wine, preferably Beaujolais or Côtes-du-Rhône. **SERVES 8 TO 10**

6 quarts Chicken Stock (page 39) or canned low-sodium
    chicken broth

4 bay leaves

2 tablespoons black peppercorns

1 large onion, halved and blackened (see Note)

2½ pounds boneless beef sirloin tip, rump roast, or
    fresh brisket, trimmed of fat

1 veal shank (about 4 pounds), trimmed of fat

1 whole chicken (3½ to 4 pounds)

2 pounds garlic sausage, homemade (page 132) or store bought

8 large carrots, peeled and cut crosswise in half

10 medium leeks, white part only, split almost to the root
    and thoroughly rinsed

Coarse (kosher) salt, to taste

1. Bring the chicken stock to a boil in a very large stockpot over high heat. Wrap the bay leaves, peppercorns, and blackened onion in a doubled square of dampened cheesecloth and knot the ends together to secure. Add it to the simmering stock along with the beef. Lower the heat and simmer, partially covered, for 20 minutes. Add the veal shank and continue simmering, partially covered, for 1¼ hours.

2. Rinse the chicken, inside and out, under cold running water, removing any excess fat. Then add the chicken to the pot and simmer for 45 minutes more, checking all the meats for doneness as you go; the beef and veal should be tender (easily pierced with a fork) but not falling apart, and the chicken is just done when the juices run clear when pierced at the thigh. Remove the meats as they are done to a platter and cover to keep them warm.

3. Add the sausages and carrots to the pot and simmer, partially covered, for 10 minutes. Add the leeks and cook until the sausage is cooked through and the vegetables are tender, about 10 minutes more.

4. Remove the pot from the heat and discard the cheesecloth bag. Slice the meats and carve the chicken, then arrange these on a large serving platter. Using a slotted spoon, remove the vegetables and sausages from the broth in the pot and arrange them on the platter with the meats and chicken. Strain the broth, season with salt, and ladle a little over the contents of the platter. Serve the meats immediately, accompanied by the remaining broth in bowls.

Note: To blacken the onion, preheat the broiler. Place the onion, cut-side up, on the rack of a broiler pan and broil until it's tender and its outside is blackened, about 15 minutes.

pot-au-feu for a party

Pot-au-feu is a homey, yet sophisticated choice to serve a crowd at a party, particularly during the festive winter holidays. You'll need a really huge pot, of course, and the basic ingredients will have to be scaled up. Pot-au-feu should always include beef and chicken, but instead of increasing the quantities, it's much nicer to introduce a wider variety of ingredients. Among the possibilities: beef short ribs, duck confit, marrow bones, a 1-pound chunk of mildly smoked ham, a beef shin, smoked pork chops, or pork ribs (cut in half).

Chilled Red-Cooked Beef

Red-cooking is a Chinese method of **braising foods slowly** in a dark, intensely flavorful soy-based cooking liquid seasoned with wine, star anise, Szechuan peppercorns, and other flavorful ingredients. Once cooked, the beef marinates for a minimum of 2 days in the same liquid in which it was braised, so plan ahead when you're preparing this recipe.

Red-cooking broth also works well with oxtails, pork shoulder, duck (page 200), chicken (page 148), squab, and even shiitake mushrooms. The broth, which is sometimes referred to in Chinese cooking as a master sauce, has an exquisite aroma and markedly exotic anise-intensive flavor. (If you're wary of so much anise, you could use ½ cup less, but the flavor will not be as good.)

There is really no good substitute for the shin of beef here. It has a tremendous amount of connective tissue, which is transformed into gelatin during the braising. Look for beef shin at a meat market or specialty food store, although you may be able to get the cut at a large supermarket with a meat department that handles special requests. When cooked correctly, beef shin is tender but chewy. It's not the type of cut that melts in your mouth. It fights back a little, and that's what it's supposed to do.

Traditionally served at Chinese banquets as part of an array of appetizers, this dish is terrific served as part of a buffet that might also include Soba Salad (page 337), Thai Seafood Salad (page 233), Honeyed-Hoisin Grilled Chicken Wings (page 189), and cold meats. Accompany it with an assortment of such condiments as Dijon mustard and several types of Chinese hot sauce.

SERVES 10 TO 12 AS PART OF A BUFFET

Staff Meals from Chanterelle

Broth for Red-Cooking (recipe follows)
1 shin of beef (4 to 5 pounds), boned, trimmed, and cut
    into 2 or 3 large pieces
Asian sesame oil, for brushing
Fresh cilantro leaves, for garnish

1. Place the unstrained broth in a large stockpot and bring to a boil over high heat. Add the beef shin and return the broth to a boil. Reduce the heat to low and simmer, partially covered, until the meat is cooked through and tender but not falling apart, about 1½ hours.

2. Remove the pot from the heat and let the beef cool in the liquid, then refrigerate the beef—still in the liquid—for at least 48 hours and up to 72.

3. To serve, remove and discard the hardened layer of fat from on top of the cold broth. Remove the beef from the broth and scrape off whatever spices and bits of jellied broth are clinging to it (see Note). Cut only as much beef as you are likely to need into very thin slices across the grain, and arrange them on a platter. Once sliced, the meat has a tendency to dry out if it's left out too long; the unsliced portion will keep, tightly wrapped, in the refrigerator for up to 3 days.

4. Just before serving, brush the meat lightly with sesame oil (don't fail to do this, because the oil tempers the anise flavor) and garnish with cilantro.

Note: Transfer the unstrained broth to a container with a tight cover and refrigerate for up to 1 week, bringing it to a boil every couple of days. If you don't think you'll be using it again for a while, it's best to freeze the broth. When frozen, it will keep for up to 6 months.

a memorable sandwich

If you're lucky enough to have leftover Chilled Red-Cooked Beef, it can be transformed into a terrific sandwich. Add a tablespoon of finely chopped fresh cilantro leaves to a cup of Basic Mayonnaise (page 360) or a good-quality commercial mayonnaise. Slather a split baguette with the mayo, add thin slices of beef shin, and top with some coleslaw.

Broth for Red-Cooking

Use this **exotic broth** to cook chicken (page 148) and duck (page 200) as well as beef. It improves with age, becoming richer and tastier, and can be used over and over again, supplemented with additional stock, water, or seasonings as needed. You need only refrigerate the broth if you use it often; freeze it if you plan to use it less frequently. **MAKES 4 QUARTS**

4 quarts Chicken Stock (page 39), canned low-sodium chicken
    broth, or a combination of stock or broth and water
2½ cups good-quality soy sauce, such as Kikkoman
½ cup black soy sauce or mushroom soy sauce
¼ cup dry sherry
1 pound Chinese rock sugar or 2¼ cups (firmly
    packed) light brown sugar
2 bunches scallions, white and green parts, trimmed
    and cut into 3-inch lengths
8 ounces whole star anise (about 2 cups; see box, page 54)
12 dried shiitake mushrooms
6 to 8 large pieces dried orange peel, softened (see box, page 51),
    or zest of 3 oranges, removed with a vegetable peeler
1 piece (4 inches) unpeeled fresh ginger, rinsed and
    cut into ¼-inch slices
2 tablespoons Szechuan peppercorns
2 cinnamon sticks (3 inches each)

1. Combine the chicken stock, soy sauces, sherry, rock sugar, scallions, star anise, mushrooms, orange peel, ginger, peppercorns, and cinnamon sticks in a large stockpot and bring to a boil over high heat. Reduce the heat to low and simmer, uncovered, for 45 minutes.

2. The broth is now ready to red-cook the desired meat. If you won't be using it immediately, transfer the broth to a storage container and refrigerate, covered, until you're ready. It will keep for up to 1 week in the refrigerator; bring it to a boil every couple of days. Frozen, it will keep for up to 6 months.

Roast Beef Hash

When it comes to roast beef, there's only one **rule of thumb** that counts—always cook a larger roast than you think you'll need. As much as my family and our staff always anticipate a good roast beef dinner, there's no question that we look forward almost as much to eating the leftovers. Remember to toss a few extra potatoes into the oven alongside the beef as it roasts and you'll be able to enjoy hash the next day.

There's nothing remotely *haute* about this hash, which is one of its virtues. Humble, economical, and satisfying, it comes out of the skillet with a wonderful golden brown crust. And the recipe can easily be doubled or tripled. Serve the hash unadorned, or topped with poached or fried eggs, and accompanied by a batch of hot homemade biscuits. Good for breakfast, lunch, or dinner!

SERVES 2

1 to 2 tablespoons olive oil
1 tablespoon unsalted butter
1 small onion, diced
1 clove garlic, minced
2 cups diced cooked waxy potatoes, such as Yukon Gold
2 cups diced cooked roast beef
¼ teaspoon dried thyme leaves
A few dashes of Tabasco sauce
Coarse (kosher) salt and freshly ground black pepper, to taste

1. Heat 1 tablespoon of the olive oil and the butter in a 10-inch nonstick or well-seasoned cast-iron skillet over medium heat. When the butter stops foaming, add the onion and sauté, stirring occasionally, until softened and browned, about 10 minutes.

2. Add the garlic, potatoes, beef, thyme, Tabasco, salt, and pepper and toss well to mix.

3. Using a metal spatula, firmly press the hash into a cake and cook until it's browned and crusty on the bottom, about 15 minutes (see Note). If the pan looks too dry, add the remaining 1 tablespoon oil. Using one or two wide spatulas, turn the hash over carefully and brown the other side, about 5 minutes.

4. Slide the hash carefully onto a platter or scoop onto individual plates and serve.

Note: Sometimes a brown crust simply won't form, in which case you can just eat the hash loose. It will still be tasty.

Italian Meatballs

Meatballs are really just miniature meat loaves with the added benefit of a shorter cooking time. Fast and easy to prepare, they're convenient to have in the freezer as emergency rations for busy days when time or energy levels are running short and the family meal can't wait. Use them for impromptu sandwiches or slice them to top a pizza.

As an alternative to roasting the browned meatballs in the oven, you could simmer them in 8 cups of tomato sauce for 20 minutes instead. **MAKES 2 DOZEN MEATBALLS**

½ cup fine dry bread crumbs (see box, page 279)
½ cup milk
1½ pounds lean ground beef (or an equal mixture
  of ground beef, ground pork, and ground veal)
1 large egg
½ cup chopped onion
1 large clove garlic, minced
¼ cup freshly grated Parmesan
1 tablespoon tomato sauce
1 teaspoon dried oregano leaves
Coarse (kosher) salt and freshly ground black pepper, to taste
Canola or other vegetable oil, for frying

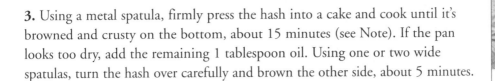

1. Combine the bread crumbs with the milk in a large bowl and let soak for 5 minutes to soften.

2. To the softened crumbs add the ground beef, egg, onion, garlic, grated Parmesan, tomato sauce, oregano, salt, and pepper. Using your hands or a wooden spoon (hands work best), mix very well. Divide the mixture into twenty-four equal portions and shape each into a ball (each will be about 1½ inches in diameter).

3. Preheat the oven to 375°F.

4. Pour oil to a depth of ¼ inch into a large skillet and heat over medium-high heat. Add only enough meatballs to the skillet to fit without crowding and brown well on all sides, using tongs to turn them, 8 to 10 minutes total. Transfer to paper towels to drain briefly, then place in a roasting pan and set aside while you brown the remaining meatballs in batches, as necessary.

5. When all the meatballs have been browned and added to the roasting pan, place them in the oven and roast until they're cooked through, about 10 minutes.

Meat Loaf, Italian Style

The thing about meat loaf is that some people like it for lunch or dinner—but others, those of us who really love it, eat meat loaf in the morning, too. Although I have nothing against breakfast, I don't care much for traditional morning foods, so I often begin the day with a meat loaf sandwich and some coleslaw.

This **herby version** of meat loaf, flecked with savory bits of prosciutto, is quick and easy to throw together. Half of the tomato sauce is blended with the meat and seasonings; the rest is poured over the top. As the meat loaf bakes, the sauce becomes concentrated and develops a wonderful, slightly sweet, roasted flavor. You can also serve this Parmesan-style by arranging a few medium-thick slices of mozzarella on top of the sauce halfway through the cooking time of the meat loaf. Serve with zucchini sautéed in olive oil and garlic. **SERVES 4 TO 6**

1 cup fine dry bread crumbs (see box, page 279)

¾ cup dry white wine

2½ pounds lean ground beef (or an equal mixture
    of ground beef, ground pork, and ground veal)

4 ounces prosciutto, cut into ¼-inch dice

1 cup Tasty Basic Tomato Sauce (page 271) or good-quality
    commercial tomato sauce

2 large eggs

1 medium onion, cut into ¼-inch dice

5 cloves garlic, minced

1 tablespoon dried oregano leaves

1 tablespoon dried basil leaves

2 teaspoons dried thyme leaves

Coarse (kosher) salt and freshly ground black pepper, to taste

1. Preheat the oven to 350°F.

2. Combine the bread crumbs and wine in a small bowl and let soak until the crumbs are soft, about 10 minutes.

3. Combine the ground beef, prosciutto, ½ cup of the tomato sauce, the eggs, onion, garlic, oregano, basil, thyme, salt, and pepper in a large bowl. Add the

maximizing dried herbs

Always be sure to use the freshest possible dried herbs (preferably ones that have been in your kitchen cupboard no longer than a few months), and always crumble them between your fingertips before using to activate their flavor. As the dried oregano, basil, and thyme are crumbled into the recipe, the air becomes delightfully suffused with their aroma. Close your eyes and sniff. It's a preview of how the dish will taste.

bread crumbs and any remaining wine. Using your hands or a wooden spoon (hands work best), mix very well to combine.

4. Shape the mixture into a loaf and place in a roasting pan or fill a glass loaf pan with it. Pour the remaining ½ cup tomato sauce over the meat loaf and bake until nicely browned and a metal skewer inserted into the center comes out hot, 1 to 1½ hours. Transfer the meat loaf to a platter and let it rest for 5 minutes before cutting it into thick slices and serving.

David's Burgers

Most chefs enjoy a **really good burger**. I certainly do. This is the method I use at home and for our staff meals to produce a straightforward hamburger with a very crisp exterior and a tender, juicy interior. It requires a cast-iron skillet, a piece of equipment every home cook should own. If you don't have one, use this recipe (and your love of a great burger) as an excuse to get one.

Try not to overhandle the beef in the course of forming the patties. The meat should be relatively loose, not tamped down and compact, so that it remains juicy as it cooks. Although most people think it's important to create a patty that fits a bun, mine are usually a bit more free-form and hang out over the bun's edges. Dusting the patties with flour ensures a crisp crust, as does cooking them in a well-seasoned cast-iron pan. How long the burgers are cooked is a matter of personal preference. My staff wryly describes the way I like mine as "burnt, but raw." But if you're like the rest of our family and staff, you'll probably want them cooked somewhat longer than the recipe specifies.

Topping a burger is a personal matter. Fans of mayo and mustard are certainly welcome to spoon them on. And if you've got some time, do prepare Yummy Onions (page 325) or Hot Dog Onions (page 324) to serve alongside. **SERVES 6**

3 pounds excellent-quality lean ground beef
¾ cup all-purpose flour, for dusting
Canola or other vegetable oil, for frying
Coarse (kosher) salt and freshly ground black pepper, to taste
6 hamburger buns, toasted
Lettuce, ripe tomato slices, and pickle slices, for serving (optional)
Ketchup, for serving

1. Divide the meat into six equal portions. Without using much pressure, gently and quickly form each portion into a thick patty. Spread the flour on a plate, then dip each burger in the flour to coat on both sides, shaking off any excess.

2. Pour oil to a depth of ¼ inch into a large cast-iron skillet. Heat over medium-high heat and, when the oil is almost smoking, add the burgers (see Note). Sprinkle one side of each burger with salt and pepper and fry that side until very brown and crusty, 3 to 4 minutes. Salt and pepper the top sides, turn the burgers over carefully, and fry until the other sides are also very brown, another 3 minutes. Do not press the burgers down with a spatula; this will only express juices and encourage them to stick. If you want the burgers cooked more than rare, lower the heat and cook for another few minutes on each side.

3. Remove the skillet from the heat and transfer each burger to a bun. If desired, top each with lettuce, a slice of tomato, and a few slices of pickle. Serve immediately, and pass the ketchup.

Note: Add the burgers to the hot oil carefully. Hot oil can spatter, so slip the burgers gently into the skillet and keep your face averted.

a slightly fancier burger

To add a bit of extra flavor to hamburgers, I sometimes place a small slice of seasoned butter in the center of each portion of ground meat and form the patty around it. To make seasoned butter, mix 4 tablespoons (½ stick) room-temperature butter with ½ teaspoon Dijon mustard, 1 chopped clove garlic, 1 tablespoon minced fresh flat-leaf parsley leaves, and a sprinkling of coarse (kosher) salt and freshly ground black pepper. Form into a log on a piece of plastic wrap, wrap tightly, and refrigerate until hardened.

Cottage Pie

After schlepping plate after luxurious plate of foie gras and truffles to our customers, we love to dig into plates heaped with this unsophisticated, **pleasingly stodgy** dish. Cottage pie originated in England as a tasty and thrifty way to use up leftover roast beef from Sunday's main meal. (Its cousin, shepherd's pie, was made with leftover lamb.) Dusted with grated Parmesan, the potato "crust" of this ground beef version turns a beautiful golden brown in the oven.

Although this isn't a fancy dish by nature, if you're feeling energetic and inspired it can be fancied up by something as simple as scoring the potato topping with a fork to create wavy patterns, or by adding a little extra warmed milk to the potatoes and piping them decoratively atop the pie. Heavy cream adds richness to the filling, while a little ketchup adds a subtle hint of sweetness. The ketchup bottle itself also makes an appearance at the table, ketchup being euphemistically referred to by family and staff as the "secret sauce" or "tomato-vinegar coulis." **SERVES 4 TO 6**

4 large Idaho potatoes of uniform size
   (about 8 ounces each), peeled
1 tablespoon canola or other vegetable oil
2½ pounds lean ground beef
¼ cup ketchup, plus additional for serving
½ teaspoon sweet Hungarian paprika
Coarse (kosher) salt and freshly ground black pepper, to taste
3 tablespoons unsalted butter
½ cup milk, warmed
½ cup frozen peas
½ cup frozen corn kernels
1 cup heavy (or whipping) cream
¼ cup freshly grated Parmesan

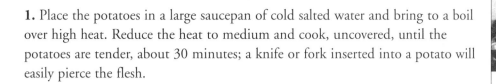

1. Place the potatoes in a large saucepan of cold salted water and bring to a boil over high heat. Reduce the heat to medium and cook, uncovered, until the potatoes are tender, about 30 minutes; a knife or fork inserted into a potato will easily pierce the flesh.

2. Meanwhile, heat the oil in a large skillet over medium heat. Add the ground beef, breaking it up well with a spoon, and cook until the meat has lost its raw color and is beginning to brown, about 15 minutes, stirring frequently to break up any clumps.

3. Remove the skillet from the heat and pour off and discard any juices and fat that have accumulated. Season the beef with the ketchup, paprika, salt, and pepper, then transfer to a 13 × 9-inch baking dish, spreading the meat in an even layer. Set aside. Wipe out the skillet and set it aside.

4. Preheat the oven to 400°F.

5. When the potatoes are done, drain them in a colander, then let them sit for a moment so that some of the moisture can evaporate. Transfer the potatoes while they're still hot to a large bowl; immediately add the butter, a bit of the milk, the salt, and pepper. Using a potato masher or an electric mixer at medium speed, mash the potatoes well but without overworking them, gradually adding the rest of the milk as you mash. Taste and adjust the seasoning, then cover and set aside.

6. Add the peas, corn, and cream to the skillet and bring to a boil over high heat. Cook until the cream is reduced and thickened, 3 to 5 minutes. Pour the mixture over the meat in the baking dish.

7. Spread the potatoes over the vegetables and sprinkle with the grated Parmesan. Bake until heated through and the potatoes are nicely browned, about 45 minutes. Serve immediately, with plenty of extra ketchup.

Sloppy Joes

The name says it all. Neatness doesn't count here, but ketchup certainly does. In fact, sloppy Joes are pretty much a defining moment for ketchup—how many other recipes can you think of that call for 2 *cups* of it? At our staff meals we're not unaware of the culinary irony represented by sloppy Joes. After all, they're the polar opposite of the refined, sophisticated dishes for which Chanterelle is so well known. With a whisper of chili powder, some garlic powder, a few hot red pepper flakes, and a dash of red wine vinegar to unite the flavors, this mildly seasoned version makes both children and adults happy. You'll probably cringe about the inclusion of garlic powder or granulated garlic, but it's a must in this recipe. Of course, for a more sophisticated flavor you might add several dashes of Tabasco sauce.

MAKES 8 TO 10 SANDWICHES, DEPENDING ON HOW SLOPPY YOU ARE

1 tablespoon canola or other vegetable oil
1 small onion, cut into ½-inch dice
2 pounds lean ground beef
2 cups ketchup, or more as needed
½ teaspoon chili powder
½ teaspoon garlic powder or granulated garlic
⅛ teaspoon hot red pepper flakes
Coarse (kosher) salt, to taste
Red wine vinegar, to taste
8 to 10 hamburger buns, toasted

1. Heat the oil in a large skillet over medium heat. Add the onion and sauté, stirring frequently, until softened and translucent, about 3 minutes.

2. Add the ground beef to the skillet, breaking it up well with a spoon, and cook until the meat has lost its raw color, about 10 minutes, stirring frequently to break up any clumps.

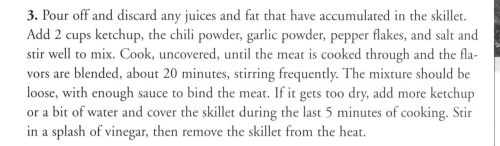

3. Pour off and discard any juices and fat that have accumulated in the skillet. Add 2 cups ketchup, the chili powder, garlic powder, pepper flakes, and salt and stir well to mix. Cook, uncovered, until the meat is cooked through and the flavors are blended, about 20 minutes, stirring frequently. The mixture should be loose, with enough sauce to bind the meat. If it gets too dry, add more ketchup or a bit of water and cover the skillet during the last 5 minutes of cooking. Stir in a splash of vinegar, then remove the skillet from the heat.

4. Taste and adjust the seasoning, then spoon onto hamburger buns and serve.

Venison Chili with Red Beans

Since virtually no ingredient goes to waste in a well-run restaurant kitchen, the instant we introduce each new monthly menu for our Chanterelle clients, the staff can tell which of our favorite dishes will soon make an appearance at our behind-the-scenes meal. When Roast Saddle of Venison with Sauce Poivrade or Sautéed Noisettes of Venison with Red Wine Braised Cèpes is on the "real people" menu, it's a sign we'll soon be setting aside venison trimmings to make this spicy but not-too-hot chili. Many chili aficionados **prefer venison** to beef because it has a stronger and more distinctive taste, as well as being leaner and lower in fat and cholesterol. In the past few years domestic free-range and farm- or ranch-raised venison have become relatively easy to find at meat markets and specialty food stores, as has Cervena, which is grass-fed venison imported from New Zealand.

The vibrant homemade chile pepper seasoning used in this dish is what makes it so good. It's a simple combination of spices and powdered dried chile peppers that's light-years more flavorful

than any supermarket chili powder (see box, page 79). Garnish the chili with dollops of sour cream and serve with Cider Vinegar Slaw (page 310) and plain white rice, a stack of warmed flour tortillas, or Cornbread (page 381). **SERVES 6 TO 8**

Canola or other vegetable oil, for sautéing
3 pounds venison stew meat, cut into ½-inch cubes (see Note)
1 medium onion, diced
2 large cloves garlic, minced
1 tablespoon good-quality chile powder
1 tablespoon ground cumin
1 teaspoon ground cinnamon
1 teaspoon cayenne pepper
½ teaspoon freshly ground black pepper
½ teaspoon dried thyme leaves
½ teaspoon dried oregano leaves
½ teaspoon unsweetened cocoa powder
2 bay leaves
4 cups Chicken Stock (page 39) or canned low-sodium
    chicken broth
½ cup canned tomato purée
Coarse (kosher) salt, to taste
1 can (19 ounces) red kidney beans, rinsed and drained
Hot cooked rice, warm tortillas, and sour cream, for serving

1. Pour vegetable oil to a depth of ⅛ inch into a large, heavy skillet and set over medium-high heat. When the oil is just beginning to smoke, add only enough of the venison pieces to fit into the skillet without crowding. Brown the meat well on all sides, 3 to 4 minutes per side, turning the pieces with tongs. As the meat is browned, transfer it to a bowl and continue browning the remaining venison in batches.

2. Heat 3 tablespoons oil in a large, heavy, nonreactive, flameproof casserole or Dutch oven over medium-low heat. Add the onion and garlic and sweat until soft and translucent but not browned, about 5 minutes.

3. Add the browned venison to the casserole, along with any juices that have accumulated, then add the chile powder, cumin, cinnamon, cayenne, black

Staff Meals from Chanterelle | beef, veal, lamb

pepper, thyme, oregano, cocoa powder, and bay leaves. Stir well to coat the meat, then add the chicken stock, tomato purée, and salt to taste and bring to a boil over high heat. Reduce the heat to low and simmer, uncovered, until the venison is tender, 2 to 2½ hours, stirring occasionally. Stir in the beans and continue cooking until they're heated through, 5 minutes more. Taste and adjust the salt, if desired.

4. Remove the chili from the heat and serve over hot cooked rice, accompanied by warm tortillas and sour cream.

Note: Farm-raised or free-range venison cooks far more quickly than its wild counterpart. If you're lucky enough to have access to some true wild venison, you may need to add up to 2 hours to the overall cooking time.

homemade chili seasoning

Commercial chili powders are just blends of spices and seasonings—usually cinnamon or allspice, garlic, onion, cumin, and/or oregano—combined with a miscellaneous mixture of powdered dried chile peppers. They're pretty blah and powdery tasting and lack fresh, clear flavor. But it takes only a few minutes, and very little effort, to create your own terrifically aromatic version by combining a good-quality, pure chile powder made from one type of dried chiles with seasonings already on hand in the spice rack. The most important ingredient is pure chile powder, which is simply finely ground dried chile peppers. Look for the powder at specialty food stores. The mixture I use in my venison chili features red New Mexico chile peppers, which are mild and full of flavor, with just a hint of heat. For more heat, you could substitute ground serranos; for a wonderfully complex smoky flavor, use chipotle powder made from smoke-dried red jalapeños.

Oxtail Stew with Olives

Our staff meals often feature **economical cuts** of meat that don't make it on our front-of-the-house menu. Oxtails, a special favorite of mine, are a good example. I would rather have them for dinner than filet mignon any time. Truly. They're a prime example of an inexpensive cut that is transformed by long, slow braising into an appealingly full-flavored, meltingly tender main course. Precut oxtails are often available at supermarkets, but if you have trouble finding meaty ones, buy the oxtails at a butcher shop and have them cut into 2-inch sections. The addition of Greek Kalamata olives and olive paste contributes a wonderful, full flavor that balances the oxtails' rich beefiness. Sucking the juices from the bones is pleasurable but messy, so set out plenty of paper napkins. Serve with Potato Gratin (see box, page 329), buttered orzo, or polenta. **SERVES 6**

2 tablespoons olive oil

3 medium onions, sliced

1 piece (4 ounces) slab bacon (with rind), cut into ¼-inch dice

2 large cloves garlic, minced

6 pounds meaty oxtails, trimmed of fat and cut into 2-inch sections

5 cups Beefed-Up Veal Stock (page 38) or canned low-sodium beef broth

4 cups canned whole tomatoes, with liquid

3 cups dry white wine

6 bay leaves

½ teaspoon dried thyme leaves

½ teaspoon dried oregano leaves

2 tablespoons olive paste (see box, facing page)

2 cups Kalamata olives, pitted

Coarse (kosher) salt and freshly ground black pepper,
    to taste

Dash of red wine vinegar

1. Heat the oil in a large stockpot over medium-low heat. Add the onions, bacon, and garlic and cook, stirring occasionally, until the onions are softened and lightly browned, about 10 minutes.

2. Add the oxtails, beef stock, tomatoes, wine, bay leaves, thyme, and oregano and bring to a boil over high heat. Reduce the heat to low and simmer, partially covered, for 2 hours, skimming frequently.

3. At this point stir in the olive paste and continue simmering until the oxtails are quite tender and the meat comes away from the bone with little prompting, about 1 hour more.

4. Add the olives and cook until heated through, about 2 minutes.

5. Remove the pot from the heat and discard the bay leaves. Season with salt and pepper and a splash of red wine vinegar, then serve.

olive paste

Although there are several flavorful dressed black olive pastes available on the market (France's *tapenade* and Italy's *olivada* come to mind), the olive paste I call for here is simply olives puréed with a little olive oil. It's easy enough to make your own using oil-cured Moroccan olives.

To pit the olives, spread out a handful on a work surface. Position the flat side of a heavy chef's knife on the olives and press down hard on the knife. This will split the olives open, allowing you to remove the pits. Purée the olives along with about 1 tablespoon extra-virgin olive oil per ½ cup olives in a food processor or blender to form a thick paste.

Braised Tripe alla Fiorentina

Although I'm very **fond of tripe,** I have to admit it's in no danger of becoming one of the most popular dishes at staff meals. Those who share my passion eat it with gusto; the others concentrate on sides and salads. In this recipe, the strips of tripe are braised in a mixture of chicken stock, wine, tomato purée, and herbs, absorbing each flavor, and creating an earthy dish that's as distinctively chewy or gelatinous as you choose it to be. The vegetables and butter lend remarkable sweetness to the braising liquid. Serve with a side of orzo and a salad of mixed greens. **SERVES 4**

¼ cup olive oil

2 medium onions, sliced

3 large cloves garlic, minced

4 cups Chicken Stock (page 39) or canned low-sodium
    chicken broth

3 cups canned tomato purée

1 cup dry white wine

4 bay leaves

¼ teaspoon dried oregano leaves

¼ teaspoon dried thyme leaves

Pinch of cayenne pepper

Pinch of sugar

2 pounds tripe, rinsed, patted dry, and cut into ½-inch strips

3 medium leeks, white part only, rinsed well,
    drained, and cut into 1 × ¼-inch strips

3 small zucchini, cut into 1 × ¼-inch strips

2 medium carrots, peeled and cut into 1 × ¼-inch strips

8 tablespoons (1 stick) unsalted butter, cut into pieces

Coarse (kosher) salt and freshly ground black pepper, to taste

Fresh lemon juice, to taste

Freshly grated Parmesan, for serving

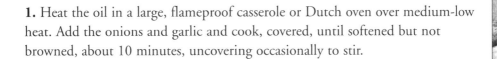

1. Heat the oil in a large, flameproof casserole or Dutch oven over medium-low heat. Add the onions and garlic and cook, covered, until softened but not browned, about 10 minutes, uncovering occasionally to stir.

2. Add the chicken stock, tomato purée, and wine and increase the heat to high. Bring to a simmer and stir in the bay leaves, oregano, thyme, cayenne, and sugar. Lower the heat and simmer, uncovered, to develop the flavors, 10 minutes.

3. Add the tripe to the casserole and return to a simmer. Reduce the heat to low and cook, covered, until the tripe is as tender as you want it, 1½ to 2 hours. (see Note).

4. Add the leeks, zucchini, and carrots to the simmering mixture and cook, covered, until tender, about 5 minutes. Uncover and add the butter a few pieces at a time, stirring until it's completely melted and incorporated.

5. Remove the casserole from the heat and season with salt and pepper and a squeeze of fresh lemon juice. Serve accompanied by grated Parmesan.

Note: The stew can be prepared through step 3 up to 2 days ahead. Refrigerate, covered, until you're ready to finish the dish. Bring to a simmer before adding the vegetables and completing the recipe.

buying and cooking tripe

Tripe is the muscular lining of two of the four stomach chambers of ruminant (cud-chewing) animals such as sheep, pigs, and cows. Thick, subtly flavored honeycomb beef tripe (named for its appearance) is the most delicate and desirable type, although, like all tripe, it's bland, chewy, and spongy, and its primary virtue is its ability to absorb other flavors. Readily available at supermarkets and butcher shops, honeycomb tripe should be ivory colored, with a fresh smell. Virtually all the fresh tripe sold in the United States has already been cleaned and parboiled and is ready to cook. Simply rinse it in cold water and pat it dry before cooking.

Determining when tripe has cooked long enough is strictly a matter of personal preference. I prefer it on the chewy side, with a slightly resilient texture that is achieved after 1 to 1½ hours of cooking. For softer, gummier tripe, a longer cooking time is necessary.

Veal Chops with Mustard and Cream

Although veal chops are a bit too pricey for our down-to-earth staff meals, they're very nice indeed for a more intimate **special** family **meal**, particularly if you're having guests. The combination of Dijon mustard and heavy cream enhanced with brandy could not be simpler, yet it makes an elegant, wonderfully flavorful sauce that tastes far more complex than the few ingredients would lead you to expect. A handful of sautéed mushrooms or a few additional herbs such as dill, basil, or thyme can be added if you wish. This recipe is also quite good made with pork chops, in which case you'll want slightly thicker chops, around about 1½ inches thick.

Either version is good served with steamed spinach and some roasted potatoes. Good crusty bread, of course, is needed to enjoy the sauce to the fullest. **SERVES 4**

3 tablespoons olive oil

4 veal chops (1 inch thick; about 10 ounces each)

2 tablespoons unsalted butter

2 tablespoons chopped shallots

1 small clove garlic, minced

2 tablespoons brandy

1 cup heavy (or whipping) cream

¼ cup Dijon mustard

Squeeze of fresh lemon juice

Coarse (kosher) salt and freshly ground black pepper, to taste

2 teaspoons mixed chopped fresh herbs, such as chives, flat-leaf parsley, tarragon, and/or chervil leaves

1. In a skillet large enough to hold the veal chops in a single layer, heat the oil over medium-high heat until it just begins to smoke. Add the chops and sauté until well browned on each side, 4 to 5 minutes per side. Transfer to a platter and cover to keep warm.

2. Discard the oil in the skillet, then wipe out the skillet with a paper towel. Set over medium heat and add the butter. When it's melted, add the shallots and garlic and sauté until aromatic but not browned, about 1 minute.

3. Remove the skillet from the heat and add the brandy; be careful here, because the brandy may ignite. Add the cream and mustard to the skillet and return the skillet to the heat, increasing the heat to high. Bring the mixture to a boil, then reduce the heat to low. Return the veal chops to the skillet, along with any accumulated juices, and simmer until the sauce has reduced enough to coat the back of a spoon and the chops are just cooked through (a hint of pink will remain when you pierce a chop with a sharp knife), 4 to 5 minutes. Turn the chops in the sauce once as they cook.

4. Remove the skillet from the heat and season the chops with lemon juice and salt and pepper. Transfer the chops to a serving platter, spoon the sauce over them, and serve immediately, sprinkled with the chopped fresh herbs.

Roasted Veal Shank

In general veal is one of the priciest meats, but veal shanks are **luxurious tasting** and inexpensive. Choosing the most effective cooking method makes all the difference. Roasting turns this mild-flavored, chewy cut into a tender silk-textured treat napped with a rich and delicious sauce. Present the whole shank on a small platter like a roast, removing the meat from the bone and carving it at the table. Serve with Creamed Spinach (page 340) and roasted potatoes. **SERVES 2**

1 veal shank (3½ to 4 pounds), trimmed of fat

4 cloves garlic, 2 thinly sliced and 2 minced

Coarse (kosher) salt and freshly ground black pepper,
   to taste

3 tablespoons olive oil

1 cup dry white wine

2 cups Chicken Stock (page 39) or canned low-sodium
   chicken broth

3 tablespoons unsalted butter

½ teaspoon chopped fresh thyme leaves or
   ¼ teaspoon dried

2 tablespoons coarsely chopped fresh flat-leaf
   parsley leaves

1. Preheat the oven to 500°F.

2. Using a small, sharp knife, make deep slits in the flesh all over the veal shank, spacing them about 1 inch apart. Insert a garlic slice into each slit, then season the meat with salt and pepper and rub it with the oil.

3. Place the shank in a flameproof roasting pan or casserole just large enough to fit it and roast, turning occasionally, until well browned and cooked through, about 45 minutes. If the meat seems to be getting too brown too quickly, reduce the oven temperature to 400°F.

4. Transfer the shank to a serving platter and set it aside, covered loosely with aluminum foil, while you prepare the sauce.

5. Pour off the fat from the roasting pan and set the pan over medium-high heat. Carefully add the wine and bring to a boil, scraping up the browned bits from the bottom of the pan. Add the chicken stock and return to a boil; cook until the liquid is reduced to about 1 cup, 10 minutes. Reduce the heat to medium and stir in the butter, minced garlic, and thyme. Cook, stirring frequently, until the butter is melted and the sauce is approximately the consistency of heavy cream and coats the back of a spoon, about 5 minutes.

6. Remove the sauce from the heat and season with salt and pepper. Stir in the parsley and pour over the veal shank to serve.

Staff Meals from Chanterelle | b e e f , v e a l , l a m b

Grilled Butterflied Leg of Lamb

Leg of lamb is **easiest to prepare** and cooks the fastest when it's boned, butterflied, and grilled over a charcoal fire. Marinating the lamb overnight in an herb-infused olive oil mixture tenderizes it and ensures terrific flavor. If you don't have a grill, sear the meat in a little canola oil in a very hot ovenproof skillet until it's quite brown and crusty, then drain off all the fat and finish it in a 450° to 475°F oven for about 15 minutes to cook it a bit more and create an even crustier exterior. Slice the meat, arrange on a warmed platter, and garnish with lemon wedges or a sprinkling of fresh cilantro leaves. Serve with orzo, rice, or Couscous (page 94) and steamed green beans. **SERVES 8 TO 10**

1 cup extra-virgin olive oil
½ cup fresh lemon juice
2 large cloves garlic, minced
1 tablespoon dried thyme leaves
1 tablespoon dried oregano leaves
1 teaspoon coarse (kosher) salt
¼ teaspoon ground cumin
Pinch of cayenne pepper
1 leg of lamb (about 5 or 6 pounds), butterflied

1. Combine the oil, lemon juice, garlic, thyme, oregano, salt, cumin, and cayenne in a small bowl and whisk thoroughly to blend. Place the lamb in a large, shallow baking dish, pour the mixture over it, and rub in well. Cover and let marinate in the refrigerator for at least 8 hours and up to 24.

2. When you're ready to cook, preheat a barbecue grill to high.

3. When the grill is ready, oil the grill rack, then place the lamb on the rack and

cook until it's somewhat charred on the outside while remaining nice and medium rare within, about 10 minutes per side. Transfer the lamb to a cutting board and let it rest for 5 minutes before slicing and serving.

Moroccan Lamb Shanks

Inexpensive and **tremendously flavorful**, lamb shanks have long been a mainstay on bistro-style restaurant menus in both France and the United States. But curiously enough, few home cooks think of preparing this rustic comfort food in their own kitchens. I hope this recipe will inspire you.

The long simmering time tenderizes the meaty shanks and creates a deep, soulful flavor intriguingly infused with Moroccan spices. Make this dish a day in advance so the flavors have time to meld and the fat solidifies on the top. To serve, remove the fat and reheat the shanks slowly, spooning the flavorful liquid over them gently and often.

At our staff meals this dish is known fondly as "Flintstone food." A single lamb shank, impressively perched atop a bed of Couscous (page 94), rice, or orzo with its bone pointing ceiling-ward, is certainly a prehistoric sight. **SERVES 6**

6 lamb shanks (about 1 pound each), trimmed of fat

¼ cup extra-virgin olive oil

2 medium onions, coarsely chopped

3 large cloves garlic, minced

2 tablespoons fresh lemon juice

1 tablespoon coarse (kosher) salt

2 teaspoons ground cumin

1 teaspoon ground coriander

1 teaspoon sweet Hungarian paprika

1 teaspoon saffron threads (see box, page 174)

½ teaspoon ground turmeric

¼ teaspoon ground ginger

1 bottle (750 ml) dry white wine

2 cups Chicken Stock (page 39) or canned low-sodium
   chicken broth

2 cups canned tomato purée

6 bay leaves

1. Preheat the oven to 500°F.

2. Rub the lamb shanks all over with 2 tablespoons of the oil and place in a roasting pan. Roast, turning shanks occasionally, until well browned, about 40 minutes. Pour off the fat, leaving the shanks in the roasting pan. Set the shanks aside. Reduce the oven temperature to 375°F.

3. Heat the remaining 2 tablespoons oil in a medium-size, heavy, nonreactive saucepan over medium heat. Add the onions and garlic and cook, stirring occasionally, until softened and lightly browned, 6 to 8 minutes.

4. Add the lemon juice, salt, cumin, coriander, paprika, saffron, turmeric, and ginger and stir well to mix, then add the wine, stock, tomato purée, and bay leaves and bring to a boil over high heat. Remove the pan from the heat and pour the mixture over the lamb shanks in the roasting pan. Cover tightly with aluminum foil and bake for 1 hour.

5. Remove the foil, reduce the oven temperature to 350°F, and continue cooking the shanks until they're quite tender (the meat should almost fall off the bones) and the sauce is reduced and thickened, about 1 hour more (see Note). Turn the shanks in the liquid occasionally as they cook.

6. Transfer the shanks to a serving platter or individual plates. Remove and discard the bay leaves. Skim the fat from the sauce and adjust the seasonings. Spoon the sauce over the shanks and serve.

Note: If the sauce hasn't thickened enough, pour it into a saucepan, bring it to a boil over high heat, and reduce it until it's the proper consistency.

Lamb Shanks with Tomato and Rosemary

The **beauty of** meats such as **lamb shanks**, which require braising to expand their flavor is that they practically cook themselves. Once they've been nicely browned and popped into a pot along with some wine, stock, and seasonings, you're free to abandon them to their destiny for several hours of simmering. In fact, there's very little sense of urgency about this dish on any front, for like all braised meats these shanks taste their best when allowed to rest, tightly covered, in the refrigerator for a day or two to further develop their lovely taste.

Just skim off the fat, reheat, and serve with plenty of plain rice, orzo, or roast potatoes. Be sure to use branches of fresh rosemary here; dried rosemary is simply worthless. It's a nice touch to use rosemary branches as a garnish atop each serving. **SERVES 4**

¼ cup canola or other vegetable oil

4 lamb shanks (about 1 pound each), trimmed of fat

2 tablespoons extra-virgin olive oil

1 medium onion, diced

3 large cloves garlic, minced

1 cup full-bodied red wine

7 cups Chicken Stock (page 39) or canned low-sodium
   chicken broth

1 can (28 ounces) whole tomatoes, drained and very roughly chopped

A few branches of fresh rosemary

3 bay leaves

1 teaspoon dried thyme leaves

Coarse (kosher) salt and freshly ground black pepper, to taste

Splash of red wine vinegar, to taste

1. Heat the canola oil in a large skillet over medium-high heat. When it's just beginning to smoke, add the lamb shanks carefully and brown well on all sides, 4 to 5 minutes per side.

2. Meanwhile, heat the olive oil in a large, heavy, nonreactive, flameproof casserole or Dutch oven over medium heat. Add the onion and garlic and sauté, stirring occasionally, until softened but not browned, about 3 minutes.

3. When the lamb shanks are nicely browned, add them to the onion and garlic in the casserole. Pour the wine over the shanks, then increase the heat to high and bring to a boil. When the wine is reduced by half, in about 5 minutes, add the chicken stock, tomatoes, rosemary, bay leaves, thyme, salt, and pepper. Return to a boil, then reduce the heat to low and simmer, partially covered, until the shanks are very tender and almost falling off the bone, about 2 hours. Check the lamb occasionally. If the liquid level seems low, add water.

4. Transfer the shanks to a platter. Increase the heat under the casserole to high and bring the cooking liquid to a boil. Reduce the heat to medium, to keep the liquid at a low boil, and cook, uncovered, until it has thickened somewhat, about 20 minutes.

5. Return the shanks to the casserole to reheat, about 5 minutes. Remove the casserole from the heat and discard the bay leaves and rosemary. Taste for seasoning, adding a splash of vinegar and more salt and pepper, if necessary. Serve immediately.

a variation

To add an extra dimension of texture and flavor to this dish, consider adding some complementary vegetables. Cube a couple of medium-size zucchini and cut several medium-size Asian eggplants into ¼-inch-thick rounds. Add them during step 4 in the recipe, after you've removed the shanks from the pot.

Lamb and Chicken Couscous

There are **infinite combinations** used in preparing couscous, varying the meats and vegetables. I think the lamb shanks, which lend a characteristic flavor to the broth base, should be a constant. You could grill kebabs of lamb or chicken and serve them on the side, using only vegetables in the stew. One tip: Give yourself time to prepare the couscous. The broth should be made the day before you plan on serving the dish.

SERVES 8

FOR THE LAMB BROTH:

4 quarts Chicken Stock (page 39), canned low-sodium
    chicken broth, or water
4 lamb shanks (about 1 pound each), trimmed of fat
2 medium onions, either puréed or grated
6 large cloves garlic, minced
Juice of 1 lemon
1 tablespoon ground cumin
1 tablespoon ground coriander
1 tablespoon ground turmeric
½ teaspoon saffron threads (see box, page 174)
½ teaspoon sweet Hungarian paprika
4 bay leaves

FOR THE COUSCOUS:

2 pounds boneless lamb leg or shoulder, trimmed of
    fat and cut into 1½-inch cubes
1 chicken (3½ pounds)
Coarse (kosher) salt and freshly ground black pepper, to taste
4 large white turnips, peeled and cut into large chunks
3 large carrots, peeled and cut into large chunks

1 large butternut squash (2 to 3 pounds), peeled, seeded, and
cut into large chunks

4 large or 8 small leeks, split, cut into 1-inch lengths, and
thoroughly rinsed and drained

3 medium zucchini, trimmed and cut into large chunks

2 cups cooked chickpeas (if using canned, rinse under cold
running water and drain)

1 cup dried currants

FOR SERVING:

Couscous (recipe follows)
Doctored Harissa (page 368)

1. The day before you plan to cook the stew, prepare the broth: Combine the chicken stock, lamb shanks, onions, garlic, lemon juice, cumin, coriander, turmeric, saffron, paprika, and bay leaves in a very large stockpot and bring to a boil over high heat. Skim the surface of foam, then reduce the heat to low and simmer, partially covered, until the lamb is tender and almost but not quite falling off the bone, 1½ hours.

2. Remove the pot from the heat. Transfer the lamb shanks to a platter to cool. Remove and discard the bay leaves and set the broth aside to cool.

3. When the shanks are cool enough to handle, pull the meat from the bones, cut it into large chunks, and refrigerate, covered, until you're ready to proceed with the recipe. When the broth is cool, transfer it to a storage container and refrigerate it, covered, overnight.

4. When you're ready to continue, remove and discard the hardened fat from the broth. Transfer the broth to a very large stockpot and bring it to a boil over high heat. Add the cubed boneless lamb leg or shoulder and return to a boil, then reduce the heat to low. Cook, partially covered, until the meat is just tender, about 45 minutes.

5. Rinse the chicken, inside and out, under cold running water, removing any excess fat. Cut the chicken into 10 pieces (see box, page 159). Add the chicken to the pot, return the broth to a boil, then season with salt and pepper and reduce the heat to low and simmer, partially covered, for 10 minutes. Add the

turnips, carrots, and squash and simmer for 10 minutes, then add the leeks, zucchini, chickpeas, reserved cooked lamb shank meat, and currants and simmer for 5 minutes more.

6. Remove the pot from the heat and taste and adjust the seasoning. Spoon the stew over the couscous on a large platter and serve, accompanied by the *harissa*.

Couscous

It's **traditional to steam** couscous in a couscousière, above the simmering stew with which it will be served, but most people don't own one, and anyway, the couscous will be bathed in the broth from the stew. I also find that steaming the couscous separately allows me to control the timing better.

I enjoy my couscous buttery and have been known to add as much as a full cup. I cut back a bit here without sacrificing too much flavor. You have my permission to add more than the 12 tablespoons suggested, but please don't use less.

MAKES 8 SERVINGS

1½ boxes (16 ounces each; 24 ounces for this recipe) couscous
2½ cups hot water
12 tablespoons (1½ sticks) unsalted butter, room temperature,
    cut into small pieces

1. Fill a large stockpot half full of water and bring to a simmer over medium heat. Select a metal colander that will fit into the stockpot and line it with several layers of dampened cheesecloth.

2. Place the couscous in a large bowl and add the hot water gradually, stirring to avoid lumps. Let the couscous stand until all the water is absorbed, about 10 minutes, then transfer it to the cheesecloth-lined colander. Cover the couscous with another piece of dampened cheesecloth and set the colander into the stockpot so it rests over, not in, the simmering water. Place a lid or piece of aluminum foil over the colander and steam the couscous for 20 minutes.

3. Remove the colander from the stockpot. Remove the cheesecloth covering the couscous and transfer the couscous to a large bowl. Use the same dampened cheesecloth to line the colander again and set aside. When the couscous is cool enough to handle (after about 5 minutes), mix in the butter, rubbing the couscous gently between your hands to break it up and incorporate the butter. If you're planning to serve the couscous immediately, return it now to the lined colander, cover it with another piece of dampened cheesecloth, and steam it over the simmering water for 20 minutes more. If you aren't planning to serve the couscous right away, cover it after you incorporate the butter and set it aside at room temperature (for up to 2 hours) until you're ready to steam it. When cool, the couscous will take 30 minutes of steaming to reheat.

about couscous

Couscous is the name of Morocco's stewlike national dish and also of the fine-grained pasta served with it. In Morocco and other areas of North Africa they are traditionally prepared together in a two-tiered pot called a couscousière. As the stew simmers in the bottom, the couscous in the perforated upper section is steamed in two stages by its vapors. Couscous grains are customarily made of semolina flour mixed with water and formed into small granules. The little yellow grains are sold loose by the pound at health food stores and also packaged (usually labeled "instant") at specialty food stores and many supermarkets. If you can buy couscous in bulk, then I urge you to do so. If you can't, then boxed is a fine second choice.

Actually, what matters most is the cooking method used; ignore the instructions on the box. You'll find that my way (page 94) is slightly less trouble than the traditional one, but more involved than the shortcut instructions on couscous boxes. The result will be couscous as it should be—light colored, fluffy, and tender.

Lamb Tagine with Prunes and Honey

Unlike other stews, it's generally unnecessary to brown the meat in the stews the Moroccans call *tagines*. But like all stews, once the ingredients of this particular irresistible *tagine* are ensconced in the pot, it gently simmers away until the lamb is meltingly tender. The sweetness of the honey and the prunes (which thicken as well as flavor the sauce) is complemented by the spices and black pepper, and the whole dish is perfumed with a drop or two of orange flower water (available at Middle Eastern markets and specialty food stores). Serve the almond-garnished tagine over Couscous (page 94) or plain or saffron rice. **SERVES 10 TO 12**

5 pounds boneless lamb stew meat, trimmed of fat and
    cut into 1-inch cubes
6 cups Chicken Stock (page 39) or canned low-sodium
    chicken broth
1 large onion, cut into ½-inch dice
4 teaspoons freshly ground black pepper
2 large cloves garlic, minced
2 teaspoons ground ginger
1 teaspoon saffron threads (see box, page 174)
Coarse (kosher) salt, to taste
12 ounces pitted prunes, coarsely chopped
2 tablespoons honey
1 tablespoon ground cinnamon
3 tablespoons chopped fresh flat-leaf parsley leaves
1 teaspoon orange flower water
Fresh lemon juice, to taste
3 tablespoons sliced almonds, for garnish

1. Place the lamb in a large stockpot along with the chicken stock, onion, pepper, garlic, ginger, saffron, and salt. Bring to a boil over high heat, then reduce the heat to low and simmer the lamb gently, uncovered, for 1½ hours.

2. Add the prunes, honey, and cinnamon to the *tagine* and stir. Continue cooking, uncovered, until the lamb is very tender, about 30 minutes more.

3. When you're ready to serve, stir in the parsley, orange flower water, and lemon juice and remove the pot from the heat. Taste and adjust the seasonings. Transfer the *tagine* to a large, shallow serving bowl or platter and garnish with the sliced almonds to serve.

cooks' conspiracy

The staff at Chanterelle is no different from any other group of people who work closely together— now and then we can't resist the urge to tease each other. When certain waiters who love say, the Lamb Tagine, take time off, we cooks, who rarely get an unscheduled day away from the restaurant, pretend that we made their favorite dish for our staff meal—and they missed it! They wander around wistfully, asking if it's true, and naturally we all say, "Oh, yes, and it was *soooo* delicious!"

Pork

Since everyone on our staff loves pork—except the vegetarians, of course—it's a frequent and very welcome main dish at staff meals. Pork has a habit of showing up in a wide range of preparations featuring every part of the pig, from chops, ribs, and roasts to bacon, ham, and sausage. In down-home mode pork is a relaxed, casual meat that loves to wallow in thick, spicy-sweet barbecue sauce. In its more elegant persona we enjoy Sautéed Pork Chops with a silky, piquant Sauce Charcutière (page 103) or pinwheel slices of Herbed Pinwheel Pork Loin (page 100). Our preference for pork also has a thrifty side, since a little goes a long way in dishes like Pork Goulash, Szeged Style (page 106), and Chinese-Style Meatballs for a Crowd (page 128).

Herbed Pinwheel Pork Loin

It takes **just a few minutes** to butterfly a boneless loin (one of the tenderest parts of the pig), spread it with garlicky herb stuffing, and roll it up pinwheel-style for roasting. When the roast is sliced, each piece reveals an attractive whirligig spiral of stuffing. Serve with polenta, Potato Gratin (see box, page 329) or Spiced Applesauce (page 303). **SERVES 4 TO 6**

1 boneless pork loin (about 2 pounds), trimmed of fat
½ cup fine dry bread crumbs (see box, page 279)
¼ cup chopped mixed fresh herbs (some combination of
    thyme, sage, and oregano leaves)
3 cloves garlic, minced
2 tablespoons unsalted butter, melted
Coarse (kosher) salt and freshly ground black pepper, to taste
½ cup dry white wine
1 cup Chicken Stock (page 39) or canned low-sodium
    chicken broth
¼ cup heavy (or whipping) cream (optional)

1. Preheat the oven to 350°F.

2. Make a deep lengthwise cut along one side of the pork loin from one end to the other and extending about two thirds of the way in. Open out the loin as you would a book. Starting on the left-hand side, at the bottom edge, slice through the thickness of the meat, easing your knife around the inner edge (what would be the spine of a book), and then along the top edge (do not slice along the outside edge). Again, open up this flap as you would a book. Repeat on the right side. Open out the right-side flap of the loin and set the loin aside while you prepare the stuffing.

3. Combine the bread crumbs, herbs, garlic, butter, salt, and pepper in a small bowl and stir well to mix. Spread the mixture over the opened-out pork loin, reserving a bit for the top of the roast. Roll up the loin from one long side and tie securely at 1-inch intervals with butcher's twine. Spread the reserved stuffing on top of the loin, then place the loin in a flameproof roasting pan. Roast until just cooked through, 50 to 60 minutes. An instant-read thermometer inserted into the thickest part of the roast will register 150°F if you like your pork slightly pink, 155°F for well done.

4. Transfer the pork to a cutting board and let it rest for a few minutes before untying and slicing.

5. Meanwhile, prepare a little sauce. Set the roasting pan over medium-high heat, pour in the wine, and bring to a boil, scraping up the little browned bits stuck to the pan. When the liquid is reduced to almost nothing, 2 to 3 minutes, pour in the chicken stock and bring to a boil. Cook until the stock is reduced by half, then stir in the cream, if desired, and reduce the sauce until a light, saucelike consistency is achieved, a minute or two more. Remove from the heat, season with salt and pepper, if necessary, and cover to keep warm.

6. Untie the pork loin, then slice it and arrange on a serving platter. Serve immediately, accompanied by the sauce in a sauceboat.

pork pointers

Today's pork is not the pork that most of us grew up eating. In the past twenty years, particularly the past ten, it has undergone a makeover. Due to changes in what hogs are fed, pork is now much higher in protein and contains far less fat, nearly 60 percent less than previously. It's also more tender, because hogs are sent to market earlier. To ensure its staying moist and flavorful, this leaner, tenderer pork requires somewhat lower cooking temperatures than were once traditional.

Roast Ham with Honey-Mustard Glaze

I think of ham as a delicious **convenience food** for our staff meals. Brushed with a simple, lively-flavored glaze and popped into the oven for only an hour or so, its preparation is nearly effortless, which makes it a handy way to feed a crowd. I buy Fleur de Lis boneless smoked ham, which is an inexpensive supermarket ham with good flavor, but you could use any ham labeled "fully cooked" or "ready to eat." The wonderful sharpness of the Dijon mustard in the glaze is mellowed just a bit by some honey and Madeira, while the balsamic vinegar–soy sauce combination broadens the spectrum of flavor and also burnishes the ham with some appetizing color. Depending on the season, serve with Summertime Creamed Corn (page 313) or Potato Gratin (see box, page 329). **SERVES 8 TO 10**

½ cup Dijon mustard
½ cup honey
2 tablespoons Madeira or medium-dry sherry
2 tablespoons balsamic vinegar
2 tablespoons good-quality soy sauce, such as Kikkoman
1 boneless cooked smoked ham (about 4 pounds)
2 cups Chicken Stock (page 39) or canned low-sodium
　　chicken broth
4 tablespoons (½ stick) unsalted butter, cut into pieces

1. Preheat the oven to 350°F.

2. Combine the mustard, honey, Madeira, vinegar, and soy sauce in a small bowl and whisk until smooth.

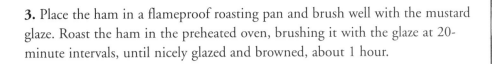

3. Place the ham in a flameproof roasting pan and brush well with the mustard glaze. Roast the ham in the preheated oven, brushing it with the glaze at 20-minute intervals, until nicely glazed and browned, about 1 hour.

4. Transfer the ham to a serving platter. Pour the chicken stock into the roasting pan, set it over high heat, and bring to a boil, scraping up the browned bits stuck to the bottom of the pan. Pour the contents of the roasting pan into a 1½-quart saucepan and return to a boil. Whisk in any unused glaze, then bring the glaze to a boil and add the butter. Stir until the butter is incorporated, then remove the pan from the heat.

5. To serve, slice the ham, arrange it on a serving platter, and pass the sauce in a gravy boat.

Sautéed Pork Chops with Sauce Charcutière

Hefty hunks of meat like these double-cut pork chops benefit from a refined, complex sauce that keeps each bite exciting. The one here is an updated, slightly lighter version of a French classic. Sherry vinegar and Dijon mustard add a distinctive piquancy to the silky sauce, as do the tart, coarsely chopped cornichons that provide surprising little pockets of crunchiness. If you prefer, the chops can be grilled rather than sautéed. Everyday Mashed Potatoes (page 334) are a must with this dish, and some lightly cooked kale, Swiss chard, or spinach would be nice as well.

SERVES 6

2 tablespoons olive oil

2 medium onions, finely chopped

½ cup dry white wine

⅓ cup sherry vinegar, or more as needed

8 cups Chicken Stock (page 39) or canned low-
   sodium chicken broth

2 bay leaves

2 tablespoons tomato paste

3 tablespoons Dijon mustard, or more as needed

½ cup coarsely chopped cornichons

Coarse (kosher) salt and freshly ground black pepper, to taste

6 double-cut loin pork chops (about 12 ounces each)

3 tablespoons canola or other vegetable oil

1. Heat the olive oil in a medium-size saucepan over medium heat. Add the onions and cook, stirring occasionally, until translucent but not browned, about 5 minutes.

2. Add the wine and ⅓ cup vinegar and bring to a boil over high heat. Cook, uncovered, until the liquid is reduced to approximately ¼ cup, about 5 minutes.

3. Add the chicken stock, bay leaves, and tomato paste and bring to a boil, then reduce the heat to low and simmer, uncovered, for 40 minutes. Whisk in 3 tablespoons mustard and the chopped cornichons and return to a boil. Continue reducing the mixture until it's slightly thickened and of a light saucelike consistency, about 45 minutes. Remove the pan from the heat and discard the bay leaves. Season the sauce with salt and pepper, adding more vinegar or mustard if needed. Set aside, covered, to keep warm.

4. Season the pork chops on both sides with salt and pepper. Heat the vegetable oil in a large, heavy skillet over high heat (see Note). When the oil has just begun to smoke, add the chops, reduce the heat to medium, and sauté until the chops are nicely browned on both sides and cooked through, about 10 minutes per side.

5. To serve, divide the chops among six dinner plates and spoon the hot sauce over them.

Note: It's important not to crowd the chops in the skillet, so you may have to use two pans. For smaller skillets, use about 2 tablespoons oil for each.

Smothered Pork Chops

In this **southern specialty** thickly cut pork chops are first browned, then simmered in a tenderizing, onion-flavored sauce. Each ingredient gives itself up to the others in a transformational exchange of flavors. The result is a homey main course that's nothing short of ambrosial. Heap the pork chops on a platter, smother them with the same hearty, gravylike sauce they were braised in, and set out a big bowl of Everyday Mashed Potatoes (page 334) or some hash browns. **SERVES 4**

3 tablespoons olive oil
4 center-cut loin pork chops (8 to 10 ounces each),
    trimmed of fat
2 medium onions, sliced lengthwise
1 heaping tablespoon all-purpose flour
2 cups Chicken Stock (page 39) or canned low-sodium
    chicken broth, or more as needed
½ cup dry white wine
1 bay leaf
¼ teaspoon dried thyme leaves
Coarse (kosher) salt and freshly ground black pepper,
    to taste
1 tablespoon balsamic vinegar

1. Heat the oil in a large, heavy skillet over medium-high heat. Add the chops and sauté until well browned on both sides, about 5 minutes per side. Remove the chops to a platter and set aside.

2. Reduce the heat to medium and add the sliced onions to the drippings in the skillet. Sauté, stirring occasionally, until tender and browned, about 10 minutes.

3. Sprinkle the onions with the flour and cook, stirring constantly, until the flour is slightly browned but not burned, about 3 minutes. Add 2 cups chicken stock, the wine, bay leaf, thyme, salt, and pepper and bring to a boil over medium-high heat, scraping up any browned bits stuck to the bottom of the skillet. Return the chops to the skillet, spooning the sauce over them, and reduce the heat so the sauce is just barely simmering. Cover and cook until the chops are cooked through, 1 to 1½ hours. Check the chops during cooking. If the liquid level seems low, add more stock to keep the chops from sticking.

4. Remove the skillet from the heat and discard the bay leaf. Add the vinegar, then taste and adjust the seasoning. Serve from the skillet, or transfer the chops to a platter and spoon the sauce over them.

Pork Goulash, Szeged Style

This is one of **my very favorite** main dishes, one that I always enjoy cooking and eating. Its simple, forthright flavors never fail to please me or the staff when it appears on the table at our meal. Simmering the sauerkraut in the stew softens the texture and mellows its distinctive taste. The combination of sweet and hot Hungarian paprikas makes this goulash, which is named for a Hungarian city renowned for paprika, just spicy enough to justify a cooling dollop of sour cream atop each serving. For more about paprika, see page 163. **SERVES 8**

¼ cup canola or other vegetable oil, or
　　more as needed
2½ pounds boneless pork shoulder, trimmed of fat
　　and cut into 1½-inch cubes
2 large onions, sliced

2 large cloves garlic, minced

3 strips thickly sliced good-quality smoked bacon,
   rind removed and discarded, cut crosswise
   into ⅛-inch pieces

4 cups Chicken Stock (page 39) or
   canned low-sodium chicken broth

¼ cup sweet Hungarian paprika,
   or more as needed

1 tablespoon hot Hungarian paprika, or
   more as needed

2 bay leaves

2 bags (16 ounces each) sauerkraut (do not use canned)

1 tablespoon red wine vinegar

Coarse (kosher) salt, to taste

½ teaspoon caraway seeds (optional)

Sour cream, for serving

1. Heat 2 tablespoons of the oil in a large, nonstick skillet over medium-high heat. Add enough of the pork to fit into the skillet comfortably and sauté until well browned on all sides, about 3 minutes per side. Remove the pork to a platter and set it aside while you brown the remaining pieces, adding more oil to the skillet, if necessary.

2. Heat the remaining 2 tablespoons oil in a large, nonreactive pot over medium heat. Add the onions, garlic, and bacon and sauté, stirring occasionally, until the bacon renders some of its fat but is not browned, about 5 minutes.

3. Add the pork to the pot along with any juices that have accumulated, as well as the chicken stock, both paprikas, and the bay leaves. Bring to a boil over high heat, then reduce the heat to low to maintain a steady simmer. Cook, uncovered, for 45 minutes, skimming off any fat as it rises to the top.

4. Stir in the sauerkraut and vinegar and continue simmering until the sauerkraut is heated through, the flavors are blended, and the pork is very tender but not falling apart, about 20 minutes.

5. Remove the pot from the heat and discard the bay leaves. Season with salt and more paprika, then add the caraway seeds, if desired, and serve. Pass a bowl of sour cream at the table.

Black Bean Stew with Pig Parts

I can no longer recall which wisecracking staff member gave this rich, **satisfying stew** its inelegant yet truthful name, but I assure you we all love the dish. The pig's feet are a must, as are the smoked ham hocks and cooked ham. The duck confit, of course, is not technically a pig part, so consider it an honored guest ingredient here. You can vary the meats, but bear in mind that the goal is to use as many smoked ones as possible so the beans have plenty of opportunities to absorb their smoky essences. Some type of garlicky sausage is also desirable, though if you dont have any, a thickly sliced frankfurter will do. Other possible additions might be bits of browned bacon, pancetta, chorizo, and leftover braised or roast pork.

Plan on making the stew 2 days ahead and refrigerating it. The fat will rise to the top and harden, making it very easy to remove. Serve with a global assortment of hot sauces and a big bowl of white rice. **SERVES A HORDE (15 TO 20 PEOPLE)**

6 cups dried black beans

2½ quarts cold water

3 pig's feet, split lengthwise, then cut crosswise
   into 2-inch pieces

3 smoked ham hocks (about 8 ounces each)

2 medium onions, coarsely chopped

4 large cloves garlic, minced

6 bay leaves

6 quarts Chicken Stock (page 39) or canned low-sodium
   chicken broth

2 cups red wine

Coarse (kosher) salt

Staff Meals from Chanterelle | p o r k

3 pounds mixed meats, including cooked ham
   cut into 1-inch cubes, thickly sliced garlic sausage, and
   several pieces Confit of Duck (page 201)
Freshly ground black pepper, to taste
Tabasco sauce, to taste
Red wine vinegar, to taste

1. Place the beans in a large bowl or other container and cover with the cold water by 2 inches. Let soak, in the refrigerator, for at least 8 hours and up to 24.

2. While the beans are soaking, prepare the stock: Combine the pig's feet, ham hocks, onions, garlic, bay leaves, chicken stock, and red wine in a very large, nonreactive stockpot and bring to a boil over high heat. Reduce the heat to low to maintain a steady simmer and cook, partially covered, until the pig's feet are tender, about 1 hour. Transfer the pig's-feet pieces to a bowl and set aside. Continue simmering the stock, partially covered, until the ham hocks are tender, 1 to 1½ hours more.

3. Transfer the ham hocks to a plate and strain the stock into one or more large containers. Refrigerate, covered, for 8 to 12 hours.

4. When it's cool enough to handle, pull the meat off the cooled ham hocks and cut it into 1-inch chunks. Add it to the bowl with the pig's feet and refrigerate, covered, until you're ready to use it.

5. When you're ready to proceed with the recipe, remove the hardened fat from the chilled stock. Return the stock to the stockpot and bring to a boil over high heat. Add the beans and a good sprinkling of salt, then reduce the heat to low and simmer, partially covered, until the beans are almost tender, 30 to 45 minutes (or longer, depending on the age of the beans). You may have to add water to keep the beans submerged.

6. Add the reserved ham hock meat and pig's feet to the beans, along with the ham, garlic sausage, confit, and any other meats you've chosen. Continue simmering the stew until the beans and all the meats are quite tender, 45 minutes more.

7. Remove the pot from the heat and season with salt, pepper, Tabasco, and a splash or two of red wine vinegar. Serve in big bowls.

Oven-Roasted Barbecued Ribs

Although barbecue seems to be firmly implanted in most people's minds as summer food, at Chanterelle we indulge our craving for it even in the dead of winter with these **succulent** oven-roasted **ribs**. Chinese hoisin sauce is the magic ingredient in the thick, spicy-sweet barbecue sauce, which is equally wonderful on chicken. The recipe makes enough sauce for three racks of ribs or two 3- to 3½-pound chickens. I like to marinate the ribs in the sauce overnight, but even if you decide to make them on the spur of the moment they'll still turn out wonderfully—burnished to a reddish sheen and thickly encrusted with sauce. Serve with traditional picnic sides like Cider Vinegar Slaw (page 310) or Slightly Southern Potato Salad (page 333). **SERVES 6**

1 cup ketchup
1 cup tomato purée
1 cup hoisin sauce
¼ cup red wine vinegar
3 tablespoons Dijon mustard
3 tablespoons dark molasses
2 tablespoons Tabasco sauce
2 large cloves garlic, minced
3 racks pork spareribs (about 2 pounds each)

1. Place the ketchup, tomato purée, hoisin sauce, vinegar, mustard, molasses, Tabasco, and garlic in a medium-size bowl and stir well to mix.

2. Place the ribs in a very large, nonreactive roasting pan. Pour the ketchup mixture over the ribs and turn to coat completely, using your hands to spread the marinade around. At this point you can marinate the ribs, covered, for up to 12 hours in the refrigerator, or you can go ahead and cook them now.

3. Preheat the oven to 450°F. Line with aluminum foil one or two shallow, nonreactive roasting pans large enough to hold the ribs in one layer.

4. Remove the racks of ribs from the pan they marinated in, reserving the marinade, and arrange, meaty-side up, in the prepared roasting pan(s), making sure they don't overlap. Roast the ribs for 20 to 30 minutes to render as much of the fat as possible; pour or spoon off the fat and discard. Reduce the oven temperature to 275°F and cook the ribs, brushing with reserved marinade every 30 minutes and turning several times, until they're tender and the glaze has caramelized and become crispy and blackened in places, 1½ to 2 hours more (see Note). Let the ribs cook for 10 minutes after the last brush with the marinade.

5. To serve, cut the racks into individual ribs and pile them on a platter.

Note: If desired, the ribs may be cooked partially on the grill. After dousing the ribs with marinade as described above, preheat the grill. Arrange the ribs, without overlapping, on the hot grill rack and cook until nicely browned on both sides, about 15 minutes per side. Transfer the ribs to foil-lined roasting pan(s) and cook in the oven for 1½ to 2 hours more, as described above.

measuring
sticky ingredients

Measuring hoisin sauce, honey, or molasses needn't be a messy proposition. Just coat the inside of the measuring cup lightly with vegetable oil and thick, sticky ingredients slide right out.

the chanterelle staff picnic

A few years ago we realized it was important for the staff to take a breather together away from the restaurant, to relax and unwind, and to enjoy being outdoors. So early one fall we held the first Chanterelle picnic at our house in Woodstock.

The group gathered at the crack of dawn in front of the restaurant to board a rickety old chartered yellow school bus. The ride turned out to be hair raising—it would become the stuff of legend—but once the survivors finally arrived, they were greeted with washtubs filled with beers, huge bowls of olives, Baba Ghanouj (page 320), Herbed Summer Hummus (page 317), and rice salad, platters loaded with local corn and tomatoes, sticky rice wrapped in lotus leaves, and Confit of Duck (page 201). The aroma of Grilled Quail with Scallions (page 204), Grilled Butterflied Leg of Lamb (page 87), and Wild Turkey Glazed Ribs (facing page) on the grills wafted in the air. Everyone doing the cooking was in an expansive mood. (That's because professional cooks spend so much time in the kitchen that they rarely have the fun of actually *seeing* people enjoy their food.) Other staff and friends contributed homemade baked goods to our decadent dessert table. The picnic was exhausting but so much fun that it became an annual affair.

The picnic has evolved over the years. Now we set up volleyball and badminton areas and have a trampoline that makes everyone giddy, especially the kids. And we rent lots of bikes so people can pedal to the nearby state park to go canoeing. Each year's picnic is more fun than the last. But one thing stays the same—as the sun sets and the evening turns chilly, we all gather around a backyard bonfire instead of a restaurant stove. It's a nice change.

Wild Turkey Glazed Ribs

The **slow-sipping**, mellow character of **bourbon** has always suited my palate, in a glass and as an ingredient. Compared to the sophisticated, somewhat standoffish refinement of brandy, bourbon is sturdy and straightforward in the kitchen. Always searching for a way to use bourbon, I've discovered that its sweet, no-nonsense flavor is perfectly at home in this garlicky glaze, where it adds depth and a sweet edge to the taste. The recipe makes enough glaze for two racks of spareribs, but it can be doubled if you need more. Serve with collard greens, Slightly Southern Potato Salad (page 333), or baked sweet potatoes. **SERVES 4**

¼ to ⅓ cup Wild Turkey or other good-quality
   bourbon, to taste
3 cloves garlic, minced
3 tablespoons honey
1 tablespoon Dijon mustard
1 tablespoon Tabasco sauce
1 tablespoon coarse (kosher) salt
1½ teaspoons Worcestershire sauce
2 racks pork spareribs (about 2 pounds each)

1. Preheat the oven to 325°F. Line with aluminum foil a shallow roasting pan large enough to hold the ribs in one layer.

2. Combine the bourbon, garlic, honey, mustard, Tabasco, salt, and Worcestershire sauce in a small bowl. Stir well to mix.

3. Brush the racks of ribs on both sides with the glaze, then arrange, meaty-side up, in the prepared pan, making sure they don't overlap. Roast the ribs for 20 to 30 minutes to render as much of the fat as possible; pour or spoon off the fat

and discard. Reduce the oven temperature to 275°F and cook the ribs, brushing with reserved marinade every 30 minutes and turning several times, until they're tender and the glaze has caramelized and become crispy and blackened in places, 1½ to 2 hours more (see Note, page 111). Let the ribs cook for 10 minutes after the last brush with the marinade.

4. To serve, cut the racks into individual ribs and pile them on a platter.

Braised Mini Ribs with Black Bean Sauce

Irresistibly tender, these diminutive **saucy riblets** are meant to be held between your fingers and gnawed on with abandon. They're perfect fare for buffet-style parties. Finger licking is inevitable, though that does not preclude the necessity of having a plentiful supply of paper napkins nearby. Unless you have a bandsaw at home, you'll need to ask the butcher to cut the racks of ribs crosswise at 1-inch intervals. He'll probably look at you like you're crazy, but be persistent. Once this is accomplished, you'll easily be able to cut in between the bones of each strip to create little bite-size riblets. Dusting the ribs with cornstarch before frying keeps them crisp on the outside without burning, and also helps thicken the braising sauce a bit. **SERVES 4 TO 6**

1 large rack lean, meaty pork ribs (about 3 pounds),
    cut into 1-inch pieces
¾ cup good-quality soy sauce, such as Kikkoman
¼ cup balsamic vinegar
2 tablespoons Asian sesame oil

2 tablespoons sugar

4¼ cups canola or other vegetable oil

½ cup cornstarch

2 bunches scallions, white and green parts, trimmed
and thinly sliced

1 piece (4 inches) fresh ginger, peeled and thinly sliced

1 medium head garlic, cloves peeled and
coarsely chopped

8 cups Chicken Stock (page 39) or canned low-sodium
chicken broth

¾ cup fermented Chinese black beans

¼ cup dry sherry

½ teaspoon hot red pepper flakes

Red wine vinegar, to taste

1. Place the rib pieces in a large bowl. Combine ¼ cup of the soy sauce with the balsamic vinegar, sesame oil, and sugar in a small bowl and whisk well to blend. Pour over the rib pieces and mix well, using your hands, until all the pieces are coated with some of the marinade. Refrigerate, covered, for at least 8 hours and up to 12.

2. When you're ready to cook the ribs, heat 4 cups of the canola oil in a deep-fryer or deep, heavy skillet until a deep-fry thermometer registers 375°F.

3. Sprinkle the cornstarch over the ribs and toss to coat. Working in batches, add the rib pieces to the hot oil and fry until well browned, 5 to 10 minutes. Remove the pieces to paper towels to drain.

4. Heat the remaining ¼ cup oil in a medium-size, heavy saucepan over medium-high heat. Add the scallions, ginger, and garlic and sauté, stirring frequently, until wilted and aromatic but not browned, 1 to 2 minutes. Add the chicken stock, black beans, remaining ½ cup soy sauce, the sherry, and pepper flakes and bring to a boil over high heat. Add the fried rib pieces and return to a boil, then reduce the heat to low and simmer, uncovered, until the meat is tender but not falling off the bone, about 45 minutes. Stir occasionally as the ribs cook, adding a little water if needed.

5. Remove the pan from the heat and add a splash or two of red wine vinegar. Transfer to a deep platter and serve immediately.

Pork Saté with Spicy Peanut Sauce

In Indonesia saté (or satay) is a traditional **snack food** of skewered tidbits grilled over hot coals and dipped in a spicy peanut sauce. Street vendors selling saté are as ubiquitous in the bazaars of Indonesia, Malaysia, and Thailand as pretzel or hot dog vendors are on the streets of New York City. In my version bite-size pieces of pork are marinated overnight in a multicultural mixture, but morsels of chicken, beef sirloin, duck, or seafood may be substituted. This is delicious as an hors d'oeuvre, but I like to pile the skewers on a platter, set out a bowl of the sauce, and serve saté as a main course along with Cucumber Salad with Red Onion and Chinese Sausage (page 314) and Thai Rice Noodles (page 284). Cold bottles of Thai Singha beer would be the perfect beverage with this meal. **SERVES 2 TO 4**

1 large onion, cut into chunks
2 cloves garlic, peeled
1 can (13 or 14 ounces) coconut milk, preferably a Thai brand
4 stalks lemongrass, trimmed and thinly sliced
3 tablespoons Thai fish sauce (nam pla)
2 tablespoons fresh lime juice
2 tablespoons sugar
1 teaspoon ground turmeric
1 teaspoon Madras-style curry powder, preferably Sun brand
1 pork tenderloin (about 1 pound), trimmed of fat
Spicy Peanut Sauce (recipe follows)

1. Combine the onion and garlic in a food processor and process to a coarse purée. Transfer to a bowl and stir in the coconut milk, lemongrass, fish sauce, lime juice, sugar, turmeric, and curry powder. Set aside.

2. Cut the pork tenderloin crosswise into 3-inch-thick pieces, then cut each piece lengthwise into ½-inch slices. Place the slices in a shallow dish and pour the marinade over them. Toss the pieces to coat thoroughly, then refrigerate, covered, for at least 8 hours and up to 12.

3. Place bamboo skewers at least 12 inches long in a baking dish long enough to hold them and cover with water. Let them soak for 2 hours.

4. Preheat a barbecue grill or preheat the broiler.

5. While the grill is preheating, drain the skewers and remove the pork from the marinade. Using one piece per skewer, thread the pork onto the skewers lengthwise like a piece of ribbon. Place the skewers on the grill rack over the hot coals or on a broiler rack in the broiler and grill or broil until nicely browned on all sides and a bit charred in places, 2 to 3 minutes per side.

6. Using tongs, transfer the skewers to a serving platter and serve immediately, accompanied by a bowl of spicy peanut sauce for dipping.

Spicy Peanut Sauce

After you've made this sauce once, you'll probably want to adjust it to **suit your taste.** This version is fairly sweet, but you can use less sugar or add some chili sauce to make it hotter. I sometimes add ¼ cup strained tamarind pulp (see box, page 372) along with the other ingredients, or sprinkle the finished sauce with chopped fresh cilantro leaves before serving it. The sauce has a tendency to thicken as it cools, but it can easily be thinned by whisking in a little water or coconut milk. It should be served at room temperature, which is when the sauce's texture is at its best. Any leftover sauce will keep well in the refrigerator in a tightly covered container for up to 2 weeks. **MAKES ABOUT 2½ CUPS**

1¼ cups chunky peanut butter

¼ cup sugar

1 can (13 or 14 ounces) coconut milk, preferably a Thai brand

2 tablespoons fresh lime juice

¾ teaspoon Madras-style curry powder,
     preferably Sun brand

½ teaspoon Thai red curry paste (optional)

¼ teaspoon minced garlic

2 tablespoons good-quality soy sauce, such as Kikkoman

2 tablespoons Thai fish sauce (nam pla)

Place all the ingredients in a large bowl and beat with the whisk attachment of an electric mixer until thoroughly blended and smooth (see Note). Taste and adjust the seasoning before serving.

Note: If you don't have a mixer, combine all the ingredients except the peanut butter in a small, nonreactive saucepan and bring just to a boil, then remove from the heat and whisk in the peanut butter. Cool to room temperature before serving.

Wiener Schnitzel

The beauty of Wiener schnitzel is its **understated**, almost chaste **character**. Unembellished and unencumbered by superfluous ingredients or garnishes, it allows the cook to concentrate exclusively on creating the crisp, grease-free crust that envelops the tender, pounded meat. Simplicity is schnitzel's charm. Once on the table, all it needs is a squirt of lemon juice to achieve perfection.

In the United States it's a common misconception that Wiener schnitzel is made only with veal. In reality it can be made with either pork or veal, and Austrian and German menus always specify which is being offered. **SERVES 4 TO 6**

2 pork tenderloins (about 1 pound each)

1 clove garlic, peeled and cut in half

Coarse (kosher) salt and freshly ground black pepper, to taste

3 large eggs

1 cup all-purpose flour

1½ cups milk

2 cups fine dry bread crumbs (see box, page 279)

1 pound (4 sticks) unsalted butter, clarified (see box, page 391;
  also see Note)

2 lemons, cut into wedges and seeded, for garnish

1. Trim the pork tenderloins of all fat and sinew, then cut them crosswise into slices 1½ inches thick. Place each slice between two sheets of waxed paper and pound thin with a meat pounder or rolling pin. Rub each piece of pork on both sides with the cut side of the garlic and sprinkle with salt and pepper.

2. Beat the eggs in a bowl. Place the flour in a shallow bowl and the bread crumbs in a second shallow bowl. Line the bowls up: first flour, then eggs, then bread crumbs. One by one, dip each piece of pork in the flour, shaking off any excess, then in the egg, then in the bread crumbs to coat on both sides, shaking gently to remove excess crumbs. Place the pork as it is breaded on a platter, without stacking or allowing the pieces to touch.

3. Preheat the oven to its lowest setting.

4. Heat 3 tablespoons of the butter in a large skillet over medium heat. The butter should be hot enough for the pork to sizzle on contact but not so hot that the butter browns. Add enough of the pork pieces to fit without crowding and sauté on both sides until a beautiful golden brown, about 3 minutes per side. Using a slotted spatula, remove the pork to a platter and keep it warm in the oven while you sauté the remaining pieces. Add more butter to the pan as necessary.

5. Arrange the Wiener schnitzel on a flat platter, without stacking, and garnish with lemon wedges. Serve immediately.

Note: Chances are you'll have some clarified butter left over. Store this extra, covered, in the refrigerator, where it will keep for 1 week. Use it to sauté thin veal and chicken scallops or tender vegetables like summer squash (sliced), or to fry up leftover potatoes into Sunday hash browns.

Chinese Eggplant with Black Beans and Pork

Although there are far more varieties of eggplant available to us now than there were in the past, only the long, slim, delicately flavored Asian ones will do for this recipe (see box, facing page). Don't be tempted to substitute the larger, more commonplace American eggplants here; they will be too bitter and watery to work well. I've made this with both ground chicken and ground turkey, but pork is the perfect choice, due to its nearly magical capacity to absorb the strong seasonings of the sauce.

For a satisfying supper, serve this with Broccoli with Oyster Sauce (page 307) and plain steamed rice. To create a multicourse feast, add such other dishes as Hot and Sour Soup (page 6), Sesame-Crusted Fish Fillets with Garlic-Ginger Sauce (page 230), and Cucumber Salad with Red Onion and Chinese Sausage (page 314).

SERVES 6

5 Chinese or Japanese eggplants (about 6 ounces each)

¼ to ½ cup canola or other vegetable oil, or more as needed

1 tablespoon grated fresh ginger

4 cloves garlic, either thinly sliced or coarsely chopped

2 tablespoons Chinese fermented black beans

8 ounces ground pork

3 tablespoons oyster sauce

2 tablespoons good-quality soy sauce, such as Kikkoman

1 tablespoon red wine vinegar or sherry vinegar

1 tablespoon sugar

Dash of Asian sesame oil

1 bunch garlic chives or scallions, white and green
    parts, trimmed and cut into ½-inch lengths

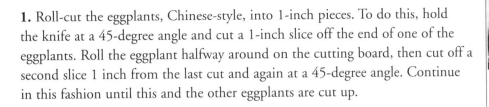

1. Roll-cut the eggplants, Chinese-style, into 1-inch pieces. To do this, hold the knife at a 45-degree angle and cut a 1-inch slice off the end of one of the eggplants. Roll the eggplant halfway around on the cutting board, then cut off a second slice 1 inch from the last cut and again at a 45-degree angle. Continue in this fashion until this and the other eggplants are cut up.

2. Heat ¼ cup of the oil in a large wok or skillet over high heat. Add half the eggplant, then reduce the heat to medium high and stir-fry until the eggplant is lightly browned and tender but not mushy, 8 to 10 minutes. Remove the cooked eggplant to a colander and repeat the process with the remaining eggplant, adding more oil if necessary.

3. When all the eggplant is cooked, there should still be some oil in the wok; if not, add a bit more, only enough for a light coating. Add the ginger and garlic and stir-fry over medium-high heat until aromatic but not browned, only a few seconds. Add the black beans, stir rapidly, and then add the pork. Cook and stir the mixture, using a wooden spoon to break up the pork, until the pork is about two thirds of the way to being fully cooked (still a little pink), 2 to 3 minutes.

4. Add the oyster sauce, soy sauce, vinegar, sugar, and sesame oil and simmer for 1 minute, stirring. Return the eggplant to the wok, tossing to reheat it and coat with the sauce. Add the garlic chives or scallions, toss again to mix, and serve immediately.

chinese and japanese eggplant

Small, thin-skinned Chinese and Japanese eggplants have fewer seeds and are sweeter than the more common and larger dark purple American eggplant. Neither type requires salting to draw out bitterness, as the American does. The lavender-colored Chinese eggplant is long, slender, and sometimes slightly curved. The deep purple Japanese eggplant, which is slightly shorter and narrower, is occasionally a bit less sweet than the Chinese kind. When shopping, look for Asian eggplants that are firm and heavy for their size, with smooth, glossy, unblemished skin.

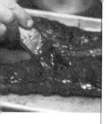

Gaby's Hungarian-Style Stuffed Cabbage

Karen's mother, Gaby, whose family came from Hungary, loves this dish. I use major amounts of both sweet and hot Hungarian paprika in the sauce, as well as in the ground pork filling, to create a big, bold flavor that is less sweet and more piquant than most versions. Although you could certainly use any type of cabbage, I prefer sweetly flavorful Savoy cabbage. Bagged sauerkraut, stocked in supermarket refrigerator cases, is the sauerkraut of choice—unless, of course, you can find old-fashioned fresh sauerkraut sold from a barrel.

The sauce can be made a day ahead and refrigerated, if you like, and leftover cabbage rolls can easily be frozen for another meal.

MAKES ABOUT 24 ROLLS; SERVES 12

FOR THE SAUCE:

3 tablespoons canola or other vegetable oil

4 medium onions, sliced

2 large cloves garlic, chopped

8 cups Chicken Stock (page 39) or canned
    low-sodium chicken broth

1/3 cup sweet Hungarian paprika

2 tablespoons hot Hungarian paprika

4 bay leaves

4 bags (16 ounces each) sauerkraut (do not use canned)

FOR THE CABBAGE ROLLS:

3 medium heads cabbage (about 4 pounds), withered or
    discolored outer leaves removed

3 medium onions, cut into large chunks

5 pounds lean ground pork

8 ounces good-quality smoked bacon, rind removed and
   discarded, finely diced

2 cups cooked long-grain rice

2 large cloves garlic, minced

¼ cup sweet Hungarian paprika

2 tablespoons hot Hungarian paprika

2 tablespoons coarse (kosher) salt

Sour cream, for serving (optional)

1. First, make the sauce: Heat the oil in a large stockpot over medium heat. Add the onions and garlic and sauté, stirring occasionally, until lightly browned, about 10 minutes. Add the chicken stock, both paprikas, and the bay leaves and bring to a boil over high heat. Reduce the heat to low to maintain a steady simmer and cook, uncovered, to develop the flavors, 10 minutes. Add the sauerkraut along with its juices and simmer for another 30 minutes. Remove from the heat and set aside while you prepare the cabbage rolls.

2. Bring a large saucepan of salted water to a boil over high heat. While it comes to a boil, cut around the core at the stem end of each cabbage without removing the core; this will facilitate removal of the leaves. Plunge 1 head of cabbage at a time into the boiling water and, using tongs, peel off the leaves from each head as they soften, avoiding the smaller core leaves; you will need 24 good-size leaves. As you remove the leaves from the water, place them in a colander to drain. When they're cool enough to handle, pat dry with paper towels and set aside while you prepare the stuffing.

3. Place the onions in a food processor and process to a purée. Transfer to a large bowl and add the pork, bacon, rice, garlic, both paprikas, and salt. Using your hands or a wooden spoon, mix well.

4. Preheat the oven to 375°F.

5. Spread a cabbage leaf, inner-side up, on your work surface, stem end toward you, first trimming away the spine of the leaf if it's very thick. Place a small handful of stuffing (about ½ cup) at the stem end of the leaf, fold the sides over the filling, and roll the leaf up. Adjust the amount of stuffing for the size of the

leaf you're working on so each roll is firmly wrapped and won't come undone. Place each roll as it is finished in a large roasting pan or casserole, setting it seam-side down and making even rows as you go; you may have to make two layers.

6. Remove the bay leaves from the sauce and discard, then ladle the sauce over the cabbage rolls. Cover the pan lightly with aluminum foil and bake until good and hot and bubbling, about 1 hour.

7. Serve the cabbage rolls directly from the casserole or arrange them on a large platter. If you're serving on the platter, spoon some of the sauce over the rolls and serve the remainder on the side. If desired, pass a bowl of sour cream.

Bell Peppers Stuffed with Rice and Sausage

Every cook needs at least a couple of recipes in his or her repertoire for transforming mundane leftover rice into **something interesting** for dinner. I rely on Highly Adaptable Shrimp Fried Rice (page 294) or this recipe, which is colorful, cheerful, and good to eat. For the best flavor, buy sweet Italian sausages made with fennel seeds.

In the summer fresh marjoram, which is spicy and a bit sweet, is a good alternative to fresh oregano. But if you can't find it fresh, don't substitute dried marjoram, which tends to taste dry and boring. If you serve the peppers with a green salad and some sautéed zucchini or green beans on the side, you'll have enough to feed four. Otherwise, serve two peppers per person.

SERVES 2 TO 4

1 tablespoon olive oil

3 sweet Italian sausages (about 1 pound total), casings
    removed

2 cloves garlic, minced

1 small onion, diced

1 carrot, peeled and grated

2 cups cooked rice

1 teaspoon chopped fresh oregano leaves or ¼ teaspoon dried
    oregano leaves

1 teaspoon chopped fresh flat-leaf parsley leaves

Coarse (kosher) salt and freshly ground black pepper, to taste

4 medium red bell peppers

1 cup dry white wine

1. Preheat the oven to 350°F.

2. Heat the olive oil in a skillet over medium heat. Add the sausage meat and sauté until browned, about 10 minutes, stirring and breaking up the pieces with a wooden spoon as it cooks.

3. Add the garlic and onion and cook, stirring often, until the onion is translucent, about 5 minutes. Add the carrot and cook another minute. Stir in the rice, oregano, parsley, salt, and pepper. Stir well to mix. Remove the skillet from the heat.

4. Slice off the tops of the peppers and discard. Use a paring knife to remove the white pith and seeds from each pepper.

5. Fill each pepper with the rice stuffing, packing it in well and mounding it over the top as much as possible. Place the stuffed peppers in a baking dish just large enough to hold them. Pour the wine into the bottom of the dish, and cover the whole dish with aluminum foil.

6. Bake until the peppers have softened and are cooked through, but not so much that they collapse, 40 to 45 minutes. Check the peppers as they cook in case you need to add a bit of water to the baking dish.

7. Carefully remove the peppers to plates or shallow bowls and serve immediately.

Alsatian Choucroute Garni

This **French classic** from Alsace is copious and satisfying, a dish to fortify body and soul on a cold, wintry day. The mellow sauerkraut provides a delicious base for an appetizing array of smoked and fresh meats, each adding another dimension to the final flavor. Some cooks rinse fresh or bagged sauerkraut before using it, but I don't bother with this since I like the way its powerful brininess complements the meats. A platter of *choucroute* is a very handy way to use up the leftover pieces of meat or poultry that have been biding their time in your refrigerator or freezer— that solitary ham end, lonely sausage, or stray chicken or duck leg. Variety is the essence of this dish. Serve with small boiled potatoes and a little pot of coarse French mustard. **SERVES 6 TO 8**

3 smoked ham hocks (about 8 ounces each)

6 cups Chicken Stock (page 39) or canned low-sodium chicken broth

3 strips thickly sliced good-quality smoked bacon, rind removed and discarded, cut into 1-inch pieces

2 medium onions, sliced

2 large cloves garlic, minced

⅓ cup gin

2 cups slightly sweet white wine, such as Riesling

1 bouquet garni (1 tablespoon each juniper berries and black peppercorns and 3 bay leaves, tied up in a piece of cheesecloth)

2 Granny Smith apples, peeled and grated

3 bags (16 ounces each) sauerkraut (do not use canned)

1 pound smoked sausage

2 pounds smoked ham, trimmed of fat and cut into 8 pieces

Coarse (kosher) salt, to taste

1. Place the ham hocks and chicken stock in a medium-size saucepan and bring to a boil over high heat. Reduce the heat to low and simmer, covered, until the hocks are tender, about 2 hours. Remove the hocks from the stock, reserving both.

2. Place the bacon in a large, nonreactive Dutch oven or other flameproof casserole and sauté over medium heat until rendered of fat and somewhat crisp, about 10 minutes. Add the onions and garlic and cook, covered, until the onions are translucent but not browned, about 5 minutes, uncovering occasionally to stir.

3. Add the reserved liquid from the ham hocks, the gin, wine, bouquet garni, apples, and sauerkraut. Bring to a boil over high heat, then reduce the heat to low and simmer, partly covered, until the flavors have blended and the sauerkraut is very tender, about 1 hour.

4. Preheat the oven to 400°F.

5. Nestle the sausage, ham, and ham hocks in the sauerkraut and bake, covered, until everything is bubbling nicely, about 45 minutes. Remove the bouquet garni, season with salt, and serve from the casserole.

buying sauerkraut

Sauerkraut ("sour cabbage" in German) is simply salted shredded cabbage that has been allowed to ferment in its own juices. It can be eaten cooked or uncooked. Prior to cooking, it has a power-fully sour mouth-puckering flavor and is tremendously salty; after cooking, it becomes pleasantly mellow. Sauerkraut is sold three ways. When I have access to it, I prefer the fresh, but it can be difficult to find. Look for it at old-fashioned delis (sometimes sold from a barrel) and Eastern European meat or specialty food shops. The next best kind, which works just fine in the recipes here, is packaged in plastic bags and can be found in supermarket or deli refrigerator cases. The canned or jarred sauerkraut at supermarkets should be avoided.

Chinese-Style Meatballs for a Crowd

These **oversize** meatballs are perfumed with fresh ginger, garlic, and Asian seasonings, pan-fried until crispy on the outside, nestled between layers of bok choy, and topped with a rich, savory sauce. They make a great party dish for an informal gathering. The recipe is a variation on a classic casserolelike Chinese dish called Lion's Head, in which the meatballs represent lions' heads and the layers of bok choy their shaggy manes.

MAKES 20 MEATBALLS; SERVES 10

TO BEGIN:

12 dried shiitake mushrooms
3 ounces dried wood ear mushrooms
3 cups chopped Savoy or napa cabbage
2 tablespoons coarse (kosher) salt

FOR THE SAUCE:

3 tablespoons vegetable oil, preferably peanut
4 large cloves garlic, minced
1 tablespoon grated fresh ginger
2½ quarts Chicken Stock (page 39) or canned low-sodium chicken broth
⅓ cup rice vinegar
⅓ cup oyster sauce
¼ cup hot bean paste
3 tablespoons good-quality soy sauce, such as Kikkoman
2 tablespoons sugar
12 dried shiitake mushrooms, reconstituted (from above, see step 1)
¼ cup cornstarch
½ cup cold water

3 pounds ground pork

3 cups chopped Savoy or napa cabbage (from To Begin),
  soaked (see step 1)

3 large cloves garlic, minced

1 piece (2 inches) fresh ginger, peeled and grated
  (1½ to 2 tablespoons)

3 ounces dried wood ear mushrooms (from To
  Begin), reconstituted (see step 1)

2 bunches scallions, white and green parts, trimmed and
  thinly sliced

⅓ cup good-quality soy sauce, such as Kikkoman

2 large egg whites

1 tablespoon Asian sesame oil

1 tablespoon coarse (kosher) salt

2 teaspoons sugar

½ teaspoon freshly ground black pepper

Canola or other vegetable oil, for frying

1 cup cornstarch, for coating the meatballs, or more
  as needed

4 large heads bok choy, leaves only

1. Place the shiitake and wood ear mushrooms in separate medium-size bowls with very warm water to cover. Let soak for 30 minutes to soften. Combine the cabbage and salt in a colander and let stand for 30 minutes in the sink to draw out some of the moisture from the cabbage.

2. Lift the mushrooms from the soaking liquid, leaving the grit behind. Trim away any stems from the shiitakes and slice the caps. Set aside. Trim away any hard parts from the wood ears, chop them, and set aside. Discard the wood ear soaking liquid and strain the shiitake soaking liquid through a strainer lined with several layers of cheesecloth. Add it to the sauce with the chicken stock in step 4 or cover, refrigerate, and save for use at another time. Rinse the cabbage, then drain, squeeze dry, and set aside.

3. Prepare the sauce: Heat the oil in a medium-size saucepan over medium-low heat. Add the garlic and ginger and cook, stirring occasionally, until softened but not browned, about 5 minutes.

4. Add the chicken stock, vinegar, oyster sauce, hot bean paste, soy sauce, sugar, and shiitake mushrooms. Increase the heat to high and bring to a boil, then reduce the heat to low and simmer the sauce, uncovered, until it's somewhat reduced and its flavors are developed, about 30 minutes.

5. Whisk the cornstarch with the water to blend. When smooth, whisk it into the simmering sauce. Continue to simmer, stirring, until the sauce thickens, about 1 minute more. Remove the saucepan from the heat and taste and adjust the seasoning. Set aside, covered, while you prepare the meatballs.

6. Place the pork in a large bowl. Add the salted cabbage, garlic, ginger, wood ears, about two thirds of the sliced scallions, the soy sauce, egg whites, sesame oil, salt, sugar, and pepper. Using your hands, mix well, then divide the mixture into twenty equal portions. Form each portion into a round ball slightly larger than a golf ball.

7. Preheat the oven to 400°F.

8. Pour canola oil into a large, deep skillet to a depth of ½ inch and heat over medium-high heat until a pinch of cornstarch sizzles on contact. While the oil heats, spread about 1 cup cornstarch on a plate and coat 6 or 7 meatballs in the cornstarch to coat completely, shaking off any excess. Add the coated meatballs to the hot oil in the skillet, being careful not to crowd them. Reduce the heat to medium and fry the meatballs, turning with tongs, until browned on all sides, about 8 minutes. Remove the meatballs to paper towels to drain while you coat and fry the remaining meatballs, working in two batches and remembering to turn up the heat to medium high before adding the next batch.

9. Wipe out the skillet and add 1 tablespoon canola oil. Heat over medium heat, then add a handful of the bok choy leaves. Sauté to wilt, 45 to 60 seconds, then remove to a bowl. Continue sautéing the remainder of the bok choy, working in batches and adding more oil as needed.

10. Spread half the bok choy leaves in a large, shallow, ovenproof casserole or baking pan. Add the meatballs in one layer, then top with the remaining bok choy. Sprinkle with the remaining sliced scallions. Pour the reserved sauce evenly over the top and bake until heated through and bubbling, about 20 minutes.

11. Serve immediately from the casserole.

Sausage and Peppers

You won't find many dishes as quick and satisfying to make as this **unfussy combination** of Italian sausages sautéed with lots of peppers, a few carefully chosen seasonings, and a little wine. If you're lucky, there'll be leftovers for sandwiches the next day. I like to use a combination of sweet and hot Italian sausages, and sometimes I substitute a yellow pepper for one of the green or red ones for additional color. The wine and tomato purée combine with the juices from the peppers and onions to create a thin yet lively-tasting gravy. **SERVES 4 TO 6**

2 tablespoons olive oil

2 pounds sweet or hot Italian sausages

2 green bell peppers, stemmed, halved, seeded, and
    cut into thin crosswise slices

2 red bell peppers, stemmed, halved, seeded, and
    cut into thin crosswise slices

1 large onion, sliced lengthwise

2 large cloves garlic, minced

½ cup dry white wine

2 bay leaves

1 teaspoon dried oregano leaves

2 tablespoons tomato purée

Coarse (kosher) salt and freshly ground black pepper,
    to taste

1. Heat the oil in a large, heavy skillet over medium-high heat. Prick each sausage in several places with the tines of a fork, then add to the hot oil and sauté until well browned on all sides, 6 to 8 minutes. Using tongs, transfer the sausages to a plate and set aside. Pour off most of the oil leaving a layer about ⅛ inch deep.

2. Add the bell peppers, onion, and garlic to the drippings in the skillet and sauté, stirring occasionally, until the onion is translucent and the vegetables are starting to brown, 5 to 10 minutes. Return the sausages to the skillet along with any juices that have accumulated on the plate. Add the wine, bay leaves, oregano, tomato purée, salt, and pepper and stir to mix. Reduce the heat to medium and cook, uncovered, stirring occasionally, until the sausages are cooked through, the sauce has thickened, and the flavors have blended, about 15 minutes.

3. Remove the skillet from the heat and discard the bay leaves. Taste and adjust the seasoning, then serve directly from the skillet, or arrange the sausages on a platter and top with the peppers and sauce.

Rustic Homemade Garlic Sausage

Once you get the hang of it, sausage making is very satisfying. It's a lot easier than you might imagine, and the results are unquestionably worth the effort. Correct equipment is essential to success—a hand-operated metal meat grinder that clamps onto the countertop makes all the difference in the world to the texture. One that comes with a sausage-stuffer attachment makes stuffing the mixture into casings much easier. Filling the casings by hand with a large pastry bag fitted with a plain ½-inch tip is certainly doable if you don't have a stuffer attachment. However, if stuffing casings seems daunting, you'll be relieved to know that any fresh sausage mixture can simply be formed into patties.

This recipe yields an ample supply of garlicky, slightly smoky sausages to eat by themselves or use in recipes. (Slab bacon gives an appetizing smokiness without the bother of having to smoke the sausages.) Devour what you can within a day or two, then freeze the remainder of the sausages (or patties) for up to 3 months. Try homemade sausages in the Pot-au-Feu (page 63), Alsatian Choucroute Garni (page 126), Black Bean Stew with Pig Parts (page 108), or Black Bean Soup (page 22). **MAKES ABOUT 10 FEET OF SAUSAGE, OR APPROXIMATELY TWENTY 6-INCH SAUSAGES**

4 pounds lean boneless pork shoulder, cut into ¾-inch cubes
  that will fit through your meat grinder
12 ounces pork fatback, cut into ¾-inch cubes that
  will fit through your meat grinder
1 pound slab bacon, rind removed, cut into ¾-inch
  cubes that will fit through your meat grinder
4 large cloves garlic, chopped
1 tablespoon chopped shallots
1 teaspoon coarsely ground black pepper
½ cup dry white wine
2 large eggs
2 teaspoons coarse (kosher) salt
1 teaspoon sugar
½ teaspoon freshly grated nutmeg
½ teaspoon ground allspice
5 lengths of sausage casing (each 2½ feet long),
  prepared for stuffing (see box, page 135)

1. Combine the shoulder, fatback, bacon, garlic, shallots, pepper, and wine in a large bowl and toss thoroughly to mix. Refrigerate, covered, for at least 8 hours and up to 12.

2. Put the mixture through a meat grinder (see box, page 135) into a large bowl. Add the eggs, salt, sugar, nutmeg, and allspice and mix thoroughly, using your hands or a wooden spoon. To check the seasoning level, remove just enough of the mixture to make a small patty, then sauté the patty in a skillet in a small amount of vegetable oil until cooked through. Taste for seasoning, then adjust the seasoning in the rest of the mixture. Refrigerate the mixture, covered, until thoroughly chilled, about 2 hours.

3. Tie one end of each length of the prepared sausage casings in a tight knot as close to the end as possible. Fit the open end onto the sausage stuffer and place

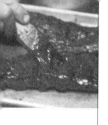

the stuffing mixture in the hopper. If you have no stuffer, fit a pastry bag (as large as you can handle) with a plain ½-inch tip. Fill it two thirds to three quarters full with the chilled sausage mixture. Carefully gather a length of sausage casing onto the tip of the pastry bag, starting from the untied end and gathering it all the way to the tied end.

4. To fill the casing, squeeze the pastry bag or operate your stuffer with one hand while using the other to guide the casing as it's being stuffed, taking care that the filled casing doesn't go shooting off the end of the bag or attachment. Fill the casing well and evenly, but don't overstuff it; if the casings are too full, they'll burst when the sausages are poached, and you'll also need some room to tie the filled casings into individual sausages. Stop filling when you're about 2 inches from the end. If you have enough room, tie a knot in the casing to close the end; if not, tie the end tightly closed with a 3-inch length of butcher's twine. Repeat the stuffing and tying procedure with the remaining casings, refilling the sausage stuffer or pastry bag with the sausage mixture as needed.

5. After all the casings are stuffed, you can divide them into individual sausages (each length should make four sausages, about 6 inches long) by tying them at the appropriate intervals with two 3-inch pieces of butcher's twine. Cut carefully between each set of ties to separate the sausages.

6. If you'll be using the sausages right away, you'll need to poach them (if you decide to freeze the sausages for later use, poach them after you thaw them). Use a wooden skewer or table fork to poke some holes in each sausage. Place the sausages in a large stockpot and cover with cold water. Place the pot over medium-high heat and bring the water to a gentle simmer, reducing the heat to maintain the simmer. Poach the sausages, uncovered, until just cooked through and firm, about 5 minutes. This precooking will release some of the fat. Remove the sausages from the water with tongs and let them cool. They are now ready to use in a recipe of your choice.

making sausages

The key to well-made sausage is the texture of the filling, which is dependent on the equipment you use to grind it. The filling should be coarsely ground into small, yet distinct bits; too fine a grind simply turns the meat and other ingredients to mush. I use an old-fashioned hand-cranked meat grinder fitted with the medium blade, grinding two thirds of the mixture coarsely, then switching blades to finely grind the last third. Slightly less good results can be obtained using an electric mixer such as a KitchenAid with the special meat-grinder attachment. A food processor fitted with a metal chopping blade should be used only if you are absolutely desperate, since it's virtually guaranteed to overgrind the filling. To follow this method, cut the meat, fatback, and bacon by hand into 1-inch pieces, then process about 2 cups at a time, pulsing at 1-second intervals.

preparing sausage casings

Natural sausage casings are simply sheep, hog, or cow intestines that have been cleaned and salted. (Synthetic casings are also available, but I don't recommend them.) I generally use medium-size 1¼-inch-diameter hog casings; these are easy to work with since they're tender but not too fragile. Casings are sold by the pound in long lengths and can be purchased from your local butcher.

With a sharp knife, cut the casing into the desired lengths (five 2½-foot lengths for Rustic Homemade Garlic Sausage, page 132) and place them in a bowl. (Wrap and freeze the rest for future use.) Cover with cold water and soak for 1 to 2 hours to remove the salt they were packed in. Drain the casings. Working with one length at a time, carefully slip one end of the casing over the end of the kitchen faucet. Slowly turn on the tap and let cold water run through for 1 minute to flush out any salt that's still inside. Hold on to the casing so it doesn't shoot off and slip down the drain! Remove from the faucet and repeat with the remaining casings. The casings don't need to be dried before they are used.

Montana Fried "Pork Chop" Sandwiches

Melicia brought the idea for these **hefty sandwiches** back from a trip to Montana, and they quickly became a staff favorite. Although this is what they're called locally, the name is a bit misleading—the sandwiches are actually made with pork cutlets, not chops, so there are no bones involved. In the supermarket pork cutlets cut from the shoulder, tenderloin, leg, or loin are often labeled "scallops" or "medallions."

Don't be tempted to make these sandwiches fancier than they're meant to be. For example, it's essential to the correct flavor that you use ordinary store-bought hamburger buns and *shredded* iceberg lettuce—nothing else will do. This version is considered "loaded," which means it's served with all the garnishes. **SERVES 4**

8 pork cutlets (about 2 ounces each)

Milk

4 hamburger buns

4 tablespoons good-quality commercial mayonnaise,
    such as Hellmann's

4 teaspoons Dijon mustard

8 pickle chips

1½ cups shredded iceberg lettuce

4 thin slices fresh, ripe tomato

4 thin slices onion

¼ cup canola or other vegetable oil

All-purpose flour, seasoned with coarse (kosher) salt
    and freshly ground black pepper, for coating

1. Place each cutlet between two sheets of waxed paper and pound with a meat pounder or rolling pin until very thin. Place the cutlets as they are pounded in a shallow dish with milk to cover while you assemble the remaining ingredients for the sandwiches.

2. Open the buns and toast them. Then lay them out on your work surface. Spread 1 tablespoon mayonnaise and 1 teaspoon mustard on the top half of each bun, then press 2 pickle slices gently into the spread on each top. Divide the lettuce among all the bun bottoms, topping each with a slice of tomato and onion.

3. Heat the oil in a large skillet over medium-high heat. While it heats, spread about ¾ cup flour on a plate and dip half the pork pieces, one by one, in the flour to coat completely, shaking off any excess. Place the cutlets in the hot oil, arranging them so they don't touch, and fry until crispy and golden, about 1 minute per side. Using a slotted spatula, transfer the cutlets to paper towels to drain while you coat and fry the remainder.

4. Place 2 fried pork cutlets on the bottom half of each bun, replace the tops, and serve immediately.

Aïoli BLTs

When a **food craving** strikes, there's no point in ignoring it—it must be satisfied. For us, quite often that means Aïoli BLTs for supper.

The success of a BLT depends, first of all, on the quality of the bacon; you want to use the best smoked bacon available to you. Although the lettuce needn't be fancy (romaine is nice, but iceberg is okay, too), the tomatoes must be ripe, and the bread firm textured but not too hard. Most important, the bread must be slathered with unctuous, garlicky Aïoli rather than mayonnaise from a jar. **SERVES 6**

1 pound good-quality, thickly sliced smoked bacon
12 slices good-quality white bread, toasted
½ cup Aïoli (page 363)
6 leaves romaine lettuce
6 large slices fresh, ripe tomato
Freshly ground black pepper

1. Preheat the oven to 350°F.

2. Cook the bacon as directed in the box on the facing page.

3. Lay out 6 of the bread slices and spread each with some of the aïoli, using about ¼ cup. Assemble the sandwiches by layering on the lettuce, tomato, and bacon, then sprinkle a healthy grinding of pepper over it all.

4. Spread the remaining aïoli on the remaining bread slices, then place 1 slice on each sandwich, aïoli-side down. Press down lightly and cut crosswise into halves to serve.

Corn Dogs

A hot dog on a mustard-slathered bun is **a great taste**, but a hot dog cloaked in buttermilk-cornmeal batter and quickly fried until it's golden and crispy is very great. Corn dogs on a stick are a traditional state- and country-fair food that dates back to the 1940s. My version eliminates the stick, and the batter contains just a pinch each of curry powder and cayenne to add interest. Kids and anyone at all young at heart will love these. Be sure to serve with plenty of mustard and ketchup. Corn dogs freeze well and can be reheated, without thawing, in a 350°F oven for 10 to 15 minutes. **MAKES 6 CORN DOGS**

¾ cup yellow cornmeal

¾ cup all-purpose flour

1 tablespoon sugar

1 teaspoon coarse (kosher) salt

1 teaspoon baking powder

¼ teaspoon baking soda

Pinch of cayenne pepper

Pinch of Madras-style curry powder, preferably Sun brand

1 large egg

1½ cups buttermilk

6 frankfurters

Canola or other vegetable oil, for frying

1. Combine the cornmeal, flour, sugar, salt, baking powder, baking soda, cayenne, and curry powder in a medium-size bowl and whisk well to mix.

2. Combine the egg and buttermilk in a second bowl and whisk thoroughly to blend. Pour this mixture into the dry ingredients and mix well.

3. Pour oil into a deep, heavy skillet to a depth of 2 inches and heat over medium heat until it registers 375°F on a deep-fry thermometer. Pat the frankfurters dry with paper towels, then dip, 2 or 3 at a time, in the batter to coat thickly, letting any excess drip back into the bowl. Place the coated frankfurters carefully in the hot oil and fry until golden brown all over, about 2 minutes per side. Transfer to paper towels to drain while you coat and fry the remaining frankfurters. Serve immediately.

the secret of perfect bacon

When restaurants use bacon, they generally need to cook a lot of it. Instead of frying it in a pan on top of the stove, professional cooks lay the bacon strips in a sheet pan (you could also use a rimmed baking sheet, such as a jelly-roll pan) and bake in a preheated 350°F oven until crisp, 15 to 20 minutes. Drain on paper towels before using. The bacon strips will curl up very little, if at all; they usually come out good and flat, which makes them easier to use.

Poultry

Poultry is the backbone of our staff meals for largely the same reasons it is in other families—it's inexpensive, always available, and highly adaptable. We enjoy exploring a wide range of ethnic cooking, and chicken's mild taste often serves as a blank canvas when we're experimenting and trying out a combination of unfamiliar seasonings. Many of the recipes in this chapter are equally delicious made with other types of domesticated poultry, such as turkey or duck, or with such game birds as pheasant, guinea hen, and partridge. Rabbit, too, can be substituted for chicken with great success in stewed or braised dishes. Although we don't often splurge on rabbit or game birds for our own meals, they're favorites on the Chanterelle menu.

Roast Chicken with Root Vegetables and Cider

This simple, comforting chicken dish will fill your home with the **autumnal aroma** of roasting sweet potatoes, parsnips, and apples. The sweet, earthy flavors of the cider and sturdy root vegetables complement one another perfectly, giving added character and depth of flavor to the bird. Serve with a simple green salad. **SERVES 4**

1 chicken (3½ pounds)
2 tablespoons unsalted butter
2 firm, tart apples, such as Granny Smith, cored,
     peeled, and cut into 1-inch dice
1 large sweet potato, peeled and cut into 1-inch dice
1 medium onion, cut into 1-inch dice
1 large parsnip, peeled and cut into 1-inch rounds
2 medium carrots, peeled and cut into 1-inch rounds
½ medium head cauliflower, cut into florets
Coarse (kosher) salt and freshly ground black pepper, to taste
2 cups apple cider

1. Preheat the oven to 400°F.

2. Rinse the chicken, inside and out, under cold running water, removing any excess fat. Pat dry with paper towels. Place the chicken in a flameproof roasting pan large enough to hold it and the vegetables without crowding. Smear the chicken skin with the butter, then surround it with the apples and vegetables, sprinkle everything with salt and pepper, and pour in the cider.

3. Place the roasting pan in the oven and roast the chicken and vegetables until the apples have practically melted away, the vegetables are browned and tender, and the chicken juices run clear when a thigh is pricked with a fork, 1¼ to 1½ hours. Stir the vegetables halfway through the roasting time so they brown evenly.

4. Carefully remove the chicken to a platter. Using a slotted spoon, remove the vegetables and place them around the chicken; cover to keep warm. Set the roasting pan over high heat and bring the cider and roasting juices to a boil over high heat, scraping up the browned bits on the bottom of the pan. Cook, uncovered, until the liquid is reduced by half, 5 to 10 minutes.

5. Remove the pan from the heat, taste for seasoning, and pour the sauce into a gravy boat. Serve the sauce to accompany the chicken. Carve the chicken in the kitchen or at the table.

how to render chicken fat

If you make roast chicken or chicken stock fairly often, it takes little extra effort to have a supply of rendered chicken fat (schmaltz) on hand for use in recipes such as chopped chicken liver and borscht. There's always surplus fat to be trimmed from whole chickens, especially from the neck, body cavity, and tail areas. I save the bits of fat in the freezer, adding to my cache until I have at least a cup or two. To render fat, defrost it slightly, cut into ½- or 1-inch pieces, and place them in a heavy skillet or saucepan over low heat. Add about ¼ cup water (to prevent the fat from sticking) and cook gently, stirring occasionally, until the fat has liquefied and the solids have shrunk and become crispy brown bits, about 10 to 15 minutes. Let the fat cool slightly before straining it through a fine-mesh strainer into a storage container with a tight-fitting cover. (In Yiddish the crunchy pieces left behind are called *gribenes,* and in the old days before cholesterol was declared the enemy they were considered quite a treat.) Store rendered fat in the refrigerator for a month or in the freezer for up to a year. To render duck or goose fat, follow the same procedure.

Chicken with Forty Cloves of Garlic

This chicken classic is a **tribute to** the transformational power of **heat**. Although raw garlic is pungent and aggressive, slow-roasted garlic is the complete opposite—it's gloriously sweet and mellow. When this dish comes out of the oven, each buttery-soft clove has become a subtle complement to the perfectly roasted chicken. **SERVES 6 TO 8**

2 chickens (3 to 3½ pounds each)
2 tablespoons rendered chicken fat or unsalted butter
Coarse (kosher) salt and freshly ground black pepper,
    to taste
6 heads garlic, blanched and peeled
    (see box, page 145)
2 cups dry white wine
2 cups Chicken Stock (page 39) or canned low-sodium
    chicken broth
1 teaspoon fresh lemon juice
3 tablespoons unsalted butter, cut into pieces

1. Preheat the oven to 450°F.

2. Rinse the chickens, inside and out, under cold running water, removing any excess fat. Pat dry with paper towels. If you wish, tuck the wing tips under the second joints and tie the legs together with butcher's twine.

3. Rub the chickens all over with the chicken fat or butter and sprinkle, inside and out, with salt and pepper. Place the birds in a flameproof roasting pan that can hold them with a little extra room to spare. Roast for 30 minutes, basting occasionally with pan drippings.

4. Add the garlic to the roasting pan, then reduce the oven temperature to 400°F and continue roasting for 15 to 20 minutes more, basting and stirring up the garlic cloves occasionally.

5. Add the wine to the roasting pan and continue roasting the chickens until they're just done (a thigh pricked with a fork will release clear juices), 15 to 20 minutes more. Transfer the chickens to a platter and keep warm, covered loosely with aluminum foil, while you prepare the sauce.

6. Put the roasting pan containing the garlic and cooking liquid on top of the stove, over two burners, if possible. Add the chicken stock and bring to a boil over high heat, scraping up the browned bits on the bottom of the pan. Cook until the liquid is reduced by about half, 10 minutes. Add the lemon juice and swirl in the butter until melted and incorporated. The sauce should thicken enough to coat the back of a spoon. Remove from the heat and season with salt and pepper.

7. To serve, cut the chickens into serving pieces and pour the sauce and garlic cloves over them.

how to peel forty cloves of garlic

It's not as time consuming as you think. To separate a head of garlic into cloves, place it root-end up on a flat surface and press forcefully down with the palm of your hand to loosen the cloves. Cut off the stringy roots, then separate the individual cloves from the head and blanch them in boiling water for 1 minute. Put the cloves in a colander and run cold water over them; the skins should slip off easily.

Roast Chicken Stuffed with Basil

This technique—creating a **boldly seasoned** butter that's "stuffed" or massaged under the skin of a whole chicken—results in a moist, succulent bird that's crisp skinned and flavorful. The melting butter bastes the chickens as they roast, while the herbs remain nestled under the skin, slowly releasing their fragrance into the meat. Any combination of herbs or seasonings that pleases you can be used, from fresh tarragon or tapenade to curry powder or roasted red peppers. The chickens taste great hot out of the oven but are even better carved and served at room temperature with a simple tomato salad. **SERVES 6 TO 8**

2 chickens (3 to 3½ pounds each)
3 large cloves garlic, peeled
2 cups fresh basil leaves, rinsed and patted dry
2 large shallots, peeled
1 cup (2 sticks) unsalted butter, at room temperature
2 teaspoons coarse (kosher) salt
¼ teaspoon freshly ground black pepper
Juice of ½ lemon

1. Rinse the chickens, inside and out, under cold running water, removing any excess fat. Pat dry with paper towels. Set aside.

2. Combine the garlic, basil, shallots, butter, salt, pepper, and lemon juice in a food processor or blender and process until smooth. Refrigerate until the mixture firms slightly, about 30 minutes.

3. Preheat the oven to 450°F.

4. Starting at the lower end of the breast on each chicken, slide your fingers under the skin and work to loosen it as much as possible over the breast and thighs, being careful not to tear it. Set 4 tablespoons of the butter mixture aside for rubbing on the outside of the chickens. Stuff the remainder under the skin of the chickens, spreading it as evenly as possible over the flesh and pressing down on the outside of the skin to distribute it further.

5. If you wish, tuck the wing tips on each chicken under their second joints and tie the legs together with butcher's twine. Rub the chickens with the reserved butter mixture and place in a roasting pan just large enough so the chickens fit without touching. Roast for 20 minutes, then reduce the oven temperature to 350°F and continue roasting, basting the chickens occasionally with pan drippings, until the juices run clear when one of the thighs is pierced by a fork, 30 to 40 minutes more.

6. Transfer the chickens to a platter and let them rest for a few minutes before carving and serving.

waste not, want not

Like any frugal home cook, a good professional cook uses almost everything, throwing out as little as possible. We transform stale bread into croutons and bread crumbs; leftover vegetables become soup ingredients; and chicken livers—well, at Chanterelle they're a delicious reason to make chopped chicken liver. Next time you roast a chicken, don't just unthinkingly toss out that little bag inside it that contains the liver, neck, gizzard, and heart. Open it up, sort the pieces, and freeze them. I keep a separate zipper-lock bag for livers in the freezer and another for those other parts that will come in handy when I make chicken stock. It's like money in the bank.

Chilled Red-Cooked Chicken

The same **dark and intriguing** broth used to make Chilled Red-Cooked Beef (page 65) will also transform a whole chicken into an unforgettable eating experience. As I roam around New York's Chinatown grocery shopping, I often see rows of these reddish brown chickens hanging in restaurant windows; they're called Soy Sauce Chicken on the restaurant menus. Make the broth from scratch or use the reserved master broth you tucked away in the freezer after making the beef version. Either way, be sure to take into account that the chicken needs to marinate for 24 hours; this is not a recipe to make on the spur of the moment. Also note that while dried shiitakes and dried orange peel usually require presoaking, this is unnecessary here due to the broth's long simmering time.

Serve this as part of an Asian-inspired buffet-style light supper that includes Soba Salad (page 337), Stir-Fried Rice Noodles with Bean Sprouts and Scallions (page 282); a platter of Ginger Pickled Vegetables (page 343), a bowl of Spicy Green Dipping Sauce (page 151), a pot of Dijon mustard, and a plate of fresh pineapple for dessert.

Since we're all hot-sauce fans at Chanterelle, there's nearly always an assortment of hot sauces set out on the staff-meal table when this is served. One of my favorites, Camel brand Chili Bean Sauce from China, is made with fermented black beans and adds just the right accent to red-cooked chicken or beef shin. It's also delicious with fried chicken. **SERVES 8 AS AN APPETIZER**

1 chicken (3 to 3½ pounds)
Broth for Red-Cooking (page 67)
Asian sesame oil, for brushing
Fresh cilantro leaves, for garnish

1. Rinse the chicken, inside and out, under cold running water, removing any excess fat. Pat dry with paper towels.

2. Place the unstrained broth in a very large stockpot and bring to a boil over high heat. Add the chicken and return the liquid to a boil. Reduce the heat to low and simmer, partially covered, for 30 minutes.

3. Remove the pot from the heat and let the chicken cool in the liquid, then refrigerate the chicken, still in the liquid, for 24 hours.

4. To serve, remove and discard the hardened layer of fat from on top of the cold broth, then remove the chicken from the broth, scraping off whatever spices and bits of jellied broth are clinging to it (see Note). Cut the chicken into 10 pieces (see box, page 159), but it's best if you can cut it even smaller (the breast in eighths, the thighs in quarters, the legs in half, and the wings in half as well) and arrange on a platter. Just before serving, brush the chicken lightly with sesame oil and garnish with cilantro.

Note: The broth will become richer and more flavorful over time, and can be used over and over again, supplemented with additional stock, water, or seasonings as needed. Transfer the broth to a container with a tight cover (don't strain it) and refrigerate for up to a week, bringing to a boil every couple of days, or freeze for up to 6 months.

happy food

In the Chinese technique known as red-cooking, ingredients are simmered in an intensely flavored dark brown, nearly black cooking liquid that contains quite a lot of soy sauce. Since the braising liquid and the finished dish are really more brown or black than red in color, you might well wonder why the technique isn't called brown-cooking. Unlike black or brown, which are considered unlucky colors in Chinese culture, red is a happy one symbolizing joy and celebration.

Chilled White-Cooked Chicken

I think boiled chicken is vastly **misunderstood**; most people dismiss it as bland and uninspiring. This version, however, is subtly flavorful and astoundingly juicy. In a variation on a classic Chinese cooking technique known as white-cut, a whole chicken is simmered in an understated water-based broth that's infused with sherry, scallions, and lots of sliced fresh ginger. Hot from the pot, the boiled chicken is plunged into an ice-water bath to cool off. This rapid cooling prompts the muscles of the meat to contract, ensuring that virtually all of the poultry's natural juices are retained. Cut into small pieces, the succulent bits of chicken are accompanied by a bowl of lively Spicy Green Dipping Sauce (page 151) seasoned with Asian sesame oil, fresh cilantro, and jalapeño pepper.

I like to serve this as part of an Asian-inspired buffet for a light supper along with Cucumber Salad with Red Onion and Chinese Sausage (page 314), Marinated Tomatoes with Balsamic Vinegar and Basil (see box, page 344) or Beets with Balsamic Vinegar (page 306), and Soba Salad (page 337). **SERVES 8 AS AN APPETIZER**

1 chicken (3 to 3½ pounds)

8 quarts water

1 cup dry sherry

1 pound fresh ginger (unpeeled), rinsed and cut into ¼-inch pieces

3 bunches scallions, white and green parts, trimmed and cut into 1-inch pieces

Fresh cilantro leaves, for garnish

Spicy Green Dipping Sauce (recipe follows)

1. Rinse the chicken, inside and out, under cold running water, removing any excess fat.

2. Combine the water, sherry, ginger, and scallions in a large stockpot. Bring to a boil over high heat and continue boiling for 10 minutes. Carefully add the chicken, return to a boil, reduce the heat to low, and simmer, covered, until the chicken is just tender, 45 minutes to 1 hour.

3. A few minutes before the chicken is done, set a very large bowl in the kitchen sink and fill it with water and plenty of ice. Carefully remove the chicken from the pot, letting the stock drip back into the pot. Immediately submerge the chicken in the ice-water bath to cool. Remove the chicken as soon as it's cool to the touch, after about 15 to 20 minutes; do not soak any longer than necessary. If you aren't sure it has cooled sufficiently, insert a metal skewer into the thickest part of the chicken—it should be cool to the touch when removed.

4. To serve, cut the chicken into at least 10 pieces (see box, page 159)—though it's best if you cut it even smaller (the breast in eighths, the thighs in quarters, the legs in half, and the wings in half as well)—and arrange on a platter. Garnish with the cilantro and serve accompanied by the dipping sauce.

Spicy Green Dipping Sauce

Set out little bowls of this **flavorful sauce** not only for white-cooked chicken but as a dip for carrot sticks, crisp jicama slices, and other favorite raw vegetables as well. **MAKES ABOUT ¾ CUP**

¼ cup tightly packed cilantro leaves and stems,
   finely chopped
1 tablespoon finely grated fresh ginger
1 large jalapeño pepper, seeded and chopped
   (about 1 tablespoon)
1 tablespoon Asian sesame oil
2 teaspoons coarse (kosher) salt
½ cup canola or peanut oil

1. Place the cilantro, ginger, jalapeño, sesame oil, and salt in a small heatproof bowl.

2. Place the canola oil in a small saucepan and heat over low heat until very hot but not smoking (a drop of water should sizzle when dropped into the oil). Carefully pour the heated oil into the bowl of cilantro mixture. Stir to combine and let cool to room temperature before serving.

Cornish Hens Provençal

The **flavors of Provence**—tomatoes, onions, garlic, and olives—were my inspiration for this robust dish, which can be quickly made with succulent little Cornish hens. To me, olives *are* Provence. I like to use Moroccan oil-cured olives in this sauce because they're wonderfully salty and meaty, but you could just as easily choose little brine-cured French Niçoise olives or Greek Kalamatas. Serve this with garlic-roasted potatoes and a dish of green beans or broccoli. **SERVES 2 TO 4**

2 Cornish hens (1 to 1½ pounds each)
2 to 3 tablespoons olive oil
1 medium onion, sliced lengthwise
2 cloves garlic, minced
1 cup canned crushed tomatoes or tomato sauce
½ cup dry white wine
½ cup Chicken Stock (page 39) or canned low-
    sodium chicken broth
½ cup pitted black olives, preferably Moroccan oil-cured
½ teaspoon dried thyme leaves
¼ teaspoon hot red pepper flakes
Coarse (kosher) salt, to taste

1. Preheat the oven to 400°F.

2. Remove the wing tips and backbones from the Cornish hens and discard, or save them for stock. Rinse the hens, inside and out, under cold running water, removing any excess fat. Cut the hens into quarters and pat dry with paper towels.

3. Heat 2 tablespoons of the oil in a large, deep cast-iron or other ovenproof skillet over medium-high heat. When it just begins to smoke, add the hen quarters, skin-side down, and sauté until well browned on all sides, about 4 minutes per side. Using tongs, transfer the hens to a platter and set aside.

4. If the oil looks burnt, wipe out the skillet and add another tablespoon of oil. Heat over medium heat, then add the onion and sauté, stirring, just until it looks a little frizzled, about 1 minute. Add the garlic and sauté until fragrant but not browned, 30 seconds more. Add the tomatoes, wine, stock, olives, thyme, pepper flakes, and salt and bring to a boil.

5. Return the Cornish hens to the skillet and place in the oven. Bake, uncovered, until the hens are cooked through (the juices will run clear when a thigh is pricked with a fork) and a nice sauce has formed, about 20 minutes. Serve immediately, directly from the skillet.

luscious little birds

Rock Cornish hens, also known as Rock Cornish game hens, are actually very young chickens that are 4 to 5 weeks old. They're a hybrid, a cross between the White Rock chicken—which accounts for their full breasts—and the flavorful Cornish hen. Until a few years ago their average weight was around a pound, but these days you're more likely to find them weighing between 1½ and 2 pounds. Their relatively smaller size makes these tasty birds ideal for serving two, or one diner with a hearty appetite.

Chicken Potpie and I Don't Care

Every family has at least one recipe with a **silly name** that's rarely as amusing to outsiders as it is to family members. This is the Waltucks'. One day as I was making this chicken potpie at home, I began singing that old childhood tune, "Jimmy crack corn and I don't care." A few minutes later, to the amusement of our children, it had new lyrics—"Chicken potpie and I don't care."

  Potpies are one of those straightforwardly homey dishes that everyone loves. They shouldn't be messed around with too much. Using roast rather than poached chicken makes a more flavorful dish. Occasionally I use the dough for Herbed Biscuits (page 382) for the crust, and at times I may add leeks, sautéed mushrooms, or fresh corn in season, but that's as much gussying up as it gets. If you like, the potpie can be frozen uncooked, then baked unthawed in a 350°F oven. **SERVES 4 TO 6**

1 chicken (3 to 3½ pounds)

Coarse (kosher) salt, to taste

6 cups Chicken Stock (page 39) or low-sodium
   chicken broth

2 large waxy potatoes, such as Yukon Gold, unpeeled,
   cut into ½-inch dice

3 medium carrots, peeled and cut into ½-inch rounds

3 tablespoons unsalted butter

3 tablespoons all-purpose flour

½ teaspoon dried thyme leaves

1 bay leaf

Freshly ground black pepper, to taste

½ cup frozen peas

½ recipe Pastry Dough (recipe follows)

1 large egg, beaten

1. Preheat the oven to 425°F.

2. Rinse the chicken, inside and out, under cold running water, removing any excess fat. Pat dry with paper towels. Sprinkle the chicken, inside and out, lightly with salt, then place in a shallow roasting pan and roast until the juices run clear when a thigh is pricked with a fork, about 1¼ hours.

3. Meanwhile, bring the chicken stock to a boil in a medium-size saucepan over medium-high heat. Add the potatoes and reduce the heat to medium low. Cook, covered, until they are just tender, 5 to 8 minutes. Using a slotted spoon, transfer the potatoes to a bowl. Add the carrots to the simmering stock and cook, covered, until they are just tender, about 5 minutes. Remove from the heat and, using the slotted spoon, transfer the carrots to the bowl with the potatoes and set aside. Reserve the stock for use in the sauce.

4. Melt the butter in a small saucepan over medium-low heat. Whisk in the flour and cook, continuing to whisk, until the mixture gives off a nutty aroma but isn't browned, about 10 minutes. Whisk in the reserved stock, then add the thyme and bay leaf and season with salt and pepper. Cook the sauce over low heat, whisking frequently, until thickened enough to coat the back of a spoon, about 5 minutes. Remove the saucepan from the heat and let cool to room temperature, stirring occasionally.

5. When the chicken is done, remove the roasting pan from the oven and transfer the chicken to a platter. Reduce the oven temperature to 400°F. When the chicken is cool enough to handle, peel off and discard the skin, then pull the meat from the bones. Discard the carcass or set aside to use for stock. Cut the meat into ¾-inch dice and place in a medium-size casserole, along with the reserved potatoes and carrots and the peas (unthawed is fine). Toss gently but thoroughly to mix. Remove the bay leaf from the sauce and pour over the mixture in the casserole, tossing gently to coat. Set aside.

6. Using a lightly floured rolling pin, roll out the pastry on a lightly floured work surface to a thickness of about ¼ inch. Cut the pastry to fit the top of the casserole with a 1-inch overhang (see Note). Brush the edge with some of the beaten egg, then carefully transfer the pastry to the top of the casserole, flipping it so the egg edge is on the underside. Press the edge of the pastry against the casserole. The egg should help seal the pastry well. Cut a few slits in the pastry, brush it all over with beaten egg, and bake the pie until the filling is bubbling and the crust is golden brown, 30 minutes. Serve immediately.

Note: You may have too much pastry, depending on the type of casserole you're using. A deeper casserole will take less pastry; a shallow one will have a wider top and take more. I prefer a shallow casserole, because I like a higher ratio of crust to filling.

Pastry Dough

This is a good **sturdy yet tender** pastry, perfect for chicken potpies. In fact, it's a good crust for any sweet or savory pie.

MAKES ENOUGH FOR TWO 9-INCH SINGLE-CRUST PIES OR ONE DOUBLE-CRUST PIE

3 cups all-purpose flour
Pinch of coarse (kosher) salt
1 cup (2 sticks) very cold unsalted butter, cut into small pieces
½ to ¾ cup ice water

1. Combine the flour and salt in a food processor (see Notes) and pulse several times just to mix. Sprinkle the pieces of butter over the mixture and pulse the machine until the butter gives the flour a mealy texture.

2. With the machine running, drizzle in the water through the feed tube, starting with ½ cup, then pulse just until the water is incorporated. The dough should be moist enough to form a ball but not be sticky. If the mixture seems dry, add more water, a tablespoon at a time. Divide the pastry in half and press into two flat disks, wrap them separately in plastic, and refrigerate for at least 1 hour before using (see Notes).

Notes: The pastry can also be made by hand, as follows: Whisk the flour and salt in a large bowl to mix, then cut in the butter, using a pastry blender or two knives, until the mixture resembles coarse meal. Sprinkle ½ cup of the water over the mixture and toss with a fork to mix. Use your hands to test a small portion of the dough; it should hold together but not be sticky. Add more water if necessary, a tablespoon at a time. Form, wrap, and refrigerate as directed above. The dough may be refrigerated for 2 to 3 days, and frozen for up to 3 months.

Staff Meals from Chanterelle | poultry

David's Famous Fried Chicken

Over the years this **delectable** fried chicken, served with Creamed Spinach (page 340) and plenty of piping hot Herbed Biscuits (page 382), has been our most requested staff meal. Depending on the season and my mood, I sometimes make Summertime Creamed Corn (page 313) or Cider Vinegar Slaw (page 310) instead of spinach.

Fried chicken, like barbecue, is one of those quintessential American dishes that all home cooks and chefs are convinced they make better than anyone else. And I'm no exception. Marinating the chicken in buttermilk boldly seasoned with Tabasco and Doctored *Harissa* (page 368) has a tenderizing effect. The buttermilk also serves as a thick coating that absorbs more flour, which is the secret to moist and crunchy fried chicken. Double-coating further ensures a nice crisp crust. The marinated pieces are coated heavily in flour and refrigerated for an hour to give the marinade time to absorb the flour, then just before frying, the pieces are lightly coated again.

This fried chicken is just as delicious at room temperature as it is served hot from the frying pan. **SERVES 6 TO 8**

2 chickens (3 to 3½ pounds each)
4 cups buttermilk
¼ cup Tabasco sauce
2 tablespoons Doctored Harissa
   (page 368)
All-purpose flour, for coating
Vegetable oil, for frying
Coarse (kosher) salt, to taste

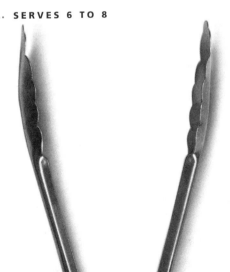

1. Rinse the chickens, inside and out, under cold running water, removing any excess fat. Cut each chicken into 8 pieces (see box, page 159) and pat dry with paper towels.

2. Combine the buttermilk, Tabasco, and *harissa* in a bowl or roasting pan large enough to hold all the chicken and whisk to blend. Add the chicken pieces, turning to coat, and refrigerate, covered, for at least 8 hours and up to 16, turning the pieces occasionally.

3. When you're ready to proceed with the recipe, spread about 1½ cups flour in a shallow dish or pie plate. Dip each piece of chicken heavily in flour to coat on all sides and arrange, without touching, on a large platter or baking sheet. Refrigerate for an hour, letting the flour absorb the buttermilk mixture.

4. If you're planning to serve the chicken hot, preheat the oven to its lowest setting. Line a large, shallow baking pan or rimmed baking sheet with paper towels.

5. Pour oil to a depth of ½ inch into a large, deep, heavy skillet and heat over medium-high heat until it's almost smoking. Just before you add each piece of chicken to the hot oil, dip it again in the flour, lightly this time, shaking off any excess. Add only enough pieces to fit into the skillet without touching; don't crowd the pan. Fry the chicken, turning as needed, until golden brown and cooked through, about 10 to 15 minutes per side (see Note). Using tongs or a slotted spatula, remove the chicken pieces to the lined baking pan and, if you're planning to serve the chicken hot, place it in the oven to keep warm while you fry the remaining chicken. Continue to fry in batches, replenishing (and reheating) the oil in the skillet as necessary and placing each batch in the oven to keep warm.

6. When all the chicken is fried, sprinkle with salt, transfer to a serving platter, and serve hot or at room temperature.

Note: Test the pieces after 20 minutes. If some pieces are done before others (white meat cooks faster than dark), remove them from the skillet. Also, if the chicken is browning too quickly, adjust the heat. You want the chicken to hit the perfect crispness and color at the same time that the meat is cooked through.

Staff Meals from Chanterelle | poultry

cutting up a whole chicken

Supermarkets have made it easy to get chicken in whatever configuration you need, but I believe it's best to buy a chicken whole and cut it up yourself. That way you know for sure where all the parts came from, and you're more likely to have a fresher-tasting final product.

Most important for chicken cutting is a good sharp knife. If I'm preparing chicken pieces for anything except fried chicken, I use a boning knife. If I'm preparing a chicken for frying, I use a chef's knife. Either way, cutting up a chicken can be greasy work, so be sure to keep plenty of paper towels around to wipe off your hands or the knife handle from time to time. Here's how to cut up a chicken into 8 pieces (for general cooking):

Place the chicken on your work surface breast-side up, legs toward you. First remove a leg by locating the joint that attaches the leg to the body. Carefully cut through that joint. Divide the leg by cutting through the joint that attaches the drumstick to the thigh. Do the same thing with the other leg.

I like to remove the breast meat from the bone, leaving just the wing bones in. To do this, I work on one half of the breast at a time.

Make a cut along one side of the breastbone near the wing end of the chicken. Ease the meat off that half of the breast by cutting down along the rib cage to the tail end of the chicken. Cut through the joint that attaches the wing to the body of the chicken and remove the breast meat half in one piece. Remove the wing tip, then divide the breast piece in half so that one half is completely boneless and the other includes the wing. Repeat this on the other side of the breast. You should have 8 pieces of chicken (4 breast pieces and 4 leg pieces).

If you're preparing chicken for frying, start with the chicken back-side up, tail end toward you. Use poultry shears to remove the backbone, cutting along each side from tail to head. Use a chef's knife to split the chicken in half through the breastbone. Remove the legs, then separate them as described above. Divide the breast pieces in half so that two have the wing portion. The other two should have a good portion of the remaining white meat. You now have 8 pieces.

To get 10 pieces, simply remove the wings from the breast pieces. Or if the thighs are meaty enough, split them in two.

Chicken with Black Mushrooms and Chinese Sausage

This nearly **effortless** one-pot meal was inspired by a steamed chicken dish I've often enjoyed in Cantonese restaurants, where it's usually made with either sausage or mushrooms, but never both. Expanding the combination of ingredients results in a dark-colored, rustically flavorful dish perfumed with the earthy undertones of the shiitakes and the slightly sweet Chinese sausage. It's long been a favorite with both the staff and my family. Our kids, Sara and Jake, are quite fond of it. In fact, for reasons I've been unable to pin down, so are most kids.

Be sure to use a casserole with a very tight-fitting lid; if it seems a bit loose, tightly cover the top with foil before putting on the lid. This dish tastes best the day it's made. The steaming creates plenty of delicious sauce, so a big bowl of plain white rice is the only essential accompaniment. **SERVES 6**

25 dried shiitake mushrooms
1 chicken (3 to 3½ pounds)
6 Chinese sausages (see box, page 161), cut
    diagonally into ⅛-inch slices
¼ cup Chicken Stock (page 39) or canned low-
    sodium chicken broth
¼ cup oyster sauce, plus additional for serving
1 bunch scallions, white and green parts, trimmed and cut into
    ¾-inch lengths, plus additional for serving
1 piece (2 inches) fresh ginger, peeled, cut in half
    crosswise, and very finely julienned
1 tablespoon Asian sesame oil
2 tablespoons good-quality soy sauce, such as Kikkoman

1. Place the shiitake mushrooms in a large bowl with very warm water to cover. Let soak for 30 minutes to soften. Lift the mushrooms from the water, leaving the grit behind. Leave the mushrooms whole, trimming away any stems. Set the caps aside. Strain the soaking liquid through a strainer lined with several layers of cheesecloth. Cover, refrigerate, and save for use at another time.

2. Preheat the oven to 400°F.

3. Rinse the chicken, inside and out, under cold running water, removing any excess fat. Cut the chicken into 10 pieces (see box, page 159) and pat dry with paper towels.

4. Combine all the ingredients in a single layer, if possible, in a large, heavy casserole with a tight-fitting lid. Bake for 1 hour, then uncover and bake for 10 minutes more.

5. Remove the pan from the oven and skim off as much of the fat as possible. Sprinkle several tablespoons of oyster sauce and a small handful of scallion pieces over the top and serve.

chinese sausage

Chinese cured pork sausages *(lop chong)*, which are a bit on the sweet side, are available at Chinese markets and some Asian specialty food stores. These hard sausages, usually red in color and about 6 inches long, are sold both in links (look for strings of them dangling in the meat section) and in vacuum-sealed packages. I prefer the kind labeled "with duck liver," because these have a little earthiness to balance their sweetness. Before you use them, the sausages must be steamed or grilled.

Chicken Paprikás

Although our menu at Chanterelle is French in spirit, for our staff meals I **love to experiment** with a wide range of ethnic cuisines. I don't claim authenticity for these forays into foreign territory; they're my own versions of dishes I've enjoyed in restaurants or seen in books.

Authentic Hungarian paprika (see box, facing page) is absolutely crucial to the success of this vividly colored, intensely flavorful dish. In fact, if you have only domestic paprika in the cupboard, don't bother making this until you have a tin of the real thing on hand. Serve the *paprikás* with rice, buttered egg noodles, or spaetzle.

SERVES 6

2 chickens (3 to 3½ pounds each)
3 tablespoons rendered chicken fat (see box, page 143),
    bacon drippings, or canola or other vegetable oil
3 large onions, sliced
2 large cloves garlic, minced
¼ cup canola or other vegetable oil
3 tablespoons sweet Hungarian paprika, or more to taste
2 tablespoons hot Hungarian paprika, or more to taste
1 teaspoon tomato paste
3 cups Chicken Stock (page 39) or canned low-sodium
    chicken broth
1 bay leaf
1 tablespoon fresh lemon juice
Coarse (kosher) salt, to taste
2 cups crème fraîche or sour cream

1. Rinse the chickens, inside and out, under cold running water, removing any excess fat. Cut each chicken into 8 pieces (see box, page 159) and pat dry with paper towels. Set aside.

2. Melt the rendered chicken fat in a Dutch oven or large, heavy pot over low heat. Add the onions and garlic and cook slowly, stirring occasionally, until very soft and lightly golden but not browned, about 20 minutes.

3. Meanwhile, heat the oil in a large, heavy skillet over medium-high heat. When it just begins to smoke, add only enough chicken pieces to fit into the skillet without touching and sauté until well browned on all sides, about 4 minutes per side. Using tongs, transfer the chicken to a platter and set aside while you sauté the remaining pieces in batches, as necessary.

4. Add the sweet and hot paprikas and tomato paste to the onions and garlic in the pot and stir to coat thoroughly. Stir in the chicken stock and bay leaf and bring to a boil over medium-high heat. Add the chicken and, when the mixture returns to a boil, reduce the heat to low and simmer, covered, until the chicken is tender and cooked through, about 30 minutes.

5. Uncover the pot, increase the heat to medium, and return to a gentle boil. Add the lemon juice, salt, and more paprika, if you wish. Stir in the crème fraîche or sour cream, bring to a simmer (do not let it boil), and cook gently for 2 minutes to allow the flavors to blend, adjusting the heat as necessary to maintain the simmer.

6. Remove from the heat, adjust the seasoning one more time, and serve immediately.

hungarian paprika

The world's finest paprika comes from Hungary, where it is processed mostly in the southern cities of Szeged and Kalocsa. Made from horn-shaped red chile pods (*Capsicum annum*) that have been dried and ground, this vivid powder comes in six strengths or grades ranging from delicate and minimally spicy to assertively hot and very spicy. The color, too, varies with each type, from orangey or bright red to a deep reddish brown. Sweet (also called noble sweet) and hot paprika are used for the recipes in this book. You'll find that the Pride of Szeged brand, packaged in bright red tins, is sold at most supermarkets and specialty food stores. (It deteriorates rapidly if exposed to air, heat, or light, and will last longer stored in the refrigerator.) Paprika is always used in generous amounts in Hungarian cooking, so don't be alarmed at the proportions called for in my recipes.

Melicia's Chicken and Dumplings

No matter how finely tuned or worldly our adult palates may become, each of us has favorite dishes from our childhoods that never fail to please. When Melicia was growing up, her grandmother and mother made this **homey dish** often. And Melicia carried on the tradition: When she joined the kitchen at Chanterelle, it was one of her first contributions to our staff meal. The light, fluffy dumplings are gently steamed on top of the simmering stew, allowing them to absorb all of the stew's wonderful aroma and flavors as they puff up, creating the epitome of comfort food. **SERVES 8**

FOR THE STEW:

2 chickens (3 to 3½ pounds each)

2 tablespoons canola or other vegetable oil

2 small onions, diced

2 large cloves garlic, minced

1 cup dry white wine

8 cups Chicken Stock (page 39), canned low-sodium chicken broth, or water

1 teaspoon dried thyme leaves

3 bay leaves

10 grinds of black pepper

Small pinch of cayenne pepper

4 medium carrots, peeled and cut into ½-inch rounds

3 large white turnips, peeled and diced

Coarse (kosher) salt, to taste

FOR THE DUMPLINGS:

2 cups all-purpose flour

4 teaspoons baking powder

1½ teaspoons salt

1 teaspoon snipped fresh chives

1 teaspoon chopped fresh flat-leaf parsley leaves

1 cup milk

Walnut-size piece of beurre manié (see box, page 62), chilled

1. Rinse the chickens, inside and out, under cold running water, removing any excess fat. Cut each chicken into 10 pieces (see box, page 159), and pat dry with paper towels.

2. Heat the oil in a large Dutch oven or large, wide, flameproof casserole over medium-high heat. When it just begins to smoke, add only enough chicken pieces to fit into the pot without touching and sauté until well browned on all sides, about 4 minutes per side. Using tongs, transfer the chicken to a platter and set aside while you sauté the remaining pieces.

3. When all the chicken pieces have been removed from the pot, add the onions and garlic and reduce the heat to medium low. Sauté, stirring occasionally, until the onions are softened but not browned, about 5 minutes.

4. Return the chicken to the pot, along with any accumulated juices, and add the wine. Increase the heat to medium high and bring to a boil. Cook, uncovered, until the wine is reduced by half, about 5 minutes, then add the chicken stock, thyme, bay leaves, black pepper, and cayenne. Bring to a boil, then reduce the heat to low and cook at barely a simmer, partially covered, until the chicken is almost done, about 1 hour, uncovering occasionally to skim any foam.

5. Add the carrots and turnips and continue simmering until the chicken is very tender and almost (but not quite) falling off the bone and the vegetables are tender, about 15 minutes.

6. Meanwhile, prepare the batter for the dumplings. Combine the flour, baking powder, salt, chives, and parsley in a medium-size bowl and whisk thoroughly to mix. Pour in the milk and stir to make a thick batter. Set aside.

7. Using a slotted spoon, gently transfer the chicken pieces to a bowl or platter and set them aside. Remove and discard the bay leaves. Taste the broth and add salt as necessary, then add the chilled *beurre manié* and whisk until it is completely incorporated and the liquid is somewhat thickened. Return the chicken to the pot and bring to a simmer.

8. Drop the dumpling batter by the tablespoonful directly onto the simmering stew. You should have sixteen dumplings. The dumplings will expand quite a bit, so don't crowd them too much; leave about an inch between them. Cover tightly and simmer over low heat for exactly 15 minutes. Don't be tempted to peek; after 15 minutes the dumplings will be perfect.

9. Remove from the heat and serve directly from the pot, or transfer the chicken and vegetables to a platter, surrounding them with the dumplings and spooning the sauce over everything.

Bistro-Style Chicken with Tomato and Tarragon

Chicken and tarragon are a **classic pairing** in French cuisine, one that results in succulent, subtle, and refined dishes. In this recipe the gutsier, bistrolike flavors of garlic, vinegar, and tomato invigorate the delicate aniselike presence of fresh tarragon.

When you're adding the sauce to the chicken, try not to completely cover the meat. The goal is to create tenderly braised pieces of chicken without losing the textural contrast of crisp chicken skin. Roasted new potatoes and sautéed zucchini are the perfect accompaniments. **SERVES 6**

2 chickens (3 to 3½ pounds each)
3 tablespoons olive oil
2 large cloves garlic, minced

1 cup dry white wine

½ cup Chicken Stock (page 39) or canned low-sodium
   chicken broth

1 can (28 ounces) whole tomatoes, undrained

¼ cup tarragon vinegar, or more as necessary

3 tablespoons unsalted butter, or more as necessary

2 teaspoons roughly chopped fresh tarragon leaves

Coarse (kosher) salt and freshly ground black pepper,
   to taste

1. Rinse the chickens, inside and out, under cold running water, removing any excess fat. Cut the chickens into 8 pieces each (see box, page 159) and pat dry with paper towels. Set aside.

2. Heat the oil in a large, heavy, nonreactive skillet over medium-high heat. When it just begins to smoke, add only enough chicken pieces to fit into the skillet without touching and sauté until well browned on all sides, about 4 minutes per side. Using tongs, transfer the chicken to a platter and set aside while you sauté the remaining pieces in batches, as necessary.

3. When all the chicken has been removed from the skillet, add the garlic to the drippings and sauté over medium heat until fragrant but not browned, about 15 seconds. Add the wine and chicken stock and bring to a boil over medium-high heat, scraping up the browned bits stuck to the bottom of the pan. Return the chicken to the skillet along with any accumulated juices and boil the liquid until it's reduced by half, about 5 minutes.

4. Add the tomatoes to the skillet, along with about half the juice in the can, ¼ cup vinegar, and 3 tablespoons butter. Return to a boil, stirring occasionally, then reduce the heat to medium low and simmer, uncovered, until the chicken is cooked through and the sauce has thickened somewhat, about 20 minutes; turn the chicken pieces once or twice during the cooking time and break up the tomatoes somewhat with your spoon. The sauce should hold together but still be rather chunky.

5. Remove the skillet from the heat and add the fresh tarragon and salt and pepper. Taste and adjust the seasoning, adding more butter if the sauce is too sharp and more vinegar if it isn't sharp enough. Serve the chicken in the skillet or transfer to a platter, topping it with the sauce.

Chicken à la Trip to Puerto Rico

I first made this chicken dish when Karen and I were vacationing in Puerto Rico, staying in a cozy rented cottage on a small, pretty island off the coast with our children, Sara and Jake. Although Karen and I love to travel, having small children has changed the way we vacation. Now, rather than experiencing a local cuisine through restaurants, we focus instead on the tastes and smells of the food markets, carrying back to our temporary kitchens whatever looks interesting and different. But even a sparsely stocked market can inspire a dish. This vibrant stew makes the most of a few simple ingredients and takes advantage of the piquant saltiness of the green olives and capers I found as I roamed our island, thinking about what we'd eat for dinner.

SERVES 6 TO 8

2 chickens (3 to 3½ pounds each)

¼ cup extra-virgin olive oil

3 medium bell peppers (can be a combination of red and green),
    stemmed, seeded, and cut into ¼-inch-wide lengthwise strips

2 medium onions, finely chopped

1 piece (4 ounces) slab bacon, rind removed, cut into small dice

2 cloves garlic, minced

2 cups Chicken Stock (page 39) or canned low-sodium
    chicken broth

2 cups canned tomato purée

2 cups chopped pitted green olives, with some of their liquid

1 cup dry white wine

¼ cup small (nonpareil) capers, with some of their liquid

4 bay leaves

Pinch of ground cinnamon

Coarse (kosher) salt, to taste, if necessary

1. Rinse the chickens, inside and out, under cold running water, removing any excess fat. Cut the chickens into 8 pieces each (see box, page 159), and pat dry with paper towels.

2. Meanwhile, heat the oil in a Dutch oven or large, heavy pot over medium-high heat. When it just begins to smoke, add half the chicken pieces and sauté until well browned on all sides, about 4 minutes per side. Using tongs, transfer the chicken to a platter and set aside while you sauté the remaining pieces.

3. When all the chicken has been removed from the pot, add the bell peppers, onions, bacon, and garlic to the drippings and reduce the heat to low. Sauté gently, stirring occasionally, until everything is very soft but not browned, about 15 minutes.

4. Return the chicken to the pot along with the chicken stock, tomato purée, olives (with some liquid), wine, capers (with some liquid), bay leaves, and cinnamon. Increase the heat to medium high and bring to a boil, then reduce the heat to low and simmer, partially covered, until the chicken is tender and cooked through, about 30 minutes.

5. Remove the pot from the heat, discarding the bay leaves. Taste and adjust the seasoning, adding salt or more liquid from the olives or capers as necessary. Serve immediately.

Dominican Chicken and Rice

As is true in most restaurants, Chanterelle's staff is like a miniature United Nations. For many years our dishwasher was a man from the Dominican Republic, and because this colorful, festive-looking dish was one of his favorites at our staff meals, we began calling it Dominican Chicken and Rice, although there's

nothing especially Dominican about it. Slices of chorizo, a spicy cured sausage often used in Spanish and Mexican cooking, add extra zip to the flavor. If unavailable, you can substitute pepperoni.

SERVES 6 TO 8

2 chickens (3 pounds each)
¼ cup canola or other vegetable oil
3 tablespoons olive oil
2 medium onions, sliced lengthwise
2 medium red bell peppers, stemmed, seeded, and
    cut into lengthwise strips
2 large cloves garlic, minced
3 cups rice
½ cup dry white wine
1 can (28 ounces) whole tomatoes, undrained
3 cups Chicken Stock (page 39) or
    canned low-sodium chicken broth
2 teaspoons coarse (kosher) salt
½ teaspoon saffron threads (see box, page 174)
¼ teaspoon ground turmeric
2 bay leaves
½ cup black olives, preferably Kalamata
6 ounces chorizo or other spicy smoked sausage,
    cut into ¼-inch slices
Freshly ground black pepper to taste
½ cup frozen peas

1. Rinse the chickens, inside and out, under cold running water, removing any excess fat. Cut each chicken into 8 pieces (see box, page 159) and pat dry with paper towels.

2. Heat the canola oil in a large, heavy skillet over medium-high heat. When it just begins to smoke, add only enough chicken pieces to fit into the skillet without touching and sauté until well browned on all sides, about 4 minutes per side. Using tongs, transfer the chicken to a platter and set aside while you sauté the remaining pieces in batches, as necessary.

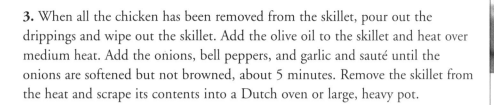

3. When all the chicken has been removed from the skillet, pour out the drippings and wipe out the skillet. Add the olive oil to the skillet and heat over medium heat. Add the onions, bell peppers, and garlic and sauté until the onions are softened but not browned, about 5 minutes. Remove the skillet from the heat and scrape its contents into a Dutch oven or large, heavy pot.

4. Add the rice to the skillet and cook, stirring, over low heat until opaque and very lightly browned, about 8 to 10 minutes. Transfer the rice to the pot.

5. Add the wine to the skillet and bring to a boil over high heat, reducing the liquid by half and scraping up any browned bits, about 3 minutes. Add the tomatoes, chicken stock, salt, saffron, turmeric, and bay leaves and bring to a boil over medium-high heat, stirring occasionally. Transfer the tomato mixture to the pot. Nestle the chicken in the pot and scatter the olives and chorizo slices over the top. Reduce the heat to low and cook, covered, for 20 minutes.

6. Uncover and taste the rice for seasoning, adding salt and pepper. Scatter the peas over the top, then cover once more and continue cooking until the rice and chicken are tender and the peas are heated through, 5 minutes more.

7. Remove the pot from the heat. Discard the bay leaves before serving the chicken and rice.

converted rice

The version of parboiled long-grain rice known as converted rice is the one made famous by Uncle Ben. Unlike regular white rice, from which the hull and layers of bran have been almost totally milled, this type has been pressure-steamed prior to milling, which forces some of the otherwise lost nutrients back into the center of the grain. During processing, the grain's starch is also gelatinized and, as a result, the pale buff-colored rice cooks up fluffy and tender, with well-separated grains that don't stick together. It's likely that the idea of parboiling rice originated centuries ago in India; in fact, many Indian curry recipes specify converted or parboiled rice, because it's important that the grains not clump together.

Chicken with Olives and Preserved Lemons

This **staff favorite** was inspired by a recipe I saw years ago in one of Paula Wolfert's classic cookbooks. The North African combination of preserved lemons and olives makes for a particularly succulent dish, with the chicken taking a real backseat to the pleasantly pungent sauce. The cooking aromas alone are enough to drive us all to distraction in the kitchen.

I prefer to make my own preserved lemons, but if you have access to a specialty food shop that carries commercial brands, save yourself the trouble and buy a jar or two. **SERVES 6 TO 8**

2 chickens (3 pounds each), with their livers
4 medium onions, either grated or chopped in a food
    processor until almost puréed
3 cloves garlic, finely chopped
½ cup olive oil
2 cups Chicken Stock (page 39) or canned low-sodium
    chicken broth
1½ teaspoons hot Hungarian paprika
½ teaspoon saffron threads (see box, page 174)
½ teaspoon ground ginger
¼ teaspoon ground coriander
3 bay leaves
2 Preserved Lemons (recipe follows), or as needed
1½ cups black olives, such as Kalamata
1 tablespoon fresh lemon juice, or more to taste
Coarse (kosher) salt, to taste
4 tablespoons (½ stick) unsalted butter, cut into pieces
Chopped flat-leaf parsley leaves, for garnish
Cilantro sprigs, for garnish

1. Trim the chicken livers, then rinse and drain well. Process the livers in a blender or food processor until puréed; set aside.

2. Rinse the chickens, inside and out, under cold running water, removing any excess fat. Cut the chickens into 8 pieces each (see box, page 159) and pat dry with paper towels. Set aside.

3. Combine half the grated onions with all the garlic, oil, chicken stock, paprika, saffron, ginger, coriander, and bay leaves in a large, heavy pot and bring to a boil over high heat. Reduce the heat to low and simmer for 15 minutes to develop the flavors.

4. Stir in the puréed chicken livers and the remaining onions, then add the chicken pieces. Increase the heat to medium and, when the mixture simmers, reduce the heat to low and cook, covered, until the chicken is very tender, 30 to 45 minutes.

5. Meanwhile, remove and discard the inner pulp from the preserved lemons, then finely chop enough of the pith and skin to make about ½ cup. Setting ½ cup of the olives aside for garnish, pit and coarsely chop the remainder.

6. When the chicken is tender, transfer it to a platter, using tongs, and set aside. Add the preserved lemons, chopped olives, and 1 tablespoon lemon juice to the pot. Bring the mixture in the pot to a boil over high heat and cook, uncovered, until it has thickened somewhat and the flavors have concentrated, about 5 minutes.

7. Remove the pot from the heat and discard the bay leaves. Season with salt and maybe a bit more lemon juice, if desired. Return the chicken to the pot, along with the butter. Set over low heat and bring to a simmer. Cook, uncovered, stirring occasionally, until the butter is melted and completely incorporated and the chicken is heated through.

8. Serve in the pot or transfer the chicken to a deep platter and pour the sauce over. Garnish with the chopped parsley, cilantro sprigs, and whole olives and serve immediately.

Preserved Lemons

Since it's pretty hard to find preserved lemons (although they are available in Middle Eastern markets and some specialty food stores), I'm including instructions for their preparation here. **MAKES 5 PRESERVED LEMONS**

15 lemons (5 to preserve, 10 for juice)
¼ to ½ cup coarse (kosher) salt
1 tablespoon whole coriander seeds
2 teaspoons whole black peppercorns

1. Scrub 5 lemons thoroughly under cold running water and pat dry with paper towels. Cut a deep X in each, starting at one end and cutting almost but not quite through to the other end; the lemons will be quartered but still attached at one end. Sprinkle the cut sides with a little salt.

2. Choose a widemouthed ceramic, glass, or plastic container for preserving the lemons. Sprinkle some salt, some coriander seeds, and some peppercorns over the bottom. Add the prepared lemons, cut-sides down, to the container, packing them in tight. If you have to do this in layers, sprinkle more of the spices between the layers, ending with a sprinkling on top of the final layer.

3. Squeeze the remaining 10 lemons to yield about 2 cups juice. Pour the juice over the lemons to cover, then weight the lemons down with a small plate to keep them from floating. Cover the container tightly and refrigerate for 3 weeks before using.

about saffron

Saffron is one of the world's most expensive spices—and worth every penny! Here's how to get the most flavor and color from each precious filament before adding it to the dish you're preparing. Place the saffron in a small bowl and cover it with a little hot water or warmed stock or red or white wine. Let the saffron soak for at least 10 minutes before using. Do not drain; just pour the saffron and soaking liquid into the dish you're preparing.

Chicken Cacciatore

This version of a classic Italian **hunter's-style** chicken and mushroom fricassee goes a bit easy on the tomatoes but is earthily redolent of mushrooms, red wine, and garlic. I use button and portobello mushrooms, but any combination would be delicious. For a more intense and woodsy mushroom flavor, soak a few dried porcinis in warm water for an hour or so, then add them along with their flavorful strained soaking liquid to the ingredients in step 3. Serve with roasted new potatoes or fettuccine or orzo, and Caesar salad. **SERVES 4**

1 chicken (about 3½ pounds)
3 tablespoons olive oil
4 small portobello mushroom caps (about 6 ounces),
    wiped clean and sliced
1 medium onion, sliced lengthwise
2 cloves garlic, minced
10 ounces small fresh cultivated white mushrooms,
    wiped clean, trimmed, and quartered
1 cup hearty red wine
1 cup Chicken Stock (page 39) or canned low-sodium
    chicken broth
1 cup Tasty Basic Tomato Sauce (page 271) or canned
    peeled tomatoes, drained and diced
1 teaspoon dried oregano leaves
¼ teaspoon hot red pepper flakes
3 bay leaves
Coarse (kosher) salt, to taste

1. Preheat the oven to 400°F.

2. Rinse the chicken, inside and out, under cold running water, removing any excess fat. Cut the chicken into 10 pieces (see box, page 159) and pat dry with paper towels.

3. Heat the oil in a large, deep, cast-iron or other ovenproof skillet over medium-high heat. When it just begins to smoke, add only enough chicken pieces to fit into the skillet without touching and sauté until well browned on all sides, about 4 minutes per side. Using tongs, transfer the chicken to a platter and set aside while you sauté the remaining pieces in batches, as necessary.

4. When all the chicken pieces have been removed from the skillet, add the portobellos and onion to the drippings and sauté, stirring occasionally, over medium-high heat until softened and lightly browned, about 3 minutes. Add the garlic and sauté, stirring, until fragrant but not browned, 1 minute or less.

5. Add the white mushrooms, wine, chicken stock, tomato sauce, oregano, pepper flakes, bay leaves, and salt and bring to a boil. Nestle the chicken pieces in among the mushrooms, leaving some of the browned chicken skin above the liquid, then transfer the skillet to the oven. Cook, uncovered, until the chicken is cooked through (the juices will run clear when a thigh is pricked with a fork), about 30 minutes.

6. Remove and discard the bay leaves, then taste and adjust the seasoning. Serve immediately, directly from the skillet.

Chicken Cordon Bleu Cheese

Staff Meals from Chanterelle | poultry

Dishes like this 1950s **banquet favorite** may seem corny, even irretrievably retro, but greet them with an unprejudiced palate and you just might be surprised at how really good some seemingly hackneyed recipes taste. Besides, how could anyone go wrong with chicken layered with slightly sweet ham and blue cheese, the whole thing breaded and sautéed to a warm golden brown?

I love blue cheese, but you may substitute goat cheese or revert to a more traditional Swiss cheese or Gruyère. **SERVES 8**

4 whole skinless, boneless chicken breasts (about 3 pounds total)
8 slices good-quality deli ham
8 ounces good-quality blue cheese, crumbled into large pieces
Freshly ground black pepper, to taste
1 cup all-purpose flour
2 cups fine dry bread crumbs (see box, page 279)
3 large eggs
3 tablespoons canola or other vegetable oil

1. Rinse the chicken under cold running water, then pat dry with paper towels. Cut the breasts in half, removing any excess fat and cartilage. Remove the chicken tenderloin from each piece and reserve them for another use (see Note). Cut each breast piece in half horizontally through its thickness. You should have 16 thin cutlets.

2. Place a cutlet between two sheets of waxed paper and pound gently with a meat pounder or rolling pin to make it an even thickness. Do this with the remaining cutlets.

3. Place 8 cutlets out on your work surface. Top each of the cutlets with 1 piece of ham. Divide the cheese among the cutlets, sprinkling it on evenly over the ham. Sprinkle pepper to taste over the cheese. Top each of the layered cutlets with one of the remaining cutlets.

4. Spread out the flour and bread crumbs on separate plates. Beat the eggs lightly in a shallow bowl.

5. Carefully dip each chicken "sandwich" in the flour to coat on all sides, shaking off any excess. Then dip each in the eggs. Lastly, dip the chicken in the bread crumbs to coat completely. Place each sandwich as it is coated on a large platter, arranging them so they don't touch. If you have the time, refrigerate the platter, uncovered, for 1 to 2 hours to let the coating dry.

6. Heat the oil in a large, heavy skillet over medium heat. Add the chicken sandwiches and sauté until golden brown and the chicken is cooked all the way through, about 4 minutes per side. Serve immediately.

Note: The chicken tenderloin is the fillet-type piece that is lightly attached to the underside of the breast.

Chicken Breasts Stuffed with Curried Couscous

This was one of Melicia's favorite staff meals to cook because the reaction is always so satisfying—the staff simply loves it. Now that Melicia is no longer at Chanterelle, I've taken her lead and continue to make it as part of the staff-meal repertoire. I think you, too, will find this **unexpected** use of couscous interesting and tasty. The couscous is stuffed underneath the breast skin so that with each bite you get a forkful of moist meat, fragrantly spiced couscous, and crispy skin.

For an attractive-looking presentation on the plate, serve the chicken with vegetables of contrasting colors, such as glazed carrots and steamed spinach. **SERVES 4**

1½ cups couscous
2 teaspoons extra-virgin olive oil
¾ cup very hot water
6 tablespoons (¾ stick) unsalted butter
¼ cup minced onion
1½ tablespoons Madras-style curry powder
1 tablespoon fresh lemon juice
Coarse (kosher) salt
3 dashes of Tabasco sauce
¼ cup toasted pine nuts (see box, page 399)
¼ cup dried currants
2 whole chicken breasts (1½ to 1¾ pounds each),
   with skin and bone

1. Place the couscous in a medium-size bowl and drizzle the olive oil over it to help keep the grains separate. Stir the couscous around until all the grains are coated with the oil. Gradually pour in the hot water, stirring as you go. When all the water has been added, let the couscous rest, stirring every few minutes, until the water is absorbed and the couscous is tender, 15 minutes.

2. Melt 4 tablespoons of the butter in a 10-inch skillet over medium-low heat. Add the onion and cook gently, stirring occasionally, until soft and translucent but not browned, about 5 minutes. Add the curry powder and cook, stirring, 2 minutes more. Be careful not to brown the curry powder or it will become bitter.

3. Add the couscous to the skillet and mix well. Stir until the couscous is hot, about 2 minutes, then add the lemon juice, ½ teaspoon salt, the Tabasco, pine nuts, and currants. Taste the couscous; it should be highly seasoned. Transfer the mixture to a bowl and let it cool to room temperature.

4. Preheat the oven to 400°F.

5. Rinse the chicken under cold running water, then pat dry with paper towels. Split each breast in half, making sure the skin is evenly divided between the two pieces. Starting from the wing socket, gently run your finger in between the skin and meat to make a pocket, being careful not to pull the skin away from around the edges.

6. Using a spoon, stuff the couscous under the skin, filling each breast piece nicely with a mound of the mixture. Try not to pull the skin away from the meat as you do this—but if you do, just smooth the skin over the stuffing as best you can. It's hard to do this neatly, but when you're finished, wipe off any couscous sticking to the outside of the breast.

7. Place the stuffed breasts on a baking sheet, dot them with the remaining 2 tablespoons butter, and sprinkle with salt. Roast until the skin is nicely browned and crisp and the chicken is done, about 30 minutes (the juices should run clear when a small cut is made in the thickest part of the breast). If the skin has browned well and the meat is still underdone, place a loose tent of aluminum foil over the chicken to prevent further browning and cook 5 minutes more before checking again. Serve immediately.

Chicken McWaltucks

Sometimes you need only replace a commonplace ingredient with an **uncommon** one to transform an ordinary recipe into something special. In this instance, breading narrow strips of chicken breast with *panko*—Japanese-style bread crumbs—rather than standard coarse dry bread crumbs makes all the difference. *Panko,* which looks like fluffy flakes of dried bread, creates an attractive extra-crispy coating on fried foods. Kids especially seem to enjoy the crunch of McWaltucks, and they're a big hit at children's birthday parties.

In Japanese cooking *panko* is frequently used as a coating for *tonkatsu* (breaded pork). Look for cellophane bags of it at Asian markets and some specialty food stores and large supermarkets. You could use regular coarse bread crumbs, of course, but the McWaltucks won't be nearly as crunchy. A word of caution: Once all the pieces of chicken are breaded and ready, don't be tempted to refrigerate them before cooking—they'll get soggy.

Serve McWaltucks with fresh lemon wedges or a bowl of Honey Mustard Dip (page 371) or Kitchen Cupboard Tartar Sauce (page 367). **SERVES 6 TO 8**

3 whole skinless, boneless chicken breasts
   (about 2¼ pounds total)
4 large eggs
1 cup milk
2 tablespoons Dijon mustard
4 to 5 cups panko (Japanese bread crumbs) or
   coarse dry bread crumbs (see box, page 279)
2 cups all-purpose flour
Canola or other vegetable oil, for frying
Coarse (kosher) salt and freshly ground black pepper,
   to taste

Staff Meals from Chanterelle | poultry

1. Rinse the chicken under cold running water, then pat dry with paper towels. Trim away any excess fat or cartilage from the breasts and cut them against the grain into ½-inch strips.

2. Combine the eggs, milk, and mustard in a wide, shallow bowl and whisk to blend. Spread half the bread crumbs in a shallow pan or pie plate (replenish the crumbs as you go along) and all the flour in another shallow pan or pie plate. Working with a few strips at a time, dip the chicken strips in flour to coat on all sides, then quickly dip in the egg mixture, and finally in the bread crumbs, to coat on all sides. Arrange the breaded strips on two large baking sheets as you work.

3. Preheat the oven to its lowest setting. Line two large baking sheets with paper towels.

4. Pour oil to a depth of 2 inches into a large, deep, heavy skillet and heat over medium-high heat until it's almost smoking (a cube of bread will brown in 30 seconds). Add only enough pieces to fit into the skillet without touching; don't crowd the pan. Fry the chicken, turning once, until GBD (golden, brown, and delicious) and cooked through, about 5 minutes. Using tongs or a slotted spatula, remove the chicken strips to the lined pans and place in the oven to keep warm while you continue to fry the remaining strips in batches.

5. When all the chicken strips are cooked, sprinkle with salt and pepper, transfer to a serving platter, and serve immediately, accompanied by lemon wedges and dips.

singing in the kitchen

The dishes at our staff meals get their names in roundabout ways. In the kitchen at Chanterelle we have a habit of idly singing ditties as we cook. When our minds roam free, old songs get new lyrics and recipes get colorful names. For example: "Old McWaltuck had a restaurant. Oy vey, oy vey, oy. . . ," you get the drift.

Chicken with Cashews

There are probably **a million versions** of this dish, and the sauce varies widely. My version is mildly spicy and abundantly dotted with crispy cashews so you'll encounter their crunch in nearly every bite. The sauce, added during the last few minutes of cooking, is made with hoisin and orange zest, a terrific combination that contributes a salty sweetness to the taste and also gives the chicken a nicely burnished reddish brown color. For the best flavor, marinate the chicken for a good long time—ideally, overnight in the refrigerator. But if you're pressed for time, marinate it for 2 hours and you'll still end up with good results.

Partially cooking the marinated chicken morsels briefly in oil, then stir-frying them with aromatics such as garlic and ginger, is a variation on a classic Chinese technique called velveting. It ensures tenderness and gives the chicken a luxurious slippery and satiny exterior. Serve with a big bowl of white rice. **SERVES 6 TO 8**

3 tablespoons cornstarch

⅓ cup plus 2 tablespoons good-quality soy sauce, such as Kikkoman

1 tablespoon Chinese black vinegar or balsamic vinegar, or more to taste

1 tablespoon dry sherry

1½ teaspoons sugar

1 teaspoon Asian sesame oil

3 whole skinless, boneless chicken breasts (about 2¼ pounds total), cut into ½-inch dice

6 cups peanut oil, for deep-frying

1½ cups (about 8 ounces) raw cashews

2 large cloves garlic, minced

1 tablespoon grated fresh ginger

Grated zest of 2 large oranges

½ teaspoon hot red pepper flakes, or more to taste

½ cup hoisin sauce

½ cup Chicken Stock (page 39) or canned low-sodium
  chicken broth

1 bunch scallions, white and green parts, trimmed and
  cut into 1-inch lengths

1. Place the cornstarch, 2 tablespoons of the soy sauce, 1 tablespoon of the vinegar, the sherry, 1 teaspoon of the sugar, and the sesame oil in a large bowl and whisk to blend. Add the diced chicken and toss thoroughly to coat. Refrigerate, covered, for at least 2 hours and up to 12.

2. Heat the oil in a wok or large, heavy saucepan until it registers 325°F on a deep-fry thermometer. Drop a test cashew in the oil; it should turn light brown in 2 to 3 minutes. Add all the cashews to the oil and fry until lightly browned, then remove them with a slotted spoon or skimmer and place on paper towels to drain; be careful not to brown the nuts too much, because they will continue to cook for a couple of minutes after they are removed from the oil.

3. Drain the chicken, then add it in batches to the hot oil. Fry until the pieces are just partially cooked but not yet browned, about 1 minute; stir constantly to keep the pieces from sticking together. Using the slotted spoon or skimmer, remove each batch from the oil to a colander set over a plate or baking sheet to drain.

4. Drain all but 3 tablespoons of the oil from the wok (see Note) and set the wok over medium-high heat. When hot but not smoking, add the garlic and ginger and stir-fry rapidly until aromatic and just slightly browned, about 15 seconds, then add the grated orange zest and pepper flakes. Stir-fry for about 10 seconds, then return the chicken to the wok and stir-fry for about 3 minutes. Add the cashews and stir-fry for 2 minutes more. Add the remaining ⅓ cup soy sauce, remaining ½ teaspoon sugar, the hoisin sauce, and chicken stock and bring to a boil, stirring.

5. Remove the wok from the heat and taste for seasoning, adding more soy or hoisin or perhaps a splash more black vinegar. Add the scallions and toss, then transfer to a serving dish and serve immediately.

Note: The leftover oil may be cooled and strained and reserved for frying at another time.

Chicken Gumbo

The **chopped vegetables** in this gumbo, significantly less brothy than most versions, meld with the roux to form a rustic, thick sauce with plenty of substance and character. The gumbo is then additionally thickened with okra or filé powder (ground dried sassafras leaves). If okra is used, it cooks along with the other ingredients, but the filé powder is stirred into the gumbo at the last moment, just as the pot is removed from the heat. I prefer to use filé because it imparts a tantalizing undercurrent of smokiness to the stew.

A bowl of rice is the classic gumbo accompaniment, but for a change of pace we enjoy it served over Cornmeal-Onion Biscuits (page 380). Split a biscuit and put the bottom half in a bowl, spoon lots of gumbo over it, then top with the other biscuit half.

SERVES 10 TO 12

12 whole chicken legs (about 6 pounds total),
    drumsticks and thighs separated
⅔ cup canola or other vegetable oil
⅔ cup all-purpose flour
3 large onions, chopped (see Note)
4 medium ribs celery, trimmed and chopped (see Note)
3 large red bell peppers, stemmed, seeded, and chopped (see Note)
2 large green bell peppers, stemmed, seeded, and chopped (see Note)
2 bunches scallions, white and green parts, trimmed and chopped
    (see Note)
½ cup chopped ham
¼ cup diced bacon
2 large cloves garlic, minced
3 bay leaves
1 tablespoon coarse (kosher) salt, or to taste
2 teaspoons cayenne pepper, or to taste
1 tablespoon freshly ground black pepper, or to taste
1 tablespoon freshly ground white pepper, or to taste

1 teaspoon dried thyme leaves

4 cups Chicken Stock (page 39) or canned low-sodium
    chicken broth, or enough to cover

1 tablespoon filé powder

1. Rinse the chicken under cold running water, removing any excess fat. Pat dry with paper towels.

2. Heat the oil in a Dutch oven or large, heavy pot over medium-high heat. When it just begins to smoke, add only enough chicken drumsticks and thighs to fit into the skillet without touching and sauté until well browned on all sides, 8 to 10 minutes total. Using tongs, transfer the pieces to a platter and set aside while you sauté the remaining pieces in batches, as necessary.

3. When all the chicken has been removed from the pot, reduce the heat a bit and sprinkle the flour over the drippings, whisking rapidly to blend. Cook the roux, whisking constantly, until it achieves a peanut-buttery color, 5 to 6 minutes. Watch carefully; you don't want to burn the roux. As soon as the roux is the right color, add the chopped vegetables along with the ham, bacon, and garlic; be careful, because steam will be created on contact with the very hot roux. Reduce the heat to very low and sauté the mixture gently, stirring frequently, until the vegetables start to soften and give off a little liquid, about 5 minutes.

4. Add the bay leaves, salt, cayenne, black and white peppers, and thyme and stir well to mix. Add 4 cups chicken stock, stirring well to mix, then return the chicken legs to the casserole. Add more stock, if necessary, to cover the chicken and bring to a boil over high heat, stirring occasionally. Reduce the heat to low and simmer, uncovered, until the chicken is very tender and almost but not quite falling off the bone, 25 minutes.

5. Using a slotted spoon, transfer the chicken legs to a platter and set them aside. Increase the heat under the pot to high and cook the sauce, uncovered, until it's reduced to a light sauce consistency, 10 to 15 minutes. Return the chicken to the pot and cook until heated through, 3 to 5 minutes. Remove the pot from the heat, stir in the filé powder, and let stand for 5 minutes before transferring to a serving dish.

Note: Vegetables chopped in a food processor usually come out too mushy for most dishes—however, that's just the texture you want for this gumbo. So if you've got a processor, use it to chop away.

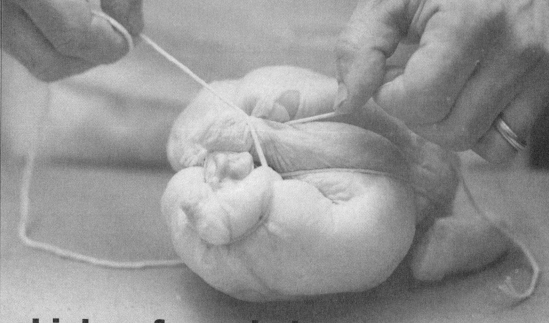

chicken for salads

Roast chicken makes the best chicken salad because it's the most flavorful, but if you don't feel like turning on the oven, use poached chicken breasts instead (see below). The salad recipes here call for 6 cups of diced chicken. As a rule of thumb, you can figure that a 6-pound roaster (or two 3- to 3½-pound broiler-fryers) will yield about 6 cups of cooked, boneless diced chicken. Four whole bone-in poached chicken breasts (4 to 4½ pounds) will also yield about 6 cups of diced chicken.

For the most flavorful poached chicken, use bone-in breasts with the skin on. Place the breasts in a large, deep saucepan or a stock-pot. Add 1 small carrot, scrubbed and sliced; 1 small onion, sliced; 1 bay leaf; 5 or 6 whole black peppercorns; and enough water to cover by about ½ inch. Bring to a boil over medium-high heat, then reduce the heat to low and simmer, partially covered, until the chicken is tender, about 10 minutes. Remove the pan from the heat and let the chicken cool in the broth. When the chicken is cool, remove it from the broth to a cutting board. Remove the skin and bones and cut the meat into bite-size pieces.

Be sure to strain the poaching liquid before storing it for another use (as a base for soup or for poaching more chicken). It will keep in the refrigerator for up to a week in a tightly covered container (be sure to bring it to a boil every 2 to 3 days; cool and refrigerate again). It can also be frozen for about a month.

Curried
Chicken Salad

The difference between a ho-hum chicken salad and an extra-ordinary one is a **flavor-packed** homemade mayonnaise. A favorite at our staff meals, this salad's terrific taste and scenic yellow hue are appetizing proof that the few extra minutes making the Curried Mayonnaise (page 361) is time well spent.

Chicken salads are simple to make and endlessly adjustable. Toss together all the ingredients of this one and present it on a platter, garnished with tomato, cucumber, alfalfa sprouts, and some avocado slices, or use the salad as a sandwich filling. Just don't bring it along to a Yankees game as a snack, as Melicia once did—the hot-dog eaters will never let you hear the end of it.

SERVES 4 TO 6

6 cups diced cooked chicken (see box, facing page)
1 cup Curried Mayonnaise (page 361)
5 scallions, white and green parts, trimmed and
    thinly sliced
¾ cup walnut pieces
¼ cup dried currants
Coarse (kosher) salt and freshly ground black
    pepper, to taste
A few dashes of Tabasco sauce
Squeeze of lemon juice

Toss the diced chicken with the mayonnaise, scallions (save a bit to sprinkle on top if you'll be serving the salad on a platter), walnuts, and currants. Season with salt, pepper, Tabasco sauce, and a squeeze of lemon and toss well to mix. Serve immediately.

Chicken Salad with Tarragon

The subtle, faintly **aniselike flavor** of homemade Tarragon Mayonnaise (page 362) contributes a bright and refreshing French accent to the tender pieces of chicken in this salad. Other fresh herbs such as basil, lemon thyme, cilantro, and chives can be used in place of the tarragon, if you wish.

SERVES 4 TO 6

6 cups diced cooked chicken (see box, page 186)
1 cup Tarragon Mayonnaise (page 362)
8 ounces green beans, steamed and chilled, for garnish
1 cucumber, peeled, halved, seeds removed, and sliced,
   for garnish
1 large fresh, ripe tomato, sliced, for garnish

1. Place the chicken and mayonnaise in a large bowl and toss well to mix. Set aside while you prepare a serving platter.

2. Artfully arrange the green beans, cucumber slices, and tomato slices around the outside edge of the platter. Spoon the chicken mixture into the center and serve immediately.

Staff Meals from Chanterelle | poultry

Honeyed-Hoisin Grilled Chicken Wings

The **intriguing combination** of ingredients in this marinade creates extraordinarily tender and tasty wings. Hoisin sauce, honey, and orange juice give the wings a deliciously dark, caramelized character, while the wine vinegar and soy and chili sauces balance the sweetness. Strong-flavored Chinese black soy sauce (sometimes called double black soy sauce) is a pivotal ingredient. It's used to add deep color and textural substance to dishes in which it's important that a sauce adhere well to slippery ingredients such as noodles or chicken. Good brands to look for are Pearl River Bridge and Koon Chun.

This marinade works equally well with bone-in chicken breasts, legs, and thighs, but it's especially good with wings served with a big bowl of room-temperature Soba Salad (page 337). **SERVES 6**

6 pounds chicken wings

3 large oranges

2 cups good-quality regular soy sauce, such as Kikkoman

½ cup red wine vinegar

¼ cup hoisin sauce

¼ cup honey

2 tablespoons black soy sauce

1 tablespoon Chinese chili sauce with garlic

1 tablespoon grated fresh ginger

2 large cloves garlic, minced

1. Trim the tips from the wings and discard or save for another purpose, such as making stock. Rinse the remaining wings under cold running water, then drain and pat dry with paper towels.

2. Grate the zest only (no white pith) from the oranges, then cut the oranges in half and squeeze the juice; you should have about 1 cup. Combine the grated zest and juice in a large bowl. Add the regular soy sauce, vinegar, hoisin sauce, honey, black soy sauce, chili sauce, ginger, and garlic and whisk thoroughly to blend. Add the chicken wings and toss to coat completely, then refrigerate, covered, for at least 8 hours and up to 24.

3. When you're ready to cook, preheat a grill.

4. When the grill is moderately hot, drain the chicken wings and arrange them on the grill rack. Cook until nicely browned and cooked through, about 10 minutes on each side. Serve with plenty of paper napkins.

hoisin sauce

Simultaneously spicy and sweet, mahogany-colored hoisin sauce is a jamlike mixture of fermented soybean paste, garlic, sugar, and five-spice powder with a hint of dried chile. You've no doubt tasted this terrifically flavorful, somewhat salty sauce many times spread on the thin pancakes that accompany mu shu pork and Peking duck (it's sometimes known as Peking sauce). Hoisin is often used as a glaze or basting sauce for grilled or roasted meats and poultry and as an ingredient in marinades and dressings. Look for glass jars of hoisin at Asian markets and large supermarkets; good brands include Koon Chun, Pearl River Bridge, and Kimlan. Stored in its glass jar, hoisin will keep indefinitely in the refrigerator.

Manhattan Buffalo Wings

When Buffalo wings first made an appearance at a staff meal, they instantly became a point of contention, sparking endless arguments on the *right*, the *only* the way to prepare them. Finally, after intense consultations with our resident Buffalonian, the following method was agreed upon and is **our official recipe**. The butter-to-hot-sauce ratio can be tinkered with, depending on how spicy (or unspicy) you like your wings. A higher proportion of butter to hot sauce, for example, makes milder, less spicy wings. It's the use of Frank's RedHot Hot Sauce, a smooth, Louisiana-style sauce with just the right amount of heat and vinegar, that makes these wings so authentic tasting. It's sold in supermarkets across America so you should have no trouble finding it, but if your local store doesn't carry it, give the company a call at (800) 841-1256. We have no compunctions about devouring a pound of wings per person at dinner (that's about 8 to 10 wings) as long as there's a salad, too. And since it's de rigueur, there are also plenty of crisp, chilled celery sticks and creamy Blue Cheese Dressing on the table.

SERVES 4 TO 8

4 pounds chicken wings
5 tablespoons unsalted butter
½ cup Frank's RedHot Hot Sauce
4 cups vegetable oil, for deep-frying
4 large ribs celery, trimmed and cut into 3-inch sticks
Blue Cheese Dressing (page 357)

1. Trim the tips from the wings and discard or save for another purpose (such as making stock), then separate the remaining part of the wings at the joint. Rinse

the wing pieces under cold running water, then drain and pat dry with paper towels.

2. Melt the butter in a small saucepan. Remove the pan from the heat and whisk in the hot sauce. Pour the mixture into a bowl deep enough to hold all the wings and set aside.

3. Heat the oil in a deep, heavy skillet or deep-fryer until it registers 375°F on a deep-fry thermometer. Add the wings, in batches so they won't touch, and fry until they're browned and quite crispy, 2 to 3 minutes per side. Transfer to paper towels to drain while you fry the remaining wings.

4. When all the wings have been fried, toss them thoroughly with the butter and hot sauce mixture. Transfer to a serving platter, arrange the celery sticks around them, and serve immediately, accompanied by the sauce. Pass the napkins!

Chopped Chicken Liver

Preparing this recipe always brings back a flood of **family memories**. When my parents entertained at home, my assigned tasks were to prepare the Manhattans and to turn the crank of the meat grinder for my mother when she made the chopped chicken liver. I regard myself as the keeper of the flame of the chopped liver recipe and try to make it for family get-togethers, especially if my brother Jonathan is in town. It's essential to use rendered chicken fat, also called schmaltz, for authentic flavor. The radishes add bite to the mixture and create a counterpoint to the richness of the liver and schmaltz. Serve this as a spread for matzoh or crackers. A schmear of chopped chicken liver on rye bread makes a great midafternoon snack. **MAKES A GOOD-SIZE BOWL**

3 pounds chicken livers
1 large sweet onion, preferably Vidalia, Maui, or Walla Walla
2 tablespoons plus ½ cup rendered chicken fat (see box, page 143)
1 teaspoon minced garlic
4 large eggs, hard cooked and peeled
6 red radishes, trimmed
Plenty of coarse (kosher) salt and freshly ground black pepper

1. Clean the chicken livers by cutting away any greenish parts and bits of fat and connective tissue. Peel the onion and cut it into pieces that will fit through your meat grinder.

2. Melt 2 tablespoons of the chicken fat in a large, heavy skillet over medium heat. Add the garlic and sauté, stirring, until aromatic but not browned, about 1 minute. Increase the heat to high, add the chicken livers, and sauté, stirring frequently, until medium rare (browned outside but still rosy inside), about 3 minutes. Transfer the livers to a colander to drain and cool.

3. When they're cool, pass the livers, onion, eggs, and radishes through a meat grinder, using the coarse blade. Alternatively, you can chop everything by hand.

4. Transfer the ground mixture to a bowl and add the remaining ½ cup chicken fat and salt and pepper. Stir gently but thoroughly to mix, then taste and adjust the seasoning. The mixture should be nicely salty, peppery, and schmaltzy.

fat equals flavor

Although fat has become distinctly unfashionable in the past decade, professional cooks have always known that the presence of some fat is fundamental to flavor. As I cook in my kitchen at Chanterelle and at home, I take advantage of the succulence of duck fat, the fruitiness of a good olive oil, the nuttiness of butter, the fullness of rendered chicken fat, and the robustness of bacon drippings. Fat makes food taste good by adding flavor, and by acting as a conduit for the good tastes that should journey across the palate with every mouthful. In baking, fat tenderizes, in sautéing it assists the transference of heat from pan to food, and in sauces and dressings it is a flavor enricher and emulsifier that also creates a beguiling appetizing sheen. I feel so strongly about fat that I once had staff sweatshirts printed with the motto "Fat = Flavor."

a waltuck family feast

One of the nicest things about owning your own restaurant is that you have room to invite as many people as you want for a holiday meal. At Thanksgiving we're surrounded by relatives and friends, plus any "orphans" who aren't traveling home to celebrate. First-timers at our Thanksgiving meal bring a special outsider energy that balances things—after all, *they* haven't heard the complete repertoire of family jokes and stories before!

Karen and I set up a very long table in the middle of the restaurant, and she creates one of her magical-looking flower arrangements for it. We scatter books and toys for the kids everywhere, and also make sure there's an ample supply of paper and crayons. Our daughter, Sara, takes the beverage orders, while our son Jake's job is to simply be himself. My cousin Linda takes charge of dessert, and there are always delicious honey cakes and traditional pumpkin pies along with a luxurious assortment of Chanterelle's sorbets and ice creams.

I love having the whole kitchen to myself, free of the rush of restaurant service. For me, relaxed and unharried time alone at Chanterelle is a luxury, so I seize this opportunity to savor the solitude of my kitchen. Over the years I've tried to introduce unorthodox dishes at our Thanksgiving table, things like venison or small birds in place of the traditional turkey, but my innovations have consistently met with such firm resistance that I've returned to roast turkey. I make a huge array of appetizers, including Ginger Pickled Salmon with Wasabi Sauce (page 214) and my brother Jonathan's favorite Chopped Chicken Liver (page 192). There are big bowls of Everyday Mashed Potatoes (page 334), giant casseroles of Cauliflower Gratin (page 310), and platters heaped with roasted root vegetables.

One of the advantages of having a powerful industrial-strength restaurant dishwasher with long spray hoses is that when the feast is finished, everyone volunteers to help clean up!

Roast Turkey the Waltuck Way

After some attempts at being innovative, I've come to be a believer in a **lavish Thanksgiving** meal that features turkey front and center. However, to be honest, I'm not a fan of turkey dark meat, so when I cook up the family bird I go for the breast. Lavishly rubbed with butter and the right selection of spices, the breast comes out moist and flavorful.

If you can't find a 14-pound breast, two 7-pounders will work just as well. And if you're a dark-meat fan, you can use this rub to flavor and roast a whole bird. The final roasting time will be different, but the taste will be just as delicious. **SERVES 12 TO 14**

1 cup canola or other vegetable oil
1 tablespoon coarse (kosher) salt
1 tablespoon sweet Hungarian paprika
1 tablespoon fresh lemon juice
2 teaspoons minced garlic
2 teaspoons freshly ground black pepper
1 whole turkey breast (about 14 pounds)

1. Preheat the oven to 400°F.

2. Combine all the ingredients except the turkey in a small bowl and whisk to combine.

3. Place the turkey in a large roasting pan skin-side up and generously rub the oil mixture over the entire breast.

4. Roast the turkey for 30 minutes, then baste with some of the remaining oil or with any juices that have accumulated in the bottom of the roasting pan. Reduce the oven temperature to 350°F and continue roasting for another hour.

Baste the turkey and roast for 30 minutes more. The skin should be beautifully crisp, and the meat tender and juicy. Test for doneness by making a small incision in the thickest part of the roast. The juices should run clear. (An instant-read thermometer should register between 160° and 165°F when inserted in the thickest part of the breast.) If the turkey isn't ready, baste again and continue roasting for another 15 minutes; then check again. Do be careful; you don't want to overroast.

5. Remove the turkey from the oven and let it rest for 20 minutes before slicing and serving.

Sara's Stuffing

From the time she was five years old my daughter, **Sara**, **and I** have been cooking Thanksgiving dinner together. We arrive at Chanterelle many hours before anyone else. There is a pleasant quietness as we unlock the door, flick on the lights, and begin our chores snugly enveloped in the stillness. We start gathering ingredients and organizing things, then move on to making this stuffing. It's a good, straightforward stuffing, filled with the earthy flavors of shiitake mushrooms, sausage, and fragrant fresh herbs. Although you could easily make it with good-quality white sandwich bread from the supermarket, I prefer to use thick-crusted, rustic white loaves from a bakery.

MAKES ENOUGH STUFFING FOR A 20-POUND TURKEY

3 large loaves (about 1 pound each) white bread

5 tablespoons unsalted butter

3 tablespoons rendered chicken fat (see box, page 143) or
    additional unsalted butter

4 large onions, diced

3 tablespoons olive oil

3 pounds fresh shiitake mushrooms, stems removed and
    discarded, caps wiped clean with a dampened paper towel,
    and sliced (see Note)

3 pounds precooked chicken sausage (or your favorite
    sausage), cut into ½-inch dice

2 cups Chicken Stock (page 39) or canned low-sodium
    chicken broth, or as needed

5 large eggs, lightly beaten

2 tablespoons chopped fresh sage leaves

1 tablespoon chopped fresh thyme leaves

Coarse (kosher) salt and freshly ground black pepper, to taste

1. Preheat the oven to 350°F.

2. Cut the bread into 1-inch cubes and scatter them over as many baking sheets as it takes; you'll probably need several. Toast the cubes in the oven until golden brown, about 15 minutes. Transfer to a large bowl and set aside.

3. Place 3 tablespoons of the butter and the chicken fat in a large skillet and melt over medium heat. Add the onions and sauté until softened but not browned, 5 to 8 minutes. Remove the skillet from the heat and add its contents to the bread in the bowl.

4. Wipe out the skillet and add the olive oil. Heat over medium-high heat and add the shiitakes. Sauté, stirring frequently, until the mushrooms are softened, about 10 minutes. Remove from the heat and add to the bowl.

5. Add the sausage to the bowl and toss with the other ingredients. Add the chicken stock ½ cup at a time to lightly moisten the mixture, then add the eggs, sage, thyme, salt, and pepper. Mix well.

6. Lightly oil a large casserole. Transfer the stuffing mixture to the casserole and dot the top with the remaining 2 tablespoons butter, cut into bits. Bake, covered, for 25 minutes. Then remove the cover and continue baking until the stuffing is nicely browned on top, 10 minutes more. Serve immediately.

Note: You can also use a mix of mushrooms in the stuffing—for example, 1 pound shiitakes and 2 pounds fresh cultivated white mushrooms. If you use white mushrooms, there's no need to discard the stems; just trim them slightly.

Thai Duck Curry

The **crisp skin** of the roast duck in this curry provides a nice contrast to the creamy, flavorful coconut milk sauce that's spooned over it just before serving. Coconut milk is an ideal base on which to build the complex flavors of classic Thai aromatics such as lemongrass, green curry paste, ginger, and kaffir lime leaves. Although duck is a perfect choice, the sauce is equally tasty with chicken or Cornish hens. For a vegetarian curry, omit the meat, increase the amount of squash, and add cauliflower and/or broccoli.

Marble-size green Thai pea eggplants, also used in chutneys and for pickling, are traditional in this curry. However, their bitterness is an acquired taste, and they're difficult to obtain, even at Asian markets. In fact, many Thai restaurants use frozen peas as a substitute, and I do the same. They don't have the same taste, of course, but they do add color to the curry. **SERVES 2 TO 4**

1 Pekin duck (about 5 pounds)

1½ tablespoons canola or other vegetable oil

6 stalks lemongrass, chopped (see box, page 236)

1 piece (3 inches) fresh ginger, unpeeled, cut into
   ⅛-inch-thick slices

2 teaspoons Thai green curry paste

1 large clove garlic, minced

3 cans (13 or 14 ounces each) coconut milk, preferably
   a Thai brand

10 fresh kaffir lime leaves (see box, page 15)

Juice of 2 limes

2 tablespoons Thai fish sauce (nam pla)

1 can (10 ounces) sliced bamboo shoots, drained

1 can (8 ounces) straw mushrooms, drained

2 medium red bell peppers, stemmed, seeded, and cut into
   julienne

Staff Meals from Chanterelle | poultry

1 medium onion, sliced

1 small zucchini, cut lengthwise in half, then cut
    crosswise into ½-inch slices

1 small yellow squash, cut lengthwise in half, then
    cut crosswise into ½-inch slices

¼ cup frozen peas

Coarse (kosher) salt, to taste (optional)

4 cups cooked rice

1. Preheat the oven to 375°F.

2. Rinse the duck, inside and out, under cold running water, removing any excess fat and skin. Pat dry with paper towels. Cut the duck into 10 pieces (see box, page 159).

3. Place the duck parts, skin-side up, in a shallow roasting pan and roast until tender and the skin is browned and crisp, about 30 minutes.

4. While the duck is roasting, heat the oil in a medium-size, heavy, nonreactive saucepan over medium-low heat. Add the lemongrass, ginger, curry paste, and garlic and sauté, stirring frequently, until fragrant and softened but not browned, about 10 minutes.

5. Add the coconut milk, lime leaves, lime juice, and fish sauce. Bring to a boil over medium-high heat, then reduce the heat to low. Simmer, uncovered, until the sauce is slightly thickened and the flavors are blended, about 20 minutes.

6. Add the bamboo shoots, mushrooms, bell peppers, onion, zucchini, and yellow squash to the sauce. Bring to a simmer over medium heat, then reduce the heat slightly and simmer, uncovered, until the vegetables are almost tender, 10 to 15 minutes. Add the peas and simmer for 5 minutes longer. Remove the pan from the heat and taste for seasoning, adding salt if necessary.

7. When the duck is ready (see Note), arrange the pieces on a serving platter and spoon the sauce over them. Serve immediately, accompanied by rice.

Note: If the duck is ready before the sauce, don't let it sit in the fatty roasting pan. Transfer the pieces to a platter and cover them lightly with aluminum foil to keep warm.

Braised Duck with Shiitakes

The basis for this dish is the same Broth for Red-Cooking used to make Chilled Red-Cooked Beef (page 65). The slight sweetness of the broth and the earthiness of the shiitakes create the perfect foil for the duck's fatty richness. When the dish is reheated after **chilling overnight** in the refrigerator, you could add a few vegetables such as snow peas, broccoli florets, and green beans if you like. When I make this in the autumn, a perfect time to enjoy it, I sometimes substitute dried chestnuts for half of the dried shiitakes. The chestnuts should be soaked overnight in warm water to cover, then drained, left whole, and stirred into the casserole after it has been in the oven for 20 minutes. (If overcooked, they will fall apart.) Serve with Broccoli with Oyster Sauce (page 307) and a big bowl of plain white rice. **SERVES 4**

24 dried shiitake mushrooms
1 Pekin duck (5 to 5½ pounds)
2 tablespoons canola or other vegetable oil
6 cups strained Broth for Red-Cooking (page 67)

1. Place the shiitake mushrooms in a large bowl with very warm water to cover. Let soak for 30 minutes to soften. Lift the mushrooms from the water, leaving the grit behind. Leave the mushrooms whole, trimming away any stems. Set the caps aside. Strain the soaking liquid through a strainer lined with several layers of cheesecloth. Add to the casserole with the mushrooms in step 5 or cover, refrigerate, and save for use at another time.

2. Preheat the oven to 350°F.

3. Trim the excess fat and skin from the duck, then cut the duck into 10 pieces

(2 drumsticks, 2 thighs, 2 wings, and 4 breast pieces; see box, page 159). Rinse under cold running water, then pat dry with paper towels.

4. Heat the oil in a large, heavy skillet over medium heat. When the oil is very hot but not yet smoking, add just enough duck pieces to fit into the skillet without touching and sauté until well browned on all sides, about 4 minutes per side. Using tongs, transfer the cooked duck to a large, nonreactive, ovenproof casserole or Dutch oven and set aside. Drain the fat from the skillet and sauté the remaining pieces, in batches if necessary, transferring the browned duck to the casserole and draining the fat from the skillet as you go along.

5. Pour the red-cooking broth over the duck and add the shiitakes. Over medium heat, bring the mixture to a simmer. Cover and transfer the casserole to the oven. Cook until the duck is tender, about 1 hour.

6. Remove the casserole from the oven and let the duck cool in the sauce for at least an hour. Then refrigerate the casserole overnight. The next day remove the layer of fat that has risen to the top. Gently reheat in the casserole on top of the stove or in a 300°F oven until warmed through.

Confit of Duck

Certainly the greatest pleasure for a cook is knowing that his or her dishes are appreciated and admired. But **other** smaller, more **casual delights** are for the cook's taste buds only. Since two of my favorite "food groups" are fat and salt, preferably in combination, it's not surprising that one of my greatest private rewards is tearing off a chunk of bread and sopping up leftover duck fat from the pan after I've made duck confit. The only higher reward might be those irresistible little bits of caramelized duck skin that cling to the sides of the pan.

The term *confit* comes from the French *confire,* which means "to preserve." A confit of pork, goose, lamb, chicken, or even

rabbit can be made using the basic technique here, but duck is the most traditional and, I think, the tastiest choice—slightly salty and very tender with a wonderfully concentrated flavor. I use Moulard duck legs, which are larger and meatier than Pekin ones. The duck legs are first salt-cured to draw out their juices. Many cooks add a lot of flavorings to the cure, but I prefer to keep it simple, using only salt and pepper. Then the legs are gently simmered in rendered fat until the meat is just shy of falling off the bone. Once cooked, the meat is transferred to a glass or ceramic storage container and the cooled fat, which acts as a preservative, is ladled over it. Tightly covered, confit can be stored for up to 6 months in the refrigerator, during which time the flavor continues to improve. Try to resist eating the confit right away—it's far better to let it age for at least a week, preferably two, before indulging.

Duck confit can be served roasted or grilled; it can be simmered in beans or soup; and, of course, it is often an ingredient in cassoulet. The flavor is very compatible with lentils, especially Warm Lentil Salad (page 322), braised cabbage, and fruits such as apples, pears, and prunes. **SERVES 8**

8 duck legs, preferably Moulard
5 tablespoons coarse (kosher) salt
1 tablespoon whole black peppercorns
8 cups rendered duck or goose fat (see box, facing page)

1. Place the duck legs in a large, nonreactive glass or ceramic baking dish and toss with the salt and peppercorns. Cover and let cure in the refrigerator for 24 hours.

2. Remove the duck from the baking dish. Rinse off the salt and pepper under cold running water and pat the duck dry with paper towels.

3. Melt the duck fat in a large, heavy pot over low heat. Add the duck legs

Staff Meals from Chanterelle | poultry

(they should be completely submerged in fat), increase the heat to medium, and bring the fat to a very slight simmer. Simmer (see Notes) until the duck is very tender but still holding together, about 2 to 2½ hours (1 to 1½ hours for Pekin legs).

4. Using a slotted spoon, gently transfer the duck to a nonreactive glass, ceramic, or stainless-steel storage container. (If your refrigerator is on the small side, you may want to use two containers.) When the fat in the saucepan has cooled to room temperature, ladle it over the duck to cover by at least 1 inch. Cover and refrigerate for at least 1 week before serving.

5. To serve, let the container of confit sit out of the refrigerator at room temperature until the fat softens enough to allow you to remove a duck leg without tearing it.

6. Preheat the oven to 375°F.

7. Place the duck legs on a rimmed baking sheet and roast until the skin is nice and crisp, 20 to 25 minutes (see Notes). If necessary, place the duck under the broiler for a few seconds for further crisping. Serve immediately.

Notes: If you prefer, the duck can be simmered in an ovenproof casserole or saucepan in a 275°F oven for 2 to 2½ hours.

If you wish, the duck can be warmed and crisped in a cast-iron skillet over medium heat for 15 to 20 minutes. Frugal cooks who want a supply of duck fat

fat for confit

A supply of rendered duck fat is essential for making duck confit. If you prepare duck occasionally and are accustomed to saving the drippings, skin, and trimmed fat in the freezer, you may want to render your own duck fat. To do this, follow the instructions in the box on page 143. If you have some duck fat but not enough for the recipe, supplement it with rendered pork or goose fat or lard (a 1-pound package of lard equals 2 cups). It's not advisable to use chicken or lamb fat.

Small tubs of duck fat are available at some specialty food stores and meat markets or by mail.

for use later should pour off and reserve the excess fat that melts off the duck after the first 2 or 3 minutes that it's heated in the pan. (Frying sliced potatoes in this fat is one of life's great treats.)

Grilled Quail with Soba Salad and Scallions

For our big annual Chanterelle staff picnic up in Woodstock, one of the first things I do is fire up the gigantic rented grill set up in our backyard and fill it with marinated quail. These **tiny game birds** (you'll need 2 per diner) are naturally tender but so delicately flavored that an assertive marinade works best. This slightly sweet one, which I jokingly refer to as Vermont teriyaki sauce since it's made with maple syrup, gives the cooked birds an attractive mahogany-colored sheen. Take care not to let the grill get too hot, though, because the marinade caramelizes quickly.

Quail have become easier to find in the past few years, so you shouldn't have difficulty buying fresh or frozen ones (defrost in the refrigerator overnight); either works for this recipe. If you're buying fresh quail from a butcher, it's nicer to have them boned. They'll leave in the tiny bones in the wings and legs but remove them from the breast and back; the cooking time is the same as for unboned birds. Cut into pieces, boned grilled quail are perfect finger food when you're entertaining. **SERVES 4**

8 quail (about 4 ounces each)
¼ cup good-quality soy sauce, such as Kikkoman
¼ cup balsamic vinegar
¼ cup plus 1 tablespoon maple syrup
1 tablespoon chopped fresh ginger
1 teaspoon Asian sesame oil
Soba Salad (page 337)
3 bunches scallions, left whole, root ends trimmed
1 tablespoon canola or peanut oil

1. Rinse the quail, inside and out, under cold running water and pat dry with paper towels. Halve each lengthwise through the breast.

2. Combine the soy sauce, vinegar, maple syrup, ginger, and sesame oil in a nonreactive bowl and whisk to combine. Pour the marinade into a large, flat-bottomed, nonreactive dish large enough to hold the quail in one layer. Add the quail and turn once to coat. Cover with plastic wrap and refrigerate for 8 hours or overnight, turning the birds in the marinade from time to time.

3. When you're ready to cook the quail, preheat the grill or broiler. Remove the quail from the marinade and drain them well, but don't pat dry. Grill or broil over medium to low heat until the skin is nicely browned and the meat is just cooked through, about 3 to 4 minutes per side.

4. While the quail are grilling, arrange the salad in a mound in the center of a large platter. When the birds are cooked, set them around the edge of the noodles.

5. Toss the scallions in the oil and grill at high heat until wilted and slightly blackened, about 3 minutes, turning as needed. Drape the scallions over the bed of noodles to garnish. Serve immediately or at room temperature.

Braised Rabbit with Dijon Mustard

I prefer to prepare this tender rabbit dish with legs only (the hind legs are the meatiest if you have a choice), which are very well suited to braising. If you use whole cut-up rabbits, be aware that the various pieces have different cooking times. Loins, for example, will cook faster than legs. You'll need to check the pieces as they cook so that each is removed from the pan as soon as it's done.

Although **assertively flavored**, the Dijon mustard sauce is quite elegant. If you like, you can eliminate the cream and finish the sauce by simply whisking in several table-spoons of unsalted butter. Sautéed mushrooms or a handful of pearl onions add delicious taste and texture to the sauce. This dish can be made 2 or 3 days ahead, but be sure to add the herbs just before serving so they taste fresh. Serve the rabbit with boiled potatoes or buttered noodles to swirl around in the satiny sauce.

SERVES 6

8 rabbit hind legs (12 to 14 ounces each)
¼ cup canola or other vegetable oil
2 cups dry white wine
3 tablespoons unsalted butter
2 medium onions, chopped
2 large cloves garlic, minced
2 tablespoons all-purpose flour
2½ quarts Chicken Stock (page 39) or canned low-sodium
   chicken broth
3 bay leaves
1 small bunch fresh thyme sprigs
3 cups heavy (or whipping) cream
¼ cup Dijon mustard

Fresh lemon juice, to taste

Coarse (kosher) salt and freshly ground black pepper,
to taste

2 tablespoons chopped mixed fresh herbs or fresh flat-leaf
parsley leaves

1. Rinse the rabbit legs under cold running water, then drain and pat dry with paper towels.

2. Heat the oil in a large, heavy, nonreactive skillet over medium-high heat. When it's almost smoking, add half the rabbit legs and sauté until well browned on all sides, about 5 minutes per side. Using tongs, transfer the legs to a platter and set aside while you brown the remaining legs.

3. When all the legs have been removed from the skillet, carefully add the wine and bring to a boil over high heat, scraping up the browned bits from the bottom of the pan. Cook until the wine is reduced by a third, 3 to 5 minutes, then remove the skillet from the heat and set aside.

4. Melt the butter in a Dutch oven or large, heavy pot over medium-low heat. Add the onions and garlic and sauté gently, stirring occasionally, until the onions are softened but not browned, 6 to 8 minutes. Sprinkle the flour over the contents of the pot and reduce the heat to low. Cook, stirring frequently, until the mixture gives off a nutty aroma but isn't browned, about 10 minutes.

5. Add the chicken stock, reduced white wine, bay leaves, and thyme and bring to a simmer over medium heat. Add the rabbit legs, along with any accumulated juices, to the pot and, when the liquid returns to a simmer, cook, partially covered, until the rabbit is tender, 45 minutes to 1 hour.

6. Using tongs or a slotted spoon, transfer the rabbit legs to a platter and set aside. Remove and discard the bay leaves and thyme. Bring the liquid to a boil over high heat and cook, uncovered, until strongly flavored and slightly thickened, about 15 minutes. Whisk in the cream, then return to a boil and cook, uncovered, whisking occasionally, until the liquid is reduced by about a third and a light, saucelike consistency is achieved, about 15 minutes.

7. Whisk in the mustard, then return the rabbit to the sauce and heat through, about 5 minutes. Season with lemon juice and salt and pepper, then stir in the herbs. To serve, transfer the rabbit to a platter and spoon the sauce over.

Staff Meals from Chanterelle

Braised Rabbit with Tomato and Olives

Rabbit is an accommodating meat, **leaner than chicken**, with a fine, somewhat firmer texture. Any of the braised chicken recipes in this chapter can be made with rabbit, especially rabbit legs. Over the years our staff has enjoyed enough variations on rabbit stew to prove to me that once the initial skepticism about rabbit is transcended, it is universally enjoyed. Serve this gutsy, olive-y stew with a simple starch side dish like Couscous (page 94), roast potatoes, fettuccine, orzo, or polenta.

SERVES 6 TO 8

8 rabbit hind legs (12 to 14 ounces each)
½ cup extra-virgin olive oil
4 medium onions, sliced
4 large cloves garlic, minced
2 tablespoons all-purpose flour
¼ cup canola or other vegetable oil
1 bottle (750 ml) dry white wine
6 cups Chicken Stock (page 39) or canned low-
    sodium chicken broth
1 can (28 ounces) whole tomatoes, drained
¼ cup brandy
1 tablespoon olive paste (see box, page 81)
5 sprigs fresh thyme
5 bay leaves
½ teaspoon dried oregano leaves
2 cups black olives, preferably Kalamata, pitted if desired
Coarse (kosher) salt and freshly ground black pepper, to taste
Red wine vinegar, to taste (optional)

1. Rinse the rabbit legs under cold running water, then pat dry with paper towels. Set aside.

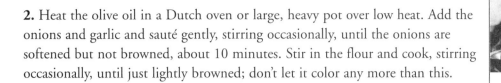

2. Heat the olive oil in a Dutch oven or large, heavy pot over low heat. Add the onions and garlic and sauté gently, stirring occasionally, until the onions are softened but not browned, about 10 minutes. Stir in the flour and cook, stirring occasionally, until just lightly browned; don't let it color any more than this.

3. Meanwhile, heat the canola oil in a large skillet over medium-high heat. When it's almost smoking, add half the rabbit legs and sauté until well browned on all sides, 8 to 10 minutes per side. Using tongs, transfer the legs to a platter and set aside while you brown the remaining legs.

4. When all the legs are removed from the skillet, pour off and discard the drippings. Add 1 cup of the wine to the skillet and carefully bring to a boil over high heat, scraping up the browned bits in the bottom of the pan. Pour the mixture into the pot with the onions and garlic. Add the remaining wine, the chicken stock, tomatoes, brandy, olive paste, thyme, bay leaves, and oregano. Bring to a boil, stirring, over high heat, then reduce the heat to low to maintain a steady simmer.

5. Add the rabbit legs and, when the mixture returns to a simmer, cook, partially covered, until the rabbit is quite tender, about 45 minutes.

6. Using tongs or a slotted spoon, remove the rabbit legs to a platter. Increase the heat under the pot to high and bring to a boil. Cook, uncovered, until the sauce has reduced by about one third, about 15 minutes. Return the rabbit legs to the casserole, along with the olives. Reduce the heat to low and continue cooking, uncovered, until the sauce has thickened somewhat further and the olives and rabbit are heated through, about 5 minutes.

7. Remove from the heat and discard the bay leaves and thyme sprigs. Season with salt and pepper, adding a little red wine vinegar if needed to balance the flavors. Serve immediately, right from the casserole.

Seafood

When it comes to food, habit is often the enemy of good taste, and there is no better example of this than seafood. Regardless of how **healthful, delicious,** and readily available it is, many Americans rarely prepare seafood at home. There has been a tendency to regard it as a treat—to enjoy seafood on special occasions, to eat it out at a restaurant like Chanterelle rather than enjoy it at home. This really is a shame, since in the past few years chefs and home cooks alike have gained access to an increasing bounty of wonderful seafood. Thus there's no reason to miss out on monkfish roasted to perfection, elegant Fresh Salmon Croquettes (page 218) with rémoulade, or a vibrant Provençal Fish Stew (page 232) fragrant with saffron and herbs.

|

Sautéed Salmon with Brown Butter, Lemon, and Capers

When you know how to prepare a good brown butter sauce, sautéed fish fillets rise above the ordinary into a more refined and elegant realm. Any fish would be honored to join it on a plate. The trick to making this sauce is allowing the butter to reach the perfect degree of golden brownness as it swirls in the pan over high heat. The wonderful, nutlike flavor and aroma that emerge at this precise point define the sauce—but be careful, since only a second or two separates brown from burnt butter. Have the lemon juice, capers, salt, pepper, and parsley ready and waiting so they can be added swiftly at just the right moment. The lemon juice halts the browning process, allowing a few seconds for you to finish the sauce.

This recipe, which is also very good made with halibut or swordfish, can easily be doubled or even tripled. Once you've made brown butter a few times, experiment with adding other flavorful ingredients like pecans or almonds, fresh tarragon or chives, shallots or garlic, depending on the type of fish. **SERVES 2**

2 salmon fillets (7 to 8 ounces each),
    skinned and boned
Coarse (kosher) salt and freshly ground black pepper,
    to taste
2 tablespoons canola or other vegetable oil
2 tablespoons unsalted butter, cut into 4 pieces
Juice of ½ lemon
1 teaspoon small (nonpareil) capers
1 teaspoon chopped fresh flat-leaf parsley leaves

1. Rinse the salmon, then pat dry. If the fish still has a few bones, remove them with tweezers or your fingers. Sprinkle the fish all over with salt and pepper.

2. Heat a large, nonstick skillet over medium-high to high heat. Add the oil and, when it's almost smoking, add the salmon and sauté until lightly browned on both sides, about 3 minutes per side. How long you need to cook the fish depends on how thick it is and how done you like it (see box, below). When it's cooked to the desired doneness, transfer the fish carefully to individual serving plates and cover lightly with aluminum foil to keep warm while you prepare the sauce.

3. Wipe out the skillet with paper towels. Place it back over medium-high to high heat and add the butter. Let the butter melt, swirling it as it foams up, then subsides. When it reaches a dark, nutty brown, a matter of mere seconds (take care that it doesn't burn), immediately add the lemon juice, capers, salt, and pepper. Cook, stirring, for a few seconds more, then add the parsley. When the parsley sizzles, remove the skillet from the heat, pour the sauce over the fish, and serve immediately.

testing fish for doneness

Fish is fragile and cooks quite quickly, often more quickly than you expect. How long it should be cooked depends on the density, thickness, and shape of the fillet or steak. It's impossible to give precise cooking times, especially for sautéing; however, the flesh is translucent before it is heated, then becomes opaque as it cooks. Use as high a heat as you dare to sear the surface of the fish so it will be lightly browned outside, moist and flavorful inside. Test for doneness by gently poking a knife or fork into the thickest part of the fish. The more resistance you feel, the less cooked it is. When checking for doneness, remember that fish continues to cook after it leaves the heat, so removing it from the pan slightly before it seems done lessens the risk of overcooking.

Gingered Pickled Salmon with Wasabi Sauce

This real front-of-the-house dish is easy to make and terrific to serve as an **unusual luncheon dish** or as a first course at dinner. Because it's prepared in advance, there's no last-minute work involved. The wasabi sauce packs a powerful punch, so be sure you tell your guests to use it sparingly. Serve the salmon with Ginger Pickled Vegetables (page 343), a tossed green salad, or potato salad. **SERVES 8 AS A FIRST COURSE OR LIGHT LUNCH**

FOR THE PICKLED SALMON:

1 piece (1½ pounds) best-quality center-cut salmon
    fillet, skin removed
Pickling Brine (recipe follows)

FOR THE WASABI SAUCE:

¼ cup wasabi powder
¼ cup rice vinegar
¼ cup water
1 tablespoon Dijon mustard
¼ cup canola or other vegetable oil
½ teaspoon coarse (kosher) salt
Finely snipped chives, for garnish

1. Run your fingers lightly over the salmon, feeling for bones. Remove any you find with tweezers or your fingers. Place the salmon in a large glass or ceramic bowl and pour the pickling brine through a colander into the bowl. Fold up a clean kitchen towel, soak it in the brine, then place it on the salmon to keep it submerged. Or place a small plate on the salmon to hold it under the brine. Cover the bowl with plastic wrap and refrigerate for at least 48 hours and as long as 3 days. The longer it stays in the brine, the more "cooked" its texture will be.

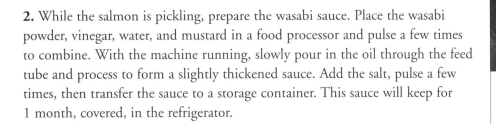

2. While the salmon is pickling, prepare the wasabi sauce. Place the wasabi powder, vinegar, water, and mustard in a food processor and pulse a few times to combine. With the machine running, slowly pour in the oil through the feed tube and process to form a slightly thickened sauce. Add the salt, pulse a few times, then transfer the sauce to a storage container. This sauce will keep for 1 month, covered, in the refrigerator.

3. When you're ready to serve, remove the salmon from the brine and pat it dry with paper towels. Using a sharp knife, slice the salmon crosswise into ⅛-inch-thick slices.

4. To serve, fan out several slices of the salmon on a plate, drizzle with the wasabi sauce, and garnish with the snipped chives.

Pickling Brine

Redolent with ginger, this brine can be used to pickle vegetables (page 343) as well as salmon. The brine takes almost no time to prepare and the flavor it gives to vegetables and fish is memorable. MAKES ABOUT 8 CUPS

1¾ pounds fresh ginger, scrubbed and thinly sliced crosswise
1 pound (2 cups) sugar
4 cups cider vinegar
4 cups water
1 clove garlic, peeled and crushed
2 tablespoons coarse (kosher) salt
1 tablespoon black peppercorns

Place all the ingredients in a large, nonreactive saucepan and bring to a boil over high heat. Boil for 5 minutes, then remove the pan from the heat and cool to room temperature. Transfer the brine to a storage container, cover, and refrigerate overnight.

Salmon with Lime Butter Sauce

Serve this **richly sauced** salmon dish the next time you have something very special to celebrate. In French cooking a thick, velvety butter sauce similar to this one is known as *beurre blanc* (white butter). Made from a reduction of vinegar, wine, or lemon juice, and chopped shallots into which a luxurious amount of butter is whisked, classic *beurre blanc* has a natural affinity for seafoods of all kinds, particularly salmon. Butter sauces can be daunting for those who haven't tried their hand at one before, but you'll find this nontraditional variation straightforward and delicious. It calls for a little cream, which acts as a stabilizer and helps prevent the mixture from separating if it gets too hot. There'll be enough warm sauce for 4 pieces of salmon; I usually allow at least ¼ cup of sauce per serving, but the recipe can successfully be doubled or tripled if you wish. **SERVES 4**

1 cup fresh lime juice
½ cup dry white wine
¼ cup heavy (or whipping) cream
1 cup (2 sticks) unsalted butter, cut into small pieces, chilled
Coarse (kosher) salt and freshly ground black pepper, to taste
4 salmon fillets with skin (6 to 8 ounces each)
3 tablespoons canola or other vegetable oil

1. Combine the lime juice and wine in a small, heavy, nonreactive saucepan. Bring to a boil over high heat and cook, uncovered, until the liquid is reduced to about ¼ cup, about 10 minutes. Be very careful, because the reduction will begin to burn in no time if it isn't watched.

2. Stir in the cream and continue reducing at a boil until the cream thickens but does not color, about 2 minutes more. Turn the heat down to very low, then vigorously whisk in the butter, a few bits at a time, waiting until the previous bits are completely incorporated before adding the next. While you're adding the butter, keep checking the temperature of the sauce. Move it on and off the heat to maintain a warm—not too hot, not too cool—temperature. If you notice the sauce getting too thick, the temperature is too low. If the sauce gets too hot, it will begin to look greasy. When all the butter has been incorporated, remove the pan from the heat. Season the sauce with salt and pepper and cover to keep warm.

3. Rinse the salmon, making sure the skin is free of scales, then pat dry. If the fish still has a few bones, remove them with tweezers or your fingers. Using a very sharp knife, score the skin with a few shallow cuts in a cross-hatch pattern.

4. Heat the oil in a large, nonstick skillet over high heat. Generously salt both sides of the salmon, then place it skin-side down in the skillet and sauté until the skin is golden brown and crispy, about 4 minutes. Adjust the heat as necessary so the skin gets crisp without overcooking the fish. Resist the urge to fiddle with the salmon too soon, or you'll tear the skin. When the skin is the right color and texture, turn the fish over and sauté on the second side for 3 to 5 minutes, depending on how done you like your fish. I prefer it rare, but this is not to everyone's taste; at 5 minutes it will be medium.

5. Ladle about ¼ cup sauce onto each serving plate and top with a piece of the fish, skin-side up. Serve immediately.

saving a separated butter sauce

If a butter sauce separates after it's made because it's being held in a pan that has become too hot, the best way to repair it is by skimming off and discarding the melted butter that has risen to the top. Then bring the remaining sauce just to a simmer over medium heat and vigorously whisk in additional cold butter, a little bit at a time, until the sauce regains the correct consistency. Taste and adjust the seasoning.

Fresh Salmon Croquettes

In the 1950s and 1960s nearly **everyone's mother** fried up croquettes. Made with canned fish, the salmon croquettes in my mom's repertoire were never one of my favorite dishes. In fact, I shudder even now at the memory of them. However, I'm a firm believer in wasting nothing, and in a restaurant kitchen that means devising recipes that use up the valuable trimmings left when preparing attractive portions for our customers. Salmon, for example. The trimmings are just too generous and rich with fish to throw out. Trimmings are a natural to use in croquettes, so my challenge was to create a recipe for croquettes that I really like . . . and these croquettes I really like. They are worthy of the center-cut portion of a salmon fillet, but if the fishmonger will sell you tail ends for less, by all means use them. In fact, these burger-shaped croquettes can also be made with leftover cooked salmon if you have some.

Serve salmon croquettes for lunch or a casual supper, with or without a bun, accompanied by a dollop of Rémoulade (page 366) or Kitchen Cupboard Tartar Sauce (page 367) and a side of Creamed Spinach (page 340) or Slightly Southern Potato Salad (page 333). **SERVES 6**

2 pounds salmon fillets, skinned and cut into 2-inch pieces
1 cup fine dry bread crumbs see box, page 279
½ cup heavy (or whipping) cream
¼ cup finely chopped shallots
1 clove garlic, minced
2 tablespoons mixed chopped fresh herbs, such as
    flat-leaf parsley, dill, and chervil leaves

Staff Meals from Chanterelle | s e a f o o d

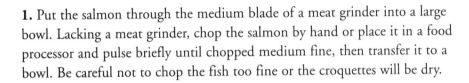

2 tablespoons Dijon mustard

2 large eggs

2 tablespoons fresh lemon juice

¼ teaspoon Tabasco sauce

Coarse (kosher) salt and freshly ground black pepper, to taste

All-purpose flour, for coating

½ cup canola or other vegetable oil

2 tablespoons unsalted butter

1. Put the salmon through the medium blade of a meat grinder into a large bowl. Lacking a meat grinder, chop the salmon by hand or place it in a food processor and pulse briefly until chopped medium fine, then transfer it to a bowl. Be careful not to chop the fish too fine or the croquettes will be dry.

2. To the salmon add the bread crumbs, cream, shallots, garlic, herbs, mustard, eggs, lemon juice, Tabasco, salt, and pepper. Using your hands or a wooden spoon, mix thoroughly. Form the mixture into six burgerlike patties, each about ¾ inch thick. Spread about ½ cup flour on a plate and dip the patties, one at a time, in it to coat on both sides, shaking off any excess.

3. Heat the oil in a large, heavy skillet over medium heat; it should be hot enough so a sprinkle of flour sizzles on contact. Add the butter to the hot oil and, as soon as it has melted, add the salmon croquettes and fry until cooked through and golden brown on both sides, about 5 minutes per side.

4. Using a slotted spatula, transfer the croquettes to paper towels to drain, then serve immediately.

real people

Restaurant kitchens are organized into "stations," each station geared to perform a specific task. Although the details of how the stations are organized varies from one restaurant to the next, it's expected that each person working a station knows precisely what to do and when to do it. As ingredients are washed, trimmed, peeled, chopped, cooked, or carved, each person keeps in mind which of the ingredients that go into the dishes being prepared will be usable for us at our staff meal. That lovely poached salmon? It's for the "real people"—the trimmings from it become our salmon croquettes!

Tuna with Two Marinades

When it comes to varying a cook's repertoire, few **flavor-enhancing** techniques are as foolproof as marination. These easy marinades take only a couple of minutes to prepare, and each imparts subtle, intriguing tastes to mild, meaty fish. Here I use tuna steaks, but red snapper or monkfish would also be good choices. Marinate overnight, if possible. If not, even an hour's worth will make a flavorful difference. Soba Salad (page 337) is a good side-dish choice for either variation. **SERVES 4**

Honey Soy Marinade or Ginger Wasabi Marinade
   (recipes follow)
4 tuna steaks (1 inch thick; 7 to 8 ounces each)

1. Pour the marinade of your choice into a sturdy plastic bag large enough to hold the tuna steaks flat. Add the tuna to the bag, gently shaking it to make sure that each piece is coated with marinade, then express the air from the bag and seal tightly with a twist-tie. Place the bag on a large plate, making sure all the pieces are lying flat so as not to bruise them. Refrigerate for at least 1 hour and up to 24 hours. (This technique ensures that the tuna is evenly immersed in the marinade, eliminating the need to turn the fish occasionally.)

2. When you're ready to cook the tuna, preheat a grill or large cast-iron skillet to very hot (see Note).

3. Remove the tuna from the marinade and pat dry. Grill or pan-fry, searing the outside and keeping the interior rosy, about 2 minutes per side. Serve immediately.

Note: Most home broilers cannot achieve a high-enough temperature to sear tuna correctly, so I prefer grilling or pan-frying in a very hot cast-iron skillet. Whichever method you use, be careful not to overcook the fish or it will be dry.

Honey Soy Marinade

The fresh lime juice and Chinese dried orange peel form the basic character of this marinade. The honey and sugar add a nice **hint of sweetness** and also help caramelize and brown the exterior of the fish a bit as it cooks. **MAKES ABOUT 2¼ CUPS**

2 cups good-quality soy sauce, such as Kikkoman
Juice of 2 limes
2 tablespoons honey
1 teaspoon grated fresh ginger
1 teaspoon hot red pepper flakes
1 clove garlic, minced
3 pieces Chinese dried orange peel (see box, page 51), softened, or
    fresh orange zest (outer skin only, no white pith)

Combine all the ingredients in a small, nonreactive saucepan and bring to just a simmer over medium heat. Remove the sauce immediately from the heat and let it cool completely before using.

Ginger Wasabi Marinade

This **marinade, is lighter** than the Honey Soy version. The mirin—a sweetened Japanese rice wine used in cooking—smooths the bite of the wasabi and ginger. **MAKES ABOUT 2½ CUPS**

2 cups good-quality soy sauce, such as Kikkoman
½ cup mirin
1 tablespoon sugar
½ teaspoon grated fresh ginger
½ teaspoon wasabi powder

Combine all the ingredients in a small bowl and stir until the sugar is dissolved. The marinade is ready to use.

Lotte with Leeks

Lotte, as it is called in France and quite often on restaurant menus here, is generally known in the United States as monkfish. In the past decade this versatile fish has enjoyed a **newfound popularity**, which it richly deserves. It's a truly delicious, sweet, firm-textured fish that easily holds its own in both refined and robust preparations. Here it's paired with slowly cooked leeks that become a meltingly sweet and tender foil for the tart butter sauce. Serve this rich dish with green beans and some roast new potatoes. **SERVES 4**

2 bunches large leeks (6 to 8 leeks total)
1 cup (2 sticks) unsalted butter, chilled
¼ cup minced shallots
1¾ cups dry white wine
½ cup white wine vinegar
3 tablespoons heavy (or whipping) cream
1 teaspoon chopped fresh tarragon leaves
Coarse (kosher) salt and freshly ground black pepper,
    to taste
3 cups water
4 monkfish fillets (about 2 inches in diameter;
    7 to 8 ounces each), trimmed of membrane and
    cut crosswise into ½-inch diagonal slices
2 teaspoons chopped fresh flat-leaf parsley leaves

1. Trim the root ends of the leeks and discard. Cut off the green tops, leaving a couple of inches attached to the white. Save the tops for stock or soup. Slice the leeks lengthwise and then crosswise into 1-inch segments. Thoroughly rinse the leeks in a colander under cold running water or, if they're particularly sandy, soak them in a bowl of cold water for 30 minutes before rinsing and draining thoroughly.

2. Melt 2 tablespoons of the butter in a medium-size, heavy, nonreactive pot over low heat. Add the leeks, cover, and cook them very slowly, uncovering occasionally to stir, until they're very soft, almost melted, about 1 hour.

3. While the leeks are cooking, prepare the sauce. Cut the remaining butter into small pieces and keep refrigerated until needed. Combine the shallots, ¾ cup of the wine, and the vinegar in a small, heavy, nonreactive saucepan and bring to a boil over high heat, then reduce the heat to maintain a steady simmer. Cook, uncovered, until the liquid is reduced to about 1 tablespoon (it will appear almost dry), about 15 minutes; be very careful not to let it burn. Add the cream and cook, uncovered, until it's reduced by half and thickens considerably, about 2 minutes. Remove the butter from the refrigerator and whisk it, bit by bit, into the reduction, adding the next bit as the previous one has been emulsified into the sauce. Keep checking the temperature of the sauce. It should stay very warm, almost but not quite hot; nor should it get too cool. To accomplish this, move the pan on and off the heat as necessary. Stir in the tarragon, season with salt and pepper, and keep warm (see Note).

4. About 15 minutes before the leeks are done, combine the water, remaining 1 cup wine, and a large pinch of salt in a large, deep, nonreactive skillet and bring to a boil over high heat, then reduce the heat to maintain a steady simmer. Add the monkfish slices to the simmering liquid and poach until just cooked through, 2 to 3 minutes (see box, page 213). Using a slotted spoon, carefully transfer the fish to a clean kitchen towel to drain.

5. Remove the leeks from the heat and season with salt and pepper, then divide among four serving plates. Spoon the sauce over the portions of leeks, dividing evenly. Sprinkle with the parsley, then top with the sliced fish. Serve immediately.

Note: A butter sauce is meant to be eaten warm, not hot. Kept covered, it should retain enough heat to last until you're ready to serve the fish.

Monkfish with Roast Shallots and Garlic

The **tail section** of monkfish is the edible part, so that portion, and only that, is what you'll find in stores. It may be sectioned into fillets, which are cut from either side of the backbone or center cartilage, or it may be the whole tail (ranging from 6 or 7 ounces to almost 10 pounds) with the center cartilage intact. In France a large tail, roasted to perfection like a leg of lamb, is called *gigot de lotte*. Because monkfish is so meaty, firm, and juicy, it's ideally suited to roasting, as you will soon taste for yourself. Although this recipe is light enough to be served year-round, I think of it as a fall or winter dish because of the earthy flavors of the roast shallots and garlic. **SERVES 4**

16 medium shallots
1 head garlic
¼ cup olive oil
Coarse (kosher) salt and freshly ground black pepper, to taste
4 monkfish fillets (about 2 inches in diameter; 7 to 8 ounces
    each), trimmed of membrane
1 large sprig fresh thyme
½ cup dry white wine
2 tablespoons unsalted butter

1. Preheat the oven to 325°F.

2. Trim the tip of the root end of each shallot, leaving just enough to hold the shallot together. Peel off the outer layers of skin, leaving the last layer or two. Separate the cloves of garlic and peel them.

3. Place the shallots and garlic in a 16 × 9-inch flameproof roasting pan and toss with 2 tablespoons of the oil and the salt and pepper, then roast until soft, about 45 minutes. Stir the shallots and garlic every so often, and if they seem to be browning too quickly, reduce the oven temperature to 300°F. When the shallots and garlic are soft, remove the pan from the oven and increase the temperature to 425°F.

4. Heat the remaining 2 tablespoons oil in a large, heavy skillet over high heat. Add the monkfish fillets, sprinkle with salt and pepper, and brown quickly on all sides, about 2 minutes per side. Remove the skillet from the heat and transfer the fillets carefully to the roasting pan with the shallots and garlic. Add the thyme, then roast the monkfish until just cooked through, about 10 minutes. Remove the roasting pan from the oven and carefully transfer the fish to a cutting board. Let it rest while you finish the dish.

5. Place the roasting pan over high heat and add the wine. Bring it to a boil and cook until reduced by half, 3 minutes. Add the butter and continue to cook, whisking until the butter is incorporated. Remove the pan from the heat and discard the thyme sprig. Season the sauce with salt and pepper.

6. To serve, divide the shallots and garlic, along with some of the sauce, among four serving plates. Cut each monkfish fillet into diagonal ½-inch slices and arrange on the plates, over the sauce and among the shallots and garlic. Serve immediately.

Fish with Ginger-Scallion Sauce

Here's a **simplified version** of one of the dishes that Karen and I most enjoy ordering at Thai restaurants. The gingery sauce is typically served over a whole fish that has been slashed to the bone with a sharp knife, then fried in oil until it's so extravagantly crisp you can practically eat the crunchy bones. Amazingly, however, the flesh remains wonderfully moist. For our staff meal, I usually serve the sauce with sautéed fish fillets, which

are easier and faster to prepare. As a special treat, try the sauce with soft-shell crabs, since their crispy exterior and soft interior are similar in texture to those of the whole fried fish. **SERVES 4**

8 dried shiitake mushrooms
2 cups Chicken Stock (page 39) or canned low-sodium
    chicken broth
¼ cup sugar
⅓ cup rice vinegar or cider vinegar
2½ tablespoons oyster sauce
2 tablespoons good-quality soy sauce, such as Kikkoman
1 tablespoon fresh lime juice
1 tablespoon Thai fish sauce (nam pla)
1 tablespoon cornstarch
2 tablespoons cold water
1 teaspoon hot red pepper flakes
1½ tablespoons grated fresh ginger
1 medium onion, sliced lengthwise
1 small red bell pepper, stemmed, seeded, and
    cut into thin strips
3 scallions, white and green parts, trimmed and cut
    into ¼-inch lengths
1 cup all-purpose flour, for coating the fish
4 mild white fish fillets (about 8 ounces each), such
    as red snapper, flounder, or bass
2 tablespoons canola or other vegetable oil
Coarse (kosher) salt, to taste

1. Place the shiitake mushrooms in a small bowl with very hot water to cover. Let soak for 30 minutes to soften. Lift the mushrooms from the soaking liquid, leaving the grit behind. Trim away any stems and slice the caps. Strain the soaking liquid through a strainer lined with several layers of cheesecloth and add to the saucepan in step 2.

2. Combine the chicken stock, shiitakes, sugar, vinegar, oyster sauce, soy sauce, lime juice, and fish sauce in a small, nonreactive saucepan and bring to a boil over high heat. Reduce the heat to low and simmer, uncovered, until the flavors have blended, about 20 minutes.

3. Whisk the cornstarch with the water to blend. When it's smooth, whisk it into the sauce, whisking constantly until the sauce thickens, 1 minute. Add the pepper flakes and ginger and simmer for 1 minute more. Add the onion, bell pepper, and scallions and cook just until heated through, another 1 to 2 minutes; the vegetables should still be very crisp. Remove from the heat and taste for seasoning. Keep warm while you prepare the fish.

4. Spread the flour on a plate and dip the fish fillets, one at a time, in it to coat on both sides, shaking off any excess.

5. Heat the oil in a large skillet over medium-high heat. Sprinkle the fish fillets lightly with salt, then add them to the skillet. Sauté until lightly browned and cooked through, 2 to 3 minutes per side.

6. Transfer the fillets to a platter or individual plates and spoon the sauce over them to serve.

fresh ginger

Pungent, peppery, and slightly sweet, ginger is one of the most extensively used flavorings in Asian cooking. There are two types of ginger, mature and young. Mature ginger is easy to find year-round in almost all supermarkets. Select firm, plump knobs with taut, unwrinkled, pale tan skin that's shiny. Avoid any that are soft or wrinkled, and bear in mind that the older the ginger, the more fibrous it will be.

Young ginger, also called stem or spring ginger, is a special treat available only twice a year, in January and February and again in July and August. Look for it in Asian markets. In contrast to mature ginger, harvested at around 10 months, tender young ginger is only 3 to 4 months old and is more perishable. It's juicy and pungent, though not as spicy and sharply flavored as mature ginger, so you'll need to use more of it in a recipe. Young ginger is lovely looking, with pale yellow skin that is paper thin to the point of translucency and rosy pink tips at the end of the knobs. No peeling is necessary.

To store ginger, wrap the knobs in paper towels (to absorb mold-inducing moisture), place in a loosely closed plastic bag, and refrigerate for up to 3 weeks in the vegetable drawer.

Crispy Fish with Spicy Sweet-and-Sour Sauce

It may seem odd, but I have a soft spot for the style of Chinese cooking that has become the **hallmark of take-out** restaurants. Although there's no question that it's an Americanized mutation of one of the world's great cuisines, I find the flavors and textures of many of the dishes appealing. It's inauthentic in the same way that take-out pizza isn't genuinely Italian, even though it can be satisfying and good to eat.

This recipe was inspired by the sweet-pungent thick sauce that characterizes a wide range of Chinese take-out dishes. It's very good with crispy fish fillets, as the recipe specifies, or served with scallops or chicken tenderloins that have been coated with flour or cornstarch and pan-fried. Although I generally use canola oil for frying, I think peanut oil works best for this dish. **SERVES 6**

2 tablespoons vegetable oil, preferably peanut, plus
    additional for frying
1 small clove garlic
¾ teaspoon grated fresh ginger
2 cups Chicken Stock (page 39) or canned low-sodium
    chicken broth
2 tablespoons white wine or rice vinegar
2 tablespoons ketchup
4 teaspoons sugar
1 tablespoon good-quality soy sauce,
    such as Kikkoman
¾ teaspoon Chinese chili paste, or other hot sauce
2 teaspoons cornstarch
3 tablespoons cold water

1 cup all-purpose flour, or more if needed, for coating
6 mild white fish fillets (6 to 8 ounces each), such as
    bass, flounder, grouper, cod, scrod, or snapper
Coarse (kosher) salt, to taste

1. Heat 2 tablespoons oil in a large skillet over medium heat. Add the garlic and ginger and cook quickly until aromatic but not browned, about 1 minute.

2. Stir in the chicken stock, vinegar, ketchup, sugar, soy sauce, and chili paste and increase the heat to high. Bring to a boil, then reduce the heat to medium low and simmer, uncovered, until the flavors have blended and the sauce has reduced slightly, about 10 minutes.

3. Whisk the cornstarch with the water to blend. When smooth, whisk it into the sauce. Reduce the heat to low and simmer the sauce, whisking constantly, until it thickens, about 1 minute. Remove the skillet from the heat and taste and adjust the seasoning. Set aside, covered, to keep warm.

4. Spread the flour on a plate and dip the fish fillets, one at a time, in it to coat on both sides, shaking off any excess.

5. Preheat the oven to its lowest setting. Line two baking sheets with several layers of paper towels.

6. Pour oil to a depth of ¼ inch into a large, heavy skillet, then set it over medium-high heat. When a drop of water sizzles rapidly on contact with the oil, sprinkle the fish with salt and add one third to one half of the fillets; do not crowd the pan. Fry until golden brown on both sides, 2 to 3 minutes per side, depending on the thickness of the fillets. Using a slotted spatula, remove the fillets to the prepared baking sheets and keep warm in the oven while you fry the rest.

7. Arrange the fillets on a serving platter or individual plates. Spoon the sauce over the fish and serve immediately.

Sesame-Crusted Fish Fillets with Garlic-Ginger Sauce

This recipe features another boldly flavored **Chinese-inspired** sauce that complements virtually any type of mild white fish fillets. The light, crispy crust on the fish is flecked with black and white sesame seeds, which add extra flavor and crunch. You could use only white sesame seeds, but it's really worth a visit to an Asian market or spice shop, for the black ones add visual drama to this simple dish. There's quite a lot of ginger in the sauce, which gives it a clean, spicy pungency. To julienne the ginger, cut the peeled knobs lengthwise along the grain into thin slices. Then stack the slices and cut them lengthwise, still along the grain, into even-size matchsticks. **SERVES 6**

6 tablespoons canola or other vegetable oil

4 teaspoons minced garlic

4 ounces fresh ginger, peeled and julienned (about 1 cup)

2 cups Fish Stock (page 41), Chicken Stock (page 39),
    or canned low-sodium chicken broth

3 tablespoons good-quality soy sauce, such as Kikkoman

2 tablespoons dry sherry

1 tablespoon sugar

1 teaspoon oyster sauce

2 teaspoons plus 1 tablespoon cornstarch

¼ cup cold water

2 large egg whites

1 cup white sesame seeds

1 cup black sesame seeds

6 mild white fish fillets (6 to 8 ounces each), such as
    flounder, cod, scrod, grouper, snapper, or bass

1. Heat 2 tablespoons of the oil in a large skillet over high heat. When a drop of water sizzles rapidly on contact with the oil, add the garlic and ginger and cook quickly until aromatic but just slightly browned, 1 to 2 minutes.

2. Add the fish stock, soy sauce, sherry, sugar, and oyster sauce and bring to a boil, stirring to dissolve the sugar. Reduce the heat to low and simmer the sauce, uncovered, until the flavors have blended and the sauce has reduced slightly, about 15 minutes.

3. Whisk 2 teaspoons of the cornstarch with the cold water to blend. When smooth, whisk the mixture into the simmering sauce, stirring until thickened, about 30 seconds. Remove the skillet from the heat and keep warm, covered, while you prepare the fish.

4. Combine the egg whites and remaining 1 tablespoon cornstarch in a wide, shallow bowl and whisk to blend. Combine the black and white sesame seeds on a plate. Dip each fish fillet first in the egg-white mixture to coat both sides, then in the sesame seeds to cover completely, shaking off any excess. Place each fillet as it is coated on a baking sheet.

5. Preheat the oven to its lowest setting.

6. Heat the remaining ¼ cup oil in a large, heavy skillet over medium-high heat. Add half the fish fillets or as many as will fit comfortably; do not crowd the pan. Sauté until lightly browned on both sides, about 3 minutes per side, depending on the thickness of the fillets. Adjust the heat as necessary so the fillets brown nicely but the seeds don't burn. Using a slotted spatula, transfer the fillets to paper towels to drain, then to a platter. Cover loosely with aluminum foil and keep warm in the oven while you sauté the remaining fillets.

7. When all the fillets are sautéed, spoon the hot sauce over them and serve immediately.

Provençal Fish Stew

Many cooks insist that authentic **bouillabaisse** be made only with specific types of fish. To me, it's the characteristic flavorings—saffron, Pernod, tomatoes—that distinguish bouillabaisse from other seafood stews. My version is in the true spirit of the practical Provençal fishermen who created this now-classic dish as a way to use up odds and ends of leftover or unsold fish. Similarly, I accumulate the trimmings and tail ends of fish at Chanterelle to make this vibrant stew for our staff meal. There's no need to peel the garlic and onions for the broth, since they'll be strained out before the fish is added. Once the fish is poaching in the broth, I like to swirl in a splash of good-quality olive oil or a few tablespoons of butter, though butter is absolutely heretical in terms of Provençal cooking. To serve, set a bowl of Aïoli (page 363) on the table along with some toasted slices of French bread. Diners can add a dollop of Aïoli to their stew or spread it on the toast and set it afloat on the stew's surface. **SERVES 8**

¼ cup extra-virgin olive oil

2 medium onions, unpeeled, roughly chopped

1 carrot, cut into ¼-inch rounds

4 heads garlic, unpeeled, roughly cut up

1 large fennel bulb, with leafy top, roughly chopped

2 cups dry white wine

1 cup Pernod or other anise-flavored liqueur, or more to taste

8 cups Fish Stock (page 41)

Zest of 2 oranges, cut into strips (no white pith)

2 cups canned whole tomatoes, with liquid, crushed

4 bay leaves

1 teaspoon saffron threads (see box, page 174)

½ teaspoon dried thyme leaves

½ teaspoon dried oregano leaves

½ teaspoon dried rosemary leaves

2 pounds mixed seafood, including mussels and clams in the shell,
scallops, firm fish fillets, and cleaned squid (see box, page 249)

Coarse (kosher) salt, to taste (optional)

Aïoli (page 363)

8 to 16 slices French bread, toasted

1. Heat the oil in a medium-size, nonreactive saucepan over medium heat. Add the onions, carrot, garlic, and fennel and sauté, stirring occasionally, until the vegetables are lightly browned, about 8 minutes.

2. Add the wine and 1 cup Pernod and increase the heat to high. Bring to a boil and cook, uncovered, until the liquid is reduced by half, about 10 minutes. Add the fish stock, orange zest, tomatoes, bay leaves, saffron, thyme, oregano, and rosemary. Bring to a boil, then reduce the heat to low and simmer, partially covered, until slightly reduced and the flavors have developed, about 1 hour.

3. While the broth is cooking, prepare the seafood. Scrub and debeard the mussels as described on page 19; scrub the clams. Trim away and discard any muscle from the scallops; cut each fish fillet into 2-inch pieces. Cut the squid bodies into ½-inch rings, and if any tentacles included are large, cut them lengthwise in half.

4. Remove the saucepan from the heat and pour the contents through a strainer into a heatproof container, pressing firmly on the solids in the strainer with the back of a wooden spoon. Discard the solids and return the broth to the saucepan. Season with salt, if necessary, and additional Pernod, if desired, then return to a simmer over low heat. Add the clams to the simmering broth and cook, covered, for 3 minutes, then add the mussels and re-cover. When the clams and mussels are just beginning to open, after 1 or 2 minutes, add the scallops and firmer fish to the pan. Cover and simmer gently until the scallops and fish are almost opaque, about 3 minutes, then add the squid. Continue simmering, covered, until all the mussels and clams have opened and the other seafood is just opaque, about 2 minutes longer.

5. Remove and discard any clams or mussels that haven't opened. Ladle the stew into large, shallow bowls and serve immediately, with a bowl of aïoli and a basket of toast for the table.

Fish 'n' Chips

This is a special treat we don't indulge in often, but always relish. The beer in the batter creates a delightfully light, crisp crust for the fish, which should be served along with heaps of fries and tartar sauce.

If you're preparing fries with the fish, make them first, then use the same oil the fries were cooked in to fry the fish. **SERVES 4**

1 bottle (12 ounces) beer
½ cup cold water
2 cups all-purpose flour
½ teaspoon baking powder
½ teaspoon sweet Hungarian paprika
Coarse (kosher) salt and freshly ground black pepper, to taste
Canola or other vegetable oil, for deep-frying
4 flounder fillets (7 to 8 ounces each), cut crosswise in half
Our Favorite Fries (page 327)
Kitchen Cupboard Tartar Sauce (page 367)

1. Place the beer and water in a medium-size bowl and stir to mix. Combine the flour, baking powder, paprika, salt, and pepper in a large bowl, whisking well to mix. Pour the beer mixture over the flour mixture and whisk just to combine.

2. Preheat the oven to its lowest setting. Line a baking sheet with several layers of paper towels.

3. Pour oil to a depth of 3 inches into a deep-fryer or deep, heavy skillet and heat over medium heat. When the temperature reaches 375°F on a deep-fry thermometer, dip a piece of flounder in the beer batter, letting the excess drip back into the bowl, then lower the fish carefully into the hot oil. Fry until golden brown all over, about 3 to 4 minutes, turning once. Fry the fillets 2 at a time to prevent crowding. Transfer the fried flounder to the prepared baking sheet and keep warm in the oven while you fry the rest. Then serve immediately, accompanied by the fries and tartar sauce.

Staff Meals from Chanterelle | seafood

Thai Seafood Salad

The **harmonious flavors** of this seafood salad will positively bounce around in your mouth. Be sure to take into account the fact that the dressing is made a day ahead so the flavors have time to mellow. Each type of seafood is poached in Lemongrass Court Bouillon (page 237), then arranged on a baking sheet to cool. Since the seafood will continue to cook until it has cooled, it's important to slightly undercook it in the bouillon. Don't stint on the intensely flavorful garnishes that add an all-important final flourish. **SERVES 4**

½ cup fresh lime juice
⅓ cup water
¼ cup sugar
4½ teaspoons Thai fish sauce (nam pla)
1½ teaspoons good-quality soy sauce, such as Kikkoman
1 teaspoon chili-garlic sauce *(sambal oelek)*
1 stalk lemongrass, trimmed and very thinly sliced (see box, page 236)
1 large clove garlic, minced
Lemongrass Court Bouillon (recipe follows)
1 monkfish fillet (8 ounces), cut into ½-inch crosswise slices
4 ounces sea scallops
8 ounces medium shrimp, peeled and deveined
4 ounces cleaned squid (see box, page 249), bodies cut into
    ½-inch rings and tentacles cut lengthwise in half if large
4 ounces lump crabmeat, picked clean
Thinly sliced cucumber, thinly sliced red onion, and
    fresh cilantro or mint leaves, for garnish

1. Place the lime juice, water, sugar, fish sauce, soy sauce, chili-garlic sauce, lemongrass, and garlic in a small bowl and whisk well to blend. Refrigerate the dressing, covered, for at least 8 hours or overnight.

2. Bring the court bouillon to a boil in a medium-size saucepan over high heat, then reduce the heat to low. Add the monkfish and poach, covered, at a gentle

simmer until almost opaque, about 5 minutes. Using a slotted spoon, transfer the fish to a shallow baking pan or rimmed baking sheet to cool. Remember that the seafood will continue cooking as it cools, so do not overcook.

3. Add the scallops to the simmering court bouillon and poach gently, covered, until almost opaque, 2 to 4 minutes, depending on their size. Using the slotted spoon, transfer the scallops to the pan with the monkfish. Add the shrimp to the court bouillon and poach, covered, until they're curled and just barely pink, about 2 minutes. Transfer the shrimp to the pan. Add the squid to the court bouillon and poach, covered, until almost opaque, 1 to 2 minutes. Transfer them to the pan and let cool for a few minutes. Refrigerate the seafood, uncovered, until thoroughly chilled, about 45 minutes (see Note).

lemongrass

Lemongrass is a staple flavoring in Thai cuisine, often used in soups, salads, and pungent curry pastes. Its flavor is bright and delicately lemony with almost perfumy floral nuances of citrus and a faint ginger undertone. It is sold fresh (best choice, of course), frozen (next best), in dried slices (these will do in a pinch if you soak them in hot water for several hours), or powdered (don't bother), and is available at Asian markets, some specialty food shops, and the occasional large supermarket. The long, dryish, fibrous stalks have a long bulblike root end, making them look like giant gray-green scallions. If you buy them fresh, you'll find them trimmed to around 6 to 8 inches above the bulbous root end.

Look for firm, greenish stalks that don't feel too light when hefted in your hand. Before using, trim off the roots and remove the tough, fibrous outer layer of each stalk. The stalks can be used whole, cut diagonally into chunks, or thinly sliced, depending on the dish. With whole or chunked lemongrass, use the blunt edge of a heavy knife to bruise the stalk and release the essential oils. This is unnecessary for thinly sliced pieces.

To store, set the stalks upright in a container with an inch of cold water or wrap them tightly in plastic wrap and refrigerate for up to 2 weeks. The stalks can also be cut into 2- or 3-inch pieces and frozen for up to a year.

4. When you're ready to serve, transfer the seafood to a shallow serving bowl. Add the crabmeat. Whisk the dressing to reblend, then strain if desired and pour over the seafood. Toss gently but thoroughly to mix, then taste and adjust the seasoning. Garnish with the cucumber, red onion, and fresh cilantro or mint leaves and serve immediately.

Note: If you won't be serving right away, cover the seafood with plastic wrap once it's cool. The seafood may be prepared up to to 24 hours ahead of time.

Lemongrass Court Bouillon

A court bouillon is an aromatic, delicately flavored poaching liquid used to enhance the flavor and color of seafood, meats, or vegetables. This one is perfumed with lemongrass, making it a good choice for poaching seafood that will be served chilled. **MAKES ABOUT 8 CUPS**

8 cups water
3 stalks lemongrass, trimmed and thinly sliced
Juice of 2 limes
3 tablespoons coarse (kosher) salt

Combine the water, lemongrass, lime juice, and salt in a medium-size, nonreactive saucepan. Bring to a boil over high heat, then reduce the heat to maintain a gentle simmer. Simmer, uncovered, for 30 minutes. Remove the pan from the heat and strain the court bouillon. Use immediately or cool and refrigerate, covered, for up to 1 week, or freeze for up to 3 months.

Crispy Cod Cakes

Making these cod cakes is not a spur-of-the-moment proposition: They're made with salt cod, and salt cod needs to be soaked for 24 hours before using. The flavor and denser texture that salt cod adds, however, make the wait **worthwhile**. Look for salt cod at Hispanic or Italian markets and some specialty food stores.

Serve the cod cakes with a bowl of Rémoulade (page 366).

MAKES SIXTEEN 3-INCH CAKES; SERVES 6 TO 8

2 pounds salt cod
1½ pounds russet potatoes, peeled
¼ cup sour cream
3 cups fresh bread crumbs (see box, page 279)
4 large eggs, lightly beaten
1 medium onion, coarsely chopped
4 cloves garlic, minced
1 bunch scallions, white and green parts, trimmed and thinly sliced
Juice of 2 lemons
5 tablespoons Worcestershire sauce
1 tablespoon Tabasco sauce
1 tablespoon Old Bay Seasoning
½ cup chopped fresh flat-leaf parsley leaves
Coarse (kosher) salt and freshly ground black pepper, to taste
2 cups all-purpose flour
1 cup cornmeal
Canola or other vegetable oil, for frying

1. Place the salt cod in a large bowl and add cold water to cover. Cover the bowl and soak the cod in the refrigerator for 24 hours, changing the water four times during the soaking.

2. Drain the cod, place it in a large stockpot, cover with fresh cold water, and bring to a boil over high heat. Reduce the heat and simmer the cod until it flakes easily with a fork, 15 minutes. Remove the cod from the pot with a slotted spoon and set aside to cool.

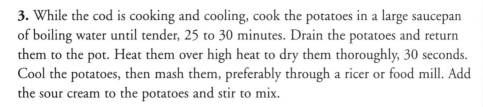

3. While the cod is cooking and cooling, cook the potatoes in a large saucepan of boiling water until tender, 25 to 30 minutes. Drain the potatoes and return them to the pot. Heat them over high heat to dry them thoroughly, 30 seconds. Cool the potatoes, then mash them, preferably through a ricer or food mill. Add the sour cream to the potatoes and stir to mix.

4. Crumble the cod into small flakes in a large bowl using your fingers or a fork. Add the potatoes and bread crumbs and mix until well blended. Mix in the eggs, onion, garlic, scallions, lemon juice, Worcestershire sauce, Tabasco, and Old Bay Seasoning. Stir in the chopped parsley and salt and pepper to taste. Form the cod mixture into cakes about 3 inches around and 1 inch thick.

5. Mix the flour and cornmeal together in a large, shallow bowl. Dip the cod cakes in the flour mixture to coat lightly, shaking off any excess.

6. Pour oil to a depth of ½ inch into a large skillet and heat over medium-high heat. Fry the cakes until crispy brown on both sides, about 3 minutes per side. You'll have to do this in batches, being sure not to crowd the pan. As they are done, remove the patties to paper towels to drain. Serve immediately.

salt cod

Dried salt-preserved cod is a staple in a number of traditional Mediterranean recipes, the most famous of which is *brandade de morue,* a specialty of Provence. Sometimes the fish is dried on the bone, but more commonly in the United States you'll find boneless and skinless fillets.

Look in ethnic markets for fish fillets that are white (gray is a sign of age) and of uniform thickness. In Italian salt cod is called *baccalà,* in Spanish *bacalao,* and in Portuguese *bacalhau.*

Before salt cod is used in a recipe, it must first be soaked to soften it and to remove the saltiness. To do this, cut the cod into a few largish pieces, arrange in a large, nonreactive glass or ceramic bowl, and cover completely with cold water. Place the bowl in the refrigerator and let the cod soak for a minimum of 24 hours, changing the water at least four or five times. The cod is ready to use when the water no longer tastes salty. Rinse under cold running water, drain well in a colander or sieve, and pat dry with paper towels before using. Check for bones before proceeding with a recipe.

Shrimp with Black Bean Sauce

The **dark and delicious** sauce in this recipe is a snap to prepare if you keep a few basic Asian ingredients, such as Thai fish sauce and Chinese fermented black beans, in your pantry. And don't reserve the sauce exclusively for shrimp. It matches up well with sautéed or steamed fish fillets; bass, grouper, cod, scrod, and snapper all take to it. For a luxurious treat, briefly sauté chunks of cooked lobster (figure on ¼ pound per person) in very hot oil, then toss with the sauce. **SERVES 6 TO 8**

½ cup canola or other vegetable oil
2½ pounds shelled and deveined medium shrimp
2 cloves garlic, minced
2 tablespoons grated fresh ginger
2 bunches scallions, white and green parts, trimmed,
    1 bunch finely chopped, 1 bunch cut into ½-inch pieces
¼ teaspoon hot red pepper flakes
2 tablespoons dry sherry
2 cups Chicken Stock (page 39) or canned low-sodium
    chicken broth
1½ tablespoons good-quality soy sauce, such as Kikkoman
1 tablespoon Thai fish sauce (nam pla)
¼ cup Chinese fermented black beans (do not rinse)
1 red bell pepper, stemmed, seeded, and cut into ⅛-inch-wide strips
1 small onion, cut lengthwise (stem to root) into ⅛-inch strips
1 tablespoon rice vinegar
Pinch of sugar
1½ teaspoons cornstarch
2 tablespoons cold water

1. Heat a large skillet or wok over high heat. When it's very hot (a drop of water sizzles rapidly on contact), add enough of the oil to coat the bottom of the pan

Staff Meals from Chanterelle | seafood

(about 2 tablespoons). Stir-fry the shrimp in batches until just cooked through, about 3 minutes per batch. As the shrimp are done, scoop them out of the skillet and set aside.

2. Wipe out the pan and return it to high heat. Add another 2 tablespoons of the oil and, when it's hot, add the garlic, ginger, chopped scallions, and pepper flakes and sauté until aromatic but not browned, about 1 minute. Add the sherry and boil for 30 seconds. Add the chicken stock, soy sauce, fish sauce, and black beans. Bring to a boil, then add the bell pepper, onion, vinegar, and sugar. Cook at a rapid boil for 3 minutes.

3. Whisk the cornstarch with the water to blend. When smooth, whisk it into the sauce in the skillet. Continue whisking until the sauce returns to a boil and thickens slightly, 2 minutes.

4. Remove the skillet from the heat, stir in the scallion pieces and the shrimp, and return the skillet to the heat. Cook until just heated through and serve.

thailand's soy sauce

Fish sauce, a universal flavoring in Southeast Asian cooking, is called *nuoc mam* in Vietnam, *tuk trey* in Cambodia, and *nam pla* in Thailand. At Chanterelle our straightforward staff simply calls it "rotten fish sauce." It's made from the liquid exuded from salted anchovies that have been left to ferment for several months. Enormously concentrated in flavor, this translucent, pale brown sauce smells awful, but don't let that stop you. The flavor becomes less powerful, even somewhat delicate, when combined with other ingredients. *Nam pla* is used in small amounts to round out the taste of Thai marinades, soups, stir-fries, and dipping sauces. It's available in Asian markets and specialty food stores. In my experience the best *nam pla* comes in glass bottles. These cost slightly more but are less salty and stay fresher longer than those in plastic. Good brands to look for include the Thai Fishsauce Company's Squid brand (my favorite), Dek, Tiparos, Ruang Tong, and Viêt Huong's Three Crabs brand. Tightly capped, *nam pla* can be stored indefinitely in a cool, dark cupboard.

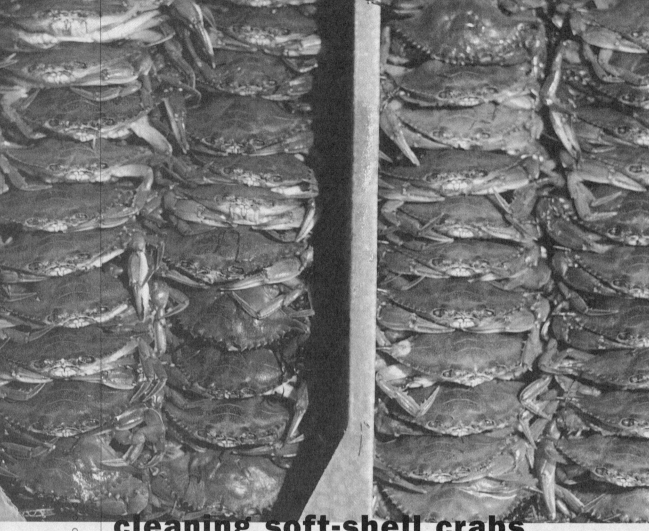

cleaning soft-shell crabs

It's best to clean soft-shell crabs as close to cooking time as possible. To prepare a live crab, place it top-side up on your work surface. Using kitchen shears, cut off the crab's face right behind the eyes; this will kill it. Right behind where the mouth was, you will find a little bubblelike sac; pull it out and discard it.

Turn the crab upside down. You will see a tail flap, called the apron; cut it off with the shears.

One at a time, fold back each pointed side of the top shell so the gills are exposed; remove and discard the gills.

Continue as directed for all your remaining crabs. Once all have been cleaned, they're ready to be cooked according to your recipe. If you aren't continuing with the recipe immediately, wrap the crabs in plastic wrap or waxed paper and refrigerate until cooking time.

Sautéed Soft-Shell Crabs with Sorrel Butter

Soft-shell crabs are blue crabs that have molted their shells and are on the verge of growing new ones. The season for this East Coast specialty is from May through August, and during that time I always put them on the menu at Chanterelle. They are a bit pricey for the usual staff meal, but we've found that we need to have a soft-shell crab dinner at least once a year as a well-deserved treat. Aside from enjoying them deep-fried and served on a bun with hot sauce (the best way, no question), we also like them sautéed and accompanied by this refined, tart, and lemony sorrel sauce. Be sure the crabs are alive when you buy them. Cleaning them is a simple-enough task but if you're the least bit squeamish have the fishmonger clean them for you. Once this is done, they must be eaten within 24 hours. A word of caution: When sautéing, use a splatter guard to prevent the sputtering crabs from spitting hot oil at you, or be prepared to duck! **SERVES 4**

8 live soft-shell crabs

¼ cup white wine vinegar

¼ cup dry white wine

2 shallots, minced

3 tablespoons heavy (or whipping) cream

4 ounces sorrel, stemmed, rinsed, and dried

1 cup (2 sticks) unsalted butter, cut into small pieces, chilled

Coarse (kosher) salt and freshly ground black pepper, to taste

Fresh lemon juice, to taste

1 cup all-purpose flour, or more if needed, for coating

Canola or other vegetable oil, for frying

1. Have the crabs cleaned by your fishmonger, or clean them yourself (see box, page 242). Rinse under cold running water and pat dry with paper towels.

2. Combine the vinegar, wine, and shallots in a small, heavy, nonreactive saucepan and bring to a boil over high heat. Cook, stirring frequently, until the liquid is reduced to about 2 tablespoons, about 5 minutes. Watch carefully to keep the reduction from burning.

3. Add the cream and sorrel to the pan and cook, stirring frequently, until the sorrel is reduced almost to a purée and the cream has thickened, about 2 minutes. (It will have an almost mushlike consistency.) Reduce the heat to low and whisk in the butter, bit by bit, adding the next bit as the previous one has been emulsified into the sauce. Keep checking the temperature of the sauce. It should stay very warm, almost but not quite hot; nor should it get too cool. To accomplish this, move the pan on and off the heat, as necessary. When all the butter has been incorporated, season with salt, pepper, and lemon juice, then set aside, covered, to keep warm while you cook the crabs.

4. Preheat the oven to its lowest setting. Line a baking sheet with several layers of paper towels.

5. Spread about 1 cup of the flour on a plate. Dip each crab in the flour to coat on both sides, shaking off any excess, and place on a platter or baking sheet while you heat the oil.

6. Pour oil to a depth of ¼ inch into a large, heavy skillet and heat over high heat. It should be hot enough so a sprinkle of flour sizzles on contact. Add half the crabs, arranging them with tongs so they're in their natural position. Sprinkle lightly with salt, place a splatter guard (if you have one) over the skillet, and reduce the heat to medium high. Sauté the crabs until they're a golden reddish brown, about 2 minutes per side. Transfer the crabs to the prepared baking sheet and keep warm in the oven while you sauté the remaining crabs.

7. Ladle about ¼ cup sauce on each of four serving plates and arrange 2 crabs over each portion of sauce. Serve immediately.

Staff Meals from Chanterelle | seafood

Deviled Crab Cakes

The seasonings in these crab cakes give them a **little kick** that enhances the natural sweetness of the crabmeat. This is a handy double-duty recipe from which you can make 3-inch crab cake patties to serve as a main course or bite-size ones suitable as an hors d'oeuvre (this recipe would make about 50 tiny cakes). The patties can be frozen, then thawed before frying. Serve the crab cakes simply, with just lemon wedges, a dollop of Rémoulade (page 366), Kitchen Cupboard Tartar Sauce (page 367) or Curried Mayonnaise (page 361), and some of Our Favorite Fries (page 327). **MAKES FOUR 3-INCH CAKES; SERVES 4**

1 pound lump crabmeat

1 large egg

½ cup fine dry bread crumbs (see box, page 279)

¼ cup good-quality store-bought mayonnaise, such as Hellmann's

¼ cup thinly sliced scallions, white and green parts

1 heaping tablespoon Dijon mustard

1 teaspoon sweet Hungarian paprika

1½ teaspoons Tabasco sauce

1 clove garlic, minced

Fresh lemon juice, to taste

Coarse (kosher) salt and freshly ground black pepper, to taste

1 cup all-purpose flour, or more if needed, for coating

2 to 3 tablespoons canola or other vegetable oil

1. Pick over the crabmeat to remove any cartilage or stray bits of shell, but try not to break it up too much. Combine the crab in a bowl with the egg, bread crumbs, mayonnaise, scallions, mustard, paprika, Tabasco, garlic, lemon juice, salt, and pepper. Using your hands or a wooden spoon, mix thoroughly, but again, try not to break up the lumps of crab.

2. Form the mixture into four 3-inch patties. Spread 1 cup flour on a plate and dip the patties, one at a time, in it to coat on both sides, shaking off any excess.

3. Heat 2 tablespoons of the oil in a large, heavy skillet over medium heat; it should be hot enough so a sprinkle of flour sizzles on contact. Add the crab cakes and sauté until golden brown on both sides and heated through, about 3 minutes per side. If the crab cakes seem to be sticking to the pan, add more oil.

4. Using a slotted spatula, transfer the crab cakes to a platter or individual plates and serve immediately.

Crab Cakes with Asian Flavors

This less traditional, somewhat more exotic crab cake recipe incorporates plenty of Asian seasonings. As with the Deviled Crab Cakes (page 245), these too can be frozen, then thawed before frying. Serve the crab cakes with wedges of lime or Curried Mayonnaise (page 361); Cucumber Salad with Red Onion and Chinese Sausage (page 314) makes an unusual accompaniment.

These crab cakes also work well as an hors d'oeuvre; the recipe yields about 50 tiny cakes. **MAKES FOUR 3-INCH CAKES; SERVES 4**

1 pound lump crabmeat

2 large eggs

¾ cup fine dry bread crumbs (see box, page 279)

½ cup thinly sliced scallions, white and green parts

2 tablespoons good-quality soy sauce,
  such as Kikkoman

1 tablespoon Thai fish sauce (nam pla)

2 teaspoons Chinese chili sauce

1½ teaspoons grated fresh ginger

1 large clove garlic, minced

Fresh lime juice, to taste

Coarse (kosher) salt and freshly ground black pepper,
to taste

1 cup all-purpose flour, or more if needed, for coating

2 to 3 tablespoons canola or other vegetable oil

1. Pick over the crabmeat to remove any cartilage or stray bits of shell, but try not to break it up too much. Combine the crab in a bowl with the eggs, bread crumbs, scallions, soy sauce, fish sauce, chili sauce, ginger, garlic, lime juice, salt, and pepper. Using your hands or a wooden spoon, mix thoroughly, but again, try not to break up the lumps of crab.

2. Form the mixture into four 3-inch patties. Spread 1 cup flour on a plate and dip the patties, one at a time, in it to coat on both sides, shaking off any excess.

3. Heat 2 tablespoons of the oil in a large, heavy skillet over medium heat; it should be hot enough so a sprinkle of flour sizzles on contact. Add the crab cakes and sauté until golden brown on both sides and heated through, about 3 minutes per side. If the crab cakes seem to be sticking to the pan, add more oil.

4. Using a slotted spatula, transfer the crab cakes to a platter or individual plates and serve immediately.

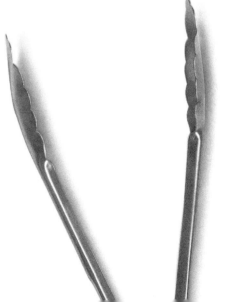

Squid Stew

This **versatile stew** is an opportunity to enjoy squid at its best, slowly cooked to perfection until it's soft and flavorful. The key to success here is understanding that squid must be either cooked very quickly, for only 2 or 3 minutes, or simmered very slowly for at least 45 minutes. There is no in-between. After the first few minutes of exposure to heat squid goes from supple to tough, chewy, and rubbery and does not relax and regain its suppleness until it has cooked for at least half an hour.

As a variation, I sometimes substitute ½ cup Pernod for half the dry white wine and add ½ cup pitted olives along with the vegetables. You might also enjoy it using a combination of scallops and squid. Serve the stew with plain rice or orzo. **SERVES 4 TO 6**

¼ cup extra-virgin olive oil

2 medium onions, coarsely chopped

4 large cloves garlic, coarsely chopped or thinly sliced

¼ teaspoon saffron threads (see box, page 174)

1 cup dry white wine

2 cups canned whole tomatoes, drained, seeded, and coarsely
   chopped (about 1 cup)

2 cups Fish Stock (page 41)

½ teaspoon dried thyme leaves

½ teaspoon dried oregano leaves

½ teaspoon hot red pepper flakes, or to taste

3 pounds cleaned fresh squid (see box, facing page), bodies cut into
   ¼-inch rings and tentacles cut lengthwise in half if large (see Note)

½ cup frozen peas (no need to thaw)

1 medium zucchini, sliced lengthwise in half, then cut crosswise
   into ¼-inch slices

2 medium carrots, peeled and cut into ¼-inch rounds

2 tablespoons unsalted butter

Coarse (kosher) salt, to taste

Fresh lemon juice, to taste

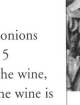

1. Heat the oil in a medium-size saucepan over medium heat. Add the onions and garlic and cook, stirring, until translucent but not browned, about 5 minutes. Add the saffron and cook, stirring, for 3 minutes more. Add the wine, increase the heat to high, and bring to a boil. Cook, uncovered, until the wine is reduced by half, about 5 minutes.

2. Add the tomatoes, fish stock, thyme, oregano, and pepper flakes and bring to a boil. Add the squid, then reduce the heat to low and simmer, uncovered, for 20 minutes. The squid will release liquid, making the mixture nice and saucy. Add the peas, zucchini, and carrots and simmer until the squid is quite tender, about 10 minutes more.

3. Remove the pan from the heat and stir in the butter. Season with salt and lemon juice and serve immediately.

Note: If fresh squid is not available, use 3 pounds thawed frozen squid that has already been cleaned, but not cut into rings.

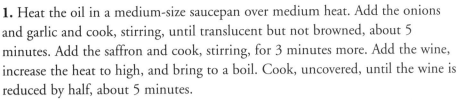

how to clean squid

Pull the head and attached tentacles from the tubelike body of the squid. As you do this, most of the innards will automatically disengage from the inside of the body and come away with the head and tentacles. With a sharp knife, cut off the tentacles just in front of the eyes. Discard the head and innards; reserve the tentacles for use in your recipe, if called for.

If you'll be using the tentacles, fold them back and, using your thumb and forefinger, gently squeeze out the beak (a small piece of cartilage).

To clean out the body, grasp the exposed end of the long, thin, transparent quill-like piece of cartilage, pull it out, and discard. Peel off as much of the skin from the body as possible; most, though not all, will come off. (Doing this under cold running water will help.) Thoroughly rinse the body, inside and out, under cold running water, pulling out and discarding any matter that has remained inside.

Leave the body whole or cut it into rings, depending on the recipe.

Clams in Black Bean Sauce

The **combination** of briny clams and salty fermented black beans is a classic one in Cantonese cooking. Try to use tiny sweet Manila clams or cockles; if these are unavailable, substitute the smallest littleneck clams you can find. Some recipes call for rinsing or chopping the black beans, but I leave them whole, balancing their pronounced, appealing saltiness with other seasonings. In fact, it is this salinity, along with the beans' rustically strong, almost musty flavor, that makes this dish so special. I like the sauce to have a noticeably spicy edge to it, so I use plenty of hot red pepper flakes, but you may prefer to use less for a milder flavor. **SERVES 4**

3 pounds small clams in the shell, preferably Manila
    or cockles
1¼ cup Chicken Stock (page 39), canned low-sodium
    chicken broth, or water
1 tablespoon cornstarch
1 tablespoon oyster sauce
1 tablespoon good-quality soy sauce,
    such as Kikkoman
2 teaspoons sugar
2 tablespoons canola or other vegetable oil
2 large cloves garlic, minced
1 tablespoon grated fresh ginger
2 bunches scallions, trimmed, white parts finely chopped and
    green parts cut separately into ½-inch lengths
3 tablespoons Chinese fermented black beans
¼ to ½ teaspoon hot red pepper flakes, to taste
2 teaspoons dry sherry
1 teaspoon Asian sesame oil

1. Using a stiff brush, scrub the clams under cold running water. Rinse them well in a colander and set aside.

2. Place the chicken stock, cornstarch, oyster sauce, soy sauce, and sugar in a bowl and stir until the cornstarch and sugar are dissolved. Set aside.

3. Set a wok or large skillet over high heat and add the oil, swirling it around to coat as much surface as possible. When a drop of water sizzles rapidly on contact with the oil, add the garlic, ginger, and scallion whites and stir-fry until aromatic but not browned, about 1 minute.

4. Add the black beans and pepper flakes and stir until aromatic, about 30 seconds. Add the sherry and cook, stirring, for 10 seconds. Add the clams, then the chicken stock mixture, giving the mixture a stir before pouring it in. Give the clams a good stir, then cover and cook, shaking the wok occasionally, until most of the clams are opened, about 5 minutes.

5. Add the scallion greens and sesame oil and cook until all the clams have opened, the sauce is lightly thickened, and everything looks beautiful, 1 minute more.

6. Turn the clams and sauce out onto a platter or into a shallow serving bowl, discarding any that didn't open. Serve immediately.

Pasta

Like most busy families, the Chanterelle family eats prodigious quantities of pasta and noodles of all kinds. They're filling, inexpensive, easy to make, and give us plenty of energy for the physically challenging work in a professional kitchen. We *need* to stoke up on carbohydrates, and there's something especially satisfying and elemental about pasta in particular. And, of course, children love it, too.

The recipes in this chapter are culled from my repertoire of the reliable, good-to-eat pasta, and almost pasta, dishes that have appeared repeatedly at our staff meals over the years—and are still enjoyed. They never fail to please, in part because they're based on flexible ingredients, ones that cut a wide swath across numerous culinary cultures. We're just as likely to feast on fragrant bowls of Thai Rice Noodles (page 284) or Singapore-Style Curried Rice Noodles (page 289) as we are to sit down to a heaping plate of Spaghetti with Potatoes and Greens (page 260), a comforting serving of old-fashioned Macaroni and Two Cheeses (page 265), or some generously cut slices of homemade Eggplant Pizza (page 297) with a green salad.

Some of the recipes are especially handy when time is short. Every smart cook should keep a supply of tortellini, ravioli, and Tasty Basic Tomato Sauce (page 271) in the freezer, and a variety of dried pastas on hand. When we've had an unusually hectic day in the kitchen at Chanterelle and time is short, that's when I whip together Ravioli with Parmesan, Butter, and Herbs (page 277) or Cheese Tortellini with Cream, Peas, and Ham (page 276).

Staff Meals from Chanterelle | pasta

Linguine Puttanesca

This robust, piquant linguine dish is for **olive lovers** only. It is, in fact, known affectionately as "salty pasta" among members of our staff, who do indeed love it. Moroccan oil-cured olives are terrific here, but you can also use a combination of good-quality brine-cured black and green olives. **SERVES 6**

⅓ cup coarse (kosher) salt, for cooking the pasta
1½ packages (16 ounces each) linguine
¼ cup olive oil
2 tablespoons unsalted butter
12 anchovy fillets packed in oil, drained but not rinsed, then mashed
2 cups olives, preferably Moroccan oil-cured olives,
    pitted and coarsely chopped
1 cup sun-dried tomatoes packed in oil, drained and coarsely chopped
¾ cup small (nonpareil) capers, rinsed, if desired, and drained
6 large cloves garlic, minced
2 teaspoons hot red pepper flakes
3 tablespoons red wine vinegar

1. Bring a very large stockpot of water and ⅓ cup salt to a boil over high heat.

2. When the water is boiling, add the linguine and cook, stirring frequently, until al dente, 8 to 10 minutes. Drain the linguine and allow it to cool slightly before continuing.

3. In a nonreactive, heavy skillet large enough to hold the pasta, heat the oil over medium-high heat. Add the butter and anchovies and cook, stirring frequently, until the butter is melted and the anchovies are beginning to soften, about 1 minute. Add the olives, sun-dried tomatoes, capers, garlic, and pepper flakes and sauté, stirring frequently, until just heated through, about 1 minute more.

4. Add the linguine to the mixture in the skillet and toss thoroughly to mix. Remove from the heat, add the vinegar, and toss again. Serve immediately, directly from the skillet.

Spaghetti with Mussels, Tomatoes, and Cream

Although any mussels would be just fine for this pasta dish, I like to use the small Prince Edward Island ones because I feel they always taste a little better than the others. The same **aromatic mixture** of white wine, shallots, and garlic that's used for steaming the mussels becomes the basis for the sauce here. Combined over high heat with the tomatoes and cream, it thickens luxuriously into a rich, mellow-tasting sauce with a hint of sweetness that perfectly complements the mussels.

SERVES 6

5 pounds mussels
4 cups dry white wine
2 large shallots, chopped
2 large cloves garlic, minced
2 cups drained, roughly chopped canned plum tomatoes
4 cups heavy (or whipping) cream
Coarse (kosher) salt
1 package (16 ounces) spaghetti or linguine
Fresh lemon juice, to taste
Freshly ground black pepper, to taste
¼ cup coarsely chopped fresh basil leaves

1. Soak, scrub, and debeard the mussels (see box, page 19).

2. Place the mussels in a large, nonreactive stockpot and add the wine, shallots, and garlic, then cover and bring to a boil over high heat. Steam the mussels until they open, 5 to 8 minutes, shaking the pot occasionally to redistribute the mussels as they steam. (Do not steam for more than 8 minutes, or the mussels will be tough.)

3. Using a slotted spoon, transfer the mussels to a large bowl, discarding any that haven't opened. When they're cool enough to handle, remove the meat from the shells, discarding the shells.

4. Pour the mussel cooking liquid through a strainer lined with a double layer of dampened cheesecloth into a medium-size, nonreactive saucepan. Bring to a boil over high heat. Add the tomatoes and cream and return to a boil, then cook, uncovered, until the mixture is reduced and thick enough to coat the back of a spoon, about 15 to 20 minutes.

5. While the sauce is reducing, bring a large stockpot of water and ¼ cup salt to a boil over high heat.

6. Add the spaghetti or linguine to the boiling salted water and cook, stirring frequently, until al dente, 8 to 10 minutes.

7. When the sauce is the proper consistency, remove it from the heat and season with lemon juice and salt and pepper. Set aside, covered, to keep warm.

8. Drain the pasta thoroughly, then transfer it to a large serving bowl. Add the reserved mussels, the sauce, and basil and toss thoroughly to mix. Serve immediately.

Linguine with Clam Sauce

I like a **robust and garlicky** clam sauce, one with a deep taste of the sea and lots of up-front brininess. Adding anchovies to the sauce enhances and adds depth to the other flavors, along with some saltiness, but doesn't result in an assertive anchovy flavor per se. (Anchovy haters should trust me about this, though I doubt they will.) Serve this pasta with a simple salad and a loaf of crusty Italian bread for sopping up the garlicky, slightly

lemony, clam-laden sauce. Whisking butter into the finished sauce may seem unusual, but it very neatly rounds off and unifies the flavors. **SERVES 6**

⅓ cup coarse (kosher) salt, for cooking the pasta
2 dozen cherrystone or other hard-shell clams
1 cup dry white wine
¼ cup extra-virgin olive oil
10 cloves garlic, thinly sliced
6 to 7 anchovy fillets packed in oil, drained but not rinsed
1 cup Chicken Stock (page 39) or canned low-sodium
   chicken broth
Juice of ½ lemon, or more to taste
1 cup (2 sticks) unsalted butter, cut into small pieces
1 package (16 ounces) linguine
1 bunch flat-leaf parsley, stemmed, leaves coarsely chopped

1. Bring a very large stockpot of water and ⅓ cup coarse (kosher) salt to a boil over high heat.

2. Meanwhile, using a stiff brush, scrub the clams well under cold running water. Rinse well in a colander, then place in a large, nonreactive saucepan or Dutch oven and add the white wine. Cover and set over medium-high heat. Steam, shaking the pan occasionally, until the clams open. Start checking after 5 minutes, removing the first-opened clams (they will not all open at the same time) to a bowl. Re-cover the pan, give it a shake, and continue to cook for another 5 to 8 minutes or so, checking every couple of minutes and transferring the clams to the bowl as they open. Clams that are reluctant to open may benefit from a smart rap on the shell with a big metal spoon; discard any that absolutely refuse to cooperate.

3. After all the clams are in the bowl, let them stand until they're cool enough to handle. Meanwhile, strain the clam broth through a sieve lined with a double thickness of dampened cheesecloth and set aside. When the clams are cool enough, remove their meat from the shells, discarding the shells, and chop coarsely. Set aside.

4. Heat the oil in a large, heavy skillet over medium heat. When it's hot but not smoking, add the sliced garlic and 6 of the anchovies and cook, stirring, until the garlic is lightly browned and the anchovies are falling apart, about 3 minutes. Add the chicken stock and reserved clam broth and bring to a boil. Cook, uncovered, until the anchovies have dissolved and the liquid is reduced by half, about 15 to 20 minutes. Remove the skillet from the heat and add the lemon juice, then whisk in the butter, a few pieces at a time, until completely incorporated. Set aside, covered, to keep warm.

5. Add the linguine to the boiling salted water and cook, stirring frequently, until al dente, 8 to 10 minutes. Drain thoroughly, then transfer to a large serving bowl.

6. Taste the sauce for seasoning, adding more lemon juice and a little chopped-up anchovy if necessary. Add the clams and set over low heat just until the clams are heated through, about 1 minute more. Remove the sauce from the heat, stir in the parsley, and pour over the linguine. Toss thoroughly and serve.

cooking pasta

The most important thing to understand about cooking pasta is that you need to use plenty of salted water. And when I say "salted," I mean *salted!* The water needs to actually taste salty to bring out the flavor of pasta. To cook 1 pound dried pasta, bring at least 6 quarts water and ¼ cup coarse (kosher) salt to a rolling boil. Add the pasta and stir gently. Many people believe that adding oil to the cooking water prevents sticking, but it doesn't. Stirring well and frequently, on the other hand, *will* prevent the pasta from sticking together.

How long to cook pasta is another story. In the recipes here I give directions for cooking pasta al dente with approximate times. But the actual cooking time will vary depending on factors such as the brand and the thickness or shape of the pasta. To be safe, test the pasta occasionally as it cooks. Bite into a piece, and when it feels right—chewable and firm to the teeth—it's done and ready to be drained. A final hint: If the pasta is to be used in a brothy medium or will be baked for a longer time with a sauce, slightly under-cook it, since the time spent in the broth or the oven will act as a second cooking and further soften it.

Spaghetti with Potatoes and Greens

Many people find broccoli rabe too bitter, but I'm very partial to its **feisty flavor** and mustardlike bite. The bitterness provides a lively contrast to the mellow starchiness of pasta and potatoes in this rustic, southern-Italian-style pasta dish. For a less aggressively flavored version, substitute somewhat milder escarole for the broccoli rabe.

You'll want to be in assembly-line mode for this recipe. First, fill two saucepans or stockpots with salted water—one for the pasta, the other for the potatoes—and set them to boil over high heat. While the water is heating, prep the ingredients and set them out on a counter near the stove. Once the pasta and potatoes are cooking, start sautéing the other ingredients. Take care not to overcook the potatoes or the broccoli rabe, which should be tender but still quite crisp. Serve for lunch or a late supper accompanied by a tomato and onion salad and a simple dessert. **SERVES 6**

Staff Meals from Chanterelle | pasta

Coarse (kosher) salt
1½ pounds broccoli rabe or escarole
6 medium waxy potatoes, such as Yukon Gold
1 package (16 ounces) spaghetti or linguine
1 cup extra-virgin olive oil
10 large cloves garlic, thinly sliced
6 anchovy fillets packed in oil, undrained
½ teaspoon hot red pepper flakes
Juice of ½ lemon
Freshly grated Parmesan, for serving

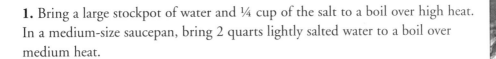

1. Bring a large stockpot of water and ¼ cup of the salt to a boil over high heat. In a medium-size saucepan, bring 2 quarts lightly salted water to a boil over medium heat.

2. Meanwhile, trim about 2 inches off the stem end of the broccoli rabe and discard. Rinse the broccoli rabe under cold running water, then drain and pat dry with paper towels or whirl dry in a salad spinner. Cut the greens into 1-inch pieces, including the remaining stems and flowerlike buds of the broccoli rabe. Set aside.

3. Add the potatoes to the boiling water in the saucepan and cook, uncovered, until tender but not falling apart, about 12 minutes. Drain and set aside. When cool enough to handle, peel and cut into ½-inch dice.

4. Add the spaghetti to the boiling salted water in the stockpot and cook, stirring frequently, until al dente, 8 to 10 minutes.

5. Meanwhile, heat the oil in a large, deep skillet over medium heat until hot but not yet smoking. Add the garlic and sauté, stirring, for about 1 minute until lightly browned, then add the anchovies and sauté, stirring, until the anchovies are falling apart, 1 to 2 minutes more. Add the pepper flakes and stir for 30 seconds.

6. Add the greens to the skillet and stir (carefully at first; the skillet will be full) until the greens are wilted and tender but still crisp, about 3 minutes for broccoli rabe, less for escarole. Remove the skillet from the heat and season with salt and a squeeze of lemon juice.

7. Drain the spaghetti thoroughly and transfer it to a large serving bowl. Add the potatoes and greens and toss thoroughly to mix. Taste for seasoning, adding more salt and lemon juice if necessary. Toss again, then serve immediately, accompanied by grated Parmesan.

Sautéed Penne with Cauliflower and Chickpeas

This **easy technique** for making toasty-tasting sautéed pasta will open the door to endless creative possibilities. The results are always fast and flavorful. If you can, buy some *merguez* or other lamb sausage to slice, sauté, and add to the other ingredients in the basic version of the recipe. If that doesn't suit you, perhaps adding sautéed red bell peppers, small cooked shrimp, and artichoke hearts will have appeal.

The technique is adaptable on every level. You can tailor the recipe to suit yourself—varying the shape of the pasta, the vegetables, seasonings, type of meat or seafood—while using up those miscellaneous ingredients lying around in the refrigerator.

SERVES 4

Coarse (kosher) salt
2 cups cauliflower florets
1 package (16 ounces) penne
3 tablespoons olive oil
1 can (12 ounces) chickpeas, rinsed and drained
2 cloves garlic, minced
½ teaspoon hot red pepper flakes
Fresh lemon juice, to taste

1. Bring a large stockpot of water and ¼ cup of the salt to a boil over high heat. In a medium-size saucepan, bring 1½ quarts water and 2 teaspoons of the salt to a boil.

2. When the water in the saucepan is boiling, add the cauliflower florets and

Staff Meals from Chanterelle | pasta

blanch until just tender but still crunchy, about 3 minutes. Drain well and set aside.

3. When the water in the stockpot is boiling, add the penne and cook, stirring frequently, until al dente, 8 to 10 minutes. Drain the penne and rinse briefly but thoroughly under cold running water. Drain again.

4. Heat the oil in a large, deep, heavy skillet over medium-high heat. Add the cooked penne and sauté for 1 minute, tossing. Add the chickpeas and reserved cauliflower florets and sauté, tossing frequently, until the ingredients are lightly browned, 3 to 4 minutes. Add the garlic and pepper flakes and continue sautéing just until the garlic is fragrant, about 30 seconds; be careful not to let the garlic burn. Remove the skillet from the heat and season with salt and a good squeeze of lemon juice. Toss once more and serve immediately, directly from the skillet.

pasta shapes

Although it's believed there are anywhere from several hundred to nearly a thousand pasta shapes in Italy, in real life most of us have far fewer choices—although those choices seem to be growing weekly. What you may not know is that there is a method for matching a pasta with its most compatible type of sauce. Some shapes, like that of fusilli, are designed to hold a lot of sauce, so you'll want to consider that when choosing. Bow ties (farfalle), which don't have many nooks and crannies, are great for sautéed dishes, where you want a little oil to cling to the pasta. Narrower, more delicate pastas such as angel-hair or thin spaghetti are complemented by light, thin sauces that will coat each strand without weighing too heavily or causing clumping. Fettuccine, egg noodles, and thicker types of spaghetti work best with tomato or cream sauces. Match rough-textured sauces that contain chunky ingredients like bits of meat or seafood with pastas that have ridges or holes or tunnels, such as rigatoni, radiatore, mostaccioli, ziti, fusilli, and penne. Versatile linguine is an appropriate choice for nearly any sauce. And we can't leave out the pastas kids like—whimsical cuts like wagon-wheel-shaped rotelle and alphabet shapes charm young appetites with any sauce.

Fried Ziti

This recipe was **inspired** by a pasta dish that Melicia discovered at Connie's, a small, old-fashioned Italian restaurant in Queens, New York. It's fast, easy, and a handy way to use up that pesky last dab of leftover tomato sauce. Connie didn't use olives in his, but since Melicia usually adds them to everything, olives naturally make an appearance here. Don't even think of using a good handmade, high-moisture mozzarella here. Supermarket mozzarella is what you want, because its low moisture quotient gives it just the right meltability factor. You'll need a skillet with a heat-resistant handle, since the pan is placed in the oven to give the pasta a last-minute roasting that heightens the flavors and makes the dish crunchy. Serve with a green salad and garlic bread.

SERVES 2

Coarse (kosher) salt
8 ounces ziti
2 tablespoons olive oil
1 cup sliced fresh cultivated white mushrooms
2 small cloves garlic, minced
¼ cup black olives, preferably Moroccan oil-cured
    or Kalamata, pitted and coarsely chopped
2 tablespoons tomato sauce
¼ teaspoon hot red pepper flakes
1 cup diced (½ inch) commercial mozzarella
3 scallions, white and green parts, trimmed and cut
    into ¼-inch slices
Fresh lemon juice, to taste

1. Preheat the oven to 400°F.

2. Bring a medium-size stockpot of water and 2 tablespoons of the salt to a boil over high heat.

3. When the water is boiling, add the ziti and cook, stirring frequently, until al dente, 8 to 10 minutes.

4. Meanwhile, heat the oil in a large, ovenproof skillet over medium-high heat. Add the mushrooms and sauté, stirring frequently, until lightly browned, about 5 minutes.

5. Drain the ziti and rinse briefly but thoroughly under cold running water. Drain again and add to the skillet with the mushrooms. Sauté, stirring frequently, over medium-high heat until the pasta begins to brown a bit, 3 to 5 minutes, then add the garlic and sauté just until fragrant, about 30 seconds; be careful not to let the garlic burn. Add the olives, tomato sauce, and pepper flakes and sauté for a minute or so more, tossing until all the ingredients are thoroughly mixed.

6. Remove the skillet from the heat and add the mozzarella, scallions, lemon juice, and salt to taste, tossing to mix. Place the skillet in the oven and bake, uncovered, until the cheese has melted and browned a bit, about 5 minutes.

7. Serve immediately, directly from the skillet.

Macaroni and Two Cheeses

Every family should have a mac-and-cheese recipe. At Chanterelle the staff and I like ours ultra-cheesy, ultra-creamy, and as rich as possible. Some cooks make theirs in a deep casserole, but I prefer to fix macaroni and cheese in a wider, shallower baking dish so there's plenty of the delightfully crusty top layer to go around. Serve this with a simple tomato salad on the side, or arrange some sliced tomatoes on top during the last 20 minutes of the baking time (the staff calls this the "fancy" version). **SERVES 6**

Coarse (kosher) salt

1 package (16 ounces) ridged elbow macaroni

3 cups heavy (or whipping) cream

2½ cups grated sharp yellow Cheddar cheese
 (about 10 ounces)

1 small onion, minced

1 small clove garlic, minced

1 teaspoon Dijon mustard

Dash of Worcestershire sauce

Dash of Tabasco sauce

Freshly ground black pepper, to taste

⅓ cup freshly grated Parmesan

⅓ cup fine dry bread crumbs (see box, page 279)

1. Preheat the oven to 400°F.

2. Bring a large stockpot of water and ¼ cup of the salt to a boil over high heat.

3. When the water is boiling, add the macaroni and cook, stirring occasionally, until flexible but very al dente, 5 to 6 minutes. Drain, then let the macaroni stand in the colander under cold running water until chilled. Drain again, then transfer to a medium-size baking dish or shallow casserole and set aside.

4. Bring the cream to a boil in a small, heavy saucepan over medium-high heat. Reduce the heat to low and stir in the grated Cheddar, onion, garlic, mustard, Worcestershire, Tabasco, pepper, and salt to taste. Stir over low heat just until the cheese is completely melted, then remove the pan from the heat and taste and adjust the seasoning; the flavor should be strong.

5. Pour the cheese sauce over the macaroni in the baking dish and stir thoroughly to coat. Sprinkle first the grated Parmesan, then the bread crumbs, over the mixture and bake until the sauce bubbles and the top is golden brown and crusty, 30 to 40 minutes. Let stand a minute or two before serving.

buying parmigiano-reggiano

Some foods are so uniquely and completely themselves that there should be no compromise about them in your kitchen—only the real thing will do. Parmigiano-Reggiano is a good example. In supermarkets and specialty food stores you'll see wedges of "Parmesan" made in the United States, South America, and even France. They're relatively inexpensive, but none come close to the complex, piquant flavor and delightfully grainy texture of Italy's most famous cheese.

In Italy the production areas and cheese-making methods for Parmigiano-Reggiano are strictly controlled by the government and overseen by a consortium of cheese makers. The enormous wheels of cheese must meet rigorous requirements before the sides of their golden rinds are stamped repeatedly with the words "Parmigiano-Reggiano." When shopping, look for this stamping; it's proof that you are buying authentic Parmigiano-Reggiano. Regardless of the size of the piece at the store, you should be able to see the lettering.

When you're shopping, look for cheese that's fresh in appearance with no white patina. If it's wrapped in plastic, the plastic should be clear, not cloudy, with no loose crumbs inside. Buy only as much as you're likely to use in a relatively short time. (Once the cheese is used up, don't toss out the rind; freeze it to use later as a soup seasoning.)

To store, wrap the cheese in a moistened piece of cheesecloth (or paper towel), then wrap it loosely in aluminum foil and keep in the special cheese or snacks compartment of the refrigerator, if yours has one, or in the vegetable compartment. Always allow Parmesan to reach room temperature before grating. A 4-ounce chunk yields approximately 1 cup of grated Parmesan.

Lasagne for a Crowd

I like this lasagne for the relative austerity of its ingredients. Unlike other, variations, it does not include Italian sausage, ground meat, or fried eggplant. It is, however, made with two delicious sauces. The béchamel is an authentic touch, since lasagne in Italy is traditionally made with it. For the tomato sauce, use Tasty Basic Tomato Sauce, Tomato-Porcini Sauce, or a good-quality commercial sauce. I use firm commercial mozzarella here because fresh mozzarella's higher water content would make the lasagne too watery and dilute the flavors.

Since this will serve at least a dozen people, you may want to divide the recipe between two pans, baking one to serve now and freezing the other for serving at another time. The frozen lasagne can be then baked unthawed, but in that case you'll have to add at least 30 minutes to the original cooking time. **SERVES 12 OR MORE**

Coarse (kosher) salt

4 tablespoons (½ stick) unsalted butter

2 tablespoons chopped shallots

¼ cup all-purpose flour

1½ cups milk

½ cup heavy (or whipping) cream

3 bay leaves

2 packages (16 ounces each) lasagne noodles

2 pounds fresh spinach

¼ cup olive oil

12 ounces fresh cultivated white mushrooms, wiped clean and sliced

Freshly ground black pepper, to taste

4 cups Tasty Basic Tomato Sauce (recipe follows), Tomato-Porcini
  Sauce (page 273), or good-quality commercial tomato sauce

1 pound Parmesan, grated (about 4 cups)

2 pounds commercial mozzarella cheese, or combination of
  mozzarella and Gruyère, grated (about 8 cups)

1. Bring a very large stockpot of water and ⅓ cup of the salt to a boil over high heat.

2. Meanwhile, make the béchamel sauce: Melt the butter in a medium-size, heavy saucepan over low heat. Add the shallots and sauté slowly, stirring frequently, until softened and translucent but not browned, about 10 minutes. Stir in the flour and cook, stirring frequently, for 10 minutes more. Take care that the flour doesn't brown.

3. Combine the milk and cream in a small saucepan and bring just to a boil over medium heat. Remove the pan from the heat immediately and whisk the liquid into the flour mixture until blended and smooth. Bring to a simmer over low heat, stirring frequently. Add the bay leaves and reduce the heat to very low. Simmer slowly, uncovered, stirring very frequently, until the sauce is smooth and has lost its floury taste, about 20 minutes.

4. Remove the pan from the heat and strain the mixture into a heatproof bowl. Set aside at room temperature and press a piece of plastic wrap on the surface to prevent a skin from forming (see Note).

5. When the water in the stockpot is boiling, add the lasagne noodles one at a time, stirring to prevent sticking. Cook until flexible but still very al dente, 5 to 6 minutes. Drain, then set the colander under cold running water and rinse the noodles until thoroughly chilled. Spread out several kitchen towels on a flat surface, then arrange the noodles in one layer on the towels to drain.

6. Clean and wilt the spinach according to the directions on page 340. After squeezing it dry, chop it coarsely and set aside.

7. Heat the oil in a large, heavy skillet over high heat. When the oil is very hot but not yet smoking, add the mushrooms and sauté, tossing, until the liquid has evaporated and the mushrooms are dry and lightly browned, about 10 minutes (for more about browning mushrooms, see box, page 272). Remove the skillet from the heat and add the reserved spinach. Season with salt and pepper, toss well to mix, and set aside.

8. Preheat the oven to 400°F.

9. Coat the bottom of a 16 × 9-inch baking pan or dish (it can be the disposable aluminum kind) lightly with some of the tomato sauce. Arrange one quarter of the reserved lasagne noodles over the sauce, then spread half the mushroom-spinach mixture in an even layer over the noodles. Drizzle about a third of the béchamel over the mushrooms and spinach and sprinkle with about 1 cup of the grated Parmesan. Add another layer of noodles, using the same number as for the first layer, and top with 1½ cups of the tomato sauce and an even sprinkling of half the mozzarella. Sprinkle another ½ cup of the grated Parmesan over the mozzarella, then use half of the remaining noodles to make another layer. Spread the remaining mushrooms and spinach over the noodles and pour on another 1½ cups of the tomato sauce. Drizzle on half the remaining béchamel.

10. To finish the lasagne, add a final layer of noodles, spreading on the remaining tomato sauce and drizzling with the remaining béchamel, then sprinkle with the remaining mozzarella and grated Parmesan. Bake until hot and bubbling and the cheese is melted and a little browned, 30 to 40 minutes. Remove the pan from the oven and let it stand for 5 minutes before cutting into squares to serve.

Note: The sauce may also be refrigerated, tightly covered, for up to a week.

the big lasagne

A good professional cook needs to have a passion for cooking, an adventurous palate (obviously)—and the strength of a stevedore. Restaurant-size pots and pans are huge and heavy. It's nothing for us to lift from the stove a filled pot that feels as if it weighs more than the chef him- or herself. And therein lies a story and a lesson.

A while back, one of our sous chefs made an enormous lasagne for our staff meal. At 2 feet long and 17 inches wide, I can only guess how much it weighed. He slaved over it for hours—simmering sauces, boiling acres of noodles, grating mountains of cheese—then monitored its progress as it baked. At last he removed it from the oven. With the utmost care he slid the huge, heavy pan from the oven, balanced it for several seconds, and then watched in disbelief as it slowly, almost majestically, tipped upside down, spilling our meal all over the floor. The lesson? Be sure you get a firm grip on heavy dishes when removing them from the oven!

Tasty Basic Tomato Sauce

This nicely seasoned, **all-purpose** tomato sauce is good to have on hand for making pasta dishes, pizza, and meat loaf. It's quite chunky, which is how I prefer it, but if you want a smoother sauce simply purée it in a food mill, food processor, or blender. Since a really good tomato sauce like this one requires long, slow simmering, it's worth your while to make a large batch. This recipe can easily be doubled, and it will keep for up to 6 months in the freezer. **MAKES ABOUT 8 CUPS**

2 tablespoons extra-virgin olive oil
2 small onions, finely diced
1 small garlic head (about 10 to 15 cloves), minced
3 cans (28 ounces each) crushed tomatoes
1 can (6 ounces) tomato paste
1 cup full-bodied red wine
2 tablespoons dried oregano leaves
1 tablespoon dried thyme leaves
3 bay leaves
½ teaspoon hot red pepper flakes
Coarse (kosher) salt, to taste

1. Heat the oil in a medium-large, heavy, nonreactive saucepan or Dutch oven over medium-low heat. Add the onions and garlic and cook, covered, until softened and translucent but not browned, about 8 minutes.

2. Add the tomatoes, tomato paste, wine, oregano, thyme, bay leaves, and pepper flakes and increase the heat to medium. Bring to a slow boil, then reduce the heat to low and simmer, uncovered, stirring occasionally, until the sauce has thickened and reduced by about one third, 2 to 3 hours, depending on the brand of canned tomatoes you're using.

3. When the sauce has reached the desired consistency, remove the pan from the heat and discard the bay leaves. Season with salt, then use immediately or store, covered, in the refrigerator for up to 3 days, or in the freezer for up to 6 months.

mushroom tricks

Here's a simple technique used in professional kitchens for sautéing fresh mushrooms, cultivated or wild. It produces nicely browned, perfectly cooked slices instead of soggy ones exuding lots of juice.

The trick is heat and plenty of it! I start with a skillet big enough to hold all of the mushrooms without crowding them. If your pan isn't big enough, simply cook the mushrooms in batches. Add just enough oil to coat the surface of the pan and heat over high heat until almost smoking. Add the mushrooms and sauté them, stirring frequently, until they're lightly browned, usually between 5 and 10 minutes, depending on the amount of mushrooms. (The mushrooms may initially give off some juice, but this will soon evaporate or be absorbed back into the mushrooms, making their flavor even more intense.) Depending on the type of mushrooms, you may need to add a bit more oil as they cook. Portobellos, for instance, will absorb the oil quite quickly, while oyster mushrooms won't.

Here's another technique that can be used for either wild or cultivated mushrooms. The method produces plenty of juices that can be used in sauces, soups, or stews. Over medium heat, heat only enough oil to lightly coat the surface of a pan large enough to hold all of the mushrooms without crowding. Add the mushrooms, then cover the pan tightly and sweat until the mushrooms are tender and their juices have been rendered, about 10 minutes. Drain the juice from the mushrooms and strain through a double layer of dampened cheesecloth (save for stocks, soups, or sauces). If you like, the mushrooms can be returned to the pan and sautéed for a few minutes in hot oil to crisp them.

Tomato-Porcini Sauce

The inclusion of dried porcini mushrooms and brandy distinguishes this **special variation** on our standard Tasty Basic Tomato Sauce. The sweetness of the brandy seems to coax extra flavor from the porcinis. For more of a mushroom presence in the flavor, add cultivated or wild mushrooms. Be sure to chop the onions by hand; if you do this in a food processor, they will release too much liquid and dilute the rich flavors here.

This sauce is terrific in lasagne, as a pizza topping, or poured over grilled polenta or meat loaf. At staff meals we're partial to enjoying it tossed with fusilli or orecchiette. **MAKES ABOUT 2½ QUARTS; ENOUGH FOR 10 TO 12 SERVINGS, OR 3 POUNDS OF PASTA**

4 ounces dried porcini mushrooms (about 2 cups)
2 cups very hot water (either from the tap or just brought
    to a boil)
¼ cup extra-virgin olive oil
2 medium onions, peeled and finely chopped (by hand,
    not processor)
2 tablespoons coarsely chopped garlic
¼ cup brandy or Madeira
3 cans (28 ounces each) plum tomatoes, drained and lightly
    crushed with your hand, but not chopped
4 cups canned tomato purée
¼ cup tomato paste
6 bay leaves
1 teaspoon dried thyme leaves
Pinch of sugar
Coarse (kosher) salt and freshly ground black pepper,
    to taste

1. Place the porcinis in a heatproof bowl and add the hot water. Let soak for at least 1 hour to soften. Using a skimmer or slotted spoon, lift the mushrooms out of the liquid and rinse under cold running water to remove any remaining

grit. Chop coarsely and set aside. Strain the liquid into another bowl through a sieve lined with a double layer of dampened cheesecloth and set aside.

2. Heat the oil in a medium-size saucepan over medium-low heat and add the onions and garlic. Sauté, stirring frequently, until aromatic and very lightly browned, about 8 minutes. Remove from the heat and add the brandy carefully, to prevent its igniting, along with the strained mushroom liquid. Return to a boil over medium-high heat. Cook, uncovered, until reduced by half, about 5 minutes.

3. Add the reserved mushrooms, the tomatoes, tomato purée, tomato paste, bay leaves, thyme, and sugar and bring to a simmer over low heat. Cook, uncovered, stirring occasionally, until the sauce has thickened and the flavors have developed nicely, about 1 hour.

4. Remove the pan from the heat, discarding the bay leaves. Season with salt and pepper, then use immediately or store, covered, in the refrigerator for up to 3 days, or in the freezer for up to 6 months.

Cheese Tortellini with Sun-Dried Tomato Cream

Although we **often make** fresh tortellini, ravioli, and other pasta for the menu at Chanterelle, we really can't spare the time to make fresh pasta for staff meals. But our taste buds are by no means deprived. There are plenty of good-quality commercial pastas—fresh, frozen, and dried—readily available at supermarkets these days, and we take full advantage of them. A quickly made rich sauce such as this combination of heavy cream, peas, and bits of sun-dried tomatoes creates a simultaneously sweet and salty flavor and is all you need. **SERVES 4**

Coarse (kosher) salt
1 tablespoon olive oil
8 fresh cultivated white mushrooms, sliced
4 cups heavy (or whipping) cream
5 cloves garlic, minced
12 sun-dried tomatoes packed in oil, undrained, roughly
    chopped
1 pound fresh cheese tortellini
½ cup frozen peas
¼ cup freshly grated Parmesan
Freshly ground black pepper, to taste

1. Bring a large stockpot of water and ¼ cup of the salt to a boil over high heat.

2. Meanwhile, heat the oil in a medium-size skillet over high heat. When it's almost smoking, add the mushrooms and sauté, stirring frequently, until lightly browned, about 5 minutes. Remove the skillet from the heat and set aside.

3. Combine the cream and garlic in a medium-size saucepan and bring to a boil over high heat. Reduce the heat to medium and cook at a slow boil until the cream is reduced by half, about 10 minutes. When it looks like it's beginning to thicken, add the sun-dried tomatoes and continue cooking, stirring occasionally, until the mixture is thick enough to coat the back of a spoon, about 8 minutes.

4. While the cream cooks, add the tortellini to the boiling salted water and cook, stirring occasionally, until just tender, about 3 minutes; test by removing one from the water and biting into it. Drain and set aside.

5. When the cream mixture has reached the proper consistency, add the tortellini, peas, reserved mushrooms, and grated Parmesan and stir well to mix. Cook for a minute or two longer, until just heated through, then remove the pan from the heat and season the mixture with salt and pepper. Transfer to a serving bowl and serve immediately.

Cheese Tortellini with Cream, Peas, and Ham

This is a **simple dish** to throw together. Any number of vegetables can be used in place of the peas—broccoli, asparagus, spinach, or red bell peppers, for example. For staff meals, I usually make this dish with leftover baked ham, but you could certainly use prosciutto or even a good-quality deli ham. **SERVES 4**

Coarse (kosher) salt
2 cups heavy (or whipping) cream
½ cup diced (¼ inch) good-quality ham
⅓ cup frozen peas
Small sprig fresh thyme
Freshly ground black pepper, to taste
Fresh lemon juice, to taste
1 pound fresh cheese tortellini
¼ cup freshly grated Parmesan

1. Bring a large stockpot of water and ¼ cup salt to a boil over high heat.

2. Meanwhile, bring the cream to a boil in a medium-size saucepan over medium-high heat. Add the ham, peas, and thyme and cook, uncovered, stirring occasionally, until the cream has thickened slightly and the peas are just tender, about 4 minutes. Remove the pan from the heat and season with pepper, salt, and lemon juice. Remove the thyme sprig and set the sauce aside, covered, to keep warm.

3. Add the tortellini to the boiling water and cook, stirring frequently, until al dente, about 3 minutes; test by removing one from the water and biting into it. Drain well and add, along with the grated Parmesan, to the cream mixture in the saucepan. Toss gently until the cheese is melted and the tortellini are coated with the sauce, then transfer to a serving bowl and serve immediately.

Staff Meals from Chanterelle | p a s t a

Ravioli with Parmesan, Butter, and Herbs

Quickly and easily prepared, this ravioli recipe can be multiplied with ease to suit your needs. The success of this dish relies on **top-quality ravioli**—I suggest pumpkin or cheese—freshly grated authentic Parmigiano-Reggiano (see box, page 267), and flavorful fresh herbs. **SERVES 4**

Coarse (kosher) salt

1 pound fresh cheese or pumpkin ravioli

6 tablespoons (¾ stick) unsalted butter, room
    temperature

½ cup freshly grated Parmesan

2 tablespoons chopped mixed fresh herbs, such as
    chives, oregano, marjoram, chervil, flat-leaf
    parsley, and tarragon leaves

Freshly ground black pepper, to taste

Fresh lemon juice, to taste

1. Bring a large stockpot of water and ¼ cup salt to a boil over high heat.

2. When the water is boiling, add the ravioli and cook, stirring frequently, until al dente, 5 to 10 minutes, depending on the size and brand of the ravioli you're using.

3. Meanwhile, combine the remaining ingredients in a large bowl.

4. Drain the ravioli well and add it to the bowl. Toss gently until the butter is melted and the ingredients are thoroughly mixed. Taste, adjust the seasoning, and serve immediately.

Eggplant Parmesan

Over the years we've always had at least one, and sometimes even a whole contingent, of vegetarians on our staff. As a result, our meals include dishes that will meet everyone's needs. This is a "crossover" dish that **always delights** both vegetarians and meat eaters. The addition of ricotta lends a touch of creaminess, making the casserole much more satisfying than the usual version. I bake this in a shallow rather than a deep pan, which prevents the eggplant from becoming too soggy. **SERVES 6**

1 cup all-purpose flour
2 cups fine dry bread crumbs (see box, facing page)
4 large eggs
2 small eggplants (about 12 ounces each), peeled
    and cut into ¼-inch rounds
⅓ to ½ cup olive oil, or more as needed
Coarse (kosher) salt, to taste
4 cups Tasty Basic Tomato Sauce (page 271) or
    good-quality commercial tomato sauce
1 container (15 ounces) ricotta cheese
1 pound commercial mozzarella cheese, sliced
¼ cup freshly grated Parmesan

1. Preheat the oven to 400°F.

2. Spread out the flour and bread crumbs on separate plates, then beat the eggs in a shallow bowl. Dip each eggplant slice first in the flour to coat lightly on both sides, then in the egg, coating completely. Finally, dip the slice in the bread crumbs to coat well on both sides, shaking off any excess. Arrange the slices as they are coated in one layer on a baking sheet, making sure they don't touch, while you coat the remaining slices.

3. Heat ⅓ cup of the oil in a large, heavy skillet over medium heat. Add only enough eggplant slices to fit into the skillet without touching and fry, sprinkling with salt, until they're golden brown on each side, about 1 minute per side. Transfer to paper towels to drain while you fry the remaining slices, adding oil to the skillet as needed.

4. Spread about ¾ cup of the tomato sauce over the bottom of a 16 × 9-inch baking pan. Add half the fried eggplant slices in an even layer, then dot the eggplant with the ricotta. Drizzle ½ cup of the tomato sauce over the ricotta. Add a layer of the remaining eggplant slices and pour the remaining tomato sauce evenly over the eggplant. Arrange the mozzarella slices over the sauce and sprinkle the Parmesan on top. Bake until hot and bubbling and the cheese is melted and a little browned, about 30 minutes.

5. Remove the dish from the oven and let stand for 5 minutes before cutting into portions to serve.

how to make bread crumbs

For fresh crumbs: I use soft, fresh bread crumbs to bind together ingredients in dishes where a slightly moist texture is desired. One slice of bread will yield a scant ½ cup of fresh bread crumbs. Use bread with a firm crumb such as a day-old peasant loaf, Italian bread, or as a last resort, a packaged sliced bread like Pepperidge Farm or Arnold. Trim away the crust, tear or cut the bread into pieces, and pulse them in a food processor fitted with the steel blade. Ideally, homemade fresh bread crumbs should be used the day they're made, but no longer than a day or two later. If this isn't possible, they can be frozen in an airtight container, where they will keep indefinitely.

For dry crumbs: To make the best dry bread crumbs, the bread must be perfectly dry. To dry it, arrange the slices in one layer on a baking sheet and place in a pre-heated 300°F oven until the bread is thoroughly dried out and lightly browned.

For coarse crumbs, break the dried bread into pieces and grind in a food processor fitted with the steel blade.

For fine crumbs, use the processor but fit it with the grating blade.

Homemade dry bread crumbs can be stored in an airtight container or zipper-lock plastic bag in the refrigerator for up to 2 weeks, or frozen for up to 6 months.

One slice of bread will yield approximately ⅓ cup of dry bread crumbs.

Stuffed Shells with Ricotta and Prosciutto

If you make a big-enough batch of these **homey, basic** stuffed shells, they become a convenience food. Divide them into individual servings and pop them into the freezer. The shells can go right from freezer to oven—though, depending on the size of the portion, you'll need to add some extra baking time. The lemon zest and freshly grated nutmeg enhance the inherent sweetness of the cheeses and generally boost the flavor a bit. **SERVES 4**

Coarse (kosher) salt
2 cups very fresh ricotta cheese
½ cup minced prosciutto, baked ham, or good-quality deli ham
2 large egg yolks
A few gratings of nutmeg
Dash of cayenne pepper
Freshly ground black pepper, to taste
⅛ teaspoon grated lemon zest
24 jumbo pasta shells
1 tablespoon olive oil
4 cups Tasty Basic Tomato Sauce (page 271)
1 pound commercial mozzarella cheese, coarsely grated

1. Preheat the oven to 350°F.

2. Bring a large stockpot of water and ¼ cup of the salt to a boil over high heat.

3. Meanwhile, combine the ricotta, prosciutto, egg yolks, nutmeg, peppers, grated lemon zest, and salt to taste in a large bowl and stir well to mix. Set aside.

4. Add the shells to the boiling salted water and cook, stirring occasionally, until flexible but very al dente, 5 to 6 minutes. Drain, then let the shells stand in the colander under cold running water until chilled. Drain again, then transfer the shells to a large bowl and toss with the oil. Set aside.

5. Spread ½ cup of the tomato sauce over the bottom of a shallow baking dish large enough to hold the shells in one layer. Gently open one shell, fill it with about 1 tablespoon of the ricotta filling, and place it in the baking dish. Repeat the procedure with the remaining shells and filling. When all the stuffed shells are in the dish, pour the remaining tomato sauce over them and sprinkle the grated mozzarella evenly over the top.

6. Bake until the sauce is bubbling and the mozzarella is nicely melted and beginning to brown slightly, 30 minutes. Let stand for a minute or two before serving.

freshly grated nutmeg

Nutmeg is the hard kernel, about the size of a marble but oval in shape, that lies within the shell of the fruit of the *Myristica fragrans,* an evergreen native to the East Indian Molucca Islands (also known as the Spice Islands). The nutmeg comes from the tree encased in a brightly colored lacy covering that, after its separation from the nutmeg, becomes a spice in its own right, called mace.

There is simply no comparison between the flavor of commercial ground nutmeg and nutmeg that's grated fresh. Special little graters, which usually have a small compartment in the top to house the nutmeg in use, are available in kitchenware stores and most other stores that carry cooking supplies. It's best to just grate what you need and store the rest of the kernel in the top of the grater.

You should be able to find small jars of whole nutmegs in the supermarket; if not, try your local specialty food store or spice store. A whole nutmeg grates down to 2 to 3 teaspoons' worth of spice.

Stir-Fried Rice Noodles with Bean Sprouts and Scallions

This is a **satisfying** rice noodle **dish** that's fairly uncomplicated yet delicious. The crunchiness of the crisp bean sprouts offers a pleasing contrast to the soft chewiness of the noodles. For some reason, perhaps because the textures are so varied and the flavor of the sauce is savory yet unidentifiable, children absolutely love this. And everyone loves noodles! If you have leftovers, serve them chilled or at room temperature. They don't reheat well. **SERVES 4**

1 pound Thai rice noodles (¼ inch wide;
   sometimes labeled "rice sticks")
2 tablespoons Asian sesame oil
4 tablespoons canola or other vegetable oil
1 cup Chicken Stock (page 39) or canned low-
   sodium chicken broth
¼ cup oyster sauce
3 tablespoons good-quality soy sauce,
   such as Kikkoman
1 tablespoon Chinese fermented black beans
2 large cloves garlic, minced
3 cups fresh bean sprouts, picked over, rinsed,
   and drained
3 bunches scallions, white and green parts, trimmed
   and cut into ½-inch lengths

1. Place the rice noodles in a large bowl with very hot water to cover. Let stand, stirring occasionally, until softened but still very chewy and not at all done, about 5 minutes. Check frequently to make sure the noodles don't get too soft.

2. Drain the noodles in a colander and rinse under cold running water until thoroughly chilled. Drain again, return to the bowl, and toss with the sesame oil and 2 tablespoons of the canola oil. Set aside until you're ready to use them (see Note).

3. Combine the chicken stock, oyster sauce, soy sauce, and black beans in a small bowl and stir well to mix. Set aside.

4. Heat the remaining 2 tablespoons canola oil in a wok or large, heavy skillet over medium-high heat. When the oil is very hot but not yet smoking, add the garlic and cook, stirring, until very lightly browned, about 10 seconds. Add the rice noodles and the chicken stock mixture and stir-fry until most of the liquid is absorbed into the noodles, 2 to 3 minutes. Stir in the bean sprouts and scallions to mix thoroughly, then remove the wok from the heat. Transfer the noodles to a serving bowl and serve immediately.

Note: The noodles may be prepared through step 2 up to 4 hours in advance. Cover and keep at room temperature until you're ready to use them.

mise en place

At first glance, recipes with a long list of ingredients—like those for Thai Rice Noodles (page 284), Hot and Sour Soup (page 6), and Two-Sides-Brown Noodles with Mushrooms (page 287)—may seem daunting. They really needn't be. This is particularly true of many stir-fried dishes, for which most of the ingredient preparation is done ahead of time so that they need only be tossed together for their final moments of cooking in a hot pan. Organization is the key. As I fix each ingredient, I place it in a small bowl, or group the ingredients together in separate piles on a large plate or platter set near the stove. In France this organizational system of laying out ingredients and equipment in a restaurant kitchen is known as *mise en place.* Once you've achieved this type of order in the culinary universe, you'll find that your frenzy level drops dramatically and cooking is more pleasurable.

Thai Rice Noodles (Pad Thai)

Karen, my wife, and I first enjoyed pad thai on a trip to Thailand in the late 1980s, back when Thai food was a relative rarity in the United States, even in large cities. These noodles are quintessential **Thai street food**, usually served up quite plain. The condiments—dried shrimp, dried hot red pepper flakes, additional fish sauce, chopped roasted peanuts, and fresh cilantro—are served on the side, added to the dish to suit the eater's taste. In my version, however, most of the condiments are combined in the dish. This is such a staff favorite that when they realize I'm fixing it for our meal, they get silly and start singing a special pad thai song of encouragement that makes no sense to anyone who doesn't work at Chanterelle. After you've made pad thai once using this recipe, you'll surely want to alter the ingredients to suit yourself, substituting chicken for the shrimp or tofu for the sausage, and so on. Serve pad thai at room temperature and don't plan on saving the leftovers, because the dish loses its allure when reheated. **SERVES 6**

1 cup boiling water, or more as needed

8 ounces dried tamarind pulp (see box, page 372)

¼ cup fresh lime juice

¼ cup sugar

¼ cup Thai fish sauce (nam pla)

¼ cup ketchup

2 tablespoons good-quality soy sauce, such as Kikkoman

2 tablespoons oyster sauce

1 pound Thai rice noodles (¼ inch wide; sometimes labeled "rice sticks")

10 tablespoons canola or other vegetable oil

3 large eggs, beaten

4 large cloves garlic, minced

1 pound large shrimp, peeled, deveined, and cut
   into ½-inch pieces

4 ounces Chinese sausage, thinly sliced (see box, page 161)

2 cups finely shredded Savoy cabbage

¼ cup diced (½ inch) extra-firm tofu

2 bunches scallions, white and green parts, trimmed and
   cut into ½-inch lengths

8 ounces fresh bean sprouts, picked over, rinsed, and drained

⅓ cup dried shrimp, pulverized in a food processor
   (see box, page 286)

¼ cup chopped salted radish

½ cup coarsely chopped fresh cilantro stems and leaves

¼ cup chopped roasted peanuts

1 teaspoon hot red pepper flakes

1. Pour the boiling water over the tamarind in a medium-size bowl and let soak until the tamarind is soft, about 15 to 20 minutes.

2. Pour the mixture into a strainer set over a second bowl and push the pulp through with a wooden spoon, discarding the fibers and seeds in the strainer. Add the lime juice, sugar, fish sauce, ketchup, soy sauce, and oyster sauce to the tamarind liquid in the bowl and whisk well to blend. Set aside.

3. Place the rice noodles in a large bowl with very hot water to cover. Let stand, stirring occasionally, until softened but still very chewy and not at all done, about 5 minutes. Check frequently to make sure the noodles don't get too soft.

4. Drain the noodles in a colander and rinse under cold running water until thoroughly chilled. Drain again, return to the bowl, and toss with 3 tablespoons of the canola oil. Set aside until you're ready to use them (see Note).

5. Heat 2 tablespoons of the canola oil in a wok or large, heavy skillet over high heat. When the oil is very hot but not yet smoking, add the beaten eggs, allowing them to set on the bottom before stirring to lightly scramble them. When they're ready, the eggs should be just cooked and a little puffy. Transfer them to a second large bowl (not the one with the noodles) and use your spoon to break them up into smaller pieces. Set aside.

6. Add another 3 tablespoons of the canola oil to the wok and heat over medium-high heat until almost smoking. Add the garlic and cook, stirring, until very lightly browned, about 10 seconds. Quickly add the fresh shrimp and sausage and stir-fry until the shrimp is just opaque, about 1 minute. Add the cabbage and tofu and stir-fry until the cabbage is wilted and the tofu is heated through, about 2 minutes. Remove the wok from the heat and transfer its contents to the bowl with the eggs.

7. Return the wok to high heat, adding the remaining 2 tablespoons canola oil. When it's almost smoking, add the noodles and tamarind liquid and cook, stirring frequently but gently to avoid breaking up the noodles too much. Cook until the noodles are tender and have absorbed most of the sauce, 2 to 3 minutes. Remove the wok from the heat and transfer the noodles and sauce to the bowl with the eggs and other ingredients. Add the scallions and half each of the bean sprouts, dried shrimp, and salted radish and toss gently but thoroughly to mix.

8. Arrange the remaining bean sprouts on a serving platter and spoon the noodle mixture over them. Sprinkle with the cilantro, peanuts, remaining dried shrimp and salted radish, and the pepper flakes. Serve immediately.

Note: The recipe may be prepared through step 4 up to 24 hours ahead of time. Cover the bowls and refrigerate.

dried shrimp

Small, salty dried shrimp are used widely in Chinese and Southeast Asian cooking, added to everything from soups, broths, and stir-fries to salads, vegetable dishes, and noodle dishes. Their strongly pungent shrimpiness adds intensity to the other flavors.

Dried shrimp are sold in approximately 8-ounce packages at Asian markets and some specialty food stores. Look for shrimp that are a healthy orangey pink color; avoid any that are brown or gray,

a sign that they're old and deteriorating. The finest, most expensive shrimp are about an inch long and very brightly colored, but I've found that the smaller, less costly ones are perfectly adequate.

When used whole, the shrimp should be softened briefly in warm water or other liquid. If they will be pulverized before using, as in the Thai Rice Noodles (Pad Thai) recipe on page 284, they require no soaking.

Two-Sides-Brown Noodles with Mushrooms

I make this **classic Chinese noodle dish** often, both at home and for our staff meals, yet we never tire of it. Devoted fans of pan-fried noodles like to argue over whether the noodles should be thin or thick, and whether or not both sides should be browned—I vote thin and both sides. The noodles are coiled in a skillet or sauté pan into a large "cake" that's fried, then flipped over, so the crispy brown outsides encase a soft center. The cake is topped with a silky mushroom sauce that clings to the noodles but doesn't soak through their crisp exterior. **SERVES 4**

10 large dried shiitake mushrooms

Coarse (kosher) salt

¾ pound fresh or frozen Chinese egg noodles
　　(sometimes labeled "lo mein"), thawed if frozen

7 tablespoons peanut, canola, or other vegetable oil

10 large fresh cultivated white or cremini mushrooms, wiped clean
　　and cut into ¼-inch-thick slices

2 cans (15 ounces each) straw mushrooms, drained

1 tablespoon grated fresh ginger

3 cloves garlic, minced

3 cups Chicken Stock (page 39) or canned low-sodium chicken broth

3 tablespoons good-quality soy sauce, such as Kikkoman

3 tablespoons oyster sauce

1 teaspoon sugar

1 teaspoon Chinese chili sauce with garlic

2 scant tablespoons cornstarch

5 tablespoons cold water

1 bunch scallions, white and green parts, trimmed and sliced

1 cup fresh bean sprouts, picked over, rinsed, and drained

1. Place the shiitake mushrooms in a medium-size bowl with very warm water to cover. Let soak for 30 minutes to soften. Lift the mushrooms from the soaking liquid, leaving the grit behind. Trim away any stems and quarter the caps. Set aside. Strain the soaking liquid through a strainer lined with several layers of cheesecloth. Add to the skillet with the chicken broth in step 7 or cover, refrigerate, and save to use at another time.

2. Preheat the oven to its lowest setting.

3. Bring a large stockpot of water and ¼ cup of the salt to a boil over high heat.

4. When the water is boiling, add the noodles and stir gently with a fork or chopsticks to separate them as they cook. Cook until al dente, 1 to 2 minutes, then drain. Transfer to a bowl and toss with 2 tablespoons of the oil.

5. Heat 3 tablespoons of the oil in a large, heavy skillet over medium-high heat. Add the noodles, using a spatula to form them into an even layer over the

how to flip a noodle cake

In the recipe for Two-Sides-Brown Noodles with Mushrooms, you're required to flip the hot noodle cake over, a feat that can be accomplished safely in two ways.

If the hot oil the noodles have been frying in has pretty much been absorbed, remove the skillet from the heat and gently run a spatula under the noodles to make sure they aren't stuck to the bottom. Invert a plate a little larger than the skillet over it. Place one hand in the center of the plate and lift the skillet with the other. Quickly invert the whole deal so you end up with the plate on the bottom and the skillet on top. The noodle cake should drop onto the plate. Set the skillet back on the heat, add some more oil, and when it's hot, slide the noodle cake, browned-side up, into the skillet, and brown the second side.

If the pan is too heavy to lift with one hand, tip the pan and use a spatula to help you slide the noodle cake onto a large plate. Place a second large plate upside down over the noodle cake and flip the cake. Remove the plate (the browned side should be facing you) and slide the noodle cake back into the skillet, browned-side up. You're now ready to brown the second side.

bottom of the skillet. Reduce the heat slightly so the noodles brown nicely but do not burn. When a handsome crust has formed on the underside of the noodle cake, after 3 to 5 minutes or so, flip the cake (see box, page 288) and brown the other side, 3 to 5 minutes more. Slide the pancake out onto a platter and keep it warm in the oven.

6. Heat the remaining 2 tablespoons oil in the skillet over medium-high heat. Add the fresh mushrooms and sauté, stirring frequently, until they are browned, about 2 minutes. Add the shiitake and straw mushrooms and sauté, stirring, until all the mushrooms are heated through, 1 minute more.

7. Add the ginger and garlic and cook, stirring, until fragrant but not browned, about 30 seconds. Add the chicken stock, soy sauce, oyster sauce, sugar, and chili sauce and bring to a boil. Cook, uncovered, stirring occasionally, for 2 minutes.

8. Whisk the cornstarch with the water to blend. When smooth, whisk it into the mixture in the skillet. Cook until thickened, about 1 minute more, then stir in the scallions and bean sprouts.

9. Remove the skillet from the heat and taste for seasoning, adding salt if necessary. Pour the sauce over the noodle cake and serve immediately.

Singapore-Style Curried Rice Noodles

This dish is an **interesting example** of the geographic mobility of cultures, from India to Singapore to China. The dish itself is Chinese, but it's called Singapore-style because of the use of curry powder to flavor the noodles. Curry, of course, had its origin in India, though no Indian cook would ever think of

using the prepared curry powder called for here; only a fresh mix of the traditional spices—among them coriander, cumin, mustard seeds, turmeric, red pepper, cinnamon, and cloves—will do.

You can use any thickness of rice noodles that you like. I prefer mine medium thick, but the thin vermicelli are more traditional. Other seafood may be used in addition to or as a substitute for the shrimp, and shredded Chinese cabbage, added at the same time as the onions and bell pepper, is a nice addition, too. **SERVES 4**

1 pound Thai rice noodles (sometimes labeled "rice sticks") of desired width

4 large eggs

2 tablespoons water

3 tablespoons Asian sesame oil

1½ cups Chicken Stock (page 39) or canned low-sodium chicken broth

2 tablespoons good-quality soy sauce, such as Kikkoman

2 tablespoons Thai fish sauce (nam pla)

2 tablespoons Madras-style curry powder, preferably Sun brand

1 tablespoon sugar

Juice of ½ lime

5 tablespoons canola or other vegetable oil

2 tablespoons coarsely chopped fresh ginger

4 large cloves garlic, coarsely chopped

1 pound large shrimp, peeled, deveined, and cut into ½-inch pieces

2 medium onions, cut into ½-inch dice

1 large red bell pepper, stemmed, seeded, and cut into julienne strips

2 bunches scallions, white and green parts, trimmed and cut into ½-inch lengths

1 cup fresh bean sprouts, picked over, rinsed, and drained

1. Place the noodles in a large bowl with very hot water to cover. Let stand, stirring occasionally, until softened but still very chewy and not at all done, about 5 minutes. Check frequently to make sure the noodles don't get too soft.

2. Meanwhile, beat the eggs with the water and 1 tablespoon of the sesame oil in a medium-size bowl. In a small bowl, combine the chicken stock, soy sauce, fish sauce, curry powder, sugar, and lime juice and whisk thoroughly to blend. Set both bowls aside.

3. Drain the noodles in a colander and rinse under cold running water until thoroughly chilled. Drain again and return to the bowl. Toss the noodles with the remaining 2 tablespoons sesame oil and 2 tablespoons of the canola oil. Set aside until you're ready to use them (see Note).

4. Heat 1 tablespoon of the canola oil in a wok or large, heavy skillet over high heat. When the oil is very hot but not yet smoking, add the beaten eggs, allowing them to set on the bottom before stirring to lightly scramble them. When they're ready, the eggs should be just cooked and a little puffy. Transfer them to a second large bowl (not the one with the noodles) and use your spoon to break them up into smaller pieces. Set aside.

5. Wipe out the wok, then add the remaining 2 tablespoons canola oil and heat over medium-high heat. When it's very hot but not yet smoking, add the ginger and garlic and stir-fry until fragrant and lightly browned, about 10 seconds. Add the shrimp, onions, and bell pepper and stir-fry until the shrimp is just opaque, about 1 minute.

6. Transfer the shrimp mixture to the bowl with the eggs and add the reserved noodles and curry sauce to the wok. Bring to a boil over medium-high heat, stirring frequently but gently to avoid breaking up the noodles too much. Cook until the noodles are tender and have absorbed most of the sauce, 2 to 3 minutes. Add the scallions and bean sprouts and stir gently to mix.

7. Remove the wok from the heat and transfer its contents to the bowl with the eggs and other ingredients. Toss gently but thoroughly to mix, then transfer to a platter and serve immediately.

Note: The noodles may be prepared through step 3 up to 4 hours in advance. Cover and keep at room temperature until you're ready to use them.

Vegetable Lo Mein

A good representative of simple, **home-style** Chinese cooking, lo mein is also a practical and delicious way to use up odds and ends of vegetables and leftover meats. Cutting the ginger into extremely narrow strips makes it less fibrous, releases more flavor, and adds nice texture to the vegetable mixture. If you wish to enjoy a long life, according to Chinese noodle wisdom, you'll eat these long noodle strands in one piece, without cutting or breaking them. **SERVES 6 TO 8**

Coarse (kosher) salt

2 pounds fresh or frozen Chinese egg noodles,
    thawed if frozen

11 tablespoons peanut, canola, or other vegetable oil

2 cups small broccoli florets

1 heaping cup shredded Savoy cabbage

1 small onion, thinly sliced lengthwise

4 ounces fresh cultivated white mushrooms, wiped
    clean and thinly sliced

4 ounces fresh snow peas, trimmed of strings and
    cut into julienne strips

1 piece (3 inches) fresh ginger, peeled and julienned

4 cloves garlic, minced

¼ cup good-quality soy sauce, such as Kikkoman

4 ounces fresh bean sprouts, picked over, rinsed, and drained

1 bunch scallions, white and green parts, trimmed and
    thinly sliced

1. Bring a very large stockpot of water and ¼ cup salt to a boil over high heat. When the water is boiling, add the noodles and stir gently with a fork or chopsticks to separate them from each other as they cook. Cook until al dente, 1 to 2 minutes, then drain. Let the noodles stand in the colander under cold running water until chilled. Drain again, then transfer to a bowl and toss with 3 tablespoons of the oil. Set aside.

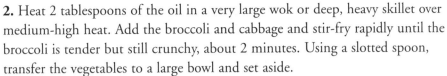

2. Heat 2 tablespoons of the oil in a very large wok or deep, heavy skillet over medium-high heat. Add the broccoli and cabbage and stir-fry rapidly until the broccoli is tender but still crunchy, about 2 minutes. Using a slotted spoon, transfer the vegetables to a large bowl and set aside.

3. Add 2 more tablespoons of the oil to the wok and return to medium-high heat. When the oil is almost smoking, add the onion and mushrooms and stir-fry until tender and lightly browned, 2 to 3 minutes. Add the snow peas and stir-fry until they turn bright green, just a few seconds.

4. Remove the wok from the heat and scrape its contents into the bowl with the broccoli and cabbage. Set aside.

5. Add the remaining ¼ cup oil to the wok and return to medium-high heat. When the oil is almost smoking, add the ginger and garlic and stir-fry rapidly for a few seconds, then add the noodles and continue to stir, making sure the garlic gets mixed in and doesn't brown. When the noodles are heated through, add the soy sauce and continue to stir-fry until the noodles are browned in a few places, about 3 minutes.

6. Remove the wok from the heat and turn the noodles into the bowl with the vegetables. Toss thoroughly to mix, then taste for seasoning, adding salt if necessary, and toss again. Transfer the mixture to a serving platter, garnish with the bean sprouts and scallions, and serve immediately.

to julienne

Ingredients such as carrots, potatoes, bell peppers, cucumbers, and ginger are often cut into matchstick pieces known as julienne. Foods cut this way look attractive (garnishes are often julienned), and they also cook quickly and evenly, which makes them ideal for stir-fried dishes. Before cutting round-sided vegetables, trim a thin strip off one side, then turn the vegetable cut-side down on the cutting board to steady it. Decide what length of pieces you will need—2 inches is a good average length—and then, using a chef's knife, cut your vegetable crosswise into sections of that length. Cut each section lengthwise into uniform slices ⅛ inch thick, then stack the slices on top of each other and make thin, even lengthwise cuts to produce strips about the size of a matchstick.

Staff Meals from Chanterelle | p a s t a

Highly Adaptable Shrimp Fried Rice

This **simple but tasty** shrimp fried rice lies somewhere between cooking from scratch and dialing for Chinese takeout. It's a terrific way to use up leftover rice, whether home cooked or from that take-out order delivered 2 days ago. If you'll be cooking the rice yourself, use long-grain Chinese rice or a slightly aromatic Thai jasmine variety. Both have superior flavor and produce grains that remain separate after cooking. The important thing is to make sure that the rice used has been thoroughly chilled before stir-frying; otherwise it will stick to the pan. Although the recipe calls for shrimp, this can be omitted, or you could add an equal amount of diced roast pork, cooked chicken, or Chinese sausage. For vegetarian fried rice, skip the shrimp and use Chinese cabbage, bok choy, and mushrooms. **SERVES 2**

3 to 4 tablespoons peanut oil, as needed

1 large egg, beaten

8 ounces medium shrimp, peeled, deveined, and split lengthwise

1 medium onion, diced

½ teaspoon grated fresh ginger

1 small clove garlic, minced

4 cups chilled cooked rice

½ cup peas, thawed if frozen

2 tablespoons good-quality soy sauce, such as Kikkoman

Coarse (kosher) salt, to taste

1. Heat 2 tablespoons of the oil in a large wok or nonstick skillet over high heat, swirling it to cover as much of the surface as possible. When it's just about smoking, add the beaten egg and stir-fry rapidly, breaking up the egg as it sets. Transfer the egg to a large bowl and keep it in a warm spot.

2. Add the shrimp to the wok, stir-frying until just pink, about 2 minutes. Transfer the shrimp to the bowl with the egg.

3. Add the onion to the wok along with another tablespoon of the oil, if needed. Stir-fry the onion until browned but still a bit crunchy, about 2 minutes. Scrape the onion into the bowl.

4. Add another tablespoon of the oil to the pan and add the ginger and garlic. When they sizzle and turn opaque, immediately add the rice. Stir-fry, making sure the rice doesn't stick to the wok. When it's beginning to brown a bit, add the peas and soy sauce. Continue stir-frying until everything is heated through, 1 to 2 minutes. Toss in the reserved shrimp mixture and stir-fry until heated through and thoroughly mixed, 1 to 2 minutes more.

5. Remove the wok from the heat and season the fried rice with salt. Transfer it to a serving bowl or platter and serve immediately.

Risotto with Porcini

This **basic technique** for risotto can be used to create numerous variations. Sometimes I substitute asparagus for the mushrooms or use a combination of chicken and fish stock and add squid. High-starch Arborio rice is essential for risotto because the short, squat grains retain their firm center while creating just the right degree of creaminess. Using a combination of dried and fresh mushrooms creates an earthier, more intense flavor, while soaking the porcinis in chicken stock rather than water further expands the mushroom essence that will slowly be absorbed as the rice cooks. Taste the rice as you add stock and stir so that you can tell when it has reached the right consistency. Properly cooked risotto should be slightly al dente, each grain coated with creamy liquid. **SERVES 6 TO 8**

8 cups Chicken Stock (page 39) or canned low-
   sodium chicken broth, or as needed
3 ounces dried porcini mushrooms
¼ cup olive oil
1 pound fresh cultivated white mushrooms, wiped
   clean and sliced
2 tablespoons unsalted butter
1 medium onion, chopped
3 cloves garlic, minced
3 cups Arborio rice
¼ cup heavy (or whipping) cream
¼ cup freshly grated Parmesan
Coarse (kosher) salt and freshly ground black pepper, to taste
3 tablespoons chopped fresh flat-leaf parsley leaves

1. Bring the chicken stock to a boil in a medium-size saucepan over high heat. Add the dried porcinis, stir, and remove from the heat. Set aside to allow the porcinis to soak in the stock, 30 minutes.

2. Heat 2 tablespoons of the oil in a large, heavy skillet over medium-high heat. Add the fresh mushrooms and sauté until lightly browned, about 5 minutes. Remove the skillet from the heat and set aside.

3. Using a skimmer or slotted spoon, remove the porcinis from the stock and coarsely chop. Strain the stock into another pot through a sieve lined with a double layer of dampened cheesecloth and set aside.

4. Combine the remaining oil and the butter in a medium-size, heavy saucepan and set over medium heat. When the butter is melted, add the onion and garlic and sauté, stirring, until the garlic is fragrant and very lightly browned, 1 to 2 minutes. Add the rice and stir until it's coated with the oil-butter mixture and also very lightly colored, about 3 minutes. Stir in the chopped porcinis.

5. Add about 1 cup of the stock to the rice mixture, stirring until it's almost completely absorbed by the rice, about 5 minutes. Continue adding stock, ½ to 1 cup at a time, stirring and adding more only when the previous addition has been absorbed; this will take approximately 45 minutes total. The rice is ready when it is creamy yet slightly al dente. You'll need most or all of the stock and perhaps a bit more, depending entirely on the brand of rice you're using.

pasta

Staff Meals from Chanterelle

6. When the rice is nearly done, stir in the sautéed fresh mushrooms. When done, remove the pan from the heat and stir in the cream, grated Parmesan, salt, and pepper. Add the parsley, give the risotto one last stir, and serve immediately.

Eggplant Pizza

Homemade **pizza is misunderstood**. Many home cooks think it's difficult to make, but it doesn't take all that much time or effort and always tastes fresh and terrific.

Knowing how to make a good crust is the key. Few home ovens are hot enough to make pizza that's really crisp, so when I make pizza for Karen and the kids, I solve the problem by partially baking the crust for about 5 minutes on a very hot preheated pan sprinkled with plenty of cornmeal. Then I add the sauce and toppings and return the pizza to the oven to finish baking.

The topping is entirely flexible, of course. Roast peppers, leftover mussels or clams, Italian sausage, olives, thin slices of salami, capers, and anchovies are all candidates for inclusion, along with or in place of the eggplant. **MAKES ONE 10-INCH PIZZA; SERVES 2**

1 large egg

2 cups fine dry bread crumbs (see box, page 279)

5 slices eggplant (about 4 inches wide and ¼ inch thick each), unpeeled

Olive oil, for frying

Cornmeal, for pan

All-purpose flour, for dusting

Pizza Dough (recipe follows)

1 cup Tasty Basic Tomato Sauce (page 271) or good-quality commercial tomato sauce

½ teaspoon hot red pepper flakes

8 ounces commercial mozzarella cheese, grated (about 2 cups)

1. Preheat the oven to 450°F.

2. Beat the egg in a shallow bowl; spread the bread crumbs on a plate.

3. Cut each eggplant slice into 1-inch-wide strips. Dip each strip first in the egg, then in the bread crumbs to coat completely, shaking off any excess. Place the strips as they are coated in a single layer on a plate.

4. Pour oil to a depth of ⅛ inch into a large, heavy skillet. Heat over medium heat until a sprinkling of bread crumbs sizzles on contact. Add enough eggplant strips to fit into the skillet without touching and fry until golden brown on both sides, about 30 seconds per side. Using a slotted spatula, transfer the strips to paper towels to drain while you fry the remaining strips.

5. Place a large, rimless baking sheet in the oven to get hot while you assemble the pizza. Place a second rimless baking sheet on your work surface to use in shaping the pizza; sprinkle this sheet liberally with cornmeal.

6. Lightly dust a work surface with flour. Place the pizza dough on the work surface and pat it into a thin 10-inch circle with your fingertips. Transfer it carefully to the cornmeal-covered baking sheet, re-forming it into a circular shape as necessary, then carry the baking sheet over to the oven and slide the dough circle onto the hot sheet already in the oven. Bake until the dough has started to puff and the surface has formed a crust that's beginning to brown just a little, about 5 minutes. Remove the baking sheet with the crust from the oven.

7. Spread the sauce evenly over the crust and sprinkle with the pepper flakes, then with the mozzarella. Arrange the fried eggplant strips over the mozzarella and return the baking sheet to the oven. Bake until the cheese has melted and is browning slightly, about 10 minutes.

8. Let the pizza rest for a minute or two before serving.

no-sauce pizza

No tomato sauce on hand? Simply cover your prebaked pizza crust with plenty of grated commercial mozzarella or imported Fontina and strew a goodly amount of chopped fresh basil leaves over it, then pop the pizza in the oven for the second baking.

Pizza Dough

Once it has risen, this dough can be punched down and used immediately or refrigerated in an airtight plastic bag for a day or two. The small amount of olive oil in it creates a crisper crust, as does prebaking the crust on a baking sheet liberally sprinkled with cornmeal. This recipe makes **enough for two** pizza crusts. The extra can be frozen for up to a month. To thaw, let the dough rest in the refrigerator for about 8 hours before using.

MAKES TWO 10-INCH PIZZA CRUSTS

1 package active dry yeast
1 cup warm water (105° to 115°F)
1 tablespoon olive oil
1 teaspoon coarse (kosher) salt
3½ cups all-purpose flour, plus additional for kneading
Canola or other vegetable oil, for the bowl

1. Sprinkle the yeast over the water in a medium-size bowl and stir to mix. Let stand until the mixture foams, about 5 minutes.

2. Add the oil and salt to the yeast mixture and stir well to blend. Add 3½ cups of the flour and stir until the dough that forms cleans the sides of the bowl. Transfer the dough to a floured work surface and knead until smooth and elastic, 8 to 10 minutes, adding flour as needed to prevent stickiness.

3. Form the dough into a ball and place in a lightly oiled large bowl, turning the dough to coat with the oil. Cover the bowl with a kitchen towel and set aside in a warm, draft-free place to rise until doubled in bulk, about 1½ hours.

4. Punch down the dough and divide it into two equal portions. Freeze one portion wrapped in freezer wrap to use within a month. Let the dough you're using rest for about 5 minutes before proceeding with the pizza recipe.

Side

s,Salads

The term *side dishes* can mean many things to us at Chanterelle, but no matter what we call them, the sides and salads served at our staff meals are usually simple ones—we rarely fix anything that's complicated or calls for a lot of ingredients. In fact, a typical staff lunch might consist of a one-pot dish with no side at all. Many of our one-pot meals are already filled with vegetables, so the side dish is less necessary—except, that is, for some crusty bread. Occasionally a big vegetable salad or some tossed greens might make an appearance.

At dinner (which we eat together at 4:30 in the afternoon), the sides become more thoughtful—some green beans or zucchini, and perhaps a big bowl of mashed potatoes in the center of the table or a baked potato at each place. And if I'm feeling particularly inspired, I whip up an extra big pot of creamed spinach or corn.

Like anyone planning a family meal, I find that time is a key. When I'm rushed, it's easy to fall into serving the same thing day after day, especially when it comes to side dishes. Although I may pull out the easy favorites more often than not, I do try to make the meal well balanced nutritionally as well as interesting to the eye and palate. No family cook likes to hear, "Oh, that again!"—and that includes a staff-family cook.

| *Staff Meals from Chanterelle* | s i d e s , s a l a d s

Spiced Applesauce

Easy to prepare and **absolutely superior** to the commercial kind, freshly made applesauce will keep for weeks in the refrigerator. I like to use spicy, slightly sweet apples that are on the crisp side, like Northern Spy, Empire, or Idared. This spiced applesauce is a must with roast pork loin or chops, sausages, and schnitzel, and it's perfect with potato pancakes, too. I sometimes use a pinch of fragrant Chinese five-spice powder in place of the cinnamon, cloves, nutmeg, and black pepper. Be sure it's just a pinch, because this is a potent spice mixture that's easy to overdo.

MAKES ABOUT 2 CUPS

1½ pounds apples of choice (see above), peeled,
     cored, and cut into large chunks
½ cup water
1 cinnamon stick (3 inches)
Pinch of ground cloves
A few gratings of nutmeg
A few grinds of black pepper
Pinch of coarse (kosher) salt

1. Combine the apples, water, cinnamon stick, cloves, nutmeg, pepper, and salt in a medium-size, heavy, nonreactive saucepan. Cover and set over medium heat. When the water begins to bubble, reduce the heat to low and cook the apples until they begin to break down, about 30 minutes; uncover occasionally to stir and prevent sticking. Remove the cover and continue cooking until the apples are chunky but soft, about another 15 minutes. Remove the cinnamon stick.

2. Put the apples through a food mill for a smooth sauce or mash them with a fork for a chunkier texture. Taste and adjust the seasoning before serving hot or cold.

Sabrina's Baked Beans

Our kitchen staff members often draw on their **personal** cooking **repertoires** when it's their turn to feed us. Sabrina was one of our first employees when we opened Chanterelle at its original SoHo location in 1979. In those early days we often enjoyed her specialty, these baked beans, as a staff-meal side dish. Feel free to adjust the balance of the seasoning. The long, slow cooking time has a miraculous effect on the beans' texture; you'll find that they are amazingly creamy. Some cooks like their beans on the spicy side, like these, while others prefer them more sweet.

My philosophy about baked beans is when you make them, you might as well make plenty. This recipe makes enough for side-dish servings at several meals. Serve with hot dogs, David's Famous Fried Chicken (page 157), or Roast Ham with Honey-Mustard Glaze (page 102). **SERVES 6 TO 8**

1 pound dried navy beans, rinsed and picked over
4 ounces slab bacon, rind removed and discarded,
    cut into 1-inch chunks
1 medium onion, chopped
½ cup (packed) light brown sugar
½ cup ketchup
⅓ cup red wine vinegar
¼ cup molasses
2 tablespoons Dijon mustard
1 tablespoon good-quality chili powder
2 teaspoons minced garlic
½ teaspoon cayenne pepper
Coarse (kosher) salt, to taste

1. Place the beans in a medium-size bowl and cover with cold water by about 3 inches. Soak for at least 8 hours or overnight.

2. Drain the beans and place in a large stockpot. Add enough fresh cold water to cover by 3 inches. Bring to a boil over high heat, then reduce the heat to low and simmer until the beans are almost tender (they should still be a little underdone), about 1 hour. Drain.

3. Preheat the oven to 325°F.

4. Combine the beans, bacon, onion, sugar, ketchup, vinegar, molasses, mustard, chili powder, garlic, cayenne, salt, and 5 cups water in a large casserole. Stir to combine and cover with a lid or aluminum foil.

5. Bake for about 4 hours, stirring every hour or so and checking the beans periodically as they bake (see Note). When done, the beans will be tender and creamy but not mushy. You can serve them right from the oven, although they improve if you refrigerate them for 1 to 2 days before serving. Let them cool, then transfer them to an airtight container before refrigerating. Reheat in a preheated 325°F oven for 20 to 30 minutes.

Note: The beans should cook slowly, the juices getting thicker and the beans creamier but holding their shape. If the beans stay too soupy, remove the lid for the last hour of baking; if they seem too dry, stir in water ¼ cup at a time and leave the cover on.

how we cook green beans

Trim the stem end of the green beans and place them in a skillet large enough to hold them in a layer not more than several green beans deep. Pour in cold water to reach about halfway up the beans—no more—then add as big a hunk of butter as you dare and a goodly amount of coarse (kosher) salt. Place the pan over high heat and bring to a boil. Cook the beans, uncovered, using tongs to fiddle with them as they cook, until they're bright green and tender but still crunchy. Lift the beans out of the pan with the tongs, letting them drip-dry a bit, and place them on a platter.

That's all there is to it; they will be very good. In fact, we have found this method to work so well that we now use it to cook zucchini and carrot rounds as well as cauliflower and broccoli florets.

Beets with Balsamic Vinegar

The **faint sweetness** and low acidity of balsamic vinegar is a perfect foil for the earthy taste of beets. For the recipe, there's no need to invest in an expensive real balsamic vinegar (labeled "*tradizionale*"); a decent mass-produced commercial brand works just fine. Baking, rather than boiling, the beets brings out their robust flavor.

Vividly colored beets "bleed," so to keep the juices in while they cook, leave on the skins, the "tails" or rootlike wisps on the bottom, and at least an inch of the green stems. After they're cooked, peel the beets over a bowl or a thick layer of paper towels, since beet juice stains are nearly impossible to remove from wood or plastic surfaces.

Karen loves beets and is happy to make a meal of this dish, with the main course there "just as an excuse." Two of the good "excuses" to serve alongside are David's Famous Fried Chicken (page 157) or Herbed Pinwheel Pork Loin (page 100). **SERVES 4**

8 medium beets (about 2 pounds total)
½ cup water
¼ cup canola or other vegetable oil
6 tablespoons balsamic vinegar
2 to 4 tablespoons extra-virgin olive oil, to taste
1 teaspoon coarse (kosher) salt
Freshly ground black pepper, to taste

1. Preheat the oven to 350°F.

2. Trim the beets, leaving on the skin, an inch of the stem, and the wispy "tail" on the bottom of each, then scrub and drain. Place the beets in a small casserole dish just big enough to hold them. Pour the water and canola oil over the beets, then cover tightly with a lid or aluminium foil and bake until tender and easily pierced with a sharp paring knife, about 1½ hours.

3. Remove the casserole from the oven and uncover the beets, keeping your face averted from the escaping steam. Allow the beets to cool completely in the casserole.

4. Meanwhile, combine the vinegar, 2 tablespoons of the olive oil, the salt, and pepper in a medium-size bowl and whisk to blend. Taste and add more olive oil, if desired.

5. Peel the cooled beets with the back of a paring knife and cut into ⅜-inch slices. Add to the dressing in the bowl and toss gently but thoroughly to coat. Serve immediately or marinate, in the refrigerator, for up to 24 hours.

Broccoli with Oyster Sauce

This is my version of a standard Chinese recipe that **never fails** to please. Most often I make it with broccoli because I always have some on hand and it's the only vegetable my son, Jake, will eat (he loves this dish), but feel free to substitute green beans, snow peas, sugar snaps, or a medley of vegetables. The combination of oyster sauce, Thai fish sauce *(nam pla),* and Chinese black vinegar is extraordinarily flavorful. For some additional zing and a touch of pepper heat, you could add hot red pepper flakes or some fresh minced chile.

With a big bowl of plain white rice, this is good as a vegetarian main course, and it's perfect alongside Chicken with Black Mushrooms and Chinese Sausage (page 160), Grilled Quail with

Soba Salad and Scallions (page 204), Sautéed Salmon with Brown Butter, Lemon, and Capers (page 212), or David's Famous Fried Chicken (page 157). **SERVES 4**

1 large bunch broccoli
½ cup canola or other vegetable oil
6 cloves garlic, minced
1 cup oyster sauce (see box, below)
2 tablespoons Thai fish sauce (nam pla)
1 tablespoon Chinese black vinegar (see box, page 49)
   or balsamic vinegar

1. Trim and discard the thick stems from the broccoli. Cut the florets from the remaining stems, then peel the stems and cut into thin slices.

2. Bring a large saucepan of salted water to a boil over high heat. Add the broccoli and blanch for 1 minute, then rinse under cold running water to stop the cooking and drain thoroughly.

3. Heat the oil in a wok or large skillet over high heat. Add the garlic and stir-fry quickly until fragrant and very lightly browned, about 15 seconds. Add the broccoli, oyster sauce, fish sauce, and vinegar and stir-fry until heated through and a light sauce has formed, about 45 seconds. Serve immediately.

Staff Meals from Chanterelle | sides, salads

oyster sauce

Thick, shiny brown oyster sauce is an all-purpose Cantonese seasoning mixture made with extract of dried oysters, salt, water, and caramel coloring, plus a little cornstarch as a stabilizer. The strong, distinctive, almost meaty flavor is simultaneously sweet and smoky. Oyster sauce is often used as a flavoring for dipping sauces, vegetable stir-fries, and various meat or broccoli dishes. The best-quality versions, such as Lee Kum Kee Premium, Hop Sing Lung Oyster Flavored Sauce, and Sa Cheng Oyster Flavored Sauce, can also be used on their own as dipping sauces. The sauce will keep indefinitely in the refrigerator.

Braised Red Cabbage

When the **weather turns cold** and it's time for hearty side dishes with deep flavor and pleasantly warming properties, nothing beats this simple, aromatic favorite. It makes a tasty accompaniment for everything from a roast pork loin or roast duck to a plate of sliced boiled beef. **SERVES 6 TO 8**

3 strips bacon, cut into ¼-inch pieces
4 tablespoons (½ stick) unsalted butter
2 medium red onions, peeled and thinly sliced
2 cloves garlic, chopped
3 tablespoons sugar
1 large head red cabbage, slivered (12 cups)
1½ cups Chicken Stock (page 39) or canned low-
    sodium chicken broth
½ cup dry red wine
¼ cup honey
2 tablespoons red wine vinegar
2 tablespoons cider vinegar
2 bay leaves
Coarse (kosher) salt and freshly ground black pepper, to taste

1. Place the bacon in a large pot and sauté over medium heat to render the fat, about 2 minutes. Add the butter and, when it has melted, add the onions. Reduce the heat to low and sweat the onions until they are translucent but not browned, 10 to 15 minutes. Add the garlic and cook for 1 minute, then stir in the sugar and cook for 2 minutes more.

2. Stir in the cabbage, then add the stock, wine, honey, both vinegars, the bay leaves, salt, and pepper. Increase the heat to high and bring the liquids to a boil, then reduce the heat to medium low, cover the pot, and simmer the cabbage until it's very tender and aromatic, 1 to 1½ hours. Taste and add more salt and pepper if needed. Remove the bay leaves and serve.

Staff Meals from Chanterelle

Cider Vinegar Slaw

This flavorful, easy-to-make **sweet-and-sour** slaw is prepared without oil, so it's a perfect foil for rich, fried, or grilled foods. Serve it with grilled hamburgers or tuna or the Fresh Salmon Croquettes on page 218. **SERVES 8 TO 10**

2 cups cider vinegar
½ cup sugar
1 teaspoon coarse (kosher) salt
10 cups shredded Savoy or green cabbage (about
    2½ pounds cabbage)
3 medium red bell peppers, stemmed, seeded, and
    cut into very thin strips
2 carrots, peeled and grated

Combine the vinegar, sugar, and salt in a large bowl and whisk until blended and the sugar is dissolved. Add the cabbage, bell peppers, and carrots and toss well to coat. Let the slaw marinate, refrigerated, for at least 2 hours or overnight before tossing again to serve, slightly chilled.

Cauliflower Gratin

With its soft, creamy **blanket of Béchamel** Sauce and generously sprinkled with two types of cheese, this gratin is a fine side dish for sautéed meats or a roast. **SERVES 6**

Coarse (kosher) salt, to taste
1 large head cauliflower, thick core removed, cut into florets
    (about 6 cups)

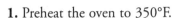

Béchamel Sauce (recipe follows)
½ cup grated Gruyère cheese
¼ cup freshly grated Parmesan

1. Preheat the oven to 350°F.

2. Bring a large saucepan of salted water to a boil over medium-high heat. Add the cauliflower florets and cook until just tender but still slightly crunchy, 3 to 5 minutes, depending on the size of the florets. Drain well and arrange in a single layer in a baking or oval gratin dish.

3. Pour the béchamel over the cauliflower and sprinkle evenly with the grated Gruyère and Parmesan. Bake until bubbly and browned and the cheeses are melted, about 20 minutes. Serve immediately.

Béchamel Sauce

Classic béchamel, that **smoothly elegant** white sauce, is made with either milk or cream. My version uses half-and-half, which, despite its modest milk-fat content, creates a sauce that's amazingly rich and luxurious in flavor and mouth feel. If you're pressed for time, make the sauce up to two days before you plan to use it and store it, tightly covered, in the refrigerator. Before storing, press a layer of plastic wrap directly on the béchamel's surface to prevent a skin from forming. Reheat béchamel in a heavy saucepan over low heat until not quite simmering. **MAKES ABOUT 4 CUPS**

5 tablespoons plus 1 teaspoon (⅔ stick) unsalted butter
⅓ cup all-purpose flour
4 cups half-and-half
2 bay leaves
2 tablespoons grated onion
Coarse (kosher) salt and freshly ground black pepper, to taste
A few gratings of nutmeg

1. Melt the butter in a small saucepan over low heat. Whisk in the flour and cook, whisking frequently, until the roux develops a nutty aroma, about 10 minutes. Be careful not to let the flour brown at all.

2. While the roux is cooking, bring the half-and-half to a simmer in a second small saucepan over high heat. Immediately remove the half-and-half from the heat and add it to the roux in a slow, steady stream, whisking constantly until blended and smooth. After all the liquid is added, continue to cook the béchamel over low heat, whisking frequently, until thickened, about 3 minutes.

3. Add the bay leaves and grated onion and continue to simmer the béchamel slowly, uncovered, whisking frequently, until the flavors are blended and it's somewhat thicker than heavy cream, about 15 minutes.

4. Remove the pan from the heat and strain the béchamel into a heatproof bowl. Season with salt, pepper, and nutmeg.

double-cutting corn

With this technique, corn kernels are removed from the cob in two steps. Holding an ear of corn upright, use a sharp knife to slice down the ear, cutting the kernels in half. Do this around the entire ear. Then slice down the ear a second time, being careful not to cut into the cob, to remove the rest of the kernels and to scrape the milk from the cob. Each ear of corn will yield ⅓ to ½ cup of kernels.

Summertime Creamed Corn

There's no point in making creamed corn unless you use **fresh corn**—frozen kernels are just not worth the effort. Standard creamed-corn recipes simply use cream or half-and-half, but mine uses a luxurious Béchamel Sauce that enhances the corn's fresh-picked sweetness without overwhelming any of its natural good taste. Fried chicken is our staff's favorite main dish, but when I make it I always struggle to decide whether to serve it with creamed corn or Creamed Spinach (page 340). Each side has its champions. **SERVES 4 TO 6**

1 tablespoon olive oil
3 tablespoons grated onion
2 small cloves garlic, minced
3 cups fresh corn kernels (6 to 8 ears; see box, page 312)
2 cups Béchamel Sauce (page 311)
2 bay leaves
Pinch of cayenne pepper
A few gratings of nutmeg
Pinch of dried thyme leaves
Coarse (kosher) salt and freshly ground black pepper, to taste
Fresh lemon juice, to taste

1. Heat the oil in a small, heavy saucepan over low heat. Add the onion and garlic and sweat, stirring occasionally, until translucent but not browned, about 5 minutes.

2. Add the corn, béchamel, bay leaves, cayenne, nutmeg, thyme, salt, and pepper. Cook, uncovered, stirring occasionally, until everything is nice and creamy, about 30 minutes.

3. Remove the pan from the heat and discard the bay leaves. Add a squeeze or two of lemon juice, then taste and adjust the seasoning before serving.

Cucumber Salad with Red Onion and Chinese Sausage

This refreshing salad is often found on Thai menus, where it's a **palate-soothing** accompaniment to highly seasoned Thai curries and barbecue. The pleasing combination of flavors makes this salad perfect buffet fare, especially in the summertime. If they're available, use seedless English (hothouse) cucumbers. You can substitute pepperoni or spicy Cajun andouille sausage for the Chinese sausage; it won't be the same, but it will still be good. Sometimes I like to chill the cucumber slices and prepare the dressing first, then add the sausage slices to the mixture while they're still very hot. The contrast between the icy cucumber and piping-hot sausage gives the salad an authentic flavor. **SERVES 4**

2 Chinese sausages (see box, page 161)
½ cup fresh lime juice
⅓ cup cold water, or more if needed
¼ cup sugar
1½ tablespoons Thai fish sauce (nam pla)
1 teaspoon chili-garlic sauce (sambal oelek)
1 clove garlic, minced
2 English cucumbers, thinly sliced, or 3 medium regular cucumbers, peeled, seeded, and thinly sliced
1 small red onion, sliced lengthwise (top to bottom)
Fresh cilantro sprigs, for garnish

1. Preheat the broiler.

2. Place the sausages on a rack on a broiler pan and broil, turning every so often, until the skin is lightly charred, 2 to 3 minutes. Let them cool, then cut them on the diagonal into ¼-inch slices. Set aside.

3. Place the lime juice, ⅓ cup water, the sugar, fish sauce, chili-garlic sauce, and garlic in a large bowl and whisk until the sugar is dissolved. Taste and add more water if the dressing is too tart.

4. Add the cucumber, onion, and sliced sausage to the dressing in the bowl and toss to coat. Arrange the salad on a platter or in a shallow bowl, garnish with the cilantro sprigs, and serve immediately.

Three-Can Curried Chickpeas

Having a few cans of chickpeas on hand in the cupboard can be **very useful**, especially when a good, simple side dish is needed for a hasty supper. I always have a supply on hand at home and in the restaurant for those times when the sides and salads get lost in the shuffle of making a main dish. Madras-style curry powder complements the nutlike taste of chickpeas, transforming the mild-flavored legumes into something genuinely interesting to eat. Heating the curry powder for a few minutes in the saucepan before adding the chickpeas and broth fully releases its flavor, and a bit of butter swirled in at the end creates a temporary emulsion that thickens the liquid, rounds out the flavors, and gives the dish a velvety feel. Serve as an accompaniment to Grilled Butterflied Leg of Lamb (page 87), plain chicken or pork dishes, or grilled steaks or hamburgers. **SERVES 8**

2 to 4 tablespoons unsalted butter

2 medium onions, cut into small dice

2 cloves garlic, minced

1 tablespoon Madras-style curry powder,
   such as Sun brand, or to taste

3 cans (15 ounces each) chickpeas,
   rinsed and drained

1 can (14½ ounces) low-sodium chicken or
   vegetable broth, or water

Fresh lemon juice, to taste

Coarse (kosher) salt, to taste

1. Melt 2 tablespoons of the butter in a medium-size saucepan over medium heat. Add the onions and garlic and sauté, stirring occasionally, until the onions are tender and golden brown, 5 to 8 minutes. Add the curry powder and cook, stirring constantly, until it's fragrant and the onions are thoroughly coated, about 3 minutes.

2. Add the chickpeas, chicken broth, and a squeeze of lemon juice and increase the heat to medium high. Bring to a boil, then reduce the heat to medium low and simmer, uncovered, stirring occasionally, until the liquid is reduced and the flavors are blended, 20 to 30 minutes.

3. Remove the pan from the heat and taste for seasoning, adding salt and more lemon juice, if desired. If you like, add the remaining 2 tablespoons butter and stir until it's melted. Serve immediately.

Staff Meals from Chanterelle | s i d e s , s a l a d s

tahini

Tahini, a paste made of untoasted ground sesame seeds, is often used as an ingredient in Middle Eastern dips and sauces. You'll find it in Middle Eastern and specialty food stores, health food stores, and large supermarkets. Asian sesame seed paste, made from roasted seeds, has a completely different flavor and cannot be used as a substitute for tahini.

Herbed Summer Hummus

In a restaurant kitchen the summer months are particularly grueling. The temperature from the ovens and stoves is intense year-round, but in the summer the kitchen thermostat soars to saunalike heights. So it's not surprising that our appetites begin to lag. During hot weather the staff meals we prepare must be sustaining (we need all the energy we can muster) yet light and cooling (we need refreshment). Hummus is one of our standby summer dishes because it's quick and easy to prepare (we can whip up a batch in the food processor early in the day), **requires no cooking**, and is good chilled. Our dinner is very likely to be a small buffet of hummus, Baba Ghanouj (page 320), Marinated Tomatoes with Balsamic Vinegar and Basil (see box, page 344), and a green salad. I like to swirl the hummus on a platter or in a shallow bowl, then garnish it with a drizzle of extra-virgin olive oil, a colorful dusting of paprika, and a few black olives. A basket of warm pita bread is all that's needed for scooping up the garlicky dip. **MAKES ABOUT 3 CUPS**

1 can (15 ounces) chickpeas, drained,
   but ½ cup liquid reserved
½ cup tahini (see box, facing page)
Juice of 1 lemon
4 to 5 cloves garlic, peeled
1 bunch fresh chives
1 cup (loosely packed) flat-leaf parsley leaves
Coarse (kosher) salt and freshly ground black pepper,
   to taste
Extra-virgin olive oil, for garnish
Sweet Hungarian paprika, for garnish

1. Combine the chickpeas, reserved ½ cup liquid, tahini, lemon juice, 4 of the garlic cloves, the chives, parsley, salt, and pepper in a food processor or blender and process to a smooth purée. Taste and adjust the seasoning, adding the remaining garlic clove as well as salt and pepper, if desired.

2. To serve, mound the hummus in a shallow bowl or platter, drizzle with the olive oil, and sprinkle with paprika.

Eggplant Caponata

Caponata, the **popular Italian** eggplant dish, is so all-purpose that it can serve as everything from appetizer to side dish to pizza topping. We enjoy it accompanying cold roast chicken, slices of pork loin, and even spread on a good, fresh hunk of crusty bread. Actually, my version is more spreadlike than a typical caponata. Fennel is an unusual ingredient for this dish, but I prefer the flavor it offers and use it instead of the classic celery. **MAKES ABOUT 6 CUPS**

2 medium eggplants

Coarse (kosher) salt

3 tablespoons extra-virgin olive oil, plus more for
    oiling the vegetables

1 red bell pepper

1 medium onion, diced

3 cloves garlic, minced

1 fennel bulb, outer leaves removed and discarded,
    coarsely diced

½ cup oil-packed green olives, pitted and chopped

¼ cup drained capers

¼ cup sugar

2 tablespoons fresh lemon juice

2 tablespoons red wine vinegar

2 tablespoons sherry vinegar

1 tablespoon good-quality soy sauce,
   such as Kikkoman

1 teaspoon crushed hot red pepper flakes

½ cup chopped fresh flat-leaf parsley leaves

3 tablespoons slivered fresh basil leaves

1. Split the eggplants in half lengthwise and score the flesh side lightly with the tip of a sharp knife. Sprinkle the cut halves with salt and place them, cut-side down, on a rack set over a baking sheet. Let them stand until the bitter juices leach from the eggplants, 1 hour. Pat dry with paper towels.

2. Preheat the oven to 450°F. Line a baking sheet with parchment paper.

3. Brush the eggplants all over with some of the olive oil. Place the eggplants skin-side down on the prepared baking sheet and roast for 10 minutes. Rub the bell pepper with some of the oil, place on the baking sheet with the eggplants, and continue roasting for 20 minutes. The eggplants and pepper should be very soft and slightly collapsed. Place the vegetables in a brown paper bag and close tightly. Let them steam in the bag.

4. Meanwhile, heat 3 tablespoons of the olive oil in a large skillet over medium-low heat. Add the onion, garlic, and fennel and sweat until soft and translucent (don't let the vegetables brown), 10 minutes.

5. When the eggplants and pepper are cool, peel off the skins and cut the flesh into ½-inch cubes. Discard the skins.

6. Add the eggplants and pepper to the skillet and stir to mix well. Add the olives, capers, sugar, lemon juice, red wine vinegar, sherry vinegar, soy sauce, and pepper flakes. Increase the heat slightly and simmer the mixture, uncovered, until the vegetables are soft, 15 minutes. Cool to room temperature, stir in the parsley and basil, and serve. Store any leftovers in a covered container in the refrigerator. The caponata will keep for up to 3 days. Let it come to room temperature before serving.

Baba Ghanouj

In the summer our staff meals become a series of cold or room-temperature dishes served **buffet-style**. Even when we're sweltering and our appetites are suppressed by the heat, we always enjoy this garlicky baba ghanouj. Scoop the dip up with warm pita bread, crudités, or crackers, or make a sandwich garnished with alfalfa sprouts or tomato and shredded lettuce.

Salting the eggplants before roasting them draws out some of their bitterness. And don't worry if the eggplant chars a bit while it's in the oven—this helps give baba ghanouj its characteristic smoky flavor. I prefer to mash the cooked eggplant by hand, which gives it a rough texture, but this can also be done in a food processor or blender. **MAKES ABOUT 6 CUPS**

3 large eggplants
Coarse (kosher) salt
5 tablespoons extra-virgin olive oil
3 tablespoons tahini
2 large cloves garlic, minced
Juice of 1 lemon
Freshly ground black pepper, to taste
For garnish: extra-virgin olive oil, sweet Hungarian paprika,
    and fresh flat-leaf parsley leaves

1. Split the eggplants in half lengthwise and score the flesh side lightly with the tip of a sharp knife. Sprinkle the cut halves with salt and place them, cut-side down, on a rack set over a baking sheet. Let them stand until the bitter juices leach from the eggplants, 1 hour. Pat dry with paper towels.

2. Preheat the oven to 450°F. Line a baking sheet with parchment paper.

3. Brush the eggplants all over with 3 tablespoons of the olive oil. Place the eggplants skin-side down on the prepared baking sheet and bake until they are very soft and slightly collapsed, about 30 minutes. Place the eggplants in a brown paper bag and close tightly. Let them steam in the bag.

4. When the eggplants are cool, scrape the flesh into a large bowl or a food processor or blender. Discard the skins. Add the tahini, the remaining 2 tablespoons olive oil, the garlic, lemon juice, and salt and pepper to taste. Mash with a fork or the back of a wooden spoon until blended, or process until smooth. Taste and adjust the seasoning, then serve, drizzled with some olive oil, dusted with paprika, and sprinkled with parsley.

Fennel Salad

I enjoy the cool crunch of fennel, and when a bulb is sliced paper thin (break out the mandoline to do the slicing, if you have one) against the grain, the crunch moves up front and center. Serve this salad on its own or as part of an antipasto platter, along with a good selection of meats, such as hard salami and prosciutto, and cheeses, such as Gruyère and aged Gouda.

SERVES 4

3 medium fennel bulbs (1¼ to 1½ pounds total)
⅓ cup extra-virgin olive oil
Juice of 2 large lemons
1 tablespoon coarse (kosher) salt
1 teaspoon freshly ground black pepper
1 piece (3 ounces) Parmesan
2 tablespoons chopped fresh flat-leaf parsley leaves

1. If the fennel still has its stalks, trim them away. Cut the bulbs into quarters, top to bottom, and remove the core and any unattractive outer leaves. Cut the fennel quarters against the grain into paper-thin slices.

2. Place the oil, lemon juice, salt, and pepper in a large bowl and whisk to combine. Add the fennel and toss to coat each slice with some of the vinaigrette. Let the fennel sit for 15 minutes to absorb some of the vinaigrette's flavor.

3. Mound the salad attractively on a platter or divide among four plates. Shave the Parmesan over the salad using a mandoline or truffle shaver. Sprinkle with parsley and serve.

Warm Lentil Salad

It's well **worth your while** to seek out small, greenish French de Puy lentils (page 24) for this recipe. Their flavor and texture are superior to those of the larger, more common brown lentils at the supermarket, although I don't hesitate to use the brown kind if that's all I have on hand.

You could say this dish is saladlike rather than a salad since it's served warm and is almost, though not quite, pourable. The butter in the recipe adds richness and mellowness to the flavors, and the balsamic vinegar adds a complementary touch of sweetness and acidity. It's lovely served with Confit of Duck (page 201), steak, lamb chops, or pork sausages. And it also makes a fine appetizer served on a bed of salad greens or cooked leafy green vegetables. When reheating leftovers, you may need to add a little water or chicken stock. **SERVES 6 TO 8**

2 cups French de Puy (green) lentils or regular brown lentils
4 cups Chicken Stock (page 39) or canned low-sodium
   chicken broth
Coarse (kosher) salt

1 cup mixed vegetables, such as leeks, carrots, zucchini, onion,
   and bell peppers, cut into ⅛-inch dice
½ teaspoon minced garlic
8 tablespoons (1 stick) unsalted butter, cut into pieces
½ cup balsamic vinegar, or more to taste
¼ cup extra-virgin olive oil
Freshly ground black pepper, to taste
2 tablespoons chopped fresh flat-leaf parsley leaves

1. Combine the lentils, chicken stock, and 1 teaspoon of the salt in a medium-size, heavy saucepan and bring to a boil over high heat. Reduce the heat to low and simmer, covered, until the lentils are cooked through and most of the liquid is absorbed, about 30 minutes.

2. Add the vegetables and garlic and cook, uncovered, until the vegetables are just tender, about 2 minutes.

3. Add the butter, ½ cup vinegar, and the olive oil and stir over low heat until the butter is melted and everything is heated through and well combined. Remove the pan from the heat and season to taste with salt and pepper and more vinegar, if needed. Stir in the parsley and serve immediately while still very warm.

Hot Dog Onions

Boredom often triggers creativity, which is how these **special onions** became a part of staff meals at the restaurant. Each summer it was the same old story—the minute the hot weather hit, our staff developed an insatiable appetite for hot dogs, and at one time or another every imaginable condiment was served. Eager to replicate those luscious, savory onions New York City hot dog vendors use to top their franks, I began fiddling around. The result was these slow-cooked, sweet-and-sour onions that are perfect with hot dogs or burgers, strewn over a grilled steak, or served alongside a thick slice of meat loaf. They can be served hot from the pan or at room temperature, and will keep, in an airtight container, for up to a week in the refrigerator. **MAKES ABOUT 2 CUPS**

1 tablespoon unsalted butter
2 tablespoons canola or other vegetable oil
2 large onions, sliced
2 tablespoons ketchup
2 teaspoons red wine vinegar
1 teaspoon Worcestershire sauce
1 teaspoon sugar
A few dashes of Tabasco sauce
Coarse (kosher) salt and freshly ground black pepper, to taste

1. Combine the butter and oil in a large skillet and heat over low heat. When the butter has melted, add the onions and cook, covered, until the onions are soft, about 1 hour, uncovering occasionally to stir. Adjust the heat during cooking so the onions don't color.

2. Stir the ketchup, vinegar, Worcestershire sauce, sugar, Tabasco, salt, and pepper into the onions and cook, uncovered, until heated through, 1 to 2 minutes, stirring occasionally. Remove the skillet from the heat and taste and adjust the seasoning as needed. Serve hot or at room temperature.

Yummy Onions

Caramelized onions are a **wonderful** example of how long, slow cooking can elevate ordinary ingredients to extraordinary heights of flavor. Here the onions' natural sugars caramelize, creating a savory dish of tender, rich, golden brown strands. A dash of balsamic vinegar accents the sweetness and adds a complementary hint of acidity.

This appetizing recipe make the leap from side dish to condiment, and you'll find that the onions are equally at home alongside roasts, mashed potatoes, and burgers. I like to fold a spoonful into green beans or lentils just before serving, or toss them with pasta. And they're terrific strewn across the top of fried eggs or tucked inside an omelet.

This recipe can easily be doubled. **MAKES ABOUT ½ CUP**

2 tablespoons unsalted butter
6 medium onions, sliced lengthwise (top to bottom)
Coarse (kosher) salt and freshly ground black pepper, to taste
Dash of balsamic vinegar

1. Melt the butter in a large, heavy skillet over medium-low heat. Add the onions and salt and pepper and cook, uncovered, stirring occasionally, until the onions are nicely browned and very tender but not mushy, about 45 minutes.

2. Remove the skillet from the heat and season the onions with a bit of vinegar, then taste and adjust the seasoning again before serving.

Staff Meals from Chanterelle

Vidalia Onion Fritters

The French term *amuse bouche* (which means "amuse the mouth") describes tiny appetizers that are served with drinks to awaken the palate. One such complimentary *amuse bouche* that we serve our Chanterelle clients as they sip their aperitifs and look over the menu is these little fritters, which come with a slightly exotic Tamarind Dipping Sauce. The restaurant staff likes them, too: After a long, late shift, when we often have snacks before we clean up and go home, we can't resist indulging in the fritters, although we usually dip them in hot sauce since there's rarely any Tamarind Dipping Sauce left in the kitchen.

Sweet Vidalia onions are harvested in the spring and are best at that time, when they're freshest. They can be found the rest of the year for as long as the supply lasts. If you can't find Vidalias, try another sweet onion like Maui (Hawaii) or Walla Walla (Washington). At other times of year you could use Spanish onions as a substitute.

MAKES ENOUGH FOR A CROWD (35 TO 40 FRITTERS)

1¾ cups all-purpose flour, or more if needed

2 teaspoons baking powder

Coarse (kosher) salt, to taste

2 to 2½ cups milk

2 large eggs

½ teaspoon white wine vinegar

¼ teaspoon Tabasco sauce or chili-garlic sauce
   (sambal oelek)

2 large Vidalia onions, sliced lengthwise (top to bottom)

Canola or other vegetable oil, for deep-frying

Tamarind Dipping Sauce (page 372), for serving

1. Place 1¾ cups flour, the baking powder, and salt in a large bowl and whisk to mix.

2. Place 2 cups of the milk, the eggs, vinegar, and hot sauce in another bowl and whisk until blended, then pour into the flour mixture and whisk until just blended; do not overmix. Stir in the sliced onions and let the batter rest for 30 minutes. It should be slightly thicker than heavy cream. If it isn't, sprinkle in a little more flour. If it's too thick, add a little more milk. The batter should look somewhat free-form, not doughy.

3. Preheat the oven to its lowest setting.

4. Pour vegetable oil to a depth of 4 inches into a large, heavy saucepan and heat to 375°F on a deep-fry thermometer. Drop the onion fritter batter into the hot oil by the tablespoonful, a few at a time, and fry, turning once, until the fritters are golden brown on both sides, about 3 minutes in all. The fritters will have an irregular, spiderlike look, with a few loose pieces of onion escaping here and there. Check a fritter by breaking it open to see if the center is cooked; if it still seems unset, cook 1 minute more. Drain on paper towels. Place the fritters in the oven to keep warm while you finish frying them all. Serve on a doily-lined platter or in a lined woven basket accompanied by the dipping sauce in one or more bowls.

Our Favorite Fries

At Chanterelle all of us love french fries, and the fact that we cook fancy food at the restaurant doesn't in the least diminish our fondness for them. Truth be told, we positively venerate our deep-fryer, and we'd be the first to concede that our favorite fries contain two of the most tempting food groups—grease and salt. Although ketchup with them is great, Aïoli (page 363) is even better. When we have Aïoli in the kitchen, we shamelessly cluster around the platter of fries, dipping each crisp morsel into the silky sauce, including even those last little fried fragments.

Everyone has a favorite fry type—some like them thick, some like them thin, and some like them curly. I like my fries to be as long as possible, and very thin. Make whichever style you prefer, but be sure not to peel the potatoes, and don't be tempted to omit the important soaking stage in this recipe. Soaking removes a great deal of the starch from the potatoes, which results in much crispier fries.

I fry my potatoes using the three-dip method. By repeatedly dipping the fries in the hot oil for a few seconds before finishing them off with a longer stay, they cook more evenly. And by eliminating some of the moisture, the slight cooling between dips prevents the potatoes from overcooking. **SERVES 2 TO 4**

4 Idaho potatoes (the longest ones you can find),
   scrubbed
2 quarts canola or other vegetable oil,
   for deep-frying
Coarse (kosher) salt

1. Using a mandoline or french-fry cutter, hold each potato lengthwise and cut the desired-size pieces for fries. Place the potatoes in a large bowl, cover with cold water, and let them soak in the refrigerator for at least 4 hours, but preferably overnight.

2. Drain the potato pieces by lifting them out of their soaking liquid and placing them in a colander to drip; do not pour the whole bowl into the colander. Pat the potatoes dry with paper towels.

3. Heat the oil in a deep-fryer or a large, deep, heavy saucepan to 375°F on a deep-fry thermometer. Place a handful or two of the potatoes in a deep-fry basket and lower them very carefully into the hot oil. Leave them there until the oil bubbles up, count to 5, then quickly lift out the basket, holding it over the pot to let the oil drip back in. Repeat the process a second and a third time. After the third dip, the fries should look translucent but not brown.

4. If you'll be finishing the fries right away, leave the oil on the heat; if you're finishing at a later time, see Note. To finish, put the fries back in the basket and dip them again in the hot oil, this time letting them brown and crisp, about 5 minutes. Don't crowd the basket; it's better to do this in batches for crispier fries. Drain the finished fries on paper towels, sprinkle with salt, and eat immediately.

Note: After their third dip in the oil, blanched fries can be held until you're ready to serve them. Gently pour them out onto paper towels and let them cool. Then cover them with plastic wrap and refrigerate for up to 3 days before their final crisping.

a master recipe for potato gratin

Many side dishes like this one don't require a recipe or, for that matter, even any measuring. All you need to know is the basic technique and how many people you want to feed. For this comfort-food potato gratin, figure on one potato per person. I use starchy Idaho (russet) potatoes, because they have the best texture for this dish. You can peel the potatoes if you want, but it's not necessary, and I prefer to leave the skins on. Cut the potatoes into very thin slices (less than ¼ inch thick), place them in a bowl, cover with cold water. Let them soak for an hour or so.

Using a slotted spoon, remove the potatoes from the water to a colander to drain. Spread several layers of paper towels (or a large clean kitchen towel) on a work surface. Place the drained potato slices on the towels and pat dry. Season the slices with plenty of salt and freshly ground black pepper, tossing them on the towel to coat evenly.

Rub the insides of a shallow casserole with the cut side of a halved garlic clove, then lightly coat with unsalted butter. Add the potatoes to the casserole, arranging them in an even layer. Pour enough heavy (or whipping) cream over the potatoes to just cover them, dot with a little butter, and bake at 375°F until the potatoes are brown and bubbly, about 45 minutes. Serve with Roast Ham with Honey-Mustard Glaze (page 102) or Roast Chicken Stuffed with Basil (page 146).

Paul's Potato Latkes

Potato latkes (pancakes) was the one dish Karen's father, Paul Brown, prepared and it was **always an event** when he did. Since restaurants rarely close for Hanukkah—and it would have been inconceivable for Paul to grate a mountain of potatoes to satisfy our entire staff—I have inherited this all-important Brown family tradition (though I add onions and Paul never did). At Hanukkah and other staff meals they become a main dish accompanied by plenty of sour cream and Spiced Applesauce (page 303). Just how much does the staff like them? We keep a running tally at our pancake dinners and compare notes at the end to see how many we've wolfed down. Let's just say the numbers are pretty scary.

There's no question that hand-grating the potatoes and vegetables produces a superior texture (that's how we make them at home), but I admit to putting the shredding disk in the food processor and doing them that way when I'm making a great quantity for our staff meal. Another tip: The more water you're able to squeeze from the shredded ingredients, the crispier the latkes will be. **SERVES 4**

4 large Idaho potatoes (about 2 pounds total), peeled
1 small onion, peeled
1 large carrot, peeled
2 large eggs
1 tablespoon chopped fresh flat-leaf parsley leaves
Coarse (kosher) salt and freshly ground black pepper, to taste
1 cup fine dry bread crumbs (see box, page 279) or matzoh meal, or as needed
Canola oil or melted rendered chicken or duck fat (see box, page 143), for frying

1. Preheat the oven to its lowest setting.

2. Using either the largest holes of a hand-grater or the shredding blade of a food processor, grate the potatoes, onion, and carrot. Place the mixture in a sieve and press to remove as much liquid as possible.

3. Combine the potato mixture in a large bowl with the eggs, parsley, salt, and pepper. Using your hands or a wooden spoon, mix well. Stir in half of the bread crumbs, then add the remainder slowly, stopping when the mixture is just thick enough to hold its shape, but not so loose that it dribbles off a spoon.

4. Pour oil or melted rendered fat to a depth of ¼ inch into a large, heavy skillet and heat over medium heat until a tiny drop of the batter sizzles upon contact. Using a ⅓-cup metal measure as a scoop, ladle the batter into the hot oil in the skillet, pressing each mound of batter into a small, flat pancake; do not crowd the skillet. Fry the pancakes until nicely browned on both sides, 4 to 5 minutes per side.

5. Transfer the pancakes to a platter and keep warm in the oven while you fry the remaining pancakes. Serve immediately.

how to bake a potato

It's easy. Somewhat mealy-textured Idahos, also called russets, are perfect baking potatoes because they bake up nice and fluffy due to their high starch and low moisture content. Scrub each potato well, then prick it once with a fork or skewer. I had always heard that this was necessary to prevent the potato from exploding in the oven, but never once had I ever seen this happen. So, after years of dutifully pricking potatoes, I decided it was just an old wives' tale and stopped doing it. More years passed. Then **one day I opened the oven to check on my baked potatoes and . . . yes, one had actually detonated! Laughing, I called over my cooks to witness the sight of all that potato skin stuck to the oven walls.**

    Anyway, onward to the next step. Place the pricked potato directly on the oven rack in a preheated 400°F oven and bake for 1 hour. Never bake potatoes wrapped in aluminum foil unless you've developed a taste for the almost steamed kind served at steakhouse chains.

how to boil a potato

Over the years I've seen chefs and home cooks boil potatoes in an astonishing number of ways, not always with successful results. This is my method and, of course, I believe it's the best. The key is to use whole *unpeeled* potatoes. Never, never cut the potatoes into smaller pieces. Cut potatoes absorb too much water, which robs them of their flavor and makes their texture mealy and mushy.

Place unpeeled potatoes in a pot with plenty of cold salted water. Bring to a boil over high heat, then reduce the heat to medium low, partially cover the pot, and boil the potatoes gently until they're tender. A fork should pierce the flesh of the potato easily, but the potato should not break apart. The cooked potatoes owe their superior texture and flavor to the fact that they are protected by their skins as they cook. This method is great for potatoes that will be used in salads. It's impractical for mashed potatoes, however, since few mortals have heat-proof fingers that can peel the potatoes while they're still hot enough for mashing.

Slightly Southern Potato Salad

Every family needs a **basic** potato salad **recipe** for casual summertime suppers and picnics with friends. I use a homemade mayonnaise but, in this recipe, a commercial one will be just fine. The sweet relish here gives the salad a southern accent, and it's very good with barbecue or cold ham. Tightly covered and refrigerated, the salad will keep for up to a week.

MAKES 4 TO 6 SERVINGS

2 pounds Yukon Gold or other waxy potatoes, scrubbed
½ cup chopped onion
¾ cup homemade Basic Mayonnaise (page 360), or a good
    quality mayonnaise, such as Hellmann's
2 tablespoons sweet relish
1 tablespoon white wine vinegar
2 teaspoons dry mustard, such as Colman's
2 teaspoons coarse (kosher) salt
1 teaspoon sweet Hungarian paprika
A few grinds of black pepper

1. Place the potatoes in a large saucepan of cold salted water and bring to a boil over high heat. Reduce the heat to medium and cook, partially covered, until the potatoes are tender, 30 to 45 minutes. Drain the potatoes in a colander. When they're cool enough to handle, remove the peels.

2. Cut the potatoes into 1-inch dice and place them in a large bowl. Let them cool to room temperature.

3. Place the onion, mayonnaise, relish, vinegar, mustard, salt, paprika, and pepper in a small bowl and stir to mix. Add the dressing to the potatoes and toss gently but thoroughly. Taste and adjust the seasoning, then cover and refrigerate for an hour before serving.

Staff Meals from Chanterelle

333

Everyday Mashed Potatoes

Not many dishes get as **enthusiastic** a **greeting** at the dinner table as a bowl of mashed potatoes. And the very best mashed potatoes are made by using an old-fashioned potato masher and elbow grease. The next best method, one that admittedly produces smoother potatoes (and the one we choose for making large quantities for our staff meal), involves using a standing mixer equipped with the paddle attachment. Whatever you do, don't use a food processor; it works the potatoes too much and makes them gummy. (Mashing potatoes after they're cooled will also result in gumminess.)

For our patrons at Chanterelle, I sometimes make a more elegant and refined potato purée by passing the boiled, drained potatoes through a food mill, then immediately stirring in some hot cream and a lot of softened butter. The finer texture allows the potatoes to hold far more butter, creating a deliciously rich purée to serve with roast beef or venison loin and flavorful sauces.

SERVES 6 TO 8

6 medium Idaho potatoes, peeled
6 tablespoons (¾ stick) unsalted butter,
   room temperature
¾ cup whole milk or half-and-half, warmed
Coarse (kosher) salt and freshly ground black pepper,
   to taste

1. Place the potatoes in a large saucepan of cold salted water and bring them to a boil over high heat. Reduce the heat to medium and cook, partially covered, until the potatoes are tender, 30 to 45 minutes. Drain the potatoes in a colander, then let them sit for a moment to let some of the moisture evaporate.

2. Transfer the potatoes while they're still hot to a large bowl; immediately add the butter, a bit of the milk, and salt and pepper. Using a potato masher or an electric mixer at medium speed, mash the potatoes well but without overworking them, gradually adding the rest of the milk as you mash. Taste and adjust the seasoning, then spoon the potatoes into a serving bowl. Serve immediately.

Coconut Rice

The floral fragrance and subtle flavor of Thai jasmine rice make it **a delightful choice** as a side dish. But adding unsweetened Thai coconut milk makes it even more appealing, contributing a bit of creaminess and more perfume to the aroma. This is a long-grain rice that cooks up nice and fluffy, with distinct grains. It does need a longer resting time (20 minutes) than short-grain rice requires, but that will ensure absolutely perfect rice every time. Coconut Rice is a fine accompaniment to Pork Saté with Spicy Peanut Sauce (page 116), Chicken with Cashews (page 182), or Oven-Roasted Barbecued Ribs (page 110).

MAKES ABOUT 7 CUPS; SERVES 6 TO 8

2 cups Thai jasmine rice or other long-grain rice
1 can (13 or 14 ounces) coconut milk, preferably a Thai brand
3⅓ cups water

1. Combine the rice, coconut milk, and water in a small, heavy saucepan. Bring to a boil over high heat, then reduce the heat to low, cover tightly, and simmer, without removing the cover, until all the liquid is absorbed, 20 minutes.

2. Remove the pan from the heat and let it stand, covered, for 20 minutes more before fluffing and serving.

Curry Rice

Plain, simple, and not very highly seasoned main dishes give a cook more room to play around when it comes to choosing a side-dish accompaniment with interesting, more assertive flavors. At home and for our staff meal I often make this versatile rice when lunch or dinner is based on a straightforward grilled meat, poultry, or fish dish. Although it's not absolutely necessary, the currants will be nicer if they're soaked in very hot water for 20 minutes or so, then drained before they're added to the rice. **MAKES ABOUT 7 CUPS; SERVES 6 TO 8**

2 tablespoons canola or other vegetable oil
1 small onion, diced
2 teaspoons Madras-style curry powder, such as Sun brand
2 cups Thai jasmine rice or other long-grain rice
1 can (13 or 14 ounces) coconut milk, preferably a Thai brand
3⅓ cups cold water
Dash of Thai fish sauce (nam pla)
½ cup dried currants

1. Heat the oil in a small, heavy saucepan over medium heat. Add the onion and sauté, stirring frequently, until softened but not browned, about 5 minutes. Add the curry powder and cook for about 1 minute, stirring to coat the onion with the powder; be careful not to let the powder burn.

2. Add the rice, coconut milk, water, and fish sauce and increase the heat to high. Bring to a boil, then reduce the heat to low, cover tightly, and simmer, without removing the cover, until the liquid is completely absorbed, 20 minutes.

3. Meanwhile, place the currants in a heatproof bowl and cover with very hot water. Let soak until softened, about 20 minutes, then drain and set aside.

4. Remove the rice from the heat and uncover to stir in the currants. Re-cover and let the dish stand for 20 minutes before fluffing and serving.

Soba Salad

Because Japanese soba noodles are made with buckwheat flour as well as wheat flour, they have a subtle, **slightly nutty flavor** with a hint of natural sweetness. This gingery dressing, made with Asian sesame oil and balsamic vinegar, echoes and complements the flavor of the noodles to perfection. I use superfine sugar in the dressing because it dissolves instantly and thoroughly. If you have none on hand, use regular granulated sugar instead; the flavor will be unaffected. I prefer imported Japanese soba noodles here, but American-made ones available in natural foods stores are fine as well.

The salad is tastiest at room temperature and fits well into a buffet-style meal that also includes Chilled Red-Cooked Beef (page 65) and Thai Seafood Salad (page 235). And, although the noodles are best eaten the day they're prepared, I must confess that I often have them the next day—for breakfast!

SERVES 4 AS PART OF A BUFFET OR DINNER WITH OTHER DISHES

1 piece (2 inches) fresh ginger, peeled and grated
  (to yield about 1 tablespoon pulp and juice)
¼ cup good-quality soy sauce,
  such as Kikkoman
2 tablespoons balsamic vinegar
2 tablespoons superfine sugar
1 tablespoon Asian sesame oil (see box,
  page 342)
Pinch of hot red pepper flakes (optional)
1 package (8.8 ounces) dried soba noodles
6 scallions, white and green parts, trimmed
  and very thinly sliced
2 tablespoons sesame seeds, toasted
  (see Note, page 342), for garnish (optional)

Staff Meals from Chanterelle | sides, salads

1. Combine the ginger, soy sauce, vinegar, sugar, oil, and pepper flakes, if desired, in a bowl and whisk thoroughly to blend. Set the dressing aside, unrefrigerated, for an hour or so to let the flavors come together.

2. Bring a large saucepan of unsalted water to a boil over high heat. Add the soba noodles and cook until just tender, 6 to 7 minutes. Drain in a colander and rinse under cold running water, then drain again thoroughly and transfer to a large bowl.

3. Add the scallions to the dressing, if you wish; otherwise, use them as a garnish. Pour the dressing over the noodles and toss gently but thoroughly to coat. Serve immediately, garnished with sesame seeds, if desired.

Rice Salad with Olives and Pine Nuts

Certain types of rice work better in some dishes than in others. For example, I like to use **converted rice** for salads like this one because the rice grains cook up separately and don't stick together, which makes them easier to toss with a dressing. I often serve this colorful salad with Grilled Butterflied Leg of Lamb (page 87); the toasty pine nuts and pungent black olives are just the right complement to this earthy meat's smoky flavor. If you plan to prepare the salad ahead of time and refrigerate it, be sure to allow it to warm to room temperature before serving. **SERVES 6**

2 cups long-grain rice
4 cups water
¾ cup extra-virgin olive oil

¼ cup red wine vinegar

1 cup pine nuts, toasted (see box, below)

½ cup black olives, preferably Kalamata or other pungent
    but not oil-cured olives, pitted and coarsely chopped

1 bunch scallions, white and green parts, trimmed and
    very thinly sliced

1 medium red bell pepper, stemmed, seeded, and
    cut into ½-inch pieces

3 tablespoons coarsely chopped fresh flat-leaf parsley leaves

2 tablespoons coarsely chopped fresh dill leaves

Coarse (kosher) salt and freshly ground black pepper, to taste

1. Place the rice and water in a small, heavy saucepan and bring to a boil over high heat. Stir, then reduce the heat to low, cover, and cook until the rice is tender and the water is fully absorbed, 15 to 20 minutes. Remove the pan from the heat, uncover, and let the rice cool for 20 minutes; it should still be a little warm. Transfer the rice to a large bowl.

2. Place the oil and vinegar in a small bowl and whisk thoroughly to combine. Add the dressing to the rice and toss to mix; the still-warm rice will absorb some of the dressing. Add the pine nuts, olives, scallions, bell pepper, parsley, dill, salt, and pepper and toss well to mix. Taste and adjust the seasoning, then serve at room temperature.

two ways to toast pine nuts

Pine nuts should always be lightly toasted to bring out their flavor. To toast the nuts on top of the stove, preheat a heavy skillet (do not add oil) over medium heat. Add the nuts in a single layer, and cook, stirring constantly, until they're lightly golden and fragrant, 4 to 5 minutes. An alternative method is to preheat the oven to 350°F. Scatter the nuts in a shallow, rimmed pan, like a jelly-roll pan, and bake, stirring occasionally, until they're lightly golden, 4 to 5 minutes. Whichever method you choose, watch the nuts carefully so they don't brown and become bitter.

Creamed Spinach

All of our staff members love this old-fashioned side dish, especially when it's served as part of our favorite fried-chicken dinner. It's best made with fresh spinach, although frozen will do in a pinch. You'll need to start with quite a large volume of fresh spinach—1 pound wilts down to approximately 1 cup of greens. **SERVES 6 TO 8**

1 tablespoon canola or other vegetable oil
3 tablespoons grated onion
1 small clove garlic, minced
4 cups wilted spinach, squeezed dry (about 4 pounds fresh
    spinach; see box, below)
1½ to 2 cups Béchamel sauce (page 311)
Pinch of cayenne pepper
A few gratings of nutmeg
Coarse (kosher) salt and freshly ground black pepper,
    to taste
Fresh lemon juice, to taste

to wilt fresh spinach

Remove the stems from the leaves and discard. Fill a sink or large bowl with cold water and drop in the spinach leaves. Swish them around in the water to loosen any grit, then drain. Repeat the procedure at least twice more, until there's no grit left in the bottom of the sink or bowl. Place the spinach, with just the water that's clinging to it, in a large saucepan or stockpot and wilt over low heat; there's no need to add any other water. Use tongs to pull up the wilted spinach on the bottom and push down the unwilted leaves. When all the spinach is just wilted, drain it; when it's cool enough to handle, squeeze it dry. I like to do this by wrapping the spinach in cheesecloth, twisting it into a ball, and wringing it.

Staff Meals from Chanterelle | s i d e s , s a l a d s

1. Heat the oil in a medium-size saucepan over medium-low heat. Add the onion and garlic and sweat, stirring occasionally, until translucent but not browned, about 5 minutes.

2. Stir in the spinach, béchamel, cayenne, nutmeg, salt, and pepper. Reduce the heat to low and cook, uncovered, stirring frequently, until the spinach is soft and creamy, about 30 minutes.

3. Add a squeeze or two of lemon juice, then taste and adjust the seasoning before serving.

Cooked Spinach Salad with Soy and Sesame

This salad of just-wilted **spinach dressed** in a sweetly pungent vinaigrette and sprinkled with toasted sesame seeds is reminiscent of one you might be served in a Japanese restaurant. The lightly cooked spinach retains all its good flavor and makes a refreshing side dish for simply prepared meat or chicken entrées. **SERVES 4**

2 pounds spinach, well rinsed, thick stems removed
1 clove garlic, very finely chopped
5 scallions, green parts only, trimmed and finely chopped
2 tablespoons balsamic vinegar
2 tablespoons good-quality soy sauce, such as Kikkoman
1 tablespoon Asian sesame oil
Squeeze of fresh lemon juice
Coarse (kosher) salt, to taste
2 tablespoons sesame seeds, toasted (see Note)

1. Wilt, drain, and squeeze dry the spinach following the directions in the box on page 340. Chop the spinach into large, uneven pieces.

2. Place the garlic, scallions, vinegar, soy sauce, and oil in a large bowl and whisk thoroughly to combine. Add the spinach and toss to evenly coat the leaves. Season with a good squeeze of lemon juice and salt and pepper; taste and adjust the seasoning.

3. To serve, divide the salad among four bowls and sprinkle each with a portion of the toasted sesame seeds.

Note: To toast sesame seeds, preheat the oven to 350°F. Scatter the seeds on a baking sheet and bake until lightly browned, 3 to 4 minutes.

asian sesame oil

Delightfully aromatic Asian sesame oil, extracted from roasted sesame seeds, adds a distinctive toasty, nutty flavor to Chinese, Japanese, and Korean dishes such as soups, noodles, and stir-fries. Amber colored with a pronounced, intriguing flavor and low burning point, it's generally used in small quantities as a seasoning rather than a cooking oil. I add it just before serving to Hot and Sour Soup (page 6) as the last fillip of flavor, and as a marinade ingredient for braised spareribs and Chinese-Style Meatballs for a Crowd (page 128). Don't confuse this wonderfully complex oil with the blander, pale yellow domestic sesame oils sold in natural food stores, which are made from unroasted seeds. Kadoya, a Japanese brand sold in glass bottles, is available at Asian markets, natural food stores, and large supermarkets. Once open, store the oil in a cool, dark cupboard or in the refrigerator (bring to room temperature before using).

Ginger Pickled Vegetables

Set out a bowl of these sweetly **pungent**, crunchy vegetables and don't be surprised if they're gone before the rest of the meal arrives on the table. At least, that's been my experience. These popular nibbles definitely fall into the "bet you can't eat just one" department. But why would you want to?

Do let the vegetables pickle for at least 24 hours before serving them. If you can wait even longer, an extra day or two will age them to gingery pickle perfection. **SERVES 6 TO 8**

Pickling Brine (page 215)
2 large carrots, peeled and cut into ¼-inch-thick rounds
2 red bell peppers, stemmed, seeded, and cut
   into ¼-inch-thick strips
½ large head cauliflower, thick core trimmed,
   cut into small florets
½ daikon radish, peeled and cut into ¼-inch-thick rounds

1. Place the pickling brine in a large, nonreactive saucepan and bring to a boil over high heat.

2. Place the vegetables in a large, nonreactive ceramic crock. Strain the boiling brine over the vegetables. Let the mixture cool, then cover and refrigerate it for 24 hours before eating. Pickled vegetables keep for a week in the refrigerator.

3. To serve, remove the vegetables from the brine to small individual serving bowls and spoon a little brine over each.

sides, salads

Staff Meals from Chanterelle

marinated tomatoes with balsamic vinegar and basil

Sometimes you don't need a formal recipe—and this is one of those times. It makes more sense for me to simply describe how I make this dish.

First of all, you'll need really good, really big, really ripe tomatoes. Stop reading and go on to another recipe if it's not tomato season, because only the plumpest, most flavor-packed tomatoes will do. Slice the tomatoes into medium-thick (about ½ inch) slabs. Place a layer of slices on a pretty porcelain or ceramic platter and sprinkle with balsamic vinegar, a good splash of olive oil, some coarse (kosher)

salt, and freshly ground black pepper. (If I'm in the mood, I add some thinly sliced red onion, too.) Continue creating more layers the same way until you've used up all of the tomatoes. Cover and let the tomatoes marinate at room temperature for several hours. Garnish with fresh basil leaves just before serving. Because chopping bruises basil and makes it discolor, I like to either tear the leaves into pieces by hand or chiffonade them. To do the latter, create a little stack of basil leaves, roll them up tightly, then slice into thin shreds. That's all there is to it!

Fried Zucchini Coins

Crispy rounds of fried zucchini make an attractive and delicious side dish with grilled or roasted meat, with pasta and tomato sauce, or as a snack. Garnish them with lemon wedges or, for a fancier presentation, serve them with a creamy salad dressing such as Green Goddess (page 352), Creamy Italian (page 358), or Horseradish Sauce (page 369) for dipping. **SERVES 6**

2 large zucchini
2 large eggs
1½ cups fine dry bread crumbs (see box, page 279)
Canola or other vegetable oil, for frying
Coarse (kosher) salt, to taste

1. Scrub the zucchini and dry them thoroughly. Slice them crosswise into rounds ¼ inch thick.

2. Beat the eggs in a shallow bowl; spread out the bread crumbs on a plate. Dip each zucchini round first in the egg, then in the bread crumbs to coat, shaking off any excess. Place each round as it is breaded on a baking sheet in a single layer.

3. Pour oil to a depth of ¼ inch in a large, heavy skillet. Heat the oil over medium-high heat until a pinch of bread crumbs sizzles on contact. Add the zucchini, in batches, without crowding the pan, and fry until nicely browned on both sides, 3 to 4 minutes per side, turning once with a slotted spatula. Remove the fried zucchini to a large plate or baking sheet lined with paper towels to drain, making sure you don't pile them on top of each other. When you're finished frying all the batches, sprinkle the zucchini with salt and serve immediately.

Dressi

ngs, Dips

We almost always have a salad at home or as part of our staff meal at Chanterelle. More often than not it's mixed greens tossed with Ultra Mustardy Vinaigrette (page 350) or David's Salad Dressing (page 349), my slightly sweet interpretation of a vinaigrette made with honey, soy sauce, and balsamic vinegar. For a change of pace we might prepare a big, crisp Caesar salad loaded with crunchy croutons, and we're certainly not above the occasional use of salad greens as an excuse to indulge in a sumptuously creamy Green Goddess (page 352) or Blue Cheese Dressing (page 357).

Many of these quick, easy-to-make dressings can also become dips or sauces for crudités, chicken wings, fried seafood, and roasted meats. The similarly versatile and

tasty dipping sauces and silken mayonnaises can be slathered on sandwiches, tossed with chicken salad, or used as a soup garnish. The appeal and usefulness of these dressings and sauces is their straightforward flavors. After all, whoever craves a raspberry–poppy seed–pineapple–thyme vinaigrette anyway? Simple nearly always tastes best.

When choosing a salad and its dressing, take into account the other dishes being served at the meal. A creamy main dish is best complemented by one with a vinaigrette rather than a creamy mayonnaise dressing. A delicate main course calls for a lighter-dressed salad as well. As a general rule, creamy dressings and dips offer a pleasing contrast to sauces and other foods that are assertive, such as barbecue and tomato sauces and fried or spicy-hot foods.

David's Salad Dressing

This is my salad dressing standby for family and staff meals. Everyone loves its forthright sweetness with hints of balsamic vinegar, soy sauce, and mustard for balance. It's a combination that perfectly complements the bitter greens in the mesclun we use at the restaurant. At home I find that it's wonderful drizzled over composed salads (see box, page 351) made with chicken, beef, or pork, cooked green beans, artichoke hearts, and tomatoes. And a little drizzled over boiled or roast beets adds a finishing touch. The dressing will keep for up to 3 days stored in a tightly covered jar in the refrigerator.

MAKES ABOUT 1½ CUPS

1 very fresh large egg (see box, page 359)
1 tablespoon Dijon mustard
1½ tablespoons honey
2½ tablespoons balsamic vinegar, or more to taste
1½ tablespoons good-quality soy sauce, such as Kikkoman
½ cup olive oil
½ cup canola or other vegetable oil
Coarse (kosher) salt (optional)

1. Place the egg, mustard, honey, 2½ tablespoons vinegar, and the soy sauce in a food processor or blender and process until blended and smooth, about 15 seconds.

2. With the machine running, slowly add the oils through the feed tube in a thin, steady stream. The dressing will emulsify nicely to a thick, smooth consistency. Taste and season with salt, if necessary, and additional vinegar, if desired. Store in an airtight container in the refrigerator for up to 3 days.

Ultra Mustardy Vinaigrette

When it comes to coating salad greens evenly and tastily, you can't beat a **good basic vinaigrette**. My family and staff agree that this one does the job with lots of finesse and flavor supplied by an ample amount of Dijon mustard. The assertive mustard calls for a less forceful oil; you'll find that the combination of extra-virgin olive oil with the neutral canola provides just the right balance. The finished dressing is as creamy looking as homemade mayonnaise, but not nearly as thick, and is lovely drizzled over salad greens, cold meats, or cooked green beans. This vinaigrette is particularly good for composed salads (see box, facing page) and makes an excellent crudité dip. Toss some of the dressing with still-hot boiled potatoes and a tablespoon or two of white wine and you've got French-style potato salad. **MAKES ABOUT 1 CUP**

3 tablespoons Dijon mustard
3 tablespoons red wine vinegar
½ cup extra-virgin olive oil
½ cup canola or other vegetable oil
Coarse (kosher) salt and freshly ground black pepper
   (optional)

1. Place the mustard and vinegar in a food processor or blender and process until blended and smooth, about 15 seconds.

2. With the machine running, slowly add the oils through the feed tube in a thin, steady stream. The vinaigrette will emulsify nicely to a thick, smooth consistency. Taste and season with salt and pepper, if desired. Store in an airtight container in the refrigerator for up to 1 week. Before using, bring to room temperature and whisk briskly to reblend the ingredients.

Staff Meals from Chanterelle | dressings, dips

composed salads

There are basically two types of salads: those consisting primarily of greens (classically known as *salade verte*), and more substantial ones, such as chef's salad or salade Niçoise, that feature a variety of other ingredients with greens playing a minor role (classically known as *salade composée*). The first type, originally served as a salad course meant to cleanse the palate, is a refreshing, understated plate of lightly dressed greens. Diners still enjoy its simplicity and straightforwardness, though it can turn up at any point in the meal and is most often served before the entrée or casually set out on the table in a big bowl.

Composed salads, on the other hand, are a culinary production number, a livelier, more intricate and exciting combination of ingredients with abundantly varied flavors, colors, and textures—foie gras, smoked trout, grilled chicken, duck, tropical fruits, goat cheese. In such salads, greens are secondary. Among the dips and dressings in this chapter that work well with these salads are Green Goddess Dressing (page 352), Ultra Mustardy Vinaigrette (page 350), and Honey Mustard Dip (page 371). Composed salads may be served at any time—scaled down as a first course, scaled up for a lunch or supper main course.

Staff Meals from Chanterelle | dressings, dips

Green Goddess Dressing

For a **change of pace** from our usual vinaigrette, we often plug in the food processor and whip up a supply of this classic American dressing with a romantic name and an appealing vivid green color. It tastes as green as it looks—abundantly herbaceous with plenty of zing. Besides salad, you can serve this dressing alongside fish and shellfish or as a sprightly dip with endive leaves and cherry tomatoes. **MAKES ABOUT 1½ CUPS**

1 bunch fresh flat-leaf parsley
3 very fresh large egg yolks (see box, page 359)
3 anchovy fillets, drained
Juice of 1 lemon
1 large clove garlic, peeled and roughly chopped
½ teaspoon Dijon mustard
½ cup extra-virgin olive oil
½ cup canola or other vegetable oil
1 teaspoon chopped fresh tarragon leaves
Coarse (kosher) salt and freshly ground black pepper, to taste
Water or milk (optional)

1. Trim the thicker stems from the parsley. Rinse the parsley and shake the water from the leaves, leaving them still a bit damp. Place the leaves in a food processor and process until they're minced. Scrape the parsley from the processor bowl into the center of a square of dampened cheesecloth. Bring the sides of the cheesecloth up around the parsley and twist to squeeze out as much parsley juice as possible into a bowl. The amount doesn't matter as long as you get some. Reserve both the juice and the minced parsley.

2. Place the egg yolks, anchovies, lemon juice, garlic, and mustard in a food processor. Process until the mixture is frothy and lightens in color, about 1 minute.

Staff Meals from Chanterelle | dressings, dips

3. With the machine running, slowly add the oils through the feed tube in a thin, steady stream until a light mayonnaise is formed, about 1 minute.

4. Add the chopped parsley, parsley juice, and tarragon and pulse a few times to thoroughly incorporate. Taste the dressing and season with salt and pepper. If the dressing seems too thick, thin it with a little water or milk. Store in an airtight container in the refrigerator for up to 3 days. The tarragon may turn a little khaki colored, but the dressing will still taste good.

anchovies and capers

It's important to let certain condiments just be themselves. As obvious as it may seem, that's really the whole point of choosing a particular ingredient in the first place and, by extension, it's what cooking is all about.

When it comes to most ingredients packed in brine or oil, I believe in using them straight from the bottle or tin—no rinsing, no wiping, no monkeying around.

Anchovy fillets, which are used in Green Goddess Dressing (facing page), Caesar Salad Dressing (page 355), and many other recipes, are a good example. They're assertively flavored, salty, oily. That's precisely what I like about them. Many cooks auto-matically blot up the oil before adding them to a dish, but I take advantage of every bit of their characteristic flavor, which means using anchovies straight from the container without draining them. I welcome their more pronounced flavor and its interaction with other ingredients.

The same goes for piquant, salty capers, which are bottled in vinegared brine. I never rinse them because I *want* that extra bit of salinity that coats them as they're spooned from the bottle dripping with brine. Old cooking habits die hard, but you owe it to yourself to try cooking with anchovies and capers this way at least once.

dressing a salad

In my experience people consume widely varying quantities of salad. Some dive right in, acting like rabbits released from a 2-week fast, while others approach the leaves with trepidation, as if they were embarking on an icy sea. The reality of how much salad to allow per person rests in the middle. For individual servings, I usually prepare 2-ounce portions (a big handful of greens), and use about 1 ounce (2 tablespoons) of dressing, just enough to provide a light coating. To make salad for a family or a crowd, simply multiply these amounts. For a Caesar salad I use a bit more dressing—about 2 ounces (¼ cup) per serving—since Caesar dressing is thicker and coats greens more densely. (And besides, I love it!)

Place the greens in a bowl, drizzle them with dressing, and toss very gently with two spoons or a pair of tongs. Take care not to crush the leaves or the salad will look bruised and unappetizing.

Toss thoroughly until the dressing lightly coats all the leaves. Serve immediately. A perfectly dressed salad will not leave a puddle in the bottom of the serving bowl.

Caesar Salad Dressing

It seems strange to me that Caesar salad has made such a big comeback in recent years, especially considering how much of its charm and taste have been lost in the course of its newfound popularity. Commercially bottled Caesar dressings have further tarnished its good name and taste. But a properly made version like this one, redolent with anchovies, Worcestershire sauce, and a good sharp Dijon mustard, is addictive.

This **strong and garlicky** dressing is best tossed with a sturdy, resilient lettuce like romaine and plenty of croutons. Frailer, more tender lettuces simply won't hold up in its powerful presence. It's definitely for anchovy lovers. If you don't care for anchovies, don't leave them out—just make another dressing. The recipe makes enough to dress two medium-size heads of romaine. **MAKES ABOUT 1½ CUPS**

3 very fresh large egg yolks (see box, page 359)
1 tablespoon mashed anchovy fillets or anchovy paste
1 teaspoon minced garlic
5 dashes of Worcestershire sauce, or more to taste
1 tablespoon Dijon mustard
¼ cup white wine vinegar
Squeeze of fresh lemon juice, or more to taste
Coarse (kosher) salt and lots of freshly ground
    black pepper, to taste
½ cup extra-virgin olive oil
½ cup freshly grated Parmesan

1. Place the egg yolks, anchovies, garlic, 5 dashes Worcestershire sauce, the mustard, vinegar, a squeeze of lemon juice, the salt, and pepper in a food

processor or blender. Process until the mixture is frothy and the anchovies are fully incorporated, about 1 minute.

2. With the machine running, slowly add the oil through the feed tube in a thin, steady stream until a light mayonnaise is formed, about 30 seconds. Add the Parmesan and pulse a few times to incorporate. Taste and adjust the seasoning, including the Worcestershire and lemon juice, if necessary. Store in an airtight container in the refrigerator for up to 3 days.

making crisp croutons

Restaurants go through incredible quantities of fresh bread every day. In fact, it would be unforgivable for us to run out of bread, so we always have far more on hand than we need, just in case. None of it goes to waste; day-old bread is routinely transformed into crisps, bread crumbs, and croutons.

To make croutons, trim the crust from day-old bread. I use a good sturdy peasant-style bread, but any kind you have on hand will do. Dice the bread into ½-inch cubes and toss with enough melted butter or olive oil (or, best of all, garlic oil) to coat, but not drench, the croutons. Sprinkle lightly with salt, spread out the croutons on a rimmed baking sheet or a jelly-roll pan, and bake in a preheated 350°F oven until just golden brown, about 15 minutes. Halfway through the baking, give the pan a shake to ensure that the croutons are toasting evenly. The secret of good croutons is to make sure they've dried out all the way through without becoming too browned. If they're browning too quickly, lower the oven temperature to 300°F. When they're done, remove the pan from the oven.

Cool the croutons completely and store in an airtight container for up to 2 weeks.

Blue Cheese Dressing

Blue cheese dressing is as **useful** as it is *tasty*. Not only is it a flavorful addition to salads, but it's also the traditional accompaniment to Buffalo chicken wings, a splendid dip for everything from crudités to potato chips, and irresistible slathered on a roast turkey sandwich. I use inexpensive Danish blue cheese to make this dressing. Authentic and expensive French Roquefort is one of the world's stellar cheeses, but the quality and subtle nuances of a finer blue cheese would just be overwhelmed by the other ingredients. **MAKES ABOUT 2 CUPS**

4 very fresh large egg yolks (see box, page 359)
1 teaspoon Dijon mustard
¼ teaspoon minced garlic
¼ cup white wine vinegar
Coarse (kosher) salt and freshly ground black pepper,
    to taste
Dash of Tabasco sauce
1½ cups canola or other vegetable oil
4 ounces blue cheese, crumbled

1. Place the egg yolks, mustard, garlic, vinegar, salt, pepper, and Tabasco in a food processor or blender. Process until the mixture is frothy and turns lighter in color, about 1 minute.

2. With the machine running, slowly add the oil through the feed tube in a thin, steady stream, about 1½ minutes. The dressing will emulsify nicely to a thick, smooth consistency. Add the blue cheese and pulse the machine a few times until it's fully incorporated. Taste and adjust the seasoning. Store in an airtight container in the refrigerator for up to 3 days.

Creamy Italian Dressing

Creamy Italian Dressing is indeed creamy, but I doubt that this, or anything remotely like it, ever originated in Italy. It's one of those commercially bottled concoctions that's been **a staple** in American kitchen pantries for generations and is still going strong on supermarket shelves. If I had to guess, I'd say it was probably the brainstorm of a product development whiz at a food manufacturing conglomerate. Like the "original," mine has no real ethnic provenance, but it's a light, flavorful, herb-flecked dressing that certainly tastes good. Use it on more delicate greens such as oakleaf, red-leaf, or Bibb lettuce. **MAKES ABOUT 1 CUP**

1 very fresh large egg (see box, facing page)
¼ cup white wine vinegar
1 teaspoon Dijon mustard
¼ cup freshly grated Parmesan
1 small clove garlic, peeled and roughly chopped
Coarse (kosher) salt and freshly ground black pepper,
    to taste
⅓ cup extra-virgin olive oil
1 teaspoon dried oregano leaves
1 teaspoon chopped fresh flat-leaf parsley leaves

1. Place the egg, vinegar, mustard, Parmesan, garlic, salt, and pepper in a food processor or blender. Process until the mixture gets frothy and lighter in color, about 1 minute.

2. With the machine running, slowly add the oil through the feed tube in a thin, steady stream, about 30 seconds. The dressing will emulsify nicely to a smooth consistency. Add the oregano and parsley and pulse a few times to just incorporate. Store in an airtight container in the refrigerator for up to 3 days.

Staff Meals from Chanterelle | dressings, dips

a note about eggs

In the past few years there has been legitimate concern over the use of raw eggs in foods that aren't cooked. Although statistics suggest that a minuscule number of eggs potentially carry the salmonella bacteria, it's believed that consuming uncooked eggs may pose a risk to the very young, the elderly, pregnant women, and anyone with a compromised immune system. Acidic ingredients such as vinegar or lemon juice may create a less hospitable environment for bacteria in uncooked egg mixtures such as mayonnaise. When shopping, buy only very fresh, refrigerated eggs with undamaged shells from top-notch purveyors.

At home, keep eggs refrigerated, use a plastic or metal egg separator, and do not allow dishes made with raw eggs to sit out at room temperature. Use eggs within a day or two of purchase if you'll be using them in a recipe calling for raw eggs.

Basic Mayonnaise

The flavor of a **homemade** mayonnaise is in a whole other realm from commercial versions. It tastes so much fresher and more interesting that it's easily worth spending the few minutes required to make it. Whether you make it in a food processor or whisk it by hand, there's always something magical about seeing the thick, creamy emulsion form. If 2 cups is too much, this recipe is easy to halve. **MAKES ABOUT 2 CUPS**

4 very fresh large egg yolks (see box, page 359)
2 tablespoons fresh lemon juice
2 tablespoons water
2 teaspoons Dijon mustard
1 cup extra-virgin olive oil
1 cup canola or other vegetable oil
Coarse (kosher) salt and freshly ground black pepper, to taste
    (optional)

1. Place the egg yolks, lemon juice, water, and mustard in a food processor or blender. Process until the mixture is frothy and turns lighter in color, about 1 minute.

2. With the machine running, slowly add the oils through the feed tube in a thin, steady stream, about 2 minutes. The mayonnaise will emulsify nicely to a thick, smooth consistency. Taste and season with salt and pepper, if desired. Store in an airtight container in the refrigerator for up to 3 days.

Staff Meals from Chanterelle | dressings, dips

Curried Mayonnaise

We use this **bright yellow** mayonnaise as the dressing for our Curried Chicken Salad (page 187), but it's also perfect with a cold roast pork sandwich or as a dipping sauce for boiled shrimp. I prefer to use Madras-style Sun brand curry powder from the south of India, which is very flavorful yet mellow, not too spicy, with just a subtle hint of extra heat. Look for it in most large supermarkets and specialty food stores. Don't skip the first step of briefly warming the curry powder in oil. The heat brings the spices to life, eliminating any powdery, uncooked taste. As with Basic Mayonnaise (page 360), this recipe is easy to halve.

MAKES ABOUT 2 CUPS

2 cups canola or other vegetable oil
2 tablespoons Madras-style curry powder, preferably Sun brand
4 very fresh large egg yolks (see box, page 359)
3 tablespoons fresh lemon juice
2 teaspoons Dijon mustard
Coarse (kosher) salt (optional)

1. Combine 6 tablespoons of the oil and the curry powder in a small, heavy saucepan and heat over low heat, stirring to release the flavor of the curry powder, 2 minutes. Be careful not to let the mixture get too hot and overcook. Remove the pan from the heat and let cool to room temperature.

2. Combine the egg yolks, lemon juice, and mustard in a food processor or blender. Process until the mixture is frothy and turns lighter in color, about 1 minute.

3. With the machine running, slowly add the remaining oil through the feed tube in a thin, steady stream, about 2 minutes. The mayonnaise will emulsify nicely to a thick, smooth consistency. Add the curry oil and continue to process until it's thoroughly blended in. Taste and season with salt, if desired. Store in an airtight container in the refrigerator for up to 3 days.

Tarragon Mayonnaise

If you rarely use fresh tarragon, the flavor of this mayonnaise will be a revelation. By nature fresh tarragon is delicate, with a **subtle and enchanting** licorice flavor that's often eclipsed when it's dried. Unlike many other herbs that easily retain their integrity of flavor when dried, tarragon tends to lose most of its allure, becoming too intense, yet with a rather lackluster, dusty taste. For this reason, only chopped *fresh* tarragon will do here. The result is an elegantly flavorful mayonnaise that can be used to create a wonderful Chicken Salad with Tarragon (page 188). It also makes a lovely sauce for cold poached salmon, chilled boiled shrimp, or room-temperature slices of roast chicken. As with the other mayonnaises, halve the recipe if you don't need quite so much. **MAKES ABOUT 2 CUPS**

4 very fresh large egg yolks (see box, page 359)
6 tablespoons tarragon vinegar, or more to taste
2 teaspoons fresh tarragon leaves
2 teaspoons Dijon mustard
Coarse (kosher) salt and freshly ground black pepper, to taste
1 cup extra-virgin olive oil
1 cup canola or other vegetable oil

1. Place the egg yolks, 6 tablespoons vinegar, the tarragon, mustard, salt, and pepper in a food processor or blender. Process until the mixture is frothy and turns lighter in color, about 1 minute.

2. With the machine running, slowly add the oils through the feed tube in a thin, steady stream, about 2 minutes. The mayonnaise will emulsify nicely to a thick, smooth consistency. Taste and adjust the vinegar and salt and pepper, if necessary. Store in an airtight container in the refrigerator for up to 3 days.

Staff Meals from Chanterelle | dressings, dips

Aïoli

This garlic mayonnaise is **our favorite dip**. I make my aïoli quite garlicky, but you can adjust the amount to make it less so if you prefer. The texture can also be varied. Mine is thick—just slightly thinner than commercial mayonnaise. That's how they do it in Provence, where a pungent bowl of aïoli is often served with crudités at the beginning of a meal. For a very snappy-tasting salad dressing, thin the mixture by using less oil or by adding some water. Thick, it makes a perfect garnish for bouillabaisse and other fish stews or soups. Simply add a dollop of aïoli to the soup—on its own or on a crusty toast round—and let it blend in as you eat. **MAKES ABOUT 2 CUPS**

4 very fresh large egg yolks (see box, page 359)
3 tablespoons white wine vinegar or fresh lemon juice
5 large cloves garlic, peeled
2 teaspoons Dijon mustard
Coarse (kosher) salt and freshly ground black pepper, to taste
1 cup extra-virgin olive oil
1 cup canola or other vegetable oil

1. Place the egg yolks, vinegar, garlic, mustard, salt, and pepper in a food processor or blender. Process until the mixture is frothy, it turns lighter in color, and the garlic is finely chopped, about 1 minute.

2. With the machine running, slowly add the oils through the feed tube in a thin, steady stream, about 2 minutes. The aïoli will emulsify nicely to a thick, smooth consistency. Taste and adjust the seasoning, if necessary. Store in an airtight container in the refrigerator for up to 3 days.

Green Sauce

Flat-leaf parsley comes into its own as an herb rather than a garnish in this vivid green sauce with its bright, **strong**, **zingy flavor**. To achieve an even brighter green, add some blanched spinach leaves. This is quite anchovy intensive, so if you don't love them, prepare the sauce with fewer than specified, then take a taste before deciding whether to add the full amount. (To tell the truth, when I make this at home I add even more anchovies!) Use the sauce the day it's made. (Refrigeration turns the color an unappetizing khaki and breaks down the mayonnaiselike texture.) Let the sauce rest, covered and at room temperature, for at least an hour before serving so the flavors have an opportunity to expand and blend. You won't find a more compatible sauce for boiled beef, fried fish, or hot or cold poached fish (especially salmon)—or a better dip for vegetables, either raw or lightly cooked. Green sauce is also a classic accompaniment for Pot-au-Feu (page 63). **MAKES ABOUT 1½ CUPS**

3 to 4 bunches fresh flat-leaf parsley
½ cup loosely packed fresh spinach leaves, rinsed
    and drained (optional)
3 large eggs
8 anchovy fillets packed in oil, drained
3 tablespoons capers, drained but not rinsed
3 tablespoons red wine vinegar
2 cloves garlic, peeled
1 tablespoon Dijon mustard
1 cup extra-virgin olive oil
Water, as needed

1. Bring a medium-size saucepan filled halfway with water to a boil over medium-high heat.

2. Meanwhile, using a sharp, heavy knife, roughly chop enough parsley, including some thinner stems, to make 4 cups loosely packed. If you wish to give the sauce an extra bright green color, use the spinach, chopping it roughly as well. Add the greens to the boiling water and blanch for a few seconds, just until they wilt and turn bright green. Drain in a colander, cool under cold running water, and drain again. Squeeze out the rest of the water, chop finely, and set aside.

3. Place the eggs in the saucepan, cover with water, and bring to a simmer over medium heat. Reduce the heat to maintain a slow but steady simmer and cook the eggs until just short of hard cooked, about 7 minutes; you want the yolks to be a little soft. Place the saucepan in the sink and run cold water into it until all the hot water is driven out; let the eggs sit in the water until cool.

4. Peel the eggs and carefully separate the yolks from the whites, discarding the whites. Place the yolks in a food processor and add the chopped greens, anchovies, capers, vinegar, garlic, and mustard. Process until the mixture forms a paste that's as fine as possible, 3 to 5 minutes (see Note).

5. With the machine running, slowly add the oil through the feed tube in a thin, steady stream, about 1 minute. The sauce will emulsify nicely to a thick, smooth consistency. If desired, thin with a little water before using.

Note: Due to the nature of flat-leaf parsley, the mixture in step 4 will be a bit grainy rather than totally smooth.

big dippers

We're constantly busy at Chanterelle, dashing around the kitchen, always in the middle of something. Our work shifts are long, so when hunger strikes we look around eagerly for tasty little snacks we can gobble on the run. That's how we became inveterate dippers. Rémoulade, tamarind sauce, aïoli, tomato-porcini sauce, simple vinaigrette—we love them all. During service, when diners are feasting and the kitchen is in high gear, the cooks pour leftover sauces from the various skillets into little dishes and set them out near bits of bread. If they're really rushed, they'll just toss a pan onto the counter and holler, "Snack!" Waiters in the nether regions of the dining room appear like magic— how do they know?

Staff Meals from Chanterelle

Rémoulade

Rémoulade is basically **French tartar sauce**. Its pleasing tartness, created by Dijon mustard, capers, and cornichons, makes it a perfect accompaniment to cold meats, shellfish, and fried or sautéed fish. And Our Favorite Fries (page 327) become unexpectedly elegant when they're served with little saucers of rémoulade instead of the usual ketchup. This recipe is a fine example of what happens when a few basic ingredients come together in precisely the right combination. **MAKES ABOUT 2 CUPS**

1 shallot, peeled and cut into large pieces
2 tablespoons small (nonpareil) capers
10 cornichons, cut into large pieces
4 very fresh large egg yolks (see box, page 359)
¼ cup white wine vinegar
1 teaspoon Dijon mustard
Coarse (kosher) salt and freshly ground black pepper, to taste
2 cups extra-virgin olive oil
Liquid from the capers or cornichons, as needed

1. Place the shallot, capers, and cornichons in a food processor or blender and pulse until they're coarsely chopped. Use a rubber spatula to scrape the mixture into a bowl and set aside.

2. Without rinsing the processor, add the egg yolks, vinegar, mustard, salt, and pepper. Process until the mixture is frothy and turns lighter in color, about 1 minute.

3. With the machine running, slowly add the oil through the feed tube in a thin, steady stream, about 2 minutes. The sauce will emulsify nicely to a thick, smooth consistency. Add the shallot mixture and pulse a few times just to incorporate. The rémoulade should be chunky. Taste and adjust the seasoning, adding some caper or cornichon liquid to increase the acidity, if necessary. Store in an airtight container in the refrigerator for up to 3 days.

Staff Meals from Chanterelle | dressings, dips

Kitchen Cupboard Tartar Sauce

Here's a **fast**, **uncomplicated**, and unfussy tartar sauce that can be made in the blink of an eye. It's infinitely finer tasting than any commercial version. Serve a bowl of this along with Fresh Salmon Croquettes (page 218), Deviled Crab Cakes (page 245), or Fish 'n' Chips (page 234). **MAKES ABOUT 1 CUP**

1 cup good-quality commercial mayonnaise,
   preferably Hellmann's
3 tablespoons commercial chopped sweet relish
3 tablespoons bottled white horseradish, measured
   after thorough draining
½ teaspoon sherry vinegar

Place all the ingredients in a small bowl and whisk thoroughly until well blended. Store in an airtight container in the refrigerator for up to 3 days.

about capers

A classic ingredient in Rémoulade (page 366), capers are the preserved flower buds of two types of trailing shrubs that grow in the Mediterranean. Glass jars of vinegar-cured capers in brine are easy to find at supermarkets and specialty food stores. (Less common salt-cured ones are sold in Italian specialty food shops.) Their nearly indescribable, slightly acidic flavor adds a bright, piquant note to sauces and *tapenade* (they have a special affinity for anchovies and olives). Capers come in a range of sizes. I always use the smallest, labeled "nonpareil," because they have a bit more flavor than larger ones. Although many cooks drain the brine and rinse capers so they're less salty, I never bother. I love the impact of their brininess and salt, especially in sauces.

Doctored Harissa

Harissa is a fiery hot red **chili paste** with roots in North Africa. It's a bold-tasting, russet-colored mixture of hot chiles ground to a paste with garlic, olive oil, paprika, coriander, cumin, and caraway seeds. *Harissa* is most often associated with couscous, the traditional dish of steamed semolina served with a vegetable or meat stew. A dab is often added to the stew broth for extra flavor before serving, and *harissa* also appears as a condiment on the table so diners can further adjust the heat to suit their palates. Excellent ready-made *harissa* from France is sold in colorful little yellow tins or convenient squeeze tubes in Middle Eastern markets, specialty food stores, and some large supermarkets. Strange as it may sound, I've found that doctoring this wonderful condiment creates an even fresher, more integrated flavor, rounding the edges of its stark heat just a bit. Stir my new and improved version sparingly (it's still *very* hot!) into scrambled eggs, rice and beans, vinaigrette, homemade mayonnaise for potato salad, marinades, or soups and stews. And black olives tossed with a little *harissa* are simply wonderful. To store, spoon into a small glass jar, pour a thin layer of olive oil on the surface, cap tightly, and refrigerate. **MAKES ABOUT ¾ CUP**

1 can (4.785 ounces) *harissa*
2 tablespoons extra-virgin olive oil
1 teaspoon tomato paste
2 tablespoons finely chopped fresh cilantro leaves
    (see Note)
Juice of 1 lemon

Combine the *harissa,* oil, tomato paste, and cilantro in a small bowl and whisk until well blended. Add the lemon juice and stir. Transfer to a pretty serving bowl and serve. Store in an airtight container in the refrigerator for up to 3 months.

Note: Adding fresh cilantro to the *harissa* will shorten its shelf life considerably, since fresh herbs tend to lose their color, texture, and potency quickly. In fact, with the herb mixed in, it's best to eat up the *harissa* within a couple of days. That very well may be out of the question, however, just a little of this stuff packs a wallop. So it's probably best to mix all the ingredients—except the cilantro—together. Then scoop out just the portion of paste you'll be serving and add a reduced amount of cilantro to it. For instance, if you think ¼ cup will meet your needs, add a couple of teaspoons of chopped cilantro and store the rest of the *harissa* cilantro-free until the next time you serve it. Don't worry about getting the amount of cilantro exactly right. Being a little off one way or the other won't matter.

Horseradish Sauce

This **sharp, piquant** sauce is perfect to serve alongside roast beef, pork, or turkey. It also makes an exceptionally tasty dip for raw vegetables. You can use either commercially bottled horseradish or much stronger fresh homemade horseradish, which is what I prefer. **MAKES ABOUT 2 CUPS**

4 very fresh large egg yolks (see box, page 359)
⅓ cup white wine vinegar, or more to taste
½ teaspoon Dijon mustard
Coarse (kosher) salt and freshly ground black pepper, to taste
1½ to 2 cups extra-virgin olive oil
¼ cup freshly ground horseradish (see box, page 370) or ½ cup
    drained, bottled horseradish, or more to taste

1. Place the egg yolks, ⅓ cup vinegar, the mustard, salt, and pepper in a food processor or blender. Process until the mixture is frothy and turns a lighter color, about 1 minute.

2. With the machine running, slowly add the oil through the feed tube in a thin, steady stream, stopping when the desired consistency is achieved, 1½ to 2 minutes. I like a loose, pourable horseradish sauce (about 1½ cups oil) rather than a thick one. Add the horseradish and pulse a few more times to thoroughly incorporate. Taste, adding more horseradish if desired, and perhaps a touch more vinegar or salt. Serve cold. Store in an airtight container in the refrigerator for up to 3 days.

fresh homemade horseradish

Large, tapered roots of fresh horseradish, which average 8 to 12 inches in length, are usually available in produce departments year-round, although they're at their best from fall through spring. Choose those that are firm, smooth, and unblemished. One root can yield anywhere from ¾ cup to 1 cup of grated horseradish.

To prepare a small amount of homemade horseradish, peel only part of the root, about 2 or 3 inches. (Wrap the unpeeled portion in plastic wrap; it will stay fresh in the refrigerator for up to 2 weeks before the flavor begins to fade.) Cut the peeled portion into ½-inch pieces and grind in a food processor, pulsing in short bursts until finely chopped or shredded but not

puréed. If it seems dry, add a few drops of water or white vinegar. The fumes from freshly ground horseradish are powerfully peppery and potent, so avert your head as you remove the food processor top. To store leftover ground horseradish, put it in an airtight glass container with just enough white vinegar to cover and refrigerate. It will keep for up to 2 months. One tablespoon of fresh homemade horseradish is equivalent to 2 tablespoons of the bottled kind.

Aside from its use as an ingredient in Horseradish Sauce (page 369), a little of the ground root will add interesting zip to applesauce, cranberry sauce or compote, plain mayonnaise, and, of course, a Bloody Mary.

Honey Mustard Dip

Quick and easy is an understatement here, since it will take you about as long to read this recipe as to make it. The sharp, full-flavored heat of Dijon mustard (I use Maille brand, which is strong) and the straightforward sweetness of honey are combined with just enough soy sauce and cider vinegar to give this versatile sauce a little kick. There's no need to rush out and buy some fancy imported, highly flavored honey that makes a statement. Supermarket honey is what you want here. This is terrific served with David's Famous Fried Chicken (page 157), fried fish fillets, or hot grilled bratwurst; as a dip for pretzels or Chicken McWaltucks (page 180); or thinly spread on a ham sandwich. Some people even put it on salad, though I think it's a bit too strong for most greens. Or you could enjoy it the way I do, by just dipping a finger in it. **MAKES ABOUT 1½ CUPS**

1 cup plus 2 tablespoons Dijon mustard
½ cup honey
2 tablespoons good-quality soy sauce, preferably Kikkoman
2 tablespoons cider vinegar

Combine all the ingredients in a food processor or blender and process until blended. Store the dip in an airtight container in the refrigerator. It will keep almost indefinitely.

Tamarind Dipping Sauce

Tamarind water gives this very **nicely balanced**, tart-yet-sweet dipping sauce its lovely deep orange color and unusual flavor. The sauce is delicious with Vidalia Onion Fritters (page 326) and other fried foods. **MAKES ABOUT 2 CUPS**

5 ounces tamarind pulp (see box, below)

2 cups plus 2 tablespoons cold water

1 piece (1 inch) fresh ginger, peeled and grated

3 cloves garlic, minced

3 tablespoons sugar, or more to taste

1 tablespoon chili-garlic sauce (sambal oelek)

2 teaspoons Thai fish sauce (nam pla)

1 teaspoon good-quality soy sauce, such as Kikkoman

2 tablespoons cornstarch

tamarind pulp

Tamarind pulp comes from the fuzzy, beanlike pods of the tamarind tree. It's used extensively in Southeast Asian cooking to add a rich, slightly sweet-sour taste to dressings, sauces, and soups. Commercially, tamarind is one of the "secret" ingredients in Worcestershire sauce. The unseeded pulp is sold in plastic-wrapped 16-ounce blocks in Asian markets and some specialty food stores. To extract the tart tamarind essence, about 1 part pulp is combined with 3 parts boiling water, and the mixture is allowed to rest briefly. The softened pulp is then strained through a sieve to extract the juice and remove any seeds and fibers before the resulting liquid is used. (A little pulp invariably ends up in the liquid, which is okay.) The seedless tamarind concentrate sold at Middle Eastern, Asian, and Caribbean markets is easier to use, but the flavor won't be quite as good as that of the blocks of Asian pulp.

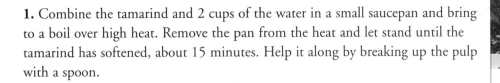

1. Combine the tamarind and 2 cups of the water in a small saucepan and bring to a boil over high heat. Remove the pan from the heat and let stand until the tamarind has softened, about 15 minutes. Help it along by breaking up the pulp with a spoon.

2. Strain the tamarind through a sieve, pressing on the pulp to extract as much water as possible. Discard the pulp and seeds and return the water to the pan. Add the ginger, garlic, 3 tablespoons sugar, the chili-garlic sauce, fish sauce, and soy sauce and bring to a boil over high heat. Reduce the heat and simmer for 5 minutes, stirring frequently.

3. Whisk the cornstarch with the remaining 2 tablespoons water. When smooth, whisk the mixture into the tamarind sauce, continuing to whisk until the sauce thickens, about 1 minute. Remove the pan from the heat and let cool. Before serving, taste and adjust the seasoning, adding more sugar if necessary to balance the tartness of the tamarind. Store tamarind sauce in an airtight container in the refrigerator for up to 1 week.

Brunc

h, Breads

Although my personal preferences in breakfast food are a bit untraditional—I'll opt for a meat loaf sandwich or cold noodles with sesame sauce rather than oatmeal or bacon and eggs anytime—at home on weekends Karen and the kids and I occasionally like to linger over a family brunch. I usually make simple but tasty versions of classics like buttermilk pancakes or French toast with challah. Some of the recipes here are old favorites that were served at Chanterelle back in the early 1990s when we briefly experimented with serving breakfast at the restaurant. Brunch recipes should be uncomplicated and not too time-consuming so the cook has plenty of time to enjoy everyone's company and catch up on their recent adventures.

The baskets of bread and other baked goods served at those early Chanterelle breakfasts were bountiful, and we still make some of those recipes for staff meals. They work as well later in the day as they do early. And since we lean toward one-pot meals for staff dining, there's always a lot of delicious sauce or gravy that needs sopping up with less sweet baked goods such as biscuits, cornbread, focaccia, and garlic bread.

Buttermilk Corn Muffins with Orange

During the brief interlude in which we served breakfast at Chanterelle, these pleasant-tasting, **not-too-sweet** muffins were part of the bread-basket assortment for each table. Orange zest complements the flavor of the cornmeal, and buttermilk ensures a tender crumb. The secret to great muffins is to avoid overmixing the wet and dry ingredients; they should be stirred, gently, until just combined. **MAKES 12 MUFFINS**

1½ cups all-purpose flour
1 cup cornmeal
½ cup sugar
2½ teaspoons baking powder
1 teaspoon baking soda
Good pinch of coarse (kosher) salt
Grated zest of 1 orange
2 large eggs
1½ cups buttermilk
4 tablespoons (½ stick) unsalted butter, melted and cooled
¼ cup canola or other vegetable oil
1 teaspoon vanilla extract

1. Preheat the oven to 350°F. Lightly butter a 12-cup muffin tin.

2. Combine the flour, cornmeal, sugar, baking powder, baking soda, salt, and orange zest in a large bowl and whisk thoroughly to mix.

3. Using the whisk, beat the eggs in a medium-size bowl, then add the buttermilk, melted butter, oil, and vanilla and whisk well to blend. Pour the

mixture into the flour mixture and whisk just until the dry ingredients are moistened; do not overmix.

4. Spoon the batter into the prepared muffin cups, filling each almost to the top. Bake until risen and very lightly browned, 15 to 20 minutes; a toothpick inserted into the center of a muffin will come out clean.

5. Serve warm or at room temperature.

Chanterelle Breakfast Scones

Back in the old days when Chanterelle was open for breakfast, and Nina Fraas was our morning chef, these scones were a big hit. Warm from the oven, they were ready to **eat as is**, in need of no butter or jam. Breakfasts at the restaurant are a thing of the past, but we still bake these scones (and Nina's waffles, see page 390) for the early-morning-staff members. It's one way to ensure that everyone shows up on time.

These scones are prepared with vanilla sugar. It's certainly easy to make, and we keep plenty of it around for flavoring desserts.

MAKES 16 TO 20 SMALL SCONES

⅔ cup heavy (or whipping) cream
1 large egg
¼ cup vanilla sugar, plus more for sprinkling on the scones
    (see box, facing page)
2½ cups all-purpose flour
1 tablespoon baking powder
½ teaspoon salt
¼ teaspoon baking soda

8 tablespoons (1 stick) unsalted butter, cut into 8 pieces, chilled
½ cup dried currants
4 tablespoons (½ stick) unsalted butter, melted

1. Preheat the oven to 400°F.

2. Place the cream, egg, and ¼ cup vanilla sugar in a medium-size bowl and whisk until fluffy and well blended.

3. Place the flour, baking powder, salt, and baking soda in a food processor and pulse to combine. Add the chilled butter, then pulse again until fairly well blended. Then add the cream mixture and pulse until the dough just holds together.

4. Transfer the dough to a lightly floured work surface. Sprinkle the currants over the dough and knead for 30 seconds, making sure the currants are well distributed throughout the dough. Pat the dough into a round about ½ inch thick.

5. Cut out the scones using a floured 2-inch round cookie cutter. Gather up the extra dough, pat it out again, and continue cutting out the scones. You should have sixteen to twenty.

6. Place the scones on an ungreased baking sheet. Brush the tops with the melted butter and sprinkle them with vanilla sugar. Bake in the oven until golden brown, 15 to 18 minutes. Remove them from the oven, place in a cloth-lined bread basket, and eat immediately.

making vanilla sugar

Place a fresh, fragrant vanilla bean into your sugar canister and let it stay there. The sugar will take on a pleasant vanilla smell and flavor. Use it in baking, on fruits, even in your coffee. Replace the vanilla bean every few months for the best results.

Cornmeal-Onion Biscuits

This recipe makes a biscuit that's **not too moist** and therefore good for sopping up the sauce from stews, such as the Chicken Gumbo on page 184. I like to place the biscuit right in the bowl with the gumbo. For an attractive glazed look, you can brush the tops of the biscuits with beaten egg before baking.

MAKES 12 BISCUITS

1½ cups all-purpose flour
1½ cups yellow cornmeal
2 tablespoons baking powder
1½ teaspoons salt
3 tablespoons unsalted butter, cut into small bits, chilled
¼ cup minced onion
2 large eggs
1½ cups half-and-half
2 tablespoons unsalted butter, melted
2 scant tablespoons honey

1. Preheat the oven to 375°F. Lightly butter a baking sheet.

2. Place the flour, cornmeal, baking powder, and salt in a large bowl and whisk thoroughly to mix. Add the cold butter and rub it in quickly with your fingers until it's fairly well blended; the texture should be mealy, but it's okay to leave a few larger lumps. Stir in the onion.

3. Using a whisk or fork, beat the eggs in a medium-size bowl, then add the half-and-half, melted butter, and honey and beat thoroughly to blend. Pour the egg mixture into the flour mixture all at once and stir with a wooden spoon until the flour is just moistened and a dough forms; do not overmix.

4. Transfer the dough to a lightly floured work surface and knead briefly, just to rid it of excess stickiness. Divide the dough into twelve pieces and, using floured hands, pat each piece into a flat, round biscuit. Place the biscuits as they are formed on the prepared baking sheet.

5. Bake until lightly browned, 15 to 20 minutes. Serve the biscuits warm from the oven or at room temperature.

Cornbread

Cornbread may well be the ultimate **quick bread**. Easy to make, this moist and light version is always a pleasing addition to our staff and family meals, especially when soup or stew is the main dish. I use regular yellow cornmeal from the supermarket, adding a little honey to complement the natural sweetness of corn. Mix the batter with a light hand—just a few strokes is sufficient to combine the ingredients—or the bread will be flat and dense.

MAKES ONE 9-INCH ROUND CORNBREAD

1¼ cups all-purpose flour
¾ cup yellow cornmeal
1 tablespoon baking powder
½ teaspoon salt
2 large eggs
1 cup whole milk
5 tablespoons unsalted butter, melted and cooled
2 tablespoons honey

skillet cornbread

For crisp-crusted cornbread, cut 2 strips of bacon into small bits and brown in a well-seasoned, heavy cast-iron skillet, then pour Cornbread batter over it and pop into a hot oven (425°F) until browned, 20 minutes. When the cornbread is inverted onto a plate, it will have a nice crusty top dotted with flavorful bacon bits.

1. Preheat the oven to 425°F. Lightly butter a 9-inch round pie pan.

2. Place the flour, cornmeal, baking powder, and salt in a large bowl and whisk to combine.

3. Using the whisk, beat the eggs in a medium-size bowl, then add the milk, melted butter, and honey and beat thoroughly to blend. Pour the egg mixture into the flour mixture all at once and stir with a wooden spoon until the dry ingredients are moistened; do not overmix.

4. Pour the batter into the prepared pan and bake until the top is lightly browned and a toothpick inserted in the center comes out clean, about 20 minutes. Cut into wedges and serve warm or at room temperature.

Herbed Biscuits

If our pastry chef has finished the preparation of her exquisite desserts and petits-fours in plenty of time *and* she's feeling benevolent, we're sometimes treated to these homey biscuits at our staff meal. We're very partial to this herbed version (it can also be used as the crust for Chicken Potpie and I Don't Care, page 154), but you could omit the herbs and make plain biscuits or substitute other flavorings like a teaspoon of coarsely ground black pepper for a change of pace. The secret to tasty biscuits is being sure to leave a few pieces of butter in the dough that seem a little bigger than you think they should be.

These biscuits are best eaten hot out of the oven. Of course, it's hard to imagine that anybody would turn down a few warmed leftover ones the next morning, especially if they were accompanied by plenty of butter and honey. **MAKES ABOUT 8 BISCUITS**

2 cups all-purpose flour

4 teaspoons baking powder

1 teaspoon salt

8 tablespoons (1 stick) unsalted butter, cut into ½-inch-thick
    pieces, chilled

3 tablespoons minced fresh herbs, such as tarragon,
    flat-leaf parsley, chives, and dill leaves

¾ cup buttermilk

1. Preheat the oven to 400°F. Lightly butter a baking sheet.

2. Place the flour, baking powder, and salt in a large bowl and whisk thoroughly to combine. Add the butter and rub it in quickly with your fingers until fairly well blended; the texture should resemble coarse meal, but it's okay to leave a few larger lumps. Add the herbs and toss to combine (see Notes). Add the buttermilk all at once and stir with a wooden spoon until the flour is just moistened and a dough forms; do not overmix.

3. Transfer the dough to a lightly floured work surface and knead briefly, just to rid it of excess stickiness. Using a lightly floured rolling pin, roll out the dough ½ inch thick. Cut it into round biscuits using a floured 3-inch biscuit cutter, or cut into 3-inch squares with a knife (see Notes).

4. Place the biscuits on the prepared baking sheet and bake until lightly browned, 15 to 20 minutes. Serve the biscuits warm from the oven or at room temperature.

Notes: If you'll be using these biscuits as a dessert topping (see Blackberry Cobbler, page 420), don't add any herbs. Just continue with the remaining recipe as written.

   If you're using a biscuit cutter, gather up the dough scraps, reroll them, and cut them into more biscuits.

Challah French Toast

When we served breakfast at Chanterelle, challah French toast quickly became **a favorite** of the morning crew. We still enjoy it now and then, mainly when there's a special party at the restaurant and the staff arrives early in the morning, usually hungry. A huge full-size sheet pan is called into action to help ready the vast quantity of French toast (or pancakes, if they are on the menu, as well). Set on the grill, it assures us that we'll all be able to sit down together, with no one stuck watching the stove. Although I make my French toast with thick, rustic slices of eggy challah, any bread you have on hand can be used. I give the bread just a quick dip in the egg mixture so it doesn't get soggy, but you might prefer a longer dunk, which results in softer toast. For breakfast or brunch, I like to serve this with a little pitcher of Spiced Maple Syrup. **SERVES 4**

3 large eggs
¼ cup milk
2 tablespoons sugar
1 tablespoon brandy
⅛ teaspoon ground cinnamon
Dash of freshly grated nutmeg
A few grinds of black pepper
Pinch of coarse (kosher) salt
2 to 4 tablespoons (¼ to ½ stick) unsalted butter,
    plus additional for serving (optional)
4 slices challah (each about 1 inch thick)
Spiced Maple Syrup (optional; recipe follows)

1. Combine the eggs, milk, sugar, brandy, cinnamon, nutmeg, pepper, and salt in a wide, shallow bowl and whisk thoroughly to blend.

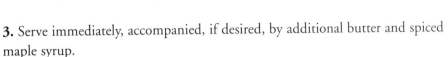

2. Melt 2 tablespoons of the butter in a large, heavy skillet over medium heat. When the foam subsides, soak (but not too long) each slice of bread in the egg mixture to coat both sides, holding it over the bowl to let the excess drain off, then place it in the hot butter. Sauté the bread slices until golden brown on both sides, 2 to 3 minutes per side. Add more butter, if necessary.

3. Serve immediately, accompanied, if desired, by additional butter and spiced maple syrup.

Spiced Maple Syrup

When pure maple syrup is embellished with just a few spices, it becomes an even more **ambrosial topping** for pancakes, waffles, and French toast. Once you've tasted this syrup, scores of other uses will spring to mind. Try brushing a little on baked squash, or adding a splash to hot apple cider served with a cinnamon stick. Tightly covered, the syrup will keep for 3 to 4 weeks in the refrigerator. **MAKES 2 CUPS**

2 cups pure maple syrup
1½ sticks cinnamon (3-inch whole sticks)
6 black peppercorns
2 whole allspice
1- to 2-inch piece of orange zest

1. Combine the syrup, cinnamon, peppercorns, allspice, and orange zest in a small, heavy saucepan and set over medium heat. When the syrup begins to simmer, reduce the heat to very low and cook, uncovered, below a simmer until the flavors are blended, about 15 minutes.

2. Remove the pan from the heat and let cool to room temperature. You can leave the spices in the syrup for a longer time if you wish a more heavily spiced flavor, but strain them out and discard before serving.

Staff Meals from Chanterelle

Ham and Cheese Crêpes with Tarragon Cream Sauce

Crêpes, which seem to go in and out of favor every decade or so, are underrated. In my experience they are always a hit with children, not to mention the staff at the restaurant, and as a consequence we enjoy them fairly often. Inexpensive, versatile, and **inherently elegant**, they're a very civilized way to use up leftovers. Once you've developed the knack of crêpe making—a batch or two is all it takes—your imagination will suggest plenty of fillings. For our staff meal, I generally make this recipe with leftover baked ham, but slices of good-quality deli ham work nicely, too. Napped with a rich, easy-to-make cream sauce, the crêpes are good at brunch with a lightly dressed salad of mixed baby greens or accompanied by steamed vegetables at dinnertime.

SERVES 4

8 Herbed Crêpes (page 389)
16 small, thin slices baked ham or good-quality deli ham
   (about 8 ounces)
8 thin slices Emmenthaler cheese (about 4 ounces)
2 cups heavy (or whipping) cream
A few gratings of nutmeg
Coarse (kosher) salt and freshly ground black pepper, to taste
Squeeze of lemon juice
1 teaspoon chopped fresh tarragon leaves

1. Preheat the oven to 350°F.

2. Arrange the crêpes, less-browned-side up, in a single layer on your work surface. Place 2 slices of ham and a slice of cheese on each and roll up.

3. Lightly oil a small baking dish and arrange the crêpes in it, seam-side down. Cover loosely with aluminum foil and bake until heated through and the cheese has melted, about 10 minutes.

4. Meanwhile, prepare the sauce: Combine the cream, nutmeg, salt, pepper, and lemon juice in a small, nonreactive skillet or wide, shallow saucepan and bring to a boil over medium-high heat. Reduce the heat to medium and cook, uncovered, until the cream is reduced by half, about 10 minutes. Remove the skillet from the heat and set aside, stirring occasionally, until the crêpes are ready.

5. Remove the crêpes from the oven and divide them among four serving plates. Taste the sauce for seasoning, adjusting as necessary. Stir in the tarragon, then spoon the sauce attractively over the crêpes and serve immediately.

cooking crêpes

Crêpe making takes a little practice initially, but once the technique is mastered you'll probably find yourself making them regularly. Luckily, the ingredients are inexpensive, so there should be no guilt about practice batches that turn out less than perfect.

The correct pan is of utmost importance. I prefer a well-seasoned French-style steel crêpe pan with a handle that slants slightly upward (to make swirling the batter easier) and angled sides that facilitate crêpe flipping. Steel is especially responsive to medium-high and high heat, but a nonstick or stainless-steel pan will also work well. The pan should be the same size as the crêpes so they'll be uniform in size; I use a 6-inch pan. Nine times out of ten the first crêpe will stick no matter how careful you are. Don't worry—just throw it out and consider it an offering to the crêpe god. If you have chronic sticking problems with a pan that doesn't have a nonstick coating, try rubbing it with a handful of kosher salt to smooth and polish the surface. Then rinse thoroughly, dry, and begin anew.

The correct temperature is also important. The pan should be hot enough to cook the crêpe within 20 seconds or so, but not so hot that it scrambles the batter. As you make crêpe after crêpe, the heat usually requires some adjusting.

(continued)

cooking crêpes, continued

With the bowl of batter conveniently near the stove, set the pan over medium-high heat. Drizzle some olive oil or clarified butter onto a folded paper towel and thoroughly rub the pan with it, taking care not to use too much. The pan is ready when the oil is hot enough for a drop of water to sizzle.

With a small ladle, scoop up enough batter for one crêpe—about 2 tablespoons per 6-inch crêpe. Remove the pan from the heat and, holding it at a 45-degree angle, quickly pour the batter into the pan at the top edge. Using your wrist, swiftly rotate the pan with a circular motion to spread a thin, even layer of batter over the bottom of the pan; do not use the ladle to spread it.

Return the pan to the heat and cook the crêpe until the surface looks almost cooked and the bottom is lightly speckled with brown, 20 to 30 seconds. Gently loosening the crêpe with a spatula, turn it over; or you can flip it by hand, grasping the edge of the crêpe with your thumb and forefinger. Cook for about 10 seconds, until the second side is lightly speckled with brown as well, then slide the crêpe out of the pan onto a plate. Repeat until the batter is used up, stacking the crêpes as they're removed from the pan.

Layered between sheets of waxed paper and covered tightly with plastic wrap, crêpes can be refrigerated for a day or two or frozen for up to 3 months.

Herbed Crêpes

This crêpe batter, seasoned with a sprinkling of fresh herbs, is meant to be used for savory main dishes. For sweet dessert crêpes, substitute canola oil for olive oil and eliminate the herbs and salt and pepper. Allowing the batter to rest in the refrigerator for at least an hour before using it ensures tender results.

MAKES ABOUT EIGHT 6-INCH CRÊPES

2 large eggs
⅔ cup water
2 tablespoons extra-virgin olive oil
Dash of brandy
Coarse (kosher) salt and freshly ground black pepper, to taste
⅓ cup all-purpose flour
2 teaspoons chopped mixed fresh herbs, such as chives, chervil,
    flat-leaf parsley, and tarragon leaves

1. Place the eggs, water, oil, brandy, salt, and pepper in a medium-size bowl and whisk thoroughly to blend. Add the flour and whisk to mix, but don't worry if there are a few lumps. Let the batter rest, covered, in the refrigerator for at least 1 hour and up to 12—the longer, the better.

2. When you're ready to make the crêpes, stir the batter and then judge its consistency. It should be relatively thin; if it has thickened upon standing, add water, a tablespoon at a time, until the batter is just about the consistency of heavy cream or slightly thicker.

3. Cook the crêpes according to the instructions in the box starting on page 387, using about 2 tablespoons batter per crêpe.

Chanterelle's Breakfast Waffles

It's wonderful when **friends from childhood** turn up again—and that's just what happened with my wife, Karen, and Nina Fraas. After years of being out of touch, Karen and Nina ran into each other and picked up the friendship as if there had been no separation. Nina, it turned out, had grown up to be a terrific chef and fortuitously reappeared when we were looking for the right person to chef our breakfasts.

Every morning at four o'clock, or maybe five, Nina would fire up the ovens and create just the kind of dishes that made getting out of bed seem like a reasonable idea. Her waffles were particularly memorable, and I offer them here. The waffles are light and bake up crisp and delicate, perfect for housing little pockets of butter and syrup. The batter is partially made the night before and develops structure and a rich flavor as it rests. Making the waffles the next morning is a breeze. Thanks, Nina.

MAKES 6 TO 8 WAFFLES, DEPENDING ON THE SIZE OF THE WAFFLE IRON

1 package active dry yeast

1 tablespoon sugar

½ cup water, at room temperature

1¾ cups whole milk, at room temperature

2 cups all-purpose flour

1 teaspoon salt

6 tablespoons (¾ stick) unsalted butter, melted

2 large eggs

½ teaspoon baking soda

Vegetable oil spray, for the waffle iron

Unsalted butter, for serving

Spiced Maple Syrup (page 385), for serving

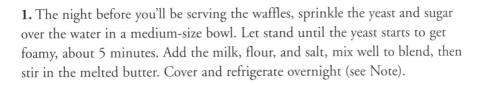

1. The night before you'll be serving the waffles, sprinkle the yeast and sugar over the water in a medium-size bowl. Let stand until the yeast starts to get foamy, about 5 minutes. Add the milk, flour, and salt, mix well to blend, then stir in the melted butter. Cover and refrigerate overnight (see Note).

2. Preheat the oven to its lowest setting.

3. When you're ready to make the waffles, beat the eggs and baking soda in a small bowl, then mix them into the batter.

4. Heat the waffle iron and bake your waffles according to the iron manufacturer's directions. If your iron is nonstick, a light spray of oil for the first waffle is all that's needed. If it isn't, you may need to spray before making each waffle. Usually each waffle uses about ⅓ to ½ cup batter. Pour it into the center of the waffle iron, spreading it out to the edges. Close the top of the iron and bake until done, about 2 minutes.

5. Place the waffles as they are baked on a platter in the oven. They can sit briefly as you prepare the others but are best eaten as soon as they finish baking. Serve the waffles with butter and maple syrup alongside.

Note: If you're making the waffles for an evening meal—say, as a dessert topped with whipped cream or ice cream and fruit—you can prepare the batter through step 1 earlier in the day. It will keep at room temperature for up to 6 hours. Do not add the eggs and baking soda until right before baking.

how to clarify butter

Clarifying butter removes milk solids and water, and allows the butter to be used at high temperatures—for sautéing, for example—without burning or scorching. One cup (2 sticks) butter will yield about ¾ cup clarified.

Cut unsalted butter into 1-inch pieces, place in a heavy saucepan, and melt over medium-low heat. Remove the pan from the heat and let the butter cool for 5 to 10 minutes, then skim the froth from the surface and discard it. Carefully pour or ladle off the clear yellow butterfat into a storage container, leaving behind any milky residue or liquid whey at the bottom of the pan. Cover and chill. Clarified butter will keep for at least 1 week stored in the refrigerator.

Half-Inch-High Buttermilk Pancakes

After a long search for the perfect pancake, my friend Leonard Lopate told me that he found this recipe in *Cook's* magazine a few years ago. At least he thinks it's the recipe he saw, because he promptly misplaced the magazine, and after changing it here and there, has no idea whether what he does now bears any similarity to the original. It was important for me to find **a good recipe** for pancakes, because my young son is a picky eater and pancakes are among the foods he has consistently eaten. He took to this version immediately and now will eat no other (as we discovered when we ordered pancakes for him in a restaurant).

Karen, Sara, and I enjoy these remarkably fluffy, soulful pancakes as much as he does. Serve the pancakes with Spiced Maple Syrup (page 385). **MAKES EIGHT 3½-INCH-WIDE PANCAKES**

1¼ cups all-purpose flour
1 tablespoon sugar
1 teaspoon salt
½ teaspoon baking soda
¼ teaspoon baking powder
5 tablespoons unsalted butter, melted and cooled
1 large egg, separated
⅔ cup buttermilk
⅓ cup milk
Canola or other vegetable oil, for greasing the griddle
Spiced Maple Syrup, for serving (optional; page 385)

1. Place the flour, sugar, salt, baking soda, and baking powder in a medium-size mixing bowl and stir to combine.

2. Place the melted butter and the egg yolk in a small bowl and whisk to blend. Add the buttermilk, milk, and egg white and whisk thoroughly to combine.

3. Pour the egg mixture into the dry ingredients and mix until combined, but do not overwork. The batter should be quite thick and very lumpy.

4. Heat a griddle over high heat until very hot (a drop of water should sizzle on contact). Lightly grease the griddle with a small amount of oil, then lower the heat to medium. Using a ¼-cup measure, pour the batter onto the griddle. Don't crowd the pancakes; you want the batter to spread comfortably, leaving enough room between cakes to be able to turn them easily.

5. Cook the pancakes until they begin to firm up and bubbles appear on the surface (watch closely; sometimes the cakes firm up before the bubbles show up), 2 to 3 minutes. Use a spatula to lift a pancake to check its bottom side; if it's nicely browned, slide the spatula all the way under and flip the cake. Check all pancakes before flipping.

6. Continue cooking the pancakes until the second side is nicely browned, about 1 minute more.

7. Serve the pancakes immediately with the syrup, if desired.

Oatmeal Pancakes

The **ground oats** in these pancakes give them a rustic, slightly earthy flavor, yet they're still light and fluffy. Like Challah French Toast (page 384), they're delicious served with warmed Spiced Maple Syrup (page 385).

MAKES SIX TO EIGHT 4-INCH PANCAKES

1 cup old-fashioned rolled oats
   (do not use instant oatmeal)
1½ cups all-purpose flour
1 tablespoon sugar
1 tablespoon baking powder
Pinch of ground cinnamon
Pinch of coarse (kosher) salt
3 large eggs
2 cups milk
4 tablespoons (½ stick) unsalted butter, melted and cooled,
   plus additional for the griddle
Spiced Maple Syrup (optional; page 385)

1. Preheat the oven to its lowest setting.

2. Place the oats in a blender or food processor and process until reduced to a fine flour. Combine in a large bowl with the flour, sugar, baking powder, cinnamon, and salt and whisk thoroughly to mix.

3. Using the whisk, beat the eggs in a medium-size bowl, then add the milk and 4 tablespoons melted butter and whisk well to blend. Pour the mixture into the oat mixture and whisk just until the dry ingredients are moistened and a medium-thick batter forms; it will be lumpy.

4. Set a pancake griddle or large, heavy skillet over medium heat and brush generously with more melted butter. When it's hot enough to sizzle a drop of batter, ladle the batter onto the griddle to form as many 4-inch pancakes as will fit (probably no more than three or four); make sure the edges don't touch. When the top of each pancake is full of little burst bubbles and the underside is lightly golden brown, 2 to 3 minutes (see Note), turn over carefully and cook until golden brown on the second side, another 2 to 3 minutes.

5. Transfer the pancakes to a platter and keep warm in the oven while you cook the remaining pancakes. Serve accompanied, if desired, by spiced maple syrup.

Note: Adjust the heat so the pancakes brown nicely but do not burn before bubbles form and burst on the surface.

Shirred Eggs with Smithfield Ham and Tarragon

This lovely baked-egg dish feels very special

Shirred eggs has an old-fashioned ring from the time of dining room sideboards laden with an expansive number of breakfast dishes prepared by the below-stairs kitchen staff. Those days may be long gone, but the romance attached isn't. Shirred eggs are ready made for an anniversary or Valentine's Day or Mother's Day brunch. Prepared and served in individual gratin dishes, the yolks finish elegantly runny, and the whites are firm but not dry. Smithfield ham is the best of our cured hams. Prosciutto makes a fine substitute.

Although the recipe makes enough to serve only one, the ingredients multiply easily to suit as many portions as are needed. Because shirred eggs should be presented with the yolks intact, break the eggs one at a time into a cup, then slide them into the baking dish. That way if one of the yolks breaks when you're cracking the egg, you won't have to try to figure out how to get it out of the gratin dish. **SERVES 1**

1 teaspoon unsalted butter

1 thin slice (approximately ½ ounce) Smithfield ham

1½ teaspoons marinara-type tomato sauce, preferably homemade

½ teaspoon fresh tarragon leaves, coarsely chopped

2 large eggs

Coarse (kosher) salt and freshly ground black pepper, to taste

1 tablespoon heavy (or whipping) cream

1. Preheat the oven to 375°F.

2. Place the butter in a single-serving, ovenproof baking dish that easily holds the eggs (a 4-inch gratin dish is perfect). Place the dish in the oven to melt the butter.

3. Place the ham on the melted butter, folding it or trimming the edges so that it fits easily in the baking dish. Spread the tomato sauce over the ham and sprinkle it with the tarragon.

4. Carefully break an egg into a small cup, then pour it into the gratin dish. Repeat this with the second egg. If a yolk breaks, save that egg for another use. Sprinkle lightly with salt and pepper, then drizzle the cream on top.

5. Bake the eggs until the whites are set and the yolks are warm but still runny, about 12 minutes. If the whites still need some firming up, run the eggs under the broiler for a few seconds. You don't want to overcook them. Serve immediately.

karen's resuscitating white wine spritzers

In the summertime, when kitchen temperatures soar mercilessly, personalities begin to kick in as the heat gets to us. It's a stage when we start wondering how we're going to get through the day. That's when my wife, Karen, has a way of miraculously appearing in the kitchen doorway bearing a silver tray of frosted, oversize snifters filled with iced white wine spritzers. They are always quintessentially thirst quenching. And it has to be Karen who makes them—no one else quite gets them right. Here is her recipe.

For each spritzer, fill a *large* goblet or snifter with ice, all the way to the top. Take 3 generous lemon twists, twist them up really well, then run them around the rim and inside top of the glass and slip them in among the ice cubes. Pour in enough white wine to come halfway up the ice, then top off with sparkling water (San Pellegrino only; accept no substitutes). Stir and serve to cranky, overheated people and watch them revive.

Mint Juleps, Chanterelle Style

For nearly two decades, Derby Day has been cause for great **celebration** among the Chanterelle staff. A week or two beforehand one of us suddenly realizes that the special day is fast approaching, and preparations are immediately launched. One of us nabs a bottle of Wild Turkey from the liquor room, bringing it to the kitchen carefully tucked under a long white apron. We open the bottle, and then, using the same butcher's twine we use for trussing chickens, we bind together the stems of a few large sprigs of mint. The bundle of mint is slid carefully inside the bottle, leaving a length of the string hanging out to ensure easy retrieval later, then the bottle is recapped. Finally, the infusion is placed, with reverence, in one of our refrigerators.

Sometime late in the evening of Derby Day, the first Saturday in May, our thoughts turn to that special bottle of Wild Turkey. If there are still diners in the restaurant, we hum our official theme song, "A Mint Julep," quietly under our breaths as we get on stealthily with the preparations; if it's just us, we put the Clovers version on full blast. Ice is fetched by one of the wait staff, who crushes it, ritualistically, in a linen napkin. Meanwhile, one of the cooks uses a silver spoon to crush several sprigs of mint in the bottom of the first of many 10-ounce rock-crystal glasses, then rubs a mint leaf around the rim. The glass is filled with crushed ice, about 4 ounces of mint-infused bourbon is added, and the whole thing is topped off with sparkling water—not too much, about 2 ounces—and, in a final festive fillip, garnished with another sprig of mint. Yes, a Chanterelle mint julep is surely refreshing. To say the least.

Polenta with Spicy Tomato Sauce and Poached Eggs

This is a **very satisfying** brunch, luncheon, or light supper dish. For dinner, serve with a big salad of fresh greens. The delicate, neutral flavor of polenta makes it a fine vehicle for the spicy sauce. Any good brand of cornmeal from the supermarket works fine here, and it makes no difference whether or not it's stone ground. For an extra bit of zip, remove and crumble the filling from several hot Italian sausages, sauté over high heat, drain, and add to the sauce.

Well wrapped and refrigerated, the unsauced polenta will keep for up to 3 days. **SERVES 6**

2 cups whole milk

2 cups water

1 tablespoon unsalted butter

Coarse (kosher) salt and freshly ground black pepper, to taste

1 cup cornmeal

Olive oil, for the baking dish

2 tablespoons freshly grated Parmesan

3 cups Tasty Basic Tomato Sauce (page 271)

1 teaspoon hot red pepper flakes

Dash of distilled white vinegar

6 large eggs

1. Combine the milk, water, butter, salt, and pepper in a medium-size, heavy saucepan and bring to a boil over medium-high heat. Reduce the heat to medium low and add the cornmeal in a slow, steady stream, whisking constantly. Continue whisking the mixture until it thickens and begins to pull away from the sides of the pan, 3 to 5 minutes.

2. Oil well a 10 × 8-inch baking dish or 9- or 10-inch glass pie plate. Remove the polenta from the heat and transfer it to the prepared dish, smoothing the top with a rubber spatula. Sprinkle it with the grated Parmesan and let cool until firm, about 15 minutes.

3. While the polenta is firming up, place the tomato sauce in a small, heavy saucepan and stir in the pepper flakes. Bring to a simmer over medium heat, then reduce the heat to low and cook, uncovered, until the sauce is slightly reduced and its flavors are developed, about 15 minutes.

4. Meanwhile, preheat the oven to 400°F. Oil a baking sheet.

5. Cut the polenta into six squares or wedges and arrange them on the prepared baking sheet. Bake until they're heated through and the Parmesan begins to brown, about 10 minutes. Remove the baking sheet from the oven and cover loosely with aluminum foil to keep warm while you poach the eggs.

6. Bring 4 cups of water to a boil in a small, heavy saucepan over medium-high heat. Add the vinegar and a pinch of salt, then reduce the heat to maintain a steady simmer. Very carefully, break an egg into a small cup, making sure the yolk doesn't break as well. Make a whirlpool in the water with a spoon and slide the egg from the cup into the center of the whirlpool. As it poaches, repeat the procedure with a second egg; you should be able to poach 2 or 3 eggs at a time. Poach the eggs for 2 to 3 minutes each for a slightly runny yolk, or to your desired doneness.

7. Using a slotted spoon, remove the eggs carefully to a plate. Cover loosely with plastic wrap to keep warm while you poach the remaining eggs.

8. When all the eggs are poached, use a kitchen scissors to trim them of any ragged edges, if desired. Place a piece of polenta on each of six serving plates, then spoon the sauce over the polenta and top with a poached egg. Serve immediately.

Herb and Garlic Focaccia

This simple-to-make Italian flatbread is **always good** and can easily be flavored in any way that suits you. This combination—fresh thyme and sage with garlic—is a favorite, but you could easily use other fresh herbs, olives, hot red pepper flakes, and a variety of spices and seeds including cumin, coriander, and even curry powder. Crisp on the outside, light and chewy inside, this focaccia is a good match for roasted or grilled lamb or fish and virtually any type or pasta or cheese. Split in half, it can also be used to create delicious, hearty sandwiches.

MAKES ONE 15 × 12 × 1-INCH BREAD

FOR THE BREAD:

1 package active dry yeast
2 cups lukewarm water
Pinch of sugar
1 tablespoon olive oil, plus additional for the bowl
¾ teaspoon coarse (kosher) salt
4 cups all-purpose flour, plus additional for kneading

FOR THE TOPPING:

1 bunch fresh thyme
6 fresh sage leaves
2 cloves garlic, peeled
¾ cup olive oil, plus additional for the pan
Coarse (kosher) salt and freshly ground black pepper, to taste

1. First, prepare the bread: Sprinkle the yeast over the water in a large bowl. Add the sugar and stir to mix. Let the mixture stand until the yeast starts to get foamy, about 5 minutes.

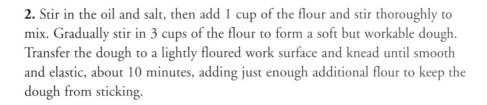

2. Stir in the oil and salt, then add 1 cup of the flour and stir thoroughly to mix. Gradually stir in 3 cups of the flour to form a soft but workable dough. Transfer the dough to a lightly floured work surface and knead until smooth and elastic, about 10 minutes, adding just enough additional flour to keep the dough from sticking.

3. Clean out the bowl, then lightly oil the inside. Form the dough into a ball and place it in the bowl, turning it to coat on all sides with oil. Cover the bowl with a dampened kitchen towel and place in a warm, draft-free spot. Let the dough rise until doubled in bulk, about 1½ hours.

4. Punch down the dough and let it rise again, covered, until doubled in bulk, about another 1¼ hours.

5. Meanwhile, prepare the topping: Strip the thyme leaves from their stems and place in a blender. Add the sage leaves, garlic cloves, and ¾ cup oil and process until the herbs and garlic are coarsely chopped. Set aside.

6. Preheat the oven to 425°F. Generously oil a 15 × 12 × 1-inch jelly-roll pan.

7. Press the dough into the prepared pan, cover with the towel, and let rise until the indentation stays when the dough is pressed with a finger, about 35 minutes.

8. Using all your fingertips, make rows of dimples in the dough. Spread the herb, garlic, and oil mixture over the dough to cover it completely, then sprinkle generously with salt and pepper.

9. Bake until the focaccia is golden brown, puffed, and fragrant, about 15 minutes. Serve hot from the oven or at room temperature.

Garlic Bread

Piping-hot garlic bread takes **no time at all** to prepare and is always a welcome addition to staff and family meals. Of course, we like ours so assertively garlicky that the second everyone's finished eating, members of the wait staff go dashing into the kitchen, grabbing sprigs of breath-freshening parsley to chew on so they won't overwhelm the unsuspecting public with garlic fumes. **SERVES 8**

2 baguettes, each about 24 inches long
¾ cup good-quality olive oil
1 medium head garlic (about 16 cloves), separated
    into cloves, peeled, and minced (about ½ cup)
2 tablespoons chopped fresh flat-leaf parsley leaves
Coarse (kosher) salt and freshly ground black pepper, to taste

1. Preheat the oven to 400°F.

2. Cut each baguette lengthwise in half and place all four halves on your work surface, cut-side up. Drizzle about 3 tablespoons of the oil over each half, then sprinkle with the garlic (about 2 tablespoons per half), parsley, salt, and pepper. Place the baguette tops on the bottoms to re-form the loaves, then wrap the loaves separately in aluminum foil. Bake until fragrant and heated through, about 10 minutes.

3. Remove the garlic bread from the oven and turn the broiler to high. When the broiler is hot enough, unwrap the loaves, separate again into halves, and place, cut-side up, under the broiler. Broil until lightly toasted, about 30 seconds.

4. Remove the garlic bread from the broiler, cut into serving-size pieces, and serve immediately.

Parmesan Bread

A sprinkling of **freshly grated**, nutty-tasting Parmigiano-Reggiano (see box, page 267) enhances the minced garlic topping here. These lightly toasted slices are perfect with pasta and a big green salad, or served as a crunchy snack with cold beer. **SERVES 8**

2 baguettes, each about 24 inches long
¾ cup good-quality olive oil
8 large cloves garlic, minced (about 2 tablespoons)
Coarse (kosher) salt and freshly ground black pepper, to taste
1 cup freshly grated Parmesan (about 4 ounces)
2 tablespoons chopped fresh flat-leaf parsley leaves

1. Preheat the oven to 400°F.

2. Cut each baguette lengthwise in half and place all four halves on your work surface, cut-side up. Drizzle about 3 tablespoons of the oil over each half, then sprinkle with the garlic (about 1½ teaspoons per half) and salt and pepper. Top each half with a sprinkling of the grated Parmesan (¼ cup per half) and some parsley.

3. Arrange the baguette halves on a large baking sheet and bake until the bread is lightly toasted and fragrant and the cheese is melted, about 10 minutes.

4. Remove the Parmesan bread from the oven, cut into serving-size pieces, and serve immediately.

Chapati

Chapati is a basic Indian flatbread that's easy to make and a great scooper-upper of curries and other fragrant, stewy dishes. It takes practically no time at all to turn out a stack to serve piping hot for dipping into sauces (the Tamarind Dipping Sauce on page 372 is a natural), for mopping up flavorful gravies (try them with Venison Chili with Red Beans, page 77, or Lamb Shanks with Tomato and Rosemary, page 90), or as a sandwich wrap filled with Cheddar cheese and a dollop of mango chutney.

If you have an Indian grocery story nearby, look for bags of chapati flour. This delicious, almost sweet whole-grain flour yields lighter results than our whole-wheat flour, but if it's unavailable a commercial whole-wheat flour, such as Gold Medal (rather than a rustic stone-ground variety), will make a good substitute.

MAKES 10 CHAPATI

3 cups chapati flour or whole-wheat flour (see Note)
1 cup all-purpose flour, plus more for dusting
1 teaspoon salt
Small pinch of cayenne pepper
⅛ teaspoon ground cumin
Small pinch of chili powder
Canola or other vegetable oil
1½ cups cold water

1. Place the chapati flour, 1 cup all-purpose flour, the salt, cayenne, cumin, and chili powder in a medium-size mixing bowl and whisk to combine.

2. Drizzle 2 teaspoons of the oil over the flour mixture and use your hands to rub it in.

3. Add the water to the flour mixture and use your hands to mix it together into a soft dough. Transfer the dough to a work surface lightly dusted with

all-purpose flour and knead just to make sure the dough is uniformly blended and not sticky, 30 seconds. Leave the dough on the board, cover it lightly with plastic wrap, and let it rest for 15 minutes.

4. Divide the dough into ten equal portions, each approximately the size of a lime. With your palms, roll each portion into a ball. Place the balls of dough in a row at the top of your work surface and cover them lightly with plastic wrap. Working with one ball of dough at a time, lightly dust the work surface again with all-purpose flour and roll each ball into a round about 8 inches wide and ⅛ inch thick. Place the chapati on a dinner plate, cover with a piece of waxed paper, and repeat with the remaining balls of dough until you have a stack of rolled chapati.

5. Heat a griddle or medium-size skillet over medium heat. When it's hot (a drop of water will sizzle on contact), pour about 1 tablespoon oil onto the griddle and spread it to coat. Carefully place one chapati onto the griddle. Fry until the chapati is slightly blistered and lightly browned, 1 to 2 minutes. Using tongs, turn the chapati and fry the second side until lightly browned, about 1 minute more. Remove the chapati from the pan, place it on a serving platter, and cover it with a clean cloth napkin while you fry the rest. If the pan gets too dry, add a bit more oil. Serve immediately.

Note: If you can't find chapati flour, use 1½ cups whole-wheat flour and increase the all-purpose flour to 2½ cups.

Desserts

Although all of us at Chanterelle love desserts, we don't often indulge in them at staff meals. They're mostly reserved for special occasions such as birthdays or holidays. Of course, there are those moments when we're inspired by the sight of a basket of sublimely ripe blackberries crying out to become a tempting cobbler or a freshly baked crisp. And sometimes, when the Chanterelle kitchen has been especially busy, we simply feel the need to indulge in a reward for our hard work and extra effort. The desserts here are not particularly fancy, but they do rely on the highest-quality ingredients. After all, it makes no sense to bake a mouthwatering chocolate cake using mediocre chocolate, or to create a fabulous cobbler with flavorless fruits.

Dried Fruits in Spiced Red Wine

This dessert says "front of the house" more than it says "staff meal," but it's a favorite of mine. **Easy to prepare**, it keeps for a long time in the refrigerator and makes a good winter holiday dish, one that you can have ready in advance. The figs and prunes rest in a dark, luscious syrup until plump and deeply flavored. In a funny way, I think this is what holiday fruitcake wished it was. Serve the fruits in their aromatic syrup accompanied by crisp Tuiles (page 427) or vanilla ice cream. **SERVES 12**

1½ pounds dried figs
1½ pounds dried pitted prunes
10 black peppercorns
2 vanilla beans
1 bottle (750 ml) dry red wine, such as an inexpensive
    California or Chilean Merlot
1 cup ruby port
½ cup brandy
1 cup sugar, or more to taste
Zest of 1 lemon, removed with a vegetable peeler
Zest of 1 orange, removed with a vegetable peeler
3 star anise
1 cinnamon stick (3 inches)
1 whole nutmeg
Chopped walnuts, for serving
Unsweetened whipped cream, for serving

1. Place the figs and prunes in a large bowl and set aside.

2. Place the peppercorns between two pieces of waxed paper and coarsely crush with a heavy mallet or the flat side of a meat cleaver. Carefully split the vanilla beans lengthwise with a sharp paring knife.

3. Place the wine, port, brandy, 1 cup sugar, the lemon and orange zests, star anise, cinnamon stick, nutmeg, crushed peppercorns, and vanilla beans in a large, nonreactive pot. Bring to a boil over high heat and reduce the liquids by half, 15 to 20 minutes. The marinade will take on a slightly syrupy consistency.

4. Strain the marinade into a small bowl and taste. It should be sweet but not cloyingly so. If necessary, add more sugar, 1 tablespoon at a time, but keep in mind that the figs and prunes will also add sweetness.

5. Pour the syrupy marinade over the dried fruit and let marinate, covered, in the refrigerator for at least 2 days and up to 3 weeks.

6. To serve, place two or three of each of the dried fruits on a plate. Drizzle with syrup, then sprinkle with chopped walnuts and top with a dollop of whipped cream.

Zesty Cranberry Soup

This easy, light dessert soup is a staff natural **in the fall** when cranberries are plentiful and festive feelings are running high. We like its tart-sweet flavor and usually serve it with a scoop of vanilla ice cream or lemon or orange sherbet midbowl, plus a few sugared cranberries on top for garnish. **SERVES 4 TO 6**

1 cinnamon stick (3 inches)
6 whole cloves
1 piece (1 inch) fresh ginger, peeled
4 long strips lemon zest, ½ inch wide
2½ cups sugar
2 cups water
2 packages (12 ounces each) fresh or frozen cranberries
3 tablespoons fresh lemon juice, or to taste

1. Place the cinnamon stick, cloves, ginger, and lemon zest in a cheesecloth square and tie together in a bundle.

2. Place 2 cups of the sugar, the spice bundle, and water in a medium-size, heavy saucepan and bring to a boil over medium-high heat. Boil, stirring constantly, to dissolve the sugar.

3. Add the cranberries and bring the mixture to a boil. Then reduce the heat to medium and cook until the berries begin to burst, 3 to 5 minutes. Remove the pan from the heat; you don't want the soup to get too thick.

4. Place the remaining ½ cup sugar on a plate. Remove ¼ cup of the cranberries and roll them in the sugar to coat. Place the plate of sugared berries in the refrigerator to chill.

5. Let the remaining berries sit for 15 minutes, then strain them through a strainer lined with cheesecloth into a medium-size bowl. Press down on the berries as you strain them to release all their juices. Discard the pressed berries. You should have about 3 cups of juice. Taste and add lemon juice a tablespoon at a time to get just the right balance of flavors. Cover the bowl and refrigerate to chill the cranberry soup.

6. When you're ready to serve, pour the soup into shallow bowls and garnish each serving with a few candied cranberries.

the emperor of ice cream

At Chanterelle there's a lot of rushing around behind the scenes, but when we step through the kitchen door to greet our clients, boom!—everything changes—it's showtime. No matter what, our job is to appear serene and friendly. This is far easier said than done on some days. And when we're frazzled, the thing that's guaranteed to calm us down and cool us off is ice cream. You cannot imagine how much we consume, and the same is true in many restaurants. Luckily, we have our own Emperor of Ice Cream, the *garde-manger*. It's the *garde-manger* who's responsible for cold or chilled foods, including desserts. For us, he or she is also the person with the scoop who obligingly indulges us. There's nothing better than bypassing adulthood just long enough to enjoy a dish of ice cream.

Staff Meals from Chanterelle | desserts

Litchi Sorbet

Fresh, sweet litchis (or lychees) are available for such a short time during early summer that it's not surprising many of us never have the opportunity to enjoy them. I always make a point of surprising Karen with fresh litchis when I see them in nearby Chinatown (she says she likes them better than flowers)! These small, succulent fruits with an easy-to-remove, reddish shell and a gel-like texture taste exotic. In fact, litchis are exotic, originally hailing from Asia.

Canned litchis, on the other hand, have lost their mystique. Still, they're available year-round and not hard to find. This sorbet gives the canned litchi back its special quality. The substantial amount of lemon juice livens up the flavor, adding a sweet-tart balance. Eat it on its own or as a garnish for a fruit soup.

MAKES 4 CUPS; SERVES 8

4 cups litchis with syrup (two 20-ounce cans; see Note)
¼ cup sugar
1 tablespoon fresh lemon juice, or more to taste

1. Purée the litchis in batches in a blender or food processor. Transfer each batch to a large bowl as it is puréed. Strain the puréed litchis through a fine sieve into another bowl.

2. Add the sugar and lemon juice and stir to blend. Taste and add more lemon juice if needed.

3. Transfer the litchi purée to an ice cream maker and freeze according to the manufacturer's directions.

Note: If you can only find 15-ounce cans of litchis, buy three and measure out 4 cups. Any extras will taste delicious in a mixed fruit salad.

Cream Cheese Pound Cake

A rich pound cake is a **perfect dessert**. It's easy to put together and needs no special attention while it bakes. You can serve it plain with cups of coffee or tea, and it will make a deliciously satisfying end to a meal. But dress up a pound cake for special occasions and it's elegance personified. When company comes, dust it with confectioners' sugar and serve slices topped with a berry compote (blueberries and blackberries are particularly appealing) or freshly poached peaches and whipped cream. If your guests are like any of us at the restaurant, the cake will be gone before the evening's out. If there's any left over for the morning, lightly toast slices and slather them with your favorite preserves. It's a sweet way to start the day. **MAKES 1 CAKE; SERVES 10**

1½ cups (3 sticks) unsalted butter, at room temperature
1 package (8 ounces) Philadelphia brand cream cheese
   (see Note), at room temperature
3 cups sugar
6 large eggs
2 teaspoons pure vanilla extract
3 cups all-purpose flour
1 teaspoon salt

1. Preheat the oven to 325°F. Lightly butter a 10-inch tube pan, then line the bottom with parchment paper.

2. Place the butter and cream cheese in a large bowl and beat with a mixer on medium speed until smooth. Add the sugar, increase the speed to high, and beat until light and airy, 5 minutes. Add the eggs, one at a time, beating after each addition and scraping down the sides of the bowl with a rubber spatula as needed. Add the vanilla, then the flour and salt all at once. Beat just until incorporated.

3. Pour the batter into the prepared pan and shake lightly to even out the top. Bake until the cake is golden brown and a toothpick inserted in the cake comes out clean, 1¼ hours.

4. Place the pan on a cake rack and cool for 20 minutes, then remove the cake from the pan and let it cool completely. Serve at room temperature.

Note: I like Philadelphia cream cheese because it contains less water than other brands. You should be able to find it in your supermarket.

Fallen Chocolate Soufflé Cake

This is the Chanterelle staff's "official" special-occasion cake; we usually whip one up for birthday celebrations or as a farewell treat for a departing staff member's last meal with us. This flourless cake's silky texture and deep, satisfying chocolate flavor belie the simplicity of its preparation. Hot from the oven, the cake is slightly puffed, but while cooling the center sinks a bit lower than the edges—hence, "fallen."

A chocolate dessert is only as good as the chocolate used to make it, so buy the best you can. We use either Valrhona, an expensive premium-quality French chocolate preferred by many chefs and bakers, or Scharffen Berger, a wonderful American boutique chocolate. We usually make this cake with Valrhona's Extra Bitter chocolate, which is actually a semisweet chocolate. Of course, another brand of semisweet chocolate may be used. However, since sweetness levels vary among brands, your cake may end up slightly sweeter. It will still be delicious. The next time you make the cake—and I believe you will make it many times— reduce the amount of sugar, if desired.

To serve, cut the cake into thin slices (it's very rich). For an extraspecial dessert, set out a bowl of Crème Anglaise (page 425). Spoon some onto each plate, then place a slice of cake on top of the sauce. **MAKES ONE 9-INCH CAKE**

1 pound best-quality semisweet chocolate, preferably
    Valrhona Extra Bitter, coarsely chopped
1 cup (2 sticks) unsalted butter
9 large eggs, separated
¾ cup plus 1 tablespoon granulated sugar
Cocoa powder, for dusting the cake
Confectioners' sugar, for dusting the cake

1. Preheat the oven to 300°F. Lightly butter and flour a 9-inch springform pan, then line the bottom with parchment paper.

2. Combine the chocolate and butter in the top of a double boiler and place over gently simmering water. When the mixture is almost completely melted, remove it from the heat. Stir with a wooden spoon until completely melted and blended together. Let cool to room temperature.

3. Combine the egg yolks and ¾ cup of the granulated sugar in a large bowl and beat with an electric mixer until light and thick enough to fall in ribbons from the mixer blades when they're lifted, 4 to 5 minutes.

4. Combine the egg whites with the remaining 1 tablespoon granulated sugar in a medium-size bowl and beat until soft peaks form, about 3 minutes.

5. Gently fold one third of the cooled chocolate mixture into the egg-yolk mixture. Then gently fold one third of the egg whites into the yolk mixture. Repeat, adding the chocolate and egg-white mixtures alternately in thirds into the egg-yolk mixture, until all the ingredients are combined.

6. Carefully pour the batter into the springform pan and bake until the edges are firm and the center is puffed but still just a big jiggly, about 30 minutes. Be sure not to overbake the cake.

7. Cool the cake on a rack before unmolding. Then dust it with a layer of cocoa powder, followed by a layer of confectioners' sugar, a second layer of cocoa, and a final layer of sugar. Serve in thin slices at room temperature.

Staff Meals from Chanterelle | d e s s e r t s

Spiced-Up Honey Cake

A well-baked honey cake was beloved in my family, and when I was growing up my aunt was the baker supreme. We all looked forward to visits to her house and thick slices of the cake for dessert. I think this honey cake is better than my Aunt Fannie's— and that's saying something. Of course, when she reads this, she may well disagree. Still, I think the inviting aroma of the spices as the cake bakes and the added touch of a slightly crusty glaze at the end will win her over. **MAKES 1 CAKE; SERVES 10**

FOR THE CAKE:

1½ cups honey
¾ cup canola oil
1 cup strong brewed coffee
2 teaspoons vanilla extract
3½ cups all-purpose flour
2 teaspoons ground cinnamon
2 teaspoons ground ginger
1 teaspoon ground nutmeg
1 teaspoon ground coriander
1 teaspoon baking soda
1 teaspoon baking powder
½ teaspoon salt
3 large eggs
¾ cup sugar

FOR THE GLAZE:

¼ cup honey
2 tablespoons sugar
2 tablespoons unsalted butter

kids and cuisine

Children often eat at Chanterelle, especially older ones of around eleven or twelve. On the whole they're very open-minded and curious about the menu, adventurously ordering squab, soft-shell crabs, foie gras, and other seemingly unlikely dishes. They tend to be incredibly well behaved, and I'm always struck by how appreciative they are of unfamiliar flavors. Of course, as a parent I know that kids go through food phases. For a while they'll eat absolutely anything, then suddenly they become picky and reluctant to experiment. Right now our daughter, Sara, adores litchis and shellfish, and she frequently orders sushi on our family's weekly visit to a Japanese restaurant. Our son, Jake, on the other hand, is a luncheonette kind of guy with a preference for simpler fare. His idea of a perfect meal away from home is pasta, bread and butter, apple juice, and pound cake.

Seeing kids with their parents at Chanterelle reminds me of my own childhood. My interest in food was sparked by eating out. I was around nine when our parents began taking my brother and me along with them to nice restaurants. From the beginning I loved every minute of it, though my brother was less entranced (I used to pay him a quarter to try something new). I relished having the opportunity to choose from a menu and to have anything I wanted to eat since, like most kids, at family meals we usually just ate what was put before us. Eating in a restaurant was a very special adventure. And I experienced the same pleasures at those dinners that our youngest Chanterelle patrons do today—a taste of the unknown, a chance to experiment, an introduction to intriguing new flavors and dishes.

1. Preheat the oven to 350°F. Oil a 12-cup Bundt pan or 13 × 9-inch rectangular cake pan.

2. First, make the cake: Combine the honey, oil, coffee, and vanilla in a small saucepan and heat, stirring constantly, until the mixture is well blended. Remove it from the heat and let cool.

3. Place the flour, cinnamon, ginger, nutmeg, coriander, baking soda, baking powder, and salt in a large bowl and stir to blend.

4. Place the eggs and sugar in a medium-size bowl and beat with a mixer on medium speed until the mixture is pale yellow and very thick, 5 minutes.

5. Pour the honey mixture into the egg mixture and beat until well incorporated, 2 minutes. Stop the mixer occasionally and scrape down the sides of the bowl with a rubber spatula. Add the flour mixture all at once and beat until fully incorporated, 2 minutes more. Spread the batter evenly in the prepared pan and bake until the cake springs back when lightly touched with your finger and a toothpick inserted in the center comes out clean, 40 to 45 minutes. Cool in the pan for 5 minutes, then place the pan on a wire rack to cool for 20 minutes. Run a long, sharp knife around the edge of the cake and invert it onto a rack to cool while you prepare the glaze.

6. Place the honey, sugar, and butter in a small saucepan and bring to a boil over medium heat, stirring constantly. Remove the glaze from the heat.

7. To glaze the cake, place it on a serving platter. Use a fork to gently poke holes all over the top of the cake. Brush on the glaze, letting it seep into the holes and down the sides. Serve the cake at room temperature.

Apple Oat Crisp

I have a **special fondness** for baked-apple desserts, and this uncomplicated, homey-tasting one is a favorite. In the family tree of all-American desserts, crisps, cobblers, and crunches are cousins. The crumbly topping of this one includes oatmeal to give it a nice crispy texture with a pleasant toastiness. Apples are usually the fruit of choice. Use tart, crisp ones such as Cortland, Granny Smith, McIntosh, Mutsu, Northern Spy, or Winesap. The crunchy topping can be used with a variety of other fruits, including pears and berries. Crisps taste best served while still slightly warm from the oven, preferably with a scoop of ice cream alongside. **SERVES 4 TO 6**

6 medium-size tart, crisp apples (3 pounds total),
   cored, peeled, and diced
Juice of 1 lemon
1 tablespoon plus ½ cup granulated sugar
6 tablespoons (¾ stick) unsalted butter, at room temperature
½ cup (firmly packed) dark brown sugar
⅓ cup all-purpose flour
1 teaspoon ground cinnamon
Pinch of salt
A few grinds of black pepper
½ cup old-fashioned rolled oats (do not use instant oatmeal)

1. Preheat the oven to 375°F.

2. Place the apples in an 8-inch square baking dish. Toss with the lemon juice and 1 tablespoon of the granulated sugar. Set aside.

3. Place the butter, remaining ½ cup granulated sugar, and the brown sugar in a medium-size bowl. Cream with an electric mixer until the mixture is light brown and crumbly, 3 to 5 minutes. Add the flour, cinnamon, salt, and pepper and stir until thoroughly incorporated. Add the oats and stir until thoroughly incorporated. Scrape down the sides of the bowl as needed.

4. Sprinkle the topping over the apples to cover. Bake until the topping is lightly browned and the apples are heated through and bubbling, 35 to 45 minutes. Let cool slightly before serving.

Our Favorite Brownies

Brownies are greeted with **universal delight** by our staff. After all, nobody is ever too grown up to enjoy them. The addition of a pinch of black pepper, which enhances the flavor of the chocolate, was inspired by a famous Maida Heatter cookie recipe. Aside from using really good chocolate, the most important trick to making great brownies is always to slightly underbake them so they remain chewy in the middle.

MAKES SIXTEEN 2-INCH-SQUARE BROWNIES

10 tablespoons (1¼ sticks) unsalted butter, cut into pieces
10 ounces best-quality bittersweet chocolate, broken into pieces
1 cup granulated sugar
½ cup (firmly packed) light brown sugar
5 large eggs
1 teaspoon vanilla extract
A few grinds of black pepper
¼ cup good-quality unsweetened cocoa powder
1½ cups all-purpose flour
1 cup walnuts or pecans, roughly chopped (optional)

1. Preheat the oven to 350°F. Lightly butter and flour an 8-inch square baking pan.

2. Combine the butter and chocolate in the top of a double boiler and place over gently simmering water. When the mixture is almost completely melted, remove it from the heat. Stir with a wooden spoon until both the butter and chocolate are completely melted and blended together. Pour the mixture into a medium-size bowl and let cool to room temperature.

3. Once the chocolate mixture is cool, add the granulated sugar, brown sugar, eggs, vanilla, and pepper and whisk well to combine.

4. Add the cocoa powder and stir until thoroughly incorporated. Add the flour ½ cup at a time, stirring well after each addition to thoroughly incorporate. Stir in the nuts, if desired. Then pour the batter into the prepared baking pan.

5. Bake until a toothpick inserted in the center of the brownies still has a light coating of batter on it when removed, but when inserted near the edge of the brownies comes out dry, 25 to 35 minutes. Let the brownies cool (the center will finish cooking to a nice chewiness), then cut them into squares to serve.

Blackberry Cobbler

We indulge in this luscious dessert only once or twice a year at our staff meal, but it's always memorable. At the height of the season, when plump, glossy blackberries are bursting with flavor, we prevail upon our pastry chef to bake this as a special treat. One good thing about a cobbler is its forgiving format—the berries need not be perfect, since they pretty much fall apart during baking anyway. Raspberries, strawberries, peaches, or plums may be used in place of the blackberries, or you could use a mixture of fruits and berries. On average, a pint yields 1½ to 2 cups berries, a pound of peaches yields about 2¾ cups sliced fruit, and a pound of plums yields around 3 cups sliced fruit.

Cobblers are best served warm from the oven accompanied by a scoop of vanilla ice cream or some unsweetened whipped cream.

SERVES 4 TO 6

6 cups fresh blackberries (about 3 pints)

¼ cup sugar, plus more for sprinkling

1½ tablespoons cornstarch, sifted

1 tablespoon brandy

Pinch of ground cinnamon

Pinch of ground cloves

Pinch of salt

Herbed Biscuits dough made without the herbs
  (page 382)

1. Preheat the oven to 375°F.

2. Place the berries in a medium-size bowl. In a small bowl, mix together ¼ cup sugar with the cornstarch, brandy, cinnamon, cloves, and salt. Add the sugar mixture to the berries and toss to coat. Transfer the berries to an 8-inch square baking dish.

3. Roll out the biscuit dough on a lightly floured work surface until it's an even ¾ inch thick. Cut out rounds using a floured 2-inch cookie cutter, placing the rounds gently over the berries as they're cut. Gather up the excess dough, roll it out again ¾ inch thick, and cut out more rounds to make a total of eight. Lightly sprinkle the tops of the rounds with sugar.

4. Bake the cobbler until the dough has risen and is lightly browned and the filling is hot and bubbly, 35 minutes. If the dough isn't browned, increase the oven temperature to 400°F and bake for 5 minutes more. Let the cobbler rest for a few minutes before serving.

the berry sweetness test

Before preparing a cobbler, be sure to taste a berry or two, then use your judgment to determine how much thickener and sugar should be used. It all depends on how sweet and juicy the berries are. I generally use just enough sifted cornstarch to dust them very lightly. If you're at all unsure, it's better to err on the side of less cornstarch than more. A runny cobbler is preferable to an overthickened, gummy one if your guess was off.

Summertime Ginger Shortcakes

When berries are in season, they naturally become an important part of the restaurant menu. Not surprisingly, they're a favorite with the staff as well, and we **keep plenty around**. Fresh summer berries don't really need help to taste terrific, but these shortcakes, with their double hit of ginger, are so easy to bake, so aromatic, and so right for a layer of berries that we treat ourselves to a batch when the mood strikes.

To serve, we set out a platter of warm shortcakes, a bowl of berries, and a bowl of whipped cream, and everyone prepares the dessert to their own liking. Some split the shortcakes, others like them whole. Some dollop on the cream, others prefer just spooning on the berries. Easy to adapt to personal preferences, this makes a very happy summer dessert. **MAKES 8 TO 10 SHORTCAKES**

2 cups all-purpose flour

1 tablespoon peeled, grated fresh ginger

1 tablespoon ground ginger

1 teaspoon ground cloves

1 teaspoon ground cinnamon

1 tablespoon baking powder

2 tablespoons granulated sugar

2 tablespoons dark brown sugar

½ teaspoon salt

8 tablespoons (1 stick) unsalted butter, cut into pieces, chilled

½ cup buttermilk

1 large egg yolk, whisked

1. Place the flour, fresh ginger, ground ginger, cloves, cinnamon, baking powder, granulated sugar, brown sugar, and salt in a bowl and stir to mix. Drop in the butter pieces and rub them into the dry ingredients using your fingers or a fork. Work quickly, rubbing until the mixture resembles coarse meal. Add the buttermilk, stirring with a wooden spoon until the dough just comes together. Cover the bowl and refrigerate the dough for 1 hour.

2. Preheat the oven to 375°F. Line a baking sheet with parchment paper.

3. Roll out the dough on a lightly floured work surface until it's an even 1 inch thick. Cut out rounds using a floured 2-inch cookie cutter, placing the rounds as they're cut onto the prepared baking sheet, about 2 inches apart. Gather up the excess dough, roll it out again 1 inch thick, and cut out more rounds to make a total of eight to ten.

4. Brush the top of the rounds with egg yolk and bake until golden, about 30 minutes. Remove the shortcakes to a cooling rack. The shortcakes can be eaten warm or at room temperature.

strawberries for the shortcakes

June is strawberry month, and when local juicy, ripe, fresh berries hit the market, you can be sure it heralds shortcake-baking season at the restaurant. Strawberries are favorites for our Summertime Ginger Shortcakes (facing page).

To have enough for the short-cakes, set out 2 pints (4 cups) of fresh berries that have been rinsed, hulled, and drained. Before adding any sugar to the berries,

taste one. Sweet berries need very little sugar; tart berries need a bit more. If the berries are very large, cut them into thick slices. If small, just halve them. Set the berries aside while making the shortcakes; by the time these are baked and cooled, the sugar will have drawn out some of the juices from the berries to make a light syrup that nicely moistens the shortcakes.

Challah Bread Pudding

Puddings and crisps are the kinds of **family desserts** that work their way into our staff meals from time to time. They add that just-right, sweet finish that makes us feel a bit pampered without feeling too full.

Bread pudding has always been a favorite of mine, and this one—flavored with brandy—separates itself from the usual nursery food style. Although it can be made with a good-quality white sandwich bread or French bread, I think a sweeter egg-enriched one, such as challah or brioche, tastes best. It's a perfect way to use up bread that's gone too stale for serving at the table. For extra texture, I sometimes add raisins or chopped nuts. The bread pudding is delicious with or without, so I've made them optional here.

When you want to go all out, top the pudding with Crème Anglaise, a lovely custard sauce that adds a very impressive final touch. **SERVES 4 TO 6**

Unsalted butter, for the pan
5 slices (½ inch thick) challah
1½ cups whole milk
⅔ cup sugar, plus more for sprinkling
2 large eggs
3 large egg yolks
¼ cup raisins (optional)
¼ cup chopped nuts, such as pecans or walnuts (optional)
¼ cup brandy
Pinch of ground cinnamon
Few gratings of fresh nutmeg
Crème Anglaise (optional; recipe follows)

1. Preheat the oven to 350°F. Lightly butter a shallow 5- or 6-cup casserole or baking dish.

2. Place the challah in the casserole, overlapping the slices and cutting them as necessary to cover the surface.

3. Place the milk, ⅔ cup sugar, the eggs, egg yolks, raisins (if desired), nuts (if desired), brandy, cinnamon, and nutmeg in a bowl and whisk well to combine. Pour the custard over the challah, making sure it's completely covered. Sprinkle the top lightly with sugar.

4. Bake until the custard is set and the pudding has puffed a bit and is lightly browned, about 30 minutes. Serve hot or at room temperature with a bowl of crème anglaise, if desired.

Crème Anglaise

Crème anglaise, a French classic, is an **uncomplicated** and very useful vanilla custard sauce that has the power to make any dish seem special. It's a sensual topping for a wide range of desserts, including cakes, soufflés, poached fruit or fruit compotes, puddings, and sweet crêpes. Make it as suggested below or create subtly flavored variations, replacing the brandy with grated orange zest or rum, cognac, or orange liqueur. Espresso-flavored crème anglaise is particularly nice drizzled over a slice of Fallen Chocolate Soufflé Cake (page 413). Dissolve 3 tablespoons instant espresso in 3 tablespoons boiling water and add it when you add the vanilla. **MAKES ABOUT 3 CUPS**

1 cup whole milk
1 cup heavy (or whipping) cream
½ cup sugar
1 vanilla bean
6 large egg yolks
1 tablespoon brandy
1 teaspoon pure vanilla extract

1. Place the milk, cream, sugar, and vanilla bean in a small saucepan and bring to a gentle simmer over low heat. Let simmer until the sugar is dissolved, about 1 minute.

2. While the milk mixture is heating, place the egg yolks in a medium-size bowl and whisk until pale yellow, about 5 minutes.

3. Remove the milk mixture from the heat; remove the vanilla bean and set it aside (see Note). To temper the eggs, slowly whisk in a small amount of the simmered milk mixture. When the eggs are warmed, slowly whisk in the remaining milk mixture. When thoroughly blended, pour the custard into the saucepan and place over low heat. Cook, stirring constantly with a wooden spoon, being sure to scrape the sides and bottom of the pan, until the custard is slightly thickened, 5 to 8 minutes. Remove the pan from the heat and continue stirring for 1 minute more.

4. Strain the crème anglaise through a strainer and let it cool, stirring occasionally to prevent a skin from forming. When it has cooled to room temperature, stir in the brandy and vanilla. Refrigerate, covered, to chill before serving.

Note: Rather than throwing out the used vanilla bean, rinse it off and let it dry. When it's thoroughly dry, place it in your sugar canister. The bean will add to the sugar a mild vanilla flavor that's particularly nice in baking as well as in a cup of coffee.

Tuiles

These graceful, **paper-thin cookies** are a French classic, named for the curved roof tiles called tuiles, which they resemble. You won't find a prettier, more elegantly understated cookie. Since tuile making can't be rushed, we rarely get to indulge in our passion for them at staff meals. However, our pastry chef bakes them regularly to serve alongside Chanterelle's special ice creams and sorbets. Needless to say, it's impossible not to raid the pastry kitchen.

After the tuile batter is mixed, it rests in the refrigerator for at least an hour (overnight is even better) so the gluten in the flour relaxes and the cookies bake up tender. Once baked, the delicate, still-hot wafers must be draped very quickly over a rolling pin or wine bottle to create their curved shape. (For other shapes, see box, page 428.) Although tuiles aren't difficult to make, the process requires a little patience and practice at first. It's worth it.

MAKES ABOUT 3 DOZEN 3-INCH TUILES

2 large egg whites
⅔ cup confectioners' sugar
½ teaspoon salt
1 teaspoon vanilla extract
⅓ cup all-purpose flour
5 tablespoons unsalted butter, melted and cooled to room
    temperature (see Note)
Blanched sliced almonds or toasted shredded coconut,
    for garnish (optional)

1. Place the egg whites, sugar, salt, and vanilla in a medium-size bowl and whisk until light and frothy, 5 minutes. Slowly add the flour, whisking until the batter is smooth, 2 to 3 minutes. Whisk in the butter until well blended, 1 minute. Cover the bowl and refrigerate for at least 1 hour and as long as overnight.

2. Preheat the oven to 350°F. Line baking sheets with parchment paper.

3. Drop teaspoonfuls of the batter onto the prepared baking sheet about 3 inches apart, then gently spread them out with the back of a spoon to form ovals. The batter should be spread very thin. Place almond slices on the tuiles or sprinkle with coconut, if desired.

4. Bake until the edges of the tuiles are browned and the center is set, about 8 minutes.

5. While the cookies are still hot, remove them from the parchment, form them over rolling pins and wine bottles, and let them cool. When set, they will have taken on their classic curved shape. Carefully remove the tuiles and stack them upside down, one on top of the other. The tuiles can be stored in airtight containers and will keep for up to 2 days. If the weather is particularly humid, it's best to eat the cookies the day they're made.

Note: If you allow the butter to brown slightly, it will give the tuiles an even nicer flavor. Just be careful not to burn the butter. As soon as it takes on color, remove it from the burner.

tuile shapes

In addition to the classic curved shape, baked tuile batter can also be rolled into "cigarettes" or molded into single-serving-size cups or baskets called *tulipes*, which are nice filled with mousse, ice cream, or sherbet. For another simple and pretty presentation, brush the basket interiors with melted chocolate, fill with whipped cream, and garnish with fresh berries.

To make cigarettes, quickly wrap a warm, pliable cookie around the handle of a wooden spoon, rolling the cookie over itself. (There should be room to form two at a time on one handle.) Leave in place until cooled and set, 30 seconds or so, then carefully slide off.

To make cups, set out several shallow teacups. Working swiftly, set a warm, pliable cookie over the outside of each cup, gently pressing it into place around the cup; the edges of the cookie should ruffle a little. Let the tuiles cool completely before removing them.

Peanut Lovers' Cookies

It's probably beyond clichéd to say that for many of us no food more than peanut butter brings out an almost aching **kidlike passion**. Well, if you love peanut butter, these are the cookies for you. They're rich and crumbly, bake up in no time, and rate about as high as you can go on the peanut-butter-flavor scale. Just make sure the milk that goes with them is icy cold.

MAKES ABOUT 3 DOZEN 2-INCH COOKIES

1 cup (2 sticks) unsalted butter, at room temperature
1 cup (firmly packed) light brown sugar
¾ cup granulated sugar
1 teaspoon salt
1 teaspoon baking soda
2 large eggs
1 jar (18 ounces) creamy peanut butter
3 cups all-purpose flour

1. Preheat the oven to 375°F. Lightly butter two baking sheets.

2. Place the butter, brown sugar, and granulated sugar in a large bowl and cream them together until light and fluffy. Add the salt and baking soda and mix well to combine. Add the eggs and mix well to combine. Add the peanut butter and mix well, scraping down the sides of the bowl until it's thoroughly incorporated.

3. Add the flour, 1 cup at a time, mixing to thoroughly incorporate it before adding more. You'll have a very thick dough.

4. Place a bowl of warm water next to your work surface. Use your fingers to roll the cookie dough into 1-inch balls. Place them on the prepared baking sheets, leaving 2 inches between cookies. Use the tines of a fork to slightly flatten each cookie, pressing gently to make a cross-hatch pattern. Lightly dip

the fork into the warm water between cookies to prevent it from sticking to the cookie dough.

5. Bake until the cookies just begin to brown, about 12 minutes. Let them cool for a few minutes before removing them to a cooling rack.

Oaty Chocolate Chip Cookies

No one outgrows chocolate chip cookies. It is the kid classic, the love of which extends way beyond childhood. This somewhat chewy, buttery version, a creation of our pastry chef, Kate, is well studded with chips, making for a satisfying chocolate experience. The oats give the cookies good texture, and the pine nuts are a nice change from pecans. **MAKES 4 DOZEN COOKIES**

1 cup (2 sticks) unsalted butter, at room temperature
1 cup (firmly packed) light brown sugar
¾ cup granulated sugar
1 teaspoon salt
1 teaspoon baking soda
2 large eggs
2 cups all-purpose flour
2 cups old-fashioned rolled oats
   (do not use instant oatmeal)
2 cups mini chocolate chips
2 cups whole pine nuts or coarsely
   chopped pecans (optional)

1. Preheat the oven to 375°F. Lightly butter two baking sheets.

2. Place the butter, brown sugar, and granulated sugar in a large bowl and cream them together until light and fluffy. Add the salt and baking soda and mix well to combine. Add the eggs and mix well to combine. Add the flour, 1 cup at a time, mixing to thoroughly incorporate it before adding more.

3. Scrape down the sides of the mixing bowl, then add the oats 1 cup at a time, mixing to thoroughly incorporate them before adding more.

4. Scrape down the sides of the bowl again and add the chips all at once, mixing until incorporated. Add the nuts, if desired, and stir until well mixed. You will have a very thick dough.

5. Drop rounded tablespoonfuls of the cookie dough onto the prepared baking sheets, leaving 2 inches between cookies.

6. Bake until the cookies just begin to brown, about 12 minutes. Let them cool for a few minutes before removing them to a cooling rack.

cookies on command

Most unbaked cookie doughs will keep nicely in the refrigerator for about 3 days, and in the freezer for around 2 to 3 months. The easiest thing to do is form the dough into a log, wrap it tightly in plastic wrap, and freeze until hard. Then, to ensure that it's airtight, transfer the frozen dough to a freezer-weight plastic bag or wrap several layers of foil around it, and return to the freezer. When it's cookie-baking time, defrost the dough by letting it set for an hour or two in the refrigerator or about half an hour out on the counter. It should only soften enough to enable you to scoop and form it into the desired shape.

Stamp-of-Approval Oatmeal Cookies

Rounding out the trio of **American classics** is this recipe for hearty oatmeal cookies. And behind the creation of this recipe is a classic Chanterelle story. Years ago one of our chefs served up deliciously comforting bowls of oatmeal for lunch. It seemed like a good idea because many staff members arrived for lunch service fairly early, with nothing in their stomachs. So why not a comforting midmorning bowl of rustic oatmeal to start the day? The lunch staff actually loved it, and in the exuberance of the moment, we bought a case of oats for what then became a regular oatmeal lunch.

As you might expect, it wasn't long before the oatmeal lunches took on the feeling of something out of *Oliver Twist*. And the buzz from the staff went from quiet mutterings to loud vocal complaints. Faced with a rebellious staff—and a whole case of oats—we quickly took oatmeal off the menu and put oatmeal cookies on. They disappeared in minutes. The staff approved, and when the staff approves, I know I have a winner.

MAKES 3 DOZEN 2-INCH COOKIES

1 cup (2 sticks) unsalted butter, at room temperature

2 cups (firmly packed) light brown sugar

1 teaspoon baking soda

1 teaspoon warm water

½ teaspoon salt

½ teaspoon ground cinnamon

2 large eggs

1 teaspoon pure vanilla extract

2½ cups all-purpose flour

2 cups old-fashioned rolled oats (do not use instant oatmeal)

1. Preheat the oven to 375°F. Lightly butter two baking sheets.

2. Place the butter and brown sugar in a large bowl and cream them together until light and fluffy.

3. Dissolve the baking soda in the warm water and add it and the salt and cinnamon to the butter mixture. Mix well to combine. Add the eggs and vanilla and mix well to combine. Add the flour 1 cup at a time, mixing to thoroughly incorporate it before adding more.

4. Scrape down the sides of the bowl and add the oats 1 cup at a time, mixing to thoroughly incorporate them before adding more. Scrape down the sides of the bowl again.

5. Drop rounded tablespoonfuls of the cookie dough onto the prepared baking sheets, leaving 2 inches between cookies.

6. Bake the cookies until they just begin to brown, about 12 minutes. Let them cool for a few minutes before removing them to a cooling rack.

conversion table

oven temperatures

fahrenheit	gas mark	celsius		fahrenheit	gas mark	celsius
250	½	120		400	6	200
275	1	140		425	7	220
300	2	150		450	8	230
325	3	160		475	9	240
350	4	180		500	10	260
375	5	190				

Note: Reduce the temperature by 20°C (68°F) for fan-assisted ovens.

liquid conversions

u.s.	imperial	metric		u.s.	imperial	metric
2 tbs	1 fl oz	30 ml		1 cup +2 tbs	9 fl oz	275 ml
3 tbs	1½ fl oz	45 ml		1¼ cups	10 fl oz	300 ml
¼ cup	2 fl oz	60 ml		1⅓ cups	11 fl oz	325 ml
⅓ cup	2½ fl oz	75 ml		1½ cups	12 fl oz	350 ml
⅓ cup +1 tbs	3 fl oz	90 ml		1⅔ cups	13 fl oz	375 ml
⅓ cup +2 tbs	3½ fl oz	100 ml		1¾ cups	14 fl oz	400 ml
½ cup	4 fl oz	125 ml		1¾ cups +2 tbs	15 fl oz	450 ml
⅔ cup	5 fl oz	150 ml		1 pint (2 cups)	16 fl oz	500 ml
¾ cup	6 fl oz	175 ml		2½ cups	1 pint	600 ml
¾ cup +2 tbs	7 fl oz	200 ml		3¾ cups	1½ pints	900 ml
1 cup	8 fl oz	250 ml		4 cups	1¾ pints	1 liter

approximate equivalents*

1 stick butter=*8 tbs =4 oz =½ cup*
1 cup all-purpose presifted flour/dried
   bread crumbs=*5 oz*
1 cup granulated sugar=*8 oz*
1 cup (packed) brown sugar=*6 oz*
1 cup confectioners' sugar=*4½ oz*

1 cup honey/syrup=*11 oz*
1 cup grated cheese=*4 oz*
1 cup dried beans=*6 oz*
1 large egg=*2 oz=about ¼ cup*
1 egg yolk=*about 1 tbs*
1 egg white=*about 2 tbs*

*Close enough to be useful when converting from one system to another.

weight conversions

u.s./u.k.	metric	u.s./u.k.	metric	u.s./u.k.	metric	u.s./u.k.	metric
½ oz	15 g	3 oz	90 g	7 oz	200 g	12 oz	350 g
1 oz	30 g	3½ oz	100 g	8 oz	250 g	13 oz	375 g
1½ oz	45 g	4 oz	125 g	9 oz	275 g	14 oz	400 g
2 oz	60 g	5 oz	150 g	10 oz	300 g	15 oz	450 g
2½ oz	75 g	6 oz	175 g	11 oz	325 g	1 lb	500 g

Staff Meals from Chanterelle | conversion table

index

aïoli, 363
    BLTs, 137–38
Alsatian choucroute garni, 126–27
Anchovies, 353
    Caesar salad dressing, 355–56
    green goddess salad dressing, 352–53
    linguine puttanesca, 255
Appetizers:
    beef, chilled red-cooked, 65–67
    chicken, chilled white-cooked, 150–52
    chicken liver, chopped, 192–93
    crab cakes, deviled, 245–46
    crab cakes with Asian flavors, 246–47
    eggplant caponata, 318–19
    see also Dips; First courses
Apple oat crisp, 418–19
Applesauce, spiced, 303
Asian ingredients:
    eggplant, Chinese and Japanese, 121
    fish sauce, 241
    ginger, fresh, 227
    kaffir lime leaves, 15
    lemongrass, 236
    panko, 180
    sesame oil, 342
    shrimp, dried, 286
    see also Chinese ingredients
Asian-style dishes:
    crab cakes, 246–47
    pork saté with spicy peanut sauce,
      116–18
    spinach salad, cooked, with soy and
      sesame, 341–42
    see also Chinese-style dishes; Thai-style
      dishes
Avocado(s):
    ripening, 36
    soup, chilled, 37

baba ghanouj, 320–21
Bacon:
    aïoli BLTs, 137–38

cooking, 138
Balsamic vinegar:
    beets with, 306–7
    marinated tomatoes with basil and, 344
Barbecued ribs, oven-roasted, 110–11
Barley-mushroom soup, 26–27
Basil:
    marinated tomatoes with balsamic
      vinegar and, 344
    roast chicken stuffed with, 146–47
Bay leaves, 21
Bean(s):
    baked, Sabrina's, 304–5
    black, soup, 22–23
    black, stew with pig parts, 108–9
    green, cooking, 305
    red, venison chili with, 77–79
    see also Black bean(s) (Chinese
      fermented); Chickpeas; Lentil
Bean sprouts, stir-fried rice noodles with
    scallions and, 282–83
Béchamel sauce, 311–12
Beef, 45–77
    borscht, hot, for Aunt Gertie, 4–5
    brisket, braised, with carrots, Mom's,
      55–56
    burgers, David's, 72–73
    cottage pie, 74–75
    crispy orange, 48–51
    fillets with star anise, 52–54
    flank steak, lime-marinated, 47
    hot and sour soup, 6–8
    meatballs, Italian, 69–70
    meat loaf, Italian style, 70–72
    pot-au-feu, 63–64
    red-cooked, chilled, 65–67
    roast, dinner, 45–46
    roast, hash, 68–69
    short ribs braised in beer, 58–59
    sloppy Joes, 76–77
    stew with red wine and vegetables,
      60–62

Beef (continued)
tripe soup with lemon, Greek-style, 12–13
Beefed-up veal stock, 38–39
Beer, beef short ribs braised in, 58–59
Beets:
with balsamic vinegar, 306–7
beef borscht, hot, for Aunt Gertie, 4–5
Beurre manié, 62
Beverages:
mint juleps, Chanterelle style, 397
white wine spritzers, 396
Biscuits:
blackberry cobbler, 420–21
cornmeal-onion, 380–81
herbed, 382–83
Bistro-style dishes:
brisket, braised, with carrots, Mom's, 55–56
chicken with tomato and tarragon, 166–67
Black bean:
soup, 22–23
stew with pig parts, 108–9
Black bean(s) (Chinese fermented):
Chinese eggplant with pork and, 120–21
sauce, braised mini ribs with, 114–15
sauce, clams in, 250–51
sauce, shrimp with, 240–41
Blackberry cobbler, 420–21
Black mushrooms, chicken with Chinese sausage and, 160–61
Black vinegar, Chinese, 49
BLTs, aïoli, 137–38
Blue cheese:
chicken cordon bleu cheese, 176–77
dressing, 357
Bok choy, in Chinese-style meatballs for a crowd, 128–30
Borscht, hot beef, for Aunt Gertie, 4–5
Bourbon:
and butternut squash soup, 34–35
mint juleps, Chanterelle style, 397
Wild Turkey glazed ribs, 113–14
Braising, 57
Bread(s), 376–85, 400–405
buttermilk corn muffins with orange, 377–78
challah, pudding, 424–26

challah French toast, 384–85
chapati, 404–5
cornbread, 381–82
cornmeal-onion biscuits, 380–81
croutons, crisp, 356
garlic, 402
herb and garlic focaccia, 400–401
herbed biscuits, 382–83
Parmesan, 403
pizza, eggplant, 297–99
scones, breakfast, Chanterelle, 378–79
stuffing, Sara's, 196–97
Bread crumbs:
making, 279
panko, 180
Breakfasts, 27
see also Brunch fare
Brine, pickling, 215
Brisket, braised, with carrots, Mom's, 55–56
Broccoli rabe, in spaghetti with potatoes and greens, 260–61
Broccoli with oyster sauce, 307–8
Broths:
lamb, 92–93
for red-cooking, 67
Brownies, our favorite, 419–20
Brunch fare, 375–405
buttermilk pancakes, half-inch-high, 392–93
challah French toast, 384–85
ham and cheese crêpes with tarragon cream sauce, 386–89
herbed crêpes, 389
oatmeal pancakes, 393–94
polenta with spicy tomato sauce and poached eggs, 398–99
shirred eggs with Smithfield ham and tarragon, 395–96
waffles, breakfast, Chanterelle's, 390–91
see also Bread(s)
Buffalo wings, Manhattan, 191–92
Burgers:
David's, 72–73
fancier, 73
Butter:
beurre manié, 62
clarifying, 391
sauces, separated, 217
seasoned, in fancier burgers, 73

Buttermilk:
    corn muffins with orange, 377–78
    pancakes, half-inch-high, 392–93
Butternut squash and bourbon soup, 34–35

Cabbage:
    beef borscht, hot, for Aunt Gertie, 4–5
    cider vinegar slaw, 310
    meatballs for a crowd, Chinese-style,
        128–30
    red, braised, 309
    stuffed, Gaby's Hungarian-style, 122–24
    Thai rice noodles (pad thai), 284–86
Caesar salad dressing, 355–56
Cakes (savory):
    cod, crispy, 238–39
    crab, deviled, 245–46
    crab, with Asian flavors, 246–47
    noodle, flipping, 288
Cakes (sweet):
    cream cheese pound, 412–13
    fallen chocolate soufflé, 413–14
    spiced-up honey, 415–17
Capers, 353, 367
    linguine puttanesca, 255
Caponata, eggplant, 318–19
Carrots:
    cider vinegar slaw, 310
    ginger pickled vegetables, 343
Cashews, chicken with, 182–83
Cauliflower:
    ginger pickled vegetables, 343
    gratin, 310–12
    sautéed penne with chickpeas and,
        262–63
Challah:
    bread pudding, 424–26
    French toast, 384–85
Chapati, 404–5
Cheese(s):
    blue, dressing, 357
    blue, in chicken cordon bleu cheese,
        176–77
    cauliflower gratin, 310–12
    cream, pound cake, 412–13
    and ham crêpes with tarragon cream
        sauce, 386–89
    lasagne for a crowd, 268–70
    ricotta, stuffed shells with prosciutto
        and, 280–81

tortellini with cream, peas, and ham,
    276
tortellini with sun-dried tomato cream,
    274–75
two, macaroni and, 265–66
see also Parmesan
Chicken, 141–93
    with black mushrooms and Chinese
        sausage, 160–61
    breasts stuffed with curried couscous,
        178–79
    cacciatore, 175–76
    with cashews, 182–83
    cordon bleu cheese, 176–77
    and dumplings, Melicia's, 164–66
    fat, rendering, 143
    with forty cloves of garlic, 144–45
    fried, David's famous, 157–58
    gumbo, 184–85
    innards, 147
    and lamb couscous, 92–95
    liver, chopped, 192–93
    McWaltucks, 180–81
    with olives and preserved lemons,
        172–74
    paprikás, 162–63
    pot-au-feu, 63–64
    potpie and I don't care, 154–56
    red-cooked, chilled, 148–49
    and rice, Dominican, 169–71
    roast, stuffed with basil, 146–47
    roast, with root vegetables and cider,
        142–43
    salad, curried, 187
    for salads, 186
    salad with tarragon, 188
    soup with fresh herbs, 9–12
    stock, 39–40
    with tomato and tarragon, bistro-style,
        166–67
    à la trip to Puerto Rico, 168–69
    white-cooked, chilled, 150–52
    whole, cutting up, 159
    wings, honeyed-hoisin grilled, 189–90
    wings, Manhattan Buffalo, 191–92
Chickpeas:
    curried, three-can, 315–16
    hummus, herbed summer, 317–18
    sautéed penne with cauliflower and,
        262–63

Children, in restaurants, 416
Chili:
    seasoning, 79
    venison, with red beans, 77–79
Chinese ingredients:
    black vinegar, 49
    five-spice powder, 54
    hoisin sauce, 190
    oyster sauce, 308
    sausages, 161
    star anise, 54
    wood ears and lily buds, 8
Chinese-style dishes:
    beef, chilled red-cooked, 65–67
    beef, crispy orange, 48–51
    beef fillets with star anise, 52–54
    broccoli with oyster sauce, 307–8
    broth for red-cooking, 67
    chicken, chilled red-cooked, 148–49
    chicken, chilled white-cooked, 150–51
    chicken wings, honeyed-hoisin grilled,
        189–90
    chicken with cashews, 182–83
    clams in black bean sauce, 250–51
    duck, braised, with shiitakes,
        200–201
    eggplant, Chinese, with black beans
        and pork, 120–21
    fish, crispy, with spicy sweet-and-sour
        sauce, 228–29
    fish fillets, sesame-crusted, with garlic-
        ginger sauce, 230–31
    hot and sour soup, 6–8
    meatballs for a crowd, 128–30
    noodles, two-sides-brown, with
        mushrooms, 287–89
    rice noodles, Singapore-style, 289–91
    shrimp fried rice, highly adaptable,
        294–95
    shrimp with black bean sauce, 240–41
    vegetable lo mein, 292–93
Chocolate:
    brownies, our favorite, 419–20
    chip cookies, oaty, 430–31
    soufflé cake, fallen, 413–14
Choucroute garni, Alsatian, 126–27
Chowder, clam, New England, 16–17
Cider, roast chicken with root vegetables
    and, 142–43
Cider vinegar slaw, 310

Cilantro, in spicy green dipping sauce,
    151–52
Citrus peel, drying, 51
Clam(s):
    in black bean sauce, 250–51
    chowder, New England, 16–17
    fish stew, Provençal, 232–33
    sauce, linguine with, 257–59
Clarifying butter, 391
Cobbler, blackberry, 420–21
Coconut rice, 335
Cod:
    cakes, crispy, 238–39
    salt, 239
Composed salads, 351
Condiments:
    citrus peel, drying, 51
    lemons, preserved, 174
    maple syrup, spiced, 385
    vanilla sugar, 379
Confit of duck, 201–4
Conversion table, 434
Cookies:
    oatmeal, stamp-of-approval, 432–33
    oaty chocolate chip, 430–31
    peanut lovers', 429–30
    refrigerating or freezing dough for, 431
    tuiles, 427–28
Corn:
    creamed, summertime, 313
    double-cutting, 312
    muffins, buttermilk, with orange,
        377–78
Cornbread, 381–82
    skillet, 381
Corn dogs, 139
Cornish hens, 153
    Provençal, 152–53
Cornmeal-onion biscuits, 380–81
Cottage pie, 74–75
Court bouillon, lemongrass, 236–37
Couscous, 95
    curried, chicken breasts stuffed with,
        178–79
    lamb and chicken, 92–95
    steaming, 94–95
Crab(meat):
    cakes, deviled, 245–46
    cakes with Asian flavors, 246–47
    seafood salad, Thai, 235–37

Staff Meals from Chanterelle | index

Crabs, soft-shell:
    cleaning, 242
    sautéed, with sorrel butter, 243–44
Cranberry soup, zesty, 409–10
Cream cheese pound cake, 412–13
Creamed:
    corn, summertime, 313
    spinach, 340–41
Crème anglaise, 425–26
Crepes:
    ham and cheese, with tarragon cream
        sauce, 386–89
    herbed, 389
    tips for, 387–88
Crisp, apple oat, 418–19
Croquettes, fresh salmon, 218–19
Croutons, crisp, making, 356
Cucumber salad with red onion and
        Chinese sausage, 314–15
Curry(ied):
    chicken salad, 187
    chickpeas, three-can, 315–16
    couscous, chicken breasts stuffed with,
        178–79
    duck, Thai, 198–99
    mayonnaise, 361
    rice, 336
    rice noodles, Singapore-style, 289–91

daikon radish, in ginger pickled
        vegetables, 343
Degreasing stock, 40
Desserts, 407–33
    apple oat crisp, 418–19
    blackberry cobbler, 420–21
    brownies, our favorite, 419–20
    challah bread pudding, 424–26
    cranberry soup, zesty, 409–10
    cream cheese pound cake, 412–13
    crème anglaise, 425–26
    dried fruits in spiced red wine, 408–9
    fallen chocolate soufflé cake, 413–14
    ginger shortcakes, summertime, 422–23
    litchi sorbet, 411
    spiced-up honey cake, 415–17
    see also Cookies
Deviled crab cakes, 245–46
Dipping sauces:
    spicy green, 151–52
    tamarind, 372–73

Dips, 348, 365
    aïoli, 363
    baba ghanouj, 320–21
    green goddess dressing, 352–53
    green sauce, 364–65
    honey mustard, 371
    horseradish sauce, 369–70
    hummus, herbed summer, 317–18
Dominican chicken and rice, 169–71
Dressing a salad, 354
Dressings, 347–62
    blue cheese, 357
    Caesar salad, 355–56
    green goddess, 352–53
    Italian, creamy, 358
    salad, David's, 349
    vinaigrette, ultra mustardy, 350
    see also Mayonnaise
Dried fruits in spiced red wine, 408–9
Duck:
    braised, with shiitakes, 200–201
    confit of, 201–4
    confit of, in black bean stew with pig
        parts, 108–9
    curry, Thai, 198–99
Dumplings, chicken and, Melicia's,
        164–66

eggplant:
    baba ghanouj, 320–21
    caponata, 318–19
    Chinese, with black beans and pork,
        120–21
    Chinese and Japanese, 121
    Parmesan, 278–79
    pizza, 297–99
Eggs:
    challah French toast, 384–85
    poached, polenta with spicy tomato
        sauce and, 398–99
    safety concerns and, 359
    shirred, with Smithfield ham and
        tarragon, 395–96
Escarole, in spaghetti with potatoes and
        greens, 260–61

fallen chocolate soufflé cake, 413–14
Fennel salad, 321–22
First courses:
    avocado soup, chilled, 37

First courses (continued)
    butternut squash and bourbon soup,
        34–35
    composed salads as, 351
    fennel salad, 320–21
    lentil salad, warm, 322–23
    salmon, gingered pickled, with wasabi
        sauce, 214–15
    see also Appetizers
Fish:
    'n' chips, 234
    cod cakes, crispy, 238–39
    crispy, with spicy sweet-and-sour sauce,
        228–29
    fillets, sesame-crusted, with garlic-ginger
        sauce, 230–31
    with ginger-scallion sauce, 225–27
    lotte with leeks, 222–23
    monkfish with roast shallots and garlic,
        224–25
    stew, Provençal, 232–33
    stock, 41
    testing for doneness, 213
    tuna with two marinades, 220–21
    see also Clam(s); Salmon; Seafood; Shrimp
Fish sauce, Asian, 241
Five-spice powder, 54
Flank steak, lime-marinated, 47
Focaccia, herb and garlic, 400–401
Food mills, 31
Frankfurters, in corn dogs, 139
French dishes:
    aïoli, 363
    brisket, braised, with carrots, Mom's,
        55–56
    chicken with tomato and tarragon,
        bistro-style, 166–67
    choucroute garni, Alsatian, 126–27
    Cornish hens, Provençal, 152–53
    crème anglaise, 425–26
    fish stew, Provençal, 232–33
    onion soup, 35–36
    pork chops, sautéed, with sauce
        charcutière, 103–4
    pot-au-feu, 63–64
    rémoulade, 366
    tuiles, 427–28
French toast, challah, 384–85
Fried rice, shrimp, highly adaptable,
    294–95

Fries, our favorite, 327–29
Fritters, Vidalia onion, 326–27

garlic:
    aïoli, 363
    bread, 402
    chicken with forty cloves of, 144–45
    ginger sauce, sesame-crusted fish fillets
        with, 230–31
    and herb focaccia, 400–401
    lentil soup with garlic vinaigrette,
        24–25
    monkfish with roast shallots and, 224–25
    peeling forty cloves of, 145
    sausage, rustic homemade, 132–34
    vinaigrette, 25
Ginger(ed), 227
    garlic sauce, sesame-crusted fish fillets
        with, 230–31
    pickled salmon with wasabi sauce,
        214–15
    pickled vegetables, 343
    scallion sauce, fish with, 225–27
    shortcakes, summertime, 422–23
    wasabi marinade, 221
Goulash, pork, Szeged style, 106–7
Gratins:
    cauliflower, 310–12
    potato, 329
Greek-style tripe soup with lemon, 12–13
Green beans, cooking, 305
Green goddess dressing, 352–53
Greens, spaghetti with potatoes and,
    260–61
Green sauce, 364–65
Grilled fare:
    beef fillets with star anise, 52–54
    chicken wings, honeyed-hoisin, 189–90
    flank steak, lime-marinated, 47
    lamb, butterflied leg of, 87–88
    quail with soba salad and scallions, 204–5
    tuna with two marinades, 220–21
Gumbo, chicken, 184–85

ham:
    black bean stew with pig parts, 108–9
    and cheese crêpes with tarragon cream
        sauce, 386–89
    cheese tortellini with cream, peas and,
        276

chicken cordon bleu cheese, 176–77
choucroute garni, Alsatian, 126–27
pea soup with, 20–21
roast, with honey-mustard glaze, 102–3
Smithfield, shirred eggs with tarragon
    and, 395–96
stock, 20–21
Harissa, doctored, 368–69
Hash, roast beef, 68–69
Herb(ed)(s):
biscuits, 382–83
crêpes, 389
dried, maximizing, 71
and garlic focaccia, 400–401
hummus, summer, 317–18
pinwheel pork loin, 100–101
ravioli with Parmesan, butter and, 277
see also specific herbs
Hoisin sauce, 190
honeyed grilled chicken wings, 189–90
Honey(ed):
cake, spiced-up, 415–17
hoisin grilled chicken wings, 189–90
mustard dip, 371
soy marinade, 221
Horseradish:
fresh homemade, 370
sauce, 369–70
Hot and sour soup, 6–8
Hot dog onions, 324
Hummus, herbed summer, 317–18
Hungarian-style dishes:
chicken paprikás, 162–63
pork goulash, Szeged style, 106–7
stuffed cabbage, Gaby's, 122–24

ice cream, 410
Indian flatbread (chapati), 404–5
Ingredients:
recipes with long list of, 283
sticky, measuring, 111
see also Asian ingredients; Chinese
    ingredients
Italian dishes:
chicken cacciatore, 175–76
eggplant caponata, 318–19
eggplant Parmesan, 278–79
eggplant pizza, 297–99
herb and garlic focaccia, 400–401
meatballs, 69–70

meat loaf, 70–72
risotto with porcini, 295–97
tripe, braised, alla Fiorentina, 82–83
see also Pasta
Italian dressing, creamy, 358

julienning, 293

kaffir lime leaves, 15

lamb:
broth, 92–93
and chicken couscous, 92–95
grilled butterflied leg of, 87–88
shanks, Moroccan, 88–89
shanks with tomato and rosemary, 90–91
tagine with prunes and honey, 96–97
Lasagne for a crowd, 268–74
Latkes, potato, Paul's, 330–31
Leek(s):
lotte with, 222–23
and potato soup, 30–31
Lemon(s):
preserved, 174
preserved, chicken with olives and,
    172–74
tripe soup with, Greek-style, 12–13
Lemongrass, 236
court bouillon, 237
Lentil:
salad, warm, 322–23
soup with garlic vinaigrette, 24–25
Lily buds, 8
hot and sour soup, 6–8
Lime:
butter sauce, salmon with, 216–17
kaffir, leaves, 15
-marinated flank steak, 47
Linguine:
with clam sauce, 257–59
puttanesca, 255
Litchi sorbet, 411
Lo mein, vegetable, 292–93
Lotte with leeks, 222–23

macaroni and two cheeses, 265–66
Manhattan Buffalo wings, 191–92
Maple syrup, spiced, 385
Marinades:
ginger wasabi, 221

Marinades *(continued)*
    honey soy, 221
Mashed potatoes, everyday, 334–35
Matzoh balls:
    chicken soup with fresh herbs, 9–10
    homemade, 11–12
Mayonnaise:
    aïoli, 363
    basic, 360
    curried, 361
    tarragon, 362
Measuring sticky ingredients, 111
Meat, 43–139
    braising, 57
    oxtail stew with olives, 80–81
    tripe, braised, alla Fiorentina, 82–83
    veal chops with mustard and cream,
        84–85
    veal shank, roasted, 85–86
    venison chili with red beans, 77–79
    see also Beef; Ham; Lamb; Pork; Sausage(s)
Meatballs:
    Chinese-style, for a crowd, 128–30
    Italian, 69–70
Meat loaf, Italian style, 70–72
Middle Eastern dishes:
    baba ghanouj, 320–21
    hummus, herbed summer, 317–18
    preserved lemons, 174
Mint:
    juleps, Chanterelle style, 397
    tomato soup, creamy, 32–33
Mirepoix, 39–40
Mise en place, 283
Monkfish:
    lotte with leeks, 222–23
    with roast shallots and garlic, 224–25
    seafood salad, Thai, 235–37
Montana fried "pork chop" sandwiches,
    136–37
Moroccan-style dishes:
    lamb shanks, 88–89
    lamb tagine with prunes and honey,
        96–97
Mushroom(s):
    barley soup, 26–27
    black, chicken with Chinese sausage
        and, 160–61
    chicken cacciatore, 175–76
    hot and sour soup, 6–8

porcini, risotto with, 295–97
porcini-tomato sauce, 273–74
sautéing, 272
stuffing, Sara's, 196–97
two-sides-brown noodles with, 287–89
Mussel(s):
    cleaning, 19
    fish stew, Provençal, 232–33
    soup with saffron, 18–19
    spaghetti with tomatoes, cream and,
        256–57
Mustard honey dip, 371
Mustardy vinaigrette, ultra, 350

n *am pla,* 241
New England clam chowder, 16–17
Noodle(s), 282–93
    cakes, flipping, 288
    rice, Singapore-style, 289–91
    rice, stir-fried, with bean sprouts and
        scallions, 282–83
    rice, Thai (pad thai), 284–86
    soba salad, 337–38
    two-sides-brown, with mushrooms,
        287–89
    vegetable lo mein, 292–93
    see also Pasta
North African–style dishes:
    chicken with olives and preserved
        lemons, 172–74
    harissa, doctored, 368–69
    lamb and chicken couscous, 92–95
    lamb shanks, Moroccan, 88–89
    lamb tagine with prunes and honey,
        Moroccan, 96–97
Nutmeg, freshly grated, 281

Oat(meal):
    apple crisp, 418–19
    chocolate chip cookies, 430–31
    cookies, stamp-of-approval, 432–33
    pancakes, 393–94
Olive(s):
    braised rabbit with tomato and, 208–9
    chicken with preserved lemons and,
        172–74
    linguine puttanesca, 255
    oxtail stew with, 80–81
    paste, 81
    rice salad with pine nuts and, 338–39

Onion(s):
    cornmeal biscuits, 380–81
    hot dog, 324
    pork chops, smothered, 105–6
    red, cucumber salad with Chinese
        sausage and, 314–15
    soup, French, 35–36
    Vidalia, fritters, 326–27
    yummy, 325
Orange:
    beef, crispy, 48–51
    buttermilk corn muffins with, 377–78
    peel, drying, 51
Oxtail stew with olives, 80–81
Oyster sauce, 308
    broccoli with, 307–8

Pad thai (Thai rice noodles), 284–86
Panacea vegetable soup, 28–29
Pancakes:
    buttermilk, half-inch–high, 392–93
    oatmeal, 393–94
    potato latkes, Paul's, 330–31
    see also Crêpes
Panko, 180
    chicken McWaltucks, 180–81
Paprika:
    chicken paprikás, 162–63
    Hungarian, 163
    pork goulash, Szeged style, 106–7
    stuffed cabbage, Gaby's Hungarian-style,
        122–24
Parmesan, 267
    bread, 403
    eggplant, 278–79
    macaroni and two cheeses, 265–66
    ravioli with butter, herbs and, 277
Parmigiano-Reggiano, 267
Parsley:
    green goddess dressing, 352–53
    green sauce, 364–65
Pasta, 253–81
    cooking, 259
    lasagne for a crowd, 268–74
    linguine puttanesca, 255
    linguine with clam sauce, 257–59
    macaroni and two cheeses,
        265–66
    penne, sautéed, with cauliflower and
        chickpeas, 262–63

ravioli with Parmesan, butter, and herbs,
    277
shapes of, 263
shells, stuffed, with ricotta and prosciutto,
    280–81
spaghetti with mussels, tomatoes, and
    cream, 256–57
spaghetti with potatoes and greens,
    260–61
tortellini, cheese, with cream, peas, and
    ham, 276
tortellini, cheese, with sun-dried tomato
    cream, 274–75
ziti, fried, 264–65
see also Noodle(s)
Pastry dough, 156
Pea(s):
    cheese tortellini with cream, ham and,
        276
    soup with ham, 20–21
Peanut:
    lovers' cookies, 429–30
    sauce, spicy, 117–18
Penne, sautéed, with cauliflower and chick-
    peas, 262–63
Peppers (bell):
    ginger pickled vegetables, 343
    red, in cider vinegar slaw, 310
    sausage and, 131–32
    stuffed with rice and sausage, 124–25
Pickled foods:
    gingered salmon with wasabi sauce,
        214–15
    vegetables, ginger, 343
Pickling brine, 215
Picnics, 112
Pies (savory):
    chicken potpie and I don't care, 154–56
    cottage, 74–75
Pine nuts:
    rice salad with olives and, 338–39
    toasting, 339
Pizza:
    dough, 299
    eggplant, 297–99
    no-sauce, 298
Polenta with spicy tomato sauce and
    poached eggs, 398–99
Porcini:
    risotto with, 295–97

Porcini *(continued)*
    tomato sauce, 273–74
Pork, 99–139
    aïoli BLTs, 137–38
    black bean stew with pig parts, 108–9
    changes in, 101
    Chinese eggplant with black beans and,
        120–21
    chops, sautéed, with sauce charcutière,
        103–4
    chops, smothered, 105–6
    "chop" sandwiches, Montana fried,
        136–37
    goulash, Szeged style, 106–7
    loin, herbed pinwheel, 100–101
    meatballs, Chinese-style, for a crowd,
        128–30
    mini ribs, braised, with black bean
        sauce, 114–15
    ribs, oven-roasted barbecued, 110–11
    ribs, Wild Turkey glazed, 113–14
    saté with spicy peanut sauce, 116–18
    stuffed cabbage, Gaby's Hungarian-style,
        122–24
    wiener schnitzel, 118–19
    see also Ham; Sausage(s)
Potato(es):
    baking, 331
    boiling, 332
    cottage pie, 74–75
    fries, our favorite, 327–29
    gratin, 329
    latkes, Paul's, 330–31
    and leek soup, 30–31
    mashed, everyday, 334–35
    roast beef hash, 68–69
    salad, slightly Southern, 333
    spaghetti with greens and, 260–61
Pot-au-feu, 63–64
Potpie, chicken, and I don't care, 154–56
Poultry:
    Cornish hens, Provençal, 152–53
    quail, grilled, with soba salad and
        scallions, 204–5
    turkey, roast, the Waltuck way, 195–96
    see also Chicken; Duck
Pound cake, cream cheese, 412–13
Prosciutto, stuffed shells with ricotta and,
    280–81
Provençal dishes:
    Cornish hens, 152–53
    fish stew, 232–33
Prunes, lamb tagine with honey and,
    96–97
Pudding, challah bread, 424–26
Puerto Rico, chicken à la trip to, 168–69

quail, grilled, with soba salad and
    scallions, 204–5

rabbit:
    braised, with Dijon mustard, 206–7
    braised, with tomato and olives, 208–9
Ravioli with Parmesan, butter, and herbs,
    277
Red beans, venison chili with, 77–79
Red cabbage, braised, 309
Red-cooked dishes, 149
    beef, chilled, 65–67
    broth for, 67
    chicken, chilled, 148–49
    duck, braised, with shiitakes, 200–201
Red wine:
    beef stew with vegetables and, 60–62
    spiced, dried fruits in, 408–9
Rémoulade, 366
Rendering chicken fat, 143
Ribs:
    beef short, braised in beer, 58–59
    mini, braised, with black bean sauce,
        114–15
    oven-roasted barbecued, 110–11
    Wild Turkey glazed, 113–14
Rice:
    bell peppers stuffed with sausage and,
        124–25
    chicken and, Dominican, 169–71
    coconut, 335
    converted, 171
    curry, 336
    risotto with porcini, 295–97
    salad with olives and pine nuts, 338–39
    shrimp fried, highly adaptable, 294–95
    stuffed cabbage, Gaby's Hungarian-style,
        122–24
Rice noodles:
    Singapore-style, 289–91
    stir-fried, with bean sprouts and
        scallions, 282–83
    Thai (pad thai), 284–86

Ricotta, stuffed shells with prosciutto and, 280–81

Risotto with porcini, 295–97

Root vegetables, roast chicken with cider and, 142–43

S affron, 174

Salads:

chicken, curried, 187

chicken, with tarragon, 188

chicken for, 186

cider vinegar slaw, 310

composed, 351

crisp croutons for, 356

cucumber, with red onion and Chinese sausage, 314–15

dressing, 354

eggplant caponata, 318–19

fennel, 321–22

lentil, warm, 322–23

potato, slightly Southern, 333

rice, with olives and pine nuts, 338–39

seafood, Thai, 235–37

soba, 337–38

soba, grilled quail with scallions and, 204–5

spinach, cooked, with soy and sesame, 341–42

see also Dressings

Salmon:

fresh, croquettes, 218–19

gingered pickled, with wasabi sauce, 214–15

with lime butter sauce, 216–17

sautéed, with brown butter, lemon, and capers, 212–13

Sandwiches:

aïoli BLTs, 137–38

beef, red-cooked, 66

burgers, David's, 72–73

"pork chop," Montana fried, 136–37

sloppy Joes, 76–77

Saté, pork, with spicy peanut sauce, 116–18

Sauces, 364–73

béchamel, 311–12

beurre manié as thickener for, 62

butter, separated, 217

crème anglaise, 425–26

green, 364–65

harissa, doctored, 368–69

horseradish, 369–70

peanut, spicy, 117–18

rémoulade, 366

spicy green dipping, 151–52

tamarind dipping, 372–73

tartar, kitchen cupboard, 367

tomato, tasty basic, 271

tomato-porcini, 273–74

wasabi, 214–15

see also Dips; Dressings; Mayonnaise

Sauerkraut, 127

choucroute garni, Alsatian, 126–27

pork goulash, Szeged style, 106–7

stuffed cabbage, Gaby's Hungarian-style, 122–24

Sausage(s):

bell peppers stuffed with rice and, 124–25

black bean stew with pig parts, 108–9

casings, 135

Chinese, 161

Chinese, chicken with black mushrooms and, 160–61

Chinese, cucumber salad with red onion and, 314–15

choucroute garni, Alsatian, 126–27

garlic, rustic homemade, 132–34

making, 135

and peppers, 131–32

pot-au-feu, 63–64

stuffing, Sara's, 196–97

Thai rice noodles (pad thai), 284–86

Scallion(s):

ginger sauce, fish with, 225–27

grilled quail with soba salad and, 204–5

stir-fried rice noodles with bean sprouts and, 282–83

Scallops:

fish stew, Provençal, 232–33

seafood salad, Thai, 235–37

Scones, breakfast, Chanterelle, 378–79

Seafood, 211–51

crab cakes, deviled, 245–46

crab cakes with Asian flavors, 246–47

mussels, spaghetti with tomatoes, cream and, 256–57

mussel soup with saffron, 18–19

salad, Thai, 235–37

soft-shell crabs, sautéed, with sorrel butter, 243–44

squid stew, 248–49

Seafood *(continued)*
    see also Clam(s); Fish; Salmon; Shrimp
Sesame:
    cooked spinach salad with soy and,
        341–42
    -crusted fish fillets with garlic-ginger
        sauce, 230–31
    oil, Asian, 342
    tahini, 316
Shallots, monkfish with roast garlic and,
    224–25
Shells, stuffed, with ricotta and prosciutto,
    280–81
Shiitakes:
    braised duck with, 200–201
    hot and sour soup, 6–8
    stuffing, Sara's, 196–97
Shortcakes:
    ginger, summertime, 422–23
    strawberries for, 423
Short ribs, beef, braised in beer, 58–59
Shrimp:
    with black bean sauce, 240–41
    dried, 286
    fried rice, highly adaptable, 294–95
    seafood salad, Thai, 235–37
    Singapore-style rice noodles, 289–91
    soup, Thai, 14–15
    Thai rice noodles (pad thai), 284–86
Side dishes, 301–45
    applesauce, spiced, 303
    baba ghanouj, 320–21
    beans, baked, Sabrina's, 304–5
    beets with balsamic vinegar, 306–7
    broccoli with oyster sauce, 307–8
    cauliflower gratin, 310–12
    chickpeas, curried, three-can, 315–16
    corn, creamed, summertime, 313
    cucumber salad with red onion and
        Chinese sausage, 314–15
    eggplant caponata, 318–19
    fennel salad, 321–22
    fries, our favorite, 327–29
    ginger pickled vegetables, 343
    green beans, 305
    hummus, herbed summer, 317–18
    lentil salad, warm, 322–23
    onion, Vidalia, fritters, 326–27
    onions, hot dog, 324
    onions, yummy, 325

potatoes, baked, 331
potatoes, boiled, 332
potatoes, mashed, everyday, 334–35
potato gratin, 329
potato latkes, Paul's, 330–31
potato salad, slightly Southern, 333
red cabbage, braised, 309
rice, coconut, 335
rice, curry, 336
rice salad with olives and pine nuts,
    338–39
slaw, cider vinegar, 310
soba salad, 337–38
spinach, creamed, 340–41
spinach salad, cooked, with soy and
    sesame, 341–42
tomatoes, marinated, with balsamic
    vinegar and basil, 344
zucchini coins, fried, 345
Singapore-style rice noodles, 289–91
Slaw, cider vinegar, 310
Sloppy Joes, 76–77
Soba salad, 337–38
    grilled quail with scallions and, 204–5
Sorbet, litchi, 411
Sorrel butter, sautéed soft-shell crabs with,
    243–44
Soufflé cake, fallen chocolate, 413–14
Soups, 3–41
    avocado, chilled, 37
    beef borscht, hot, for Aunt Gertie,
        4–5
    black bean, 22–23
    butternut squash and bourbon, 34–35
    chicken, with fresh herbs, 9–12
    clam chowder, New England, 16–17
    cranberry, zesty, 409–10
    hot and sour, 6–8
    leek and potato, 30–31
    lentil, with garlic vinaigrette, 24–25
    matzoh balls for, homemade, 11–12
    mushroom-barley, 26–27
    mussel, with saffron, 18–19
    onion, French, 35–36
    pea, with ham, 20–21
    shrimp, Thai, 14–15
    tomato mint, creamy, 32–33
    tripe, with lemon, Greek-style, 12–13
    vegetable, panacea, 28–29
    see also Stocks

Staff Meals from Chanterelle | index

Southern fare:
    pork chops, smothered, 105–6
    potato salad, slightly Southern, 333
Soy honey marinade, 221
Spaghetti:
    with mussels, tomatoes, and cream,
        256–57
    with potatoes and greens, 260–61
Spiced-up honey cake, 415–17
Spices:
    chili seasoning, 79
    five-spice powder, Chinese, 54
    ginger, fresh, 227
    nutmeg, freshly grated, 281
    paprika, Hungarian, 163
    saffron, 174
    star anise, 54
Spinach:
    cooked, salad with soy and sesame,
        341–42
    creamed, 340–41
    fresh, wilting, 340
    green sauce, 364–65
Spritzers, white wine, 396
Squash, butternut, and bourbon soup,
        34–35
Squid:
    cleaning, 249
    fish stew, Provençal, 232–33
    seafood salad, Thai, 235–37
    stew, 248–49
Star anise, 54
    beef fillets with, 52–54
Stews:
    beef, with red wine and vegetables, 60–62
    beurre manié as thickener for, 62
    black bean, with pig parts, 108–9
    chicken à la trip to Puerto Rico, 168–69
    chicken and dumplings, Melicia's, 164–66
    choosing meat for, 61
    fish, Provençal, 232–33
    lamb tagine with prunes and honey,
        96–97
    oxtail, with olives, 80–81
    pork goulash, Szeged style, 106–7
    pot-au-feu, 63–64
    rabbit, braised, with tomato and olives,
        208–9
    squid, 248–49
    venison chili with red beans, 77–79

Stir-fried rice noodles with bean sprouts
        and scallions, 282–83
Stocks:
    chicken, 39–40
    degreasing, 40
    fish, 41
    ham, 20–21
    veal, beefed-up, 38–39
    see also Broths
Strawberries, for shortcakes, 423
Stuffed:
    bell peppers, with rice and sausage,
        124–25
    cabbage, Gaby's Hungarian-style, 122–24
    shells with ricotta and prosciutto,
        280–81
Stuffing, Sara's, 196–97
Sugar, vanilla, 379
Sweating vegetables, 29
Sweet-and-sour sauce, spicy, crispy fish
        with, 228–29
Syrup, spiced maple, 385

tagine, lamb, with prunes and honey,
        96–97
Tahini, 316
Tamarind:
    dipping sauce, 372–73
    pulp, 372
Tangerine peel, drying, 51
Tarragon:
    chicken salad with, 188
    chicken with tomato and, bistro-style,
        166–67
    cream sauce, ham and cheese crêpes
        with, 386–89
    mayonnaise, 362
    shirred eggs with Smithfield ham and,
        395–96
Tartar sauce:
    kitchen cupboard, 367
    rémoulade, 366
Thai-style dishes:
    duck curry, 198–99
    fish with ginger-scallion sauce, 225–27
    pork saté with spicy peanut sauce,
        116–17
    rice noodles (pad thai), 284–86
    seafood salad, 235–37
    shrimp soup, 14–15

Thanksgiving fare, 194
    stuffing, Sara's, 196–97
    turkey, roast, the Waltuck way, 195–96
Tomato(es):
    marinated, with balsamic vinegar and
        basil, 344
    mint soup, creamy, 32–33
    peeling and seeding, 33
    porcini sauce, 273–74
    sauce, tasty basic, 271
Tomato(es), sun-dried:
    cream, cheese tortellini with, 274–75
    linguine puttanesca, 255
Tortellini, cheese:
    with cream, peas, and ham, 276
    with sun-dried tomato cream, 274–75
Tripe:
    braised, alla Fiorentina, 82–83
    buying and cooking, 83
    soup with lemon, Greek-style, 12–13
Truffles, black, matzoh balls with, 11
Tuiles, 427–28
Tuna with two marinades, 220–21
Turkey:
    roast, the Waltuck way, 195–96
    stuffing for, Sara's, 196–97
Two-sides-brown noodles with mushrooms,
        287–89

Vanilla sugar, 379
Veal:
    chops with mustard and cream, 84–85
    pot-au-feu, 63–64

    shank, roasted, 85–86
    stock, beefed-up, 38–39
Vegetable(s):
    ginger pickled, 343
    lo mein, 292–93
    soup, panacea, 28–29
    sweating, 29
    see also Side dishes; specific vegetables
Venison chili with red beans, 77–79
Vidalia onion fritters, 326–27
Vinaigrettes:
    garlic, 25
    ultra mustardy, 350
Vinegar:
    Chinese black, 49
    see also Balsamic vinegar

Waffles, breakfast, Chanterelle's, 390–91
Wasabi:
    ginger marinade, 221
    sauce, 214–15
White wine spritzers, 396
Wiener schnitzel, 118–19
Wild Turkey glazed ribs, 113–14
Wine:
    red, beef stew with vegetables and, 60–62
    red, spiced, dried fruits in, 408–9
    white, spritzers, 396
Wood ear mushrooms, 8
    hot and sour soup, 6–8

Ziti, fried, 264–65
Zucchini coins, fried, 345

Staff Meals from Chanterelle | index

RD1LFF